Unruly Ideas

NEW AFRICAN HISTORIES

SERIES EDITORS: JEAN ALLMAN, ALLEN ISAACMAN, DEREK R. PETERSON, AND CARINA RAY

David William Cohen and E. S. Atieno Odhiambo, *The Risks of Knowledge*
Belinda Bozzoli, *Theatres of Struggle and the End of Apartheid*
Gary Kynoch, *We Are Fighting the World*
Stephanie Newell, *The Forger's Tale*
Jacob A. Tropp, *Natures of Colonial Change*
Jan Bender Shetler, *Imagining Serengeti*
Cheikh Anta Babou, *Fighting the Greater Jihad*
Marc Epprecht, *Heterosexual Africa?*
Marissa J. Moorman, *Intonations*
Karen E. Flint, *Healing Traditions*
Derek R. Peterson and Giacomo Macola, editors, *Recasting the Past*
Moses E. Ochonu, *Colonial Meltdown*
Emily S. Burrill, Richard L. Roberts, and Elizabeth Thornberry, editors, *Domestic Violence and the Law in Colonial and Postcolonial Africa*
Daniel R. Magaziner, *The Law and the Prophets*
Emily Lynn Osborn, *Our New Husbands Are Here*
Robert Trent Vinson, *The Americans Are Coming!*
James R. Brennan, *Taifa*
Benjamin N. Lawrance and Richard L. Roberts, editors, *Trafficking in Slavery's Wake*
David M. Gordon, *Invisible Agents*
Allen F. Isaacman and Barbara S. Isaacman, *Dams, Displacement, and the Delusion of Development*
Stephanie Newell, *The Power to Name*
Gibril R. Cole, *The Krio of West Africa*
Matthew M. Heaton, *Black Skin, White Coats*
Meredith Terretta, *Nation of Outlaws, State of Violence*
Paolo Israel, *In Step with the Times*
Michelle R. Moyd, *Violent Intermediaries*
Abosede A. George, *Making Modern Girls*
Alicia C. Decker, *In Idi Amin's Shadow*
Rachel Jean-Baptiste, *Conjugal Rights*
Shobana Shankar, *Who Shall Enter Paradise?*
Emily S. Burrill, *States of Marriage*
Todd Cleveland, *Diamonds in the Rough*
Carina E. Ray, *Crossing the Color Line*
Sarah Van Beurden, *Authentically African*
Giacomo Macola, *The Gun in Central Africa*
Lynn Schler, *Nation on Board*
Julie MacArthur, *Cartography and the Political Imagination*
Abou B. Bamba, *African Miracle, African Mirage*
Daniel Magaziner, *The Art of Life in South Africa*
Paul Ocobock, *An Uncertain Age*
Keren Weitzberg, *We Do Not Have Borders*
Nuno Domingos, *Football and Colonialism*
Jeffrey S. Ahlman, *Living with Nkrumahism*
Bianca Murillo, *Market Encounters*
Laura Fair, *Reel Pleasures*
Thomas F. McDow, *Buying Time*
Jon Soske, *Internal Frontiers*
Elizabeth W. Giorgis, *Modernist Art in Ethiopia*
Matthew V. Bender, *Water Brings No Harm*
David Morton, *Age of Concrete*
Marissa J. Moorman, *Powerful Frequencies*
Ndubueze L. Mbah, *Emergent Masculinities*
Judith A. Byfield, *The Great Upheaval*
Patricia Hayes and Gary Minkley, editors, *Ambivalent*
Mari K. Webel, *The Politics of Disease Control*
Kara Moskowitz, *Seeing Like a Citizen*
Jacob Dlamini, *Safari Nation*
Alice Wiemers, *Village Work*
Cheikh Anta Babou, *The Muridiyya on the Move*
Laura Ann Twagira, *Embodied Engineering*
Marissa Mika, *Africanizing Oncology*
Holly Hanson, *To Speak and Be Heard*
Paul S. Landau, *Spear*
Saheed Aderinto, *Animality and Colonial Subjecthood in Africa*
Katherine Bruce-Lockhart, *Carceral Afterlives*
Natasha Erlank, *Convening Black Intimacy*
Morgan J. Robinson, *A Language for the World*
Faeeza Ballim, *Apartheid's Leviathan*
Nicole Eggers, *Unruly Ideas*

Unruly Ideas

A History of Kitawala in Congo

Nicole Eggers

OHIO UNIVERSITY PRESS
ATHENS, OHIO

Ohio University Press, Athens, Ohio 45701
ohioswallow.com
© 2023 by Ohio University Press
All rights reserved

To obtain permission to quote, reprint, or otherwise reproduce or distribute material from Ohio University Press publications, please contact our rights and permissions department at (740) 593-1154 or (740) 593-4536 (fax).

Printed in the United States of America
Ohio University Press books are printed on acid-free paper ∞ ™

31 30 29 28 27 26 25 24 23 22 21 5 4 3 2 1

Library of Congress Cataloging-in-Publication Data

Names: Eggers, Nicole, author.
Title: Unruly ideas : a history of Kitawala in Congo / Nicole Eggers.
Other titles: New African histories series.
Description: Athens, Ohio : Ohio University Press, 2023. | Series: New African histories | Includes bibliographical references and index.
Identifiers: LCCN 2023012176 (print) | LCCN 2023012177 (ebook) | ISBN 9780821426081 (paperback) | ISBN 9780821426074 (hardcover) | ISBN 9780821426098 (pdf)
Subjects: LCSH: Kitawala—Congo (Democratic Republic)—History. | Christianity and politics—Congo (Democratic Republic) | Power (Social sciences)
Classification: LCC BR1430 .E37 2023 (print) | LCC BR1430 (ebook) | DDC 276.751—dc23/eng/20230626
LC record available at https://lccn.loc.gov/2023012176
LC ebook record available at https://lccn.loc.gov/2023012177

Contents

List of Illustrations — vii

Acknowledgments — ix

Introduction — 1

PART 1: BEGINNINGS AND DESTINATIONS

Chapter 1 Transmissions — 25

Chapter 2 Healing — 58

PART 2: VIOLENCE AND POWER

Chapter 3 Violence — 87

Chapter 4 Unruliness — 110

Chapter 5 Relegation — 141

PART 3: POSTS AND PRESENTS

Chapter 6 Posts — 175

Chapter 7 Presents — 195

Conclusion — 210

Notes — 219

Bibliography — 273

Index — 287

Illustrations

MAPS

1.1.	Map of Kitawalist arrest records	27
5.1.	Map of Kitawalist prisoners' relegation sites	148
5.2.	Map of prisoners' villages of origin	157

FIGURES

1.1.	Marginalia in the pages of Pastor Mulongo's copy of *Kitawala: Roman*	55
2.1.	A robe worn by a member of EDAC	61
2.2.	A woman during a spirit possession at a Kitawalist mass	68
5.1.	The prison inside of COLAGREL	143
5.2.	Entry to a "special cell" in COLAGREL	143
5.3.	The prison director's office	144
5.4.	COLAGREL guards stationed outside of the prison director's office	145
5.5.	Original planning sketch for COLAGREL	153
5.6.	The tree-lined road between the prisoners' barracks in COLAGREL	154
5.7.	The grave of Mama Saint Nkulu Kwamwanya Adolphine	169
5.8.	A Watchtower pamphlet	171
5.9.	The watch tower at COLAGREL	171

Acknowledgments

This book has been with me for more than a decade. It began way back in 2007, after I stumbled upon an archive rich with Kitawala documents (the DeRyck collection) at the University of Wisconsin–Madison (UW–Madison). That year, I wrote my first graduate seminar paper about the 1944 Kitawalist uprising in Lobutu-Masisi. I was hooked by the story. It has since become the subject of a master's thesis, a doctoral dissertation, two articles, and now this book. The project has been with me through four research trips to Congo (2008, 2010, 2014, 2018), four trips to the colonial archives in Belgium (2008, 2011, 2014, 2016), two jobs (Loyola University New Orleans, University of Tennessee, Knoxville [UTK]), a global pandemic, and virtually every milestone of my adult life. Without this time—and the myriad relationships, experiences, challenges, and insights it encompassed—this book would not be the same. Academia has a way of demanding and rewarding fast publication. I am, thus, grateful for the time I have had to sit and grow with the (unruly) ideas in this book.

Many people have made this study possible. First and foremost, I must thank the many individuals and communities—the everyday intellectuals—in Congo who took time out of their lives to speak with me, enduring my ceaseless questioning with kindness and patience, and offering me an invaluable chance to learn from their knowledge, experiences, and expertise. Without them, this project would not have been possible and I am forever indebted to them. In particular, I want to thank the Kitawalist leaders—PP2, Théophile Mulongo, Amani Simbi, Kibasombo-Wakilongo, Kabanga Kamalondo, Ilunga Wesele Joseph, and many others—who welcomed me into their communities and generously offered me their time and their knowledge about Kitawalist beliefs, practices, and history. In the years since we met, some of these individuals have passed away—namely PP2 and Kabanga Kamalondo—and I hope this book can, in some way, be a tribute to their memories. I am also indebted to the many Kitawalist women—in particular,

Maman Kalema—who shared with me their knowledge of Kitawalist healing and prayer. And I am also grateful to the members of the Wamalkia wa Ubembe community—especially Tata Wahiselelwa and his family and the Wazee 24 (in particular, Mzee 24 Ngandu)—who welcomed me openly into their community as well and graciously offered me the use of their archives. Although I have not featured their histories in this book, our conversations shaped my understandings of power, prayer, and Congolese history in profound ways. Inevitably, these individuals and communities will not agree with every word written within these pages, for historical interpretation can never fully account for faith. Yet, I hope I have nonetheless conveyed how profoundly I respect them, their beliefs, and their histories.

I am equally indebted to my friends and colleagues in Congo, without whom it would have been impossible for me to navigate the complex and conflicted social context of contemporary eastern Congo. Some of them—namely Marceline Kongolo, Amisi Mas, Michael Ahuka, and Sermy Nsenga—I discuss in the introduction, where I highlight their roles as coproducers of this research. But there are others to thank. In Uvira, I must thank Vincent Elocho and Reuben Abandelwa for the hours of lively and informed conversation. I must also thank Mama Nyota, who welcomed me into her home and her life as guest in Kalemie, and her son, Ken Muyumba, who offered aid and friendship to a raggedy researcher who wandered into the United Nations Mission in the Democratic Republic of Congo one day in Lubumbashi in 2010. Also in Lubumbashi, I am thankful to the Peres Salesian de Don Bosco for welcoming me into their guest house and to Donatien Dibwe at the University of Lubumbashi for his important historical insights and his aid in acquiring visas on multiple occasions. I must also thank my dear friend Patrick Kazadi. I could not have asked for a better friend with whom to explore and appreciate Lubumbashi—and all the places we have met since. Finally, in Kinshasa, I am thankful to Kiangu Sindano for his time and patience in facilitating my brief archival research in 2010.

A number of institutions have supported this project. I am especially grateful to have benefited from the aid of a Fulbright-Hays Doctoral Dissertation Research Abroad fellowship, which funded a year of field research in 2010. In 2008, the UW–Madison African History program awarded me the Vansina Fund, which facilitated a brief period of predissertation fieldwork that was crucial in convincing many people (including myself) and institutions that field research in eastern Congo was feasible. The UW–Madison Department of History also granted me both a single-semester write-up grant in spring of 2012 and the Doris Quinn Dissertation Completion Fellowship for 2012–13, which allowed for the completion of the dissertation version of this project. I must also thank the Wissenschaftskolleg research institute in Berlin, which funded my participation in the Berlin Meets Congo workshop in the summer of 2011 (and by proxy my first extensive period of archival work in Brussels). I am particularly thankful to Nancy Hunt for inviting me to that workshop and to the distinguished participants, whose feedback at that early stage was invaluable. In 2014, Loyola awarded me the Marquette Faculty Fellowship for summer research in the Democratic Republic of the Congo (DRC) and in Belgium, and, in 2016, they awarded me both a Bobet fellowship and a Faculty Research Fellowship, which funded a particularly crucial period of archival research in Belgium. I am also grateful to the UTK Department of History, which gave me the start-up funds that paid for a transformative period of field research in 2018, and the UTK Humanities Center, which awarded me a year-long writing fellowship in 2018–19. For aid in archival research, I am particularly grateful to Pierre Dandoy and Alain Gérard at the Archives africaines in the Ministère belge d'affaires étrangères in Brussels, as well as Albert van Eydne, who very kindly reached out to me and gave me access to his father's personal archive. I am also grateful to the Kitawalist communities in Kalemie and Lubumbashi who shared their own archives with me. Without the support of all these institutions, programs, and individuals, I could not have completed this project.

In the process of conceptualizing and writing this study, I have also benefited greatly from numerous editors, colleagues, and teachers who have shared with me their time and their feedback and inspired me in this work. I am grateful to the editors and staff at Ohio University Press—in particular, the editorial board of the New African Histories series—who took a chance on a first-time book author and pushed me to make it clearer and better. Nick di Liberto likewise helped me to sharpen both my prose and my arguments. I also owe a special thanks to Neil Kodesh, who was my adviser at UW–Madison and has always been incredibly helpful and encouraging, both during my graduate studies and beyond. I am likewise thankful to Florence Bernault, who has consistently supported, encouraged, and inspired me in this research, including reading drafts and offering feedback. Jim Sweet has also long been supportive of my work and career. At the UW–Madison, these three scholars taught me to open my eyes so that I might see something new and interesting in the history of Kitawala. Over the years, I have also benefited from conversations and interactions with a variety of colleagues who study Congo and Central Africa: Katrien Pype, Pedro Monaville, David Gordon, Miles Larmer, Emery Kalema, Vicky Van Bockhaven, Nancy Hunt, Benoit Henriet, Didier Gondola, and many others who have either read or attended presentations on various parts of this project over the years and/

or whose work generally inspires me. My colleague friends at both UTK and Loyola have likewise inspired me in their work and invigorated me with their conversation. My undergraduate professor of African history, Victoria Tashjian, and my high school history teacher, Jeff Ryan, were ideal mentors to a young and curious mind and first sparked in me a love of history. Aliko and Emilie Songolo, as well as Ned Meerdink, not only shared with me their contacts in South Kivu, but also their friendship, thoughts, and encouragement.

Writing is always easier and more productive when you have brilliant colleagues and friends you can bounce ideas off of. I am particularly indebted to Gillian Mathys, a fellow historian of eastern DRC and dear friend. Our transcontinental Zoom writing sessions and WhatsApp conversations helped me to think through and sharpen key concepts in the book at crucial moments. Roger Alfani is also a deeply valued friend and colleague, whose insights I have greatly benefited from in the late writing stages of this project. Although we were working on conceptualizing a new project (stay tuned), our conversations about the nature and power of religious community helped me to hone my ideas at important moments. Sarah Eldridge read multiple chapters for me during the revision process and offered me the keen and useful feedback of a qualified nonexpert reader. Aris Clemmons, Anne Langendorfer, and Kristen Block were my writing retreat buddies and offered much-needed conversation and encouragement in key moments of late-stage revision.

Finally, I must thank my family and friends. I have been blessed in life with the most supportive and encouraging parents a person could hope for, and without their constant love and encouragement, I would not be the person I am today. It is why I have dedicated this book to them. Even when my ambitions have taken me to places they could not imagine for reasons they could not fathom, they have never once done anything but encourage my passion and curiosity. To my Prescott ladies, the Krewe des Cartes in New Orleans, the Usual Suspects in Knoxville, my dear friend Annie Helke, and my many other cherished friends, old and new: life is richer and work is more meaningful when one benefits from such a wealth in community. And finally, to my beloved partner, Derek Yeadon, who has endured many months of separation, flown halfway around the world to see me, and never once been anything but supportive and encouraging. He is my support, my love, my life, and there is no one else with whom I would rather share my days.

I saddle none of these incredible people and institutions that have helped me along the way with the shortcomings of this book, but I thank all of them for making it possible.

Introduction

PAULO KANUMBI was born in Kinshasa (then Leopoldville) in 1930.[1] His parents had come from the region around Kabalo, a small outpost along the Lualaba, a major tributary in the vast Congo River network. When he was a young boy in the city, Kanumbi had a terrible accident in which he fell into a hole and split open his stomach, exposing his intestines. Everyone thought he would die, but miraculously he survived. When he reached school age, Kanumbi enrolled at the Catholic school, where he became close with a Catholic priest. One day he decided to ask the priest to teach him the secrets (*fumbu*) of the Holy Spirit. The priest grabbed him by the ears and shouted at him: "What are you? Kitawala?" Then he kicked him out of school. It was the first time that Kanumbi had ever heard the term and he was confused.

Following this incident, Kanumbi decided to become a soldier. In 1948, he joined the Force Publique. He was sent to Kisangani (then Stanleyville). There, his religious curiosity and zeal once again led to confrontation with authorities. When he was assigned the task of clearing weeds one Sunday, he refused the job because it was "God's day." For his insolence, his superior officers beat him unconscious, and he awoke in a prison cell two days later. This happened several more times until finally his commanding officer gave up and allowed him Sundays off to pray.

Shortly thereafter, he was examined by doctors who told him that his old stomach injuries would likely kill him within five years. He was discharged from service and decided to make his way back to his ancestral home in Kabalo. Along the way, he met an old woman living in the streets, and he helped her when no one else would. She blessed him.

By 1949, Kanumbi managed to make it back to Kabalo. Shortly after his arrival, he heard news of some "godly things" (*mambo ya mungu*) called *Stawal* (Kitawala). Remembering what the priest had said to him, he set off in search of it along with his brother, Kalenga Andre. They arrived in Ankoro where they met two "Christians of Stawal," Josepha Ngaluma and Kalumba Jakob. These two Kitawalist proselytizers told Kanumbi and his brother that they saw "two bibles" in their heads but that they would not be able to access them in Ankoro. After just two days, they sent Kanumbi and his brother away and told them they should "go to their mountains" to pray because "God is everywhere." Before they left, however, the two teachers gave them an object, which they claimed had been given to them in a cave outside of Manono. There, they had been visited by two Americans—white apparitions who had given them the object. They were warned that it was an empowering object, but also a dangerous object. If turned one way, it could release devastating floods. If turned another, it could release destructive fires. They charged Kanumbi and his brother with the object's safekeeping.

After this, Kanumbi and his brother returned to their home outside of Kabalo. Kanumbi started to sleep in the wilderness, on top of a nearby mountain called Kakasebi, which locals knew to be a place where ancestral spirits could be evoked. One night, it began to pour rain, soaking him to the bone and putting out his fire. Then suddenly, he heard a bird cry out and the rain stopped. Immediately, he dried out and his fire came back to life. In that moment, the Holy Spirit descended upon him and spoke with him for three days. Afterward, Kanumbi returned from the mountain with his revelations—his bible, which he had written down under the guidance of the Holy Spirit. Among these revelations were three very specific commandments: (1) it is forbidden to enter into political parties, (2) it is forbidden to get vaccines, and (3) it is forbidden to pay taxes. With these guiding directives, Kanumbi founded the community of Kitawala-Filadelfie.

BEGINNINGS

Pastor Paul II, known by most as PP2, narrated the above history to me as we sat in the courtyard of a tiny hotel in Kabalo in the summer of 2018. When we sat down to discuss the history of his community, the very first thing PP2 said to me was "if we begin with my father's birth, we will arrive well to our destination." For PP2, the story of his Kitawalist community began not with the African Watchtower (Jehovah's Witness) movement but with the story of his father, Paulo Kanumbi. It began with Kanumbi's path to religious revelation, and his journey to intellectual and spiritual leadership.

Woven into that story are the narrative threads of other beginnings, of different histories emphasizing other origins. The history of the African Watchtower movement and, more specifically, of Kitawala in Congo is part of this narrative. It is implied in the moment the priest asked him "What are you, Kitawala?" and implanted the idea of Kitawala into his memory. Drawing on the colonial discourse of that era, the priest understood *Kitawala* to mean insolence and religious dissidence. In Kanumbi's memory of that incident, however, the term *Kitawala* must have come to signify something quite different: the search for spiritual truth and power, and the panic that search induced in the agents of colonialism. The broader history of Kitawala is also reflected in the rumors of mambo ya mungu (godly things) that drew Kanumbi to Ankoro and introduced him to the network of Kitawalist proselytizers who were spread across the region in that era and were themselves connected to a long line of transmission stretching back to Watchtower in America. That thread of transmission is likewise revealed in the appearance of the "American apparitions," who offered an empowered and dangerous object to the Kitawalists in a cave. The very name taken by PP2's community, Kitawala-Filadelfie, a reference to Philadelphia, also points to Watchtower's American origins.

Still other narratives, other beginnings, are woven into Kanumbi's story. The history of the movement and migration in colonial Congo in the 1930s and 1940s is recorded in the story of PP2's grandparents, who migrated to the city in search of work, and in that of Kanumbi, whose diverse experiences as a young boy in a growing capital city, as a student interacting with White colonialist priests, and as a soldier traversing the colony undoubtedly shaped his understandings of power, politics, and possibility.[2]

Equally crucial to the richness of PP2's story are the threads of transmission originating in Central African discourses and practices of power that long predate the colonial era and the arrival of Watchtower. Such threads are present in his account of prayer and mediumship performed in caves or on sacred mountains; in his story of the miraculous appearance and diffusion of an empowered object that possessed the capacity to both protect and destroy, to heal and harm; and in the connections his story highlights between prophecy, shifting authority, and institutional innovation. PP2 understood the significance of each of these threads. But he also understood, like any good historian, that where one begins a story shapes its destination.

Unruly Ideas is about this multifaceted history of Kitawala—from its moments of rebellion and repression to its stories of revival and remedy. It follows Kitawala's history from its origins in the colonial context of the 1920s, through to its continued practice in some of the most conflict-affected parts of the eastern Democratic Republic of Congo today, providing a lens through which we may examine the complex and intersecting relationships between politics, religion, healing, and violence in Central African history. Like PP2, it begins with a premise: that placing the stories of individuals like Paulo Kanumbi at the center is the best way to arrive at a more nuanced study of Congolese history that, above all, highlights the experiences of Kitawalist men, women, and children as diverse thinkers, rebels, healers, and seekers, whose lives have intersected with and helped to redefine other, more familiar currents of Congolese history over the past century.

KITAWALA

The history of Kitawala is not unknown, but neither is it well-known outside of Congo.[3] In Congolese historiography, it has most often appeared in lists of anticolonial religious movements, often alongside much more widely recognized movements such as Kimbanguism. One particularly important exception is the Congolese sociologist Mwene-Batende's foundational work on Kitawala, which very meticulously reconstructs the political and economic context of the region touched by the 1944 Lobutu-Masisi revolt led by Kitawalists.[4] There is also excellent work on the history of African Watchtower, in which Kitawala has undeniable roots. Karen Fields's groundbreaking work, for example, illuminated the centrality of antiwitchcraft discourse to the broader movement and the particular challenge it posed to British attempts to secularize colonial rule.[5]

John Higginson's work on history of Kitawala among migrant workers in Katanga, which centers on the economic context of Kitawala's initial spread into Congo, has provided an equally enduring image of the movement as one of male African laborers engaged in anticolonial religious resistance.[6] And in many ways this image is accurate. Kitawalists were associated with a number of significant uprisings during the colonial era, and the majority of individuals arrested for those activities were men, many of them migrant laborers, who had moved from rural areas to cities like Elizabethville (Lubumbashi) or mining encampments, like those near Manono or Lubutu. Belgian colonial authorities imprisoned and/or displaced thousands of them for espousing ideas that they considered "subversive." They viewed these Kitawalists as unruly in the most rebellious sense of the word. From the Belgian perspective, *unruly* was a pejorative descriptor, signaling their frustration with intractable Kitawalist dissent. For the Kitawalists, however, unruliness, or unwillingness to be ruled, was a spiritual and political imperative: Congolese Kitawalist oral tradition holds that the very name *Kitawala* derives from the Swahili verb *kujitawala*—to rule oneself.[7]

But just as Kitawalists have never been exclusively male migrant workers, their teachings and activities have never been directed solely at resisting the Belgian colonial state, and their yearnings for self-rule have never been entirely about political self-determination. As PP2's story makes clear, Kitawala's history must be understood as containing multiple narrative threads. It is equally part of longer history of movements and institutions in Congo—and Central Africa more broadly—that have articulated critiques of moral and immoral uses of power and authority, and sought to transform the political, spiritual, and material status quo. In their use of medicines (*dawas*) to heal and power objects (*nkisi*) to protect, as well as their use of prayer, prophesy, and spirit possession to mediate the power of God and the ancestors for the guidance and protection of themselves and their communities, Kitawalists have historically rooted their faith in a very old language of power, ritual, and legitimacy.[8] Their interpretations of Christianity—like those of Simon Kimbangu and countless other independent African Christian intellectuals, prophets, and practitioners—have historically left room for traditional spiritual practice, even as they have called for renovation and renewal. Indeed, they have queried and theorized the very nature of tradition, and in so doing, participated in the long history of both preservation and innovation.

As a result, there was historically and is today a great deal of doctrinal diversity under the umbrella of Kitawala. And many have characterized it as a "syncretic" movement—a term that this book rejects. Although there is a need to describe processes of blending and exchange in human interactions, I, like many scholars of religion, particularly in Africa, find the term *syncretism* wanting—especially when used (like it often was by Belgian colonial officials) to imply confusion.[9] It occludes the complexity of the intellectual work done by those who develop, transmit, and practice blended faiths. Indeed, most Kitawalists today talk about Kitawala as both Christian and *ya asili* (traditional)—not a mixture of these things, but both of these things at once. Considering its connections to both Christian and Central African strands of transmission certainly matters—and is a major theme in this book. But these strands cannot be unraveled just to expose them as pure objects of analysis. Rather, what is more interesting are the ways that people in different times and places have woven them together, in the process demonstrating both the durability and the flexibility of the materials out of which they have been composed.

Such an understanding of processes of blending and exchange builds on the works of scholars like Birigit Meyer, Paul Landau, and Walima Kalusa, who have effectively illustrated both the expandability of African semantic and semiotic worlds and how such expansions have historically been shaped by specific (and often unequal) political and social interactions.[10] It likewise draws on the works of numerous scholars of Central African history who have noted this dynamism: the ability to borrow, merge, and invent, often in ways that were simultaneously innovative and conservative, has long been a core feature of Central African traditions and institutions.[11] Acknowledging this dynamism not only helps to make sense of the specific theories through which the blending of Christianity and *asili* was possible but also illustrates how Kitawala is part of what Steve Feierman has called an African "macro-history of power and knowledge."[12] It points to long histories of "hybridity" and multidirectional "transaction" across social and cultural contexts, without erasing the violence and destruction colonialism wrought on African communities and institutions.[13] And it also illustrates that Kitawala is part of an African intellectual history that is grounded in a deep regional past just as much as it is part of a global history of moving ideas.

Although Kitawala's preachers, prophets, and practitioners have articulated innumerable interpretations, most of which differ notably from Watchtower Christianity, some Watchtower ideas endured across communities. "The idea of the unmitigated equality of peoples in Christ" was perhaps the most enduring.[14] Critique of "this worldly" authorities (particularly colonial authorities, but also "customary" authorities) was also central to most iterations.[15] Emphasis on baptism as the path to salvation and the Bible as a source of truth (which White missionaries tried to obfuscate) were broadly accepted teachings. The promise of a new order, an era free from the "spiritual and physical slavery" of immoral secular rule (particularly of colonial states), was also widely articulated. Such beliefs are often described as "millenarian," although I also avoid this term in general. While it has some comparative value, it tends to emphasize ideas about the future (specifically an impending apocalypse) over interpretations of the past and present—both of which, this book reveals, were equally, if not more, central to Kitawalist thought.

In the end, the question of whether Kitawala is or is not Watchtower Christianity—and the parsing of which Watchtower ideas endured and how—is not the focus of this study.[16] *Unruly Ideas* is less a book about Kitawala, its theology, doctrine, and rituals, than it is a book about the people who have practiced different versions of Kitawala and the many ways they have interpreted and utilized theology, doctrine, and ritual to specific ends, in particular contexts.

It looks beyond doctrine to see the unruliness of Kitawalist ideas as they have been wielded by a variety of different people in different places and times. This includes a wide range of figures: clerks and miners in Elizabethville (Lubumbashi) and Manono in the 1920s and 1930s, rebel prophets and young girls in search of healing around Lobutu in the 1940s, prisoners in a penal colony in Kasaji in the 1950s, enclave communities in Equateur escaping Mobutu's state in the 1970s, mamas in prayer chambers in Uvira and Fizi in 2010, and a community of COVID-restriction refusers in Kabalo in 2020. Their stories span a century of Congo's history and touch many corners of the eastern part of the country, from Katanga to the Kivus to Orientale to Equateur. Through these diverse stories, this study emphasizes connections and continuities, but also ruptures and innovations, in the processes of transmitting and practicing Kitawala.

A central premise of this book is that Kitawalists were and are everyday intellectuals who engaged actively and creatively with the political, economic, and spiritual contexts in which they lived, who theorized and experimented. Like Paulo Kanumbi, some were prophetic figures who, after initial conversion and tutelage under Kitawalist proselytizers, received visions from God that guided them in developing their own doctrinal interpretations and founding their own Kitawalist communities. Such figures connected their interpretations of Kitawala—the "bible in their head"—to those of previous prophets or teachers, even as they transformed it to fit their particular spiritual, social, and political context. Others were not leaders at all, but nonetheless debated, parsed, and interpreted Kitawalist ideas as they encountered and transformed them.

This book is about this wider history of Kitawala and the individuals and communities whose pursuits defined it. It is about Kitawala's connection to deeply rooted Congolese histories of spiritual, political, and therapeutic power, as well as its transformation of and by colonial and postcolonial realities. More than a case study of a particular religious movement, it is a history of theories and practices of power that investigates the ways that communities and individuals in eastern Congo have historically imagined it and sought to access it, wield it, and police the morality of its uses.

POWER AND CONCEPT-WORK

One of the most striking characteristics of both archival and oral evidence from Kitawala's history is the sheer ubiquity of references to power. It shows up in a dizzying array of places and times and evokes a myriad of meanings:

spiritual power (of God, of ancestral spirits), authority, coercion, capacity to heal, capacity for malevolence. Frequently, it defies easy separation of those meanings. But such elision is in some cases the point. It can be used to invoke multiple registers of meaning, and to play with the tension between those registers. It is a language of overt and covert meanings—of inference, innuendo, and sometimes accusation. It often plays with temporality, juxtaposing older meanings with new, slipping between translations and muddying semantic fields. I have heard Kitawalists use *nguvu* and *uwezo* (Kiswahili), and *-anga* (Kiluba), as well as *puissance, force,* and *pouvoir* (French), interchangeably, often in the same conversation. Usually, its intended meaning seemed to be something that could be translated as "spiritual power"—a kind of innate capacity that comes from within, originating from God and/or the ancestors. But it has often also evoked other meanings—of authority, of capacity for persuasion and even coercion—simultaneously touching different but connected edges of the semantic field, sometimes signaling one meaning overtly (authority, resilience), but implying another (use of spiritual force, morally or immorally) under the surface. I have also heard it used as a critique—inferring its potential nefariousness, its connections to *bulozi* (often translated as "witchcraft") and the devil. And I have heard people refute that dichotomy, collapsing categories: "What is bulozi? It is the power of our ancestors. God gave us that power."[17] Often, it has been uttered with a sort of inflection meant to signal the gravity of it, its central importance. Vocal emphasis, body language—people used these modes to signal meaning.[18] Not just power, but "*that kind of* power."[19] It also emerges from the evidence as something that is embodied, something that can be transmitted, and/or something that can be exchanged or "transacted."[20] Like the object that Kanumbi was handed in the cave, it can exist somewhere in between metaphor ("the object is the Word," PP2 later told me) and physical manifestation.[21]

Tracing these many iterations of power over the course of Kitawala's history is a core project of this book. The term is thus used very deliberately throughout, appearing almost exclusively in moments when it evokes one (or more) of the particular meanings it carries within its Central African conceptual field and highlighting the variety of ways that Kitawalists themselves have sought to debate and delineate the nature of power.[22] Readers are thus invited to reflect on its intended meaning(s) in each context and consider how different preachers, prophets, healers, and everyday practitioners within the movement preserved, debated, and innovated these meanings. Power was not simply a set of forces—visible and invisible—that people imagined acted on them and/or could be wielded in a variety of ways. Nor was it just a set of changing institutional forces, shaping and reshaping their material, political, and social worlds. It was those things, but it was also a field of experience and meaning that they queried and debated.

This latter point is central to the underlying historical approach of this book, which borrows from the field of conceptual history. Conceptual history—which comes from the German *Begriffsgeschichte*—is not a new approach to studying the past. It was originally developed by historians of modern Europe, reflecting on the way concepts like *progress* or *citizen* shifted in meaning to reflect changing economic (industrialization) and political (nationalism) circumstances. As Axel Fleisch and Rhiannon Stephens helpfully explain, the approach works by following the usage of particular concepts across a defined linguistic, geographic, and/or temporal range. It emphasizes the "intellectual work" that everyday (i.e., nonelite) actors engage in as they both "contest" and "ensure the continuity" of the meanings of particular concepts. It is intended to "engage with people's intellectual lives and explore how their ideas shaped their history without the reductionism of exclusively studying elite thought." It focuses on the ways that language is used in particular places and times, how that usage both changes and endures, and how "meanings are always renegotiated in the process of translation."[23]

Fleisch and Stephens argue convincingly that conceptual history offers a promising new pathway in the study of African history because it "helps foreground the ways in which the intellectual work of Africans shaped their worlds," ensuring that they "are not relegated to a reactive position." But more than that, they argue that the study of African history can also enrich conceptual history by reckoning with the complex ways that Africans have both preserved and innovated concepts in their linguistically diverse contexts, where people—like Kitawalists—regularly move between languages, in ways that complicate theories of translation.[24] These contexts, they suggest, may "provide exactly those examples in which conceptual trends and ideas transcend language boundaries and afford the possibility of studying concepts that are constantly being translated."[25]

What makes conceptual history especially helpful for thinking through the history of Kitawala is its attention to the significance of translation and the ways that both overlap and slippage between different words for the same concept—in this case, power—create the space where people interpret, debate, and adapt meaning. This is where they do what I call concept-work—the agentive work of conceptualization—as materially new circumstances (and sometimes new languages to describe them) call for reassessment of meaning.[26] But this process is by no means linear and it is

Introduction 〜 9

always contested. There are often subtle—and sometimes big—differences in what people mean when they discuss power. It would be easy enough to signal some of these differences by retaining the particular words people use (nguvu, uwezo, puissance) in the sources, rather than translating them to "power." However, the parsing of difference is also the parsing of similarity, and I translate these various terms to "power" throughout the book as a reminder of the fact that identifying and interrogating the nature and meaning of such similarities was often central to the concept-work Kitawalists engaged in.

To better understand the concept-work that Kitawalists engaged in, however, it is necessary to consider the historically and contextually situated conceptions of power with which they were working. There is a rich body of literature outlining the history of political, religious, and healing traditions in Central Africa that can help to illuminate these diverse conceptions of power.[27] This literature has demonstrated that, as far back in the historical record as scholars have been able to discern, power in Central Africa was composed in fields of meaning that entwined religion, politics, healing, and violence, both dissolving and enforcing the boundaries between them. Drawing from a wealth of historical linguistic data, David Schoenbrun has highlighted what he terms "the contradictory historical character of power" in the early history of the region.[28] Power, in his configuration, took two forms: instrumental, such as "patron-client relationships," redistribution of wealth, and military power; and creative, the "words, pauses, and gestures used by healers and political orators to make people well and sway opinion."[29] Although often linked and sometimes embodied in the same person, these forms of power were also often at odds with each other. The "instrumental" power of family heads and chiefs (sometimes also priests), for example, depended on connection with the "creative" power of spirit mediums. But as wielders of creative spiritual forces, mediums could also challenge or undermine those holding instrumental power by using their creative power—their ability to access spirits—to establish alternative (and often subversive) nodes of authority and to mediate various relationships, including generational, kinship-based, and gendered relationships.[30] The push and pull between these forms of power, and the boundaries it both created and defied, constituted a central form of what Schoenbrun calls "groupwork" in the region.[31]

Although Schoenbrun's work focuses more specifically on the Great Lakes region, the model he describes is relevant to the broader region of Central Africa.[32] And this interplay—between instrumental and creative power—can help to elucidate much about Kitawala's history. Competing and overlapping claims to these kinds of power were central to the "groupwork" that Kitawalists engaged in, as they sought to delineate—and sometimes dissolve—boundaries between their communities and those around them.[33] For example, it offers some insight into the reasons why in some villages Kitawala's strong claims to creative power would at times be co-opted by existing authorities and used to bolster the legitimacy of their instrumental power. Meanwhile, in other villages Kitawalists would find themselves directly opposed to existing authorities and sometimes, as a result, use violence against those authorities. It is also useful for making sense of the role of women as wielders of creative power in Kitawalist history—a facet of Kitawala's history that has been hitherto ignored. If, as one Kitawalist leader told me in 2010, the success of Kitawalist men in their most political endeavors to undermine the colonial state depended on the creative power of the "mamas in the prayer chambers," then the history becomes much more complicated than rebellious Kitawalist men resisting the colonial government.[34]

Another important insight that has emerged from this scholarship on conceptions of power in Central Africa is that it has long been understood, in the language and philosophy of the region, to have a dual character, manifesting varyingly (or even simultaneously) as protection and predation, benevolence and malevolence, healing and "eating." The question of which manifestation of power is presumed in a given circumstance has been central to debates about the morality and legitimacy of its exercise. Scholars like Wyatt MacGaffey and Simon Bockie, for example, have demonstrated how, in western Congo, the term for power—"*kindoki* or a cognate term"—has historically been understood to be both the root of "all exceptional success" and the source of evil.[35] In eastern Congo, a similar term, *bwanga*, can also be translated as "witchcraft/power/force," and carries similar connotations of both exceptional and malevolent abilities.[36] Indeed, it shares the same root as a widespread Bantu term for healer: *nganga*. In short, this dual nature of power is inherent in the language people have used to discuss it—a language that, as MacGaffey puts it, has been one of "conflict and negotiation, not consensus."[37]

That last point is important because it underlines the ambivalence of these conceptions of power. This is not to suggest that such concepts are chaotic or without boundaries, but that they are manipulable and contingent and therefore doubtable and debatable. This has made them volatile, especially within the context of colonial violence, but not exclusively. Scholars like Michael Schatzberg, Stephen Ellis, and Gerrie ter Haar have argued that this volatility has carried into the postcolonial era as well, where it has shaped public discourses of legitimacy and illegitimacy.[38] Those perceived to use their power to protect, fulfilling the role of providing for their community, have been seen as legitimate. Those who used their power—often theorized as "the occult"—to "eat" resources have been deemed illegitimate. And disagreement about which side of that binary a given public authority represents has animated debate about the morality of their political agendas. Meanwhile, other scholars, like Joseph Tonda and Peter Geschiere, have noted how such forms of malevolence have come to occupy a prominent position in the Central African *imaginaire,* at the intersection of the public and private spheres, where accusations of persecution and affliction have been animated and distorted by postcolonial economic failures and global capitalist exploitation.[39] However, I am not really interested in discussing the "occult" as a discrete category, separate from the interplay with the broader conceptual world of power, divorced from the contingent ways that people theorize it in context. Such nefarious manifestations of power are certainly part of Kitawalist thought on the subject, including PP2's accusations that the current government of the DRC is a "DEMONcratic" regime that harms the people through malfeasance and extraction (see chapter 7). But this is where the parsing of similarity—the space of overlap—matters, because such accusations are inevitably subjective. At the same time that PP2 has accused the government of maleficence, others have accused Kitawalists of similar moral transgression (see chapter 2).

Moreover, the ambiguity of such conceptions of power in Central Africa has also made them incredibly generative—filled with possibilities for exercising agency. The power of spirits or of God may be harnessed to heal or cleanse people through conversion, initiation, or other rituals of transformation. Those who can wield, or direct, such forces may bring about revelation, revolution, and what lies between. For better or worse, spirits themselves may be put to work as "invisible agents" in people's everyday lives, transforming the worlds they inhabit.[40] Such agentive forms of spirits do emerge in Kitawalist stories—the American apparitions in PP2's story, for example, or the figure of Simon Kimbangu appearing in a prison cell (see chapter 6). But power might also be contained and transmitted via objects (medicines or nkisi or dangerous objects bequeathed in caves).[41] Central Africans have historically understood such objects to contain power that can be accessed, more or less successfully, by skilled healers, mediums, or, in the case of religious movements like Kitawala, pastors. In this configuration, power is something that can be exchanged, acquired, or accessed in what might be called an "economy of power."[42] In their search to find communal and individual health or to understand the source of their ills, people engaged in what Bernault has called "transactions" within that economy that, in a given historical circumstance, were perceived to best fit their needs.[43] And that economy of power could and did include forms of power (and its wielders) that came from outside Congo—increasingly so during the colonial era. Trying to illuminate what, at a given moment in Congolese history, Kitawala had to offer in the economy of power can go a long way toward understanding how people perceived their ills and why they were attracted to the movement (see chapter 3). And it speaks once again to the importance of the intellectual work Kitawalists did in parsing similarity.

Of course, power is not the only concept that Kitawalists thought about. They have, for example, done similar concept-work around the very names they have called themselves. As Osumaka Likaka has argued, naming, which situates new experiences and ideas within a conceptual world, constitutes an important Central African practice of meaning-making.[44] It opens up space to debate their significance and interpret their meaning, while simultaneously embedding them in the existing social and semantic world. In Central Africa, practices like punning and onomatopoeia are common, using familiar and related sounds to evoke multiple registers of meaning, making space for varied, intersecting, and changing etymologies. Kitawala has taken many names over the course of its history. Often, they have played with similarities in sound: Kitower signals the English word *tower*, for Watchtower; Kitawala signals the Kiswahili root *-tawala,* meaning "rule," "govern," or "dominate"; Kitabala (which also appears regularly in archives) signals the Tshiluba root *-tabala,* meaning to "open the eyes," "pay attention," or "wake up."[45] At other times, it has taken completely different names: EDAC (see chapter 2) connotes particular attention to the ancestors; *Dini ya Hoki/Haki* (see chapter 1) seems to play with the American word *okay* (hoki) and the Swahili word for *rights* (haki); *Mapendo* (chapter 3) signals the Swahili word for *love,* with contextual connotations of "self-love." Together these various names have constituted a rich semantic field that those who practiced, proselytized, and prophesied Kitawala (and its aliases) have drawn on to signal and/or reinterpret its meaning. Moreover, such concept-work around naming invariably intersected with that around the nature and purpose of power.

EVERYDAY THEORISTS AND TRANSMISSION

A central claim this book makes is that Kitawalists (and other everyday theorists like them, past and present) were and are intellectual agents and that understanding their concepts as theories does more than illuminate emic categories of meaning; it expands our understanding of African intellectual history. It recasts a movement traditionally understood as "resistance" as part of a much more multifaceted realm of lively debate, experimentation, and critical thought and action within African communities.

In recent years, other scholars have sought to expand the field of African intellectual history. Dan Magaziner, for example, has looked at the history of young Black Consciousness activists in South Africa, who put a vast array of "books and ideas"—including Christian theology—to "work in their particular historical contexts."[46] Derek Peterson has looked at the variety of "moral arguments" that Africans conducted in their own languages, as they elaborated a "patriotic theory" of what their families and political communities should look like.[47] Outside of Africa, feminist intellectual historians like Sadaf Jaffer, have emphasized how activities like life-writing and other forms of self-narration constitute a form of "claim making" that can be considered a kind of everyday theory. As Jaffer writes, expanding our definition of theory and theorists in this way helps us to "unsettle the notion that only certain designated theorists are generators of ideas."[48]

Evidence for these kinds of contemplation, moral argumentation, and claim making can certainly be recovered from oral and archival sources relating to Kitawalists, who likewise put ideas to work in their particular contexts. The writings of Kitawalists themselves are a particularly rich source for investigating their thought—their theories of power, their narratives of history, and their conceptions of moral community and moral action. Scattered throughout such sources is ample evidence of the questions people were contemplating about the nature of power—about its morality and the efficacy of its various sources and manifestations. Where does it come from? Who can and should wield it and to what ends? What are examples of how it has been wielded in a moral way and how can those examples be applied in context? There is also ample evidence in both the texts that they have written and the ways that they have interpreted other texts (the Bible, colonialist novels, etc.) of debate, doubt, and radical reinterpretation. Their critics have (particularly in the colonial context) read this as incoherence.[49] But I would instead argue that it is evidence of experimentation and adaptation. Kitawalist ideas were certainly unruly in the sense that they were in a constant state of interrogation, but that unruliness is precisely why they offer a useful framework for theorizing power. The multiplication of meanings in this context suggests active engagement.

As everyday intellectuals, theorists of Kitawala have been altogether less tied to books and writing as markers of intellectual legitimacy. Steve Feierman's work on "peasant intellectuals" is useful as a comparison here.

Feierman describes peasant intellectuals as those who "engage in socially recognized organizational, directive educative, or expressive activities."[50] This broad definition, which draws on the work of Gramsci, certainly fits many Kitawalists—particularly the (usually male) leaders, whose public activities emerge quite vividly from the archives. It opens up space for an approach to "intellectual work" that aligns more with that of conceptual history. In Feierman's approach, African actors (public healers) could and did revise and deploy historically rooted, but dynamic, categories of analysis and action (healing and harming the land) to address emergent and pressing social and political issues. But the definition also assumes a kind of "publicness" as requirement for intellectual influence, which potentially obscures the more intimate forms of contemplation that could and did generate theories of power and action.

This is where transmission—discussed in chapter 1—enters as a useful concept. Transmission stresses the movement of ideas through processes of translation, circulation, exchange, conveyance, and even contagion. It not only allows texts, transcription, and translation—writing and recording—to be part of the historical record but also spontaneous, contextually specific interpretation, as well as orality and aurality. It emphasizes reception, intimate contemplation, and individual innovation as things that happen both within and outside of the textual world, and it recognizes that ideological innovation can be something that happens in commune with spirits and spiritual forces, as much as texts. In short, transmission asserts that everyday people—not just men, not just literate thinkers, not just public figures—theorize about the world around them, and make decisions about how to imagine and enact their desired futures.

However, Kitawalists did not transmit their ideas absent of the influence and obstacles often inherent in uneven structural relationships and the "shrunken milieu" of possibility they have so often created in Congo.[51] The century of time this book weaves through has witnessed immense violence and upheaval in Congo. Its stories begin not long after Belgium annexed Congo from its notorious king, Leopold II, whose violent tenure ruling over the Congo Free State as his personal domain was infamously dubbed the "red rubber" era for the amount of Congolese blood that was spilled in pursuit of resource extraction.[52] They end in the midst of the global COVID-19 pandemic, itself situated in the context of a decades-long period of conflict and instability in eastern Congo characterized by neocolonial forms of extraction that have purchased precious minerals for global consumers at the cost of millions of Congolese lives.[53] The years in between featured the development of Belgium's notoriously repressive "nervous state," the "Congo

Crisis" after independence and the wars that followed, and three decades of autocratic rule under Mobutu.[54]

The historical context in which Kitawala emerged, spread, and developed certainly provided ample obstacles and challenges, and making sense of how to navigate those obstacles and challenges was central to the intellectual work Kitawalists were engaged in across these eras. But as Nancy Hunt has recently argued, the history of Congo must not be read as a "history moving from violence to violence, malfeasance to malfeasance."[55] Eastern Congo's history has been particularly prone to this approach, with a historiography largely revolving around histories of conflict and its causes.[56] But there are so many other stories to tell—stories that can lead us into what Hunt calls an "unresolved set of spaces, dynamics, and lives."[57] Although there have historically been a myriad of structural violences shaping both their desires and their endeavors to transmit ideas, Kitawalists have nonetheless done so in ways that signal discernment and creativity, as much as they do distress. Moreover, the ideas—and the actions—that emerged from such transmissions have not always been easy to categorize. They could be messy, unruly.

UNRULY IDEAS

Unruliness emerges as an important concept in this book. As an approach to histories of religion, it holds that what are often called doctrines—bundles of ideas transmitted between and taught within communities—were as often fuel for debate and fodder for revision as they were guiding sets of beliefs. They provided vibrant—but also volatile—fields for contemplation and action. Transmission, as a process of exchange and engagement, rendered them contingent but also relevant to context. They provided contours for defining and policing the boundaries of moral community, but in their infinite interpretability, also became subjects of radical contestation, refusal, and sometimes transgression.[58] Unruly ideas, then, are ideas in flux, shaped by the context and agency of those who encounter, adopt, and alter them.

This kind of unruliness is no way unique to Kitawala. It could be said about most systems of belief and is certainly inherent in the long history of Christianity. This inconvenient fact was a source of discomfort to missionaries and colonial officials across Africa, who were quick to dismiss or repress what they saw as incoherent—and therefore dangerous—African beliefs, but loath to recognize the incoherence of their own beliefs. To call Kitawalist ideas unruly is not to accept these colonial categories of what constituted legitimate religious expression. Rather, it is to simultaneously acknowledge the anxiety they caused Belgian authorities—how successful Kitawalists were at disturbing colonial order—and to upend the meaning of the word. *Unruliness* is a subjective term; it is only derogatory if you are invested in the order being upheld. As this book illustrates, Kitawalists were definitively not invested in upholding existing orders at many points in Congo's history— in both the colonial and the postcolonial eras. They have at various points in time pushed back against colonial authorities, against customary patriarchal authorities, and against postcolonial authorities. But more than that, they have pushed back against what Frantz Fanon and Steve Biko both theorized as the "colonization of the mind."[59] Their ideas were also unruly in the sense that they insisted on thinking freely—beyond the rules and deceptions of colonizers, missionaries, and anyone else they deemed oppressive.

Like Aparicio et al. in *Ethnographic Refusals, Unruly Latinidades*, this book puts forth a vision of community formation—in this case Kitawalist community formation—that is and was "always socially contingent, contextual and framed by both erasures and violences, from without and within, in a word, unruly."[60] It involved boundary-making and boundary-enforcing, but also flexibility, creativity, contestation, and refusal. Kitawala represented an alternative to, or revision of, other forms of "groupwork" taking place in Congo during the colonial era, such as emergent ethnic categorization, labor/class solidarity, mainstream Christian conversion, and the imposition of gender categories and expectations. The flexibility of its ideas and their transmission had the capacity to disturb other regimes of authority, whether colonial and missionary or "customary" and patriarchal.

As noted above, Kitawala's history has often been read as a history of resistance—specifically to colonial rule.[61] This was certainly how the Belgian colonial government viewed it. As we will see in chapter 4, Belgian colonial officials were deeply concerned that Kitawala was not only anticolonial but (particularly in the 1950s) also a nascent form of nationalism or communism. While there were officials who pondered to what extent Kitawala was "purely religious" and could be potentially cleansed of its radicalism through education, the overwhelming consensus in colonial circles was that Kitawalists were irredeemable "xenophobes" and "anarchists."[62] This is the stance that ultimately shaped policies of surveillance, displacement, and incarceration that underlay their approach to the "Kitawala Problem."

Kitawalists, in turn, have employed a number of tactics, particularly in their relationship to the state (both colonial and postcolonial) that could be fruitfully interpreted as resistance. Their repertoires of resistance have included tactics ranging from rebellion (chapter 3) to refusal (chapter 7) to remembering (chapter 5). And they have employed a variety of tools—spiritual (prayer, evocations, revival), intellectual (letter writing, clandestine teaching and preaching, human rights discourse), and physical (violence, self-marginalization)—in their pursuits. In the end, however, "resistance" fails to capture the multidirectionality of the moral (and immoral) projects Kitawalists pursued, and it occludes the reality that those "moral projects," which sometimes directed violence toward other Congolese people, created diversity of discontents.[63] Resistance slips too easily into binaries—oppression and liberation, colonizer and colonized, moral and immoral—that reduce the complexity of the religious, political, and social worlds in which Kitawalists have lived, and the futures they have hoped to create. It also leaves little room for interrogating the ways in which violences—state, gendered, boundary-enforcing—could be compounded and ultimately reiterative in circumstances of deep structural inequality. Unruliness could be much more "illegible" than resistance implies.[64]

ARCHIVES, ORAL HISTORIES, AND "ACCOMPANIMENT"

Unruly Ideas is the product of over a decade of multisited, archival, oral, and "ethnographic" research.[65] The bulk of archival sources consulted come out of Archives africaines, the administrative archives of the Belgian colonial government.[66] These archives constitute a rich trove of information about Congo's colonial past. They are also profoundly and irreparably shaped by the anxieties and obsessions of colonial rulers and their descendants. The last point is important because "former" colonial states can be notoriously anxious about when, where, and who they allow to see particular colonial archives, and have been known to suppress unsavory evidence.[67] Judging by the number of *sûreté* (classified) files relating to Kitawala I was not allowed to see, because they remained protected more than fifty years after Congo's independence, Belgium has retained a level of this anxiety.[68]

As many historians have pointed out, such archives are notoriously reproductive of the silences and violences that undergirded colonial power (see chapter 4).[69] They create "invisibilities" that become particularly pronounced when considering the history of women (see chapter 2).[70] As a result, we are left to work through what Bernault has called "the gaps and knots" of our evidence in pursuit of "the fierce elusiveness of the past."[71] Despite these shortcomings, colonial archives nonetheless remain sites where African representations of self can be glimpsed, where their voices can be heard and their ambitions can be witnessed. This study makes particular use of interrogation records, for example. The self-representations in such sources are always informed and often deeply tainted by the power dynamics of their production. Arrest records and prison reports are likewise important "second-hand" sources for things Africans said and did, but also invariably suffused by obvious colonial biases. Although flawed, these sources are nonetheless precious and can be read "against the grain" as windows into the social, political, and intellectual lives of Kitawalist actors.[72] Such sources can also situate people in space and time—a reality I have taken advantage of to produce the GIS maps exhibited in this book.

Some of the richest archival sources in this book are not from colonial archives at all, however; they are from Kitawalist archives. They are "tin trunk" histories that have been written by Kitawalist historians and circulated within Kitawalist communities.[73] The authors of these works are always anonymous—a reality that seems to reflect an understanding that these histories are not the possession of a particular author; rather, they belong to the community. It is in these histories—and in the oral histories that constitute the third main source from which I have composed this history—that some of the most vivid renderings of Kitawalist thought can be seen.

The oral histories featured in this study were collected over successive periods of field research in 2008, 2010, 2014, and 2018.[74] This research involved travel to a number of (sometimes remote) locations, largely in South Kivu, Haut Katanga, Tanganyika, and Lualaba Provinces.[75] I have visited several of the Kitawalist communities in these regions multiple times over the years; others I have not been able to return to because of both personal and financial constraints, as well as the infrastructural and political complexities of conducting research in eastern Congo. There are many other places I would have liked to conduct research—particularly Masisi in North Kivu—but was unable to because of the realities of continued conflict in the region. As a result, the oral evidence presented in this study and the archival evidence do not always overlap geographically.

To find a methodological language through which these sources could speak to each other, I have relied on the important body of literature that historians of Africa have developed over the past few decades related to techniques of analysis for oral and written texts. In particular, this study benefits from the work these scholars have done to liberate the oral histories from earlier notions of the oral as "traditions," which could be stripped of the contingencies of their production to reveal unified oral narratives, or "traditions" that were "true" and could be proven when compared with other kinds of sources.[76] Such a notion of oral history, beyond ignoring the very centrality of performance and subjectivity in the creation of oral texts, offers little that is analytically useful for thinking about oral texts produced via interviews and informal conversations with people who are not keepers of formal traditions, but rather—as is the case with most of the interviews featured in this study—keepers of their own experiences and interpretations of the past and present. I rely instead on the work that has been done to frustrate distinctions between truth and falsity, to render rumors reliable sources, and to recognize that while oral texts are inevitably subjective, they are also subject to the conformities of genre that render them comparable across time and space.[77]

Luise White's attention to genre in the reading of oral and archival texts has offered a particularly useful way to think about the relationships between these different kinds of texts not as sources for "proving" each other, but as a means of "refracting" each other: "they provide ways in which to read each other."[78] Thus attention to the ways in which certain "phrases, images, attitudes, and memories" are shared across the genres of archival and oral sources can help to illuminate something new about their common subject. If attention to genre can illuminate something new about these various texts across the temporal and cultural space dividing the archival and oral, then I would argue that it can do the same across geographic space.[79] Oral texts and fragments of evidence—rumors, images, attitudes—collected among Kitawalist communities in Fizi, Tanganyika, Kabalo, and Kasaji cannot "prove" anything about the experiences of Kitawalists in Elizabethville in the 1930s or North Kivu and Oriental in the 1940s and 1950s. But oral evidence can help us to "read" the archives anew and, in the process, write a history that neither could reveal on its own. This not only allows for the possibility of writing a history of Kitawala in the challenging research context of conflict in eastern Congo, but suggests that perhaps that very context can both inform and be informed by that history in revealing ways.

Other recent scholarship on field research methods, particularly in the field of anthropology, has emphasized how fieldwork involves "bodywork." This literature insists on acknowledging the embodied and relational nature of fieldwork and implores researchers to consider the ethical and methodological implications thereof.[80] This includes reflecting on what Adrian van Klinken calls the "messiness" of fieldwork in ways that draw on the postmodern insights of feminist, postcolonial, and queer studies scholars.[81] The present study draws insights from these works and, when possible, reflects on how my race, nationality, education level, language (my research was conducted almost entirely in Swahili), religion (agnostic raised Catholic), and gender, in particular, shaped (and sometimes defied) the expectations of the people I interacted with during my fieldwork.[82] Moreover, fieldwork in a region where long years of periodic political instability and its concomitant infrastructural decay could and did disrupt, alter, and upend travel plans, and was frequently messy in a more conventional sense of the term. It is not a stretch to call fieldwork in these circumstances improvisational.

But in some ways this kind of messiness altered the meaning of my embodied presence: that I showed up in places where people did not expect me (because of the distance and difficulty of travel) mattered, and altered my relationship to the Kitawalist communities I had traveled to find. It did this in part by inserting me into what I discuss in chapter 6 as their "profound histories," or the plane of history in which "spirits, ancestors, and God intervene in human actions."[83] That is, my presence was sometimes read as sign from God—particularly because of my habit of showing up, by complete chance, at auspicious moments—a subject I expand on in chapter 1. Grappling with this reality matters not just because of how it shaped my relationship to Kitawalist communities, but because it reminds historians that we are not the only creators of narratives of history, and our conventions of historical causation and meaning are not the only ones operating in the world. It is, moreover, a good example of how my interlocutors at all times retained the right and the capacity to "talk back" about the meaning of this research.[84]

Such acknowledgments do not, however, negate the very real inequalities that have shaped the research processes out of which this study was born. Power dynamics between me, as a White American researcher, and my interlocutors, as a relatively marginalized group within Congo, were and are inherently unequal. I have tried, on all occasions, to conduct research in an ethical way (with institutional review board approval, and attention to risk) and to mitigate the worst consequences of such inequalities by practicing what Aparicio et al. call "accompaniment"—"discernment, careful listening, and physical and social proximity with others to challenge the asymmetries of power that lead to structural violence."[85] I have done this by sharing language, sharing meals, and traveling with Kitawalists, and by genuinely trying to humble myself to their expertise about their own history. In the end, however, any claim of success in such endeavors is not mine to make.

Furthermore, it must be acknowledged that this research is not something I achieved on my own. I frequently traveled and worked with Congolese companions who aided me in both "fixing" and conducting the research. Some of them—particularly Amisi Mas, Marceline Kongolo, and Michael Ahuka—were not themselves "researchers" in the sense that they do not work in the academic field. Marceline and Amisi, for example, were and are involved in NGO work in the region.[86] Michael is Marceline's brother, and largely involved in odd transportation jobs for a living. Sermy Nsenga, himself a trained historian and affiliated with the university in Kalemie, has also worked graciously with me to arrange visits to Kitawalist communities in Tanganyika and accompanied me on several occasions. All have become close friends and companions who I trust and on whom I have relied to execute this research.[87] Without their work in finding Kitawalist communities (by asking around), helping to arrange transport, and substantively shaping many of the interviews (interjecting, clarifying, asking their own questions), it would not have been possible.[88] As recent conversations about decolonizing research in Africa—and particularly in the conflict zones of eastern Congo—have made clear, discussions about the crucial role that such individuals play in successfully conducting research belong not just in the acknowledgments, but at the center of conversations about how—and with whose labor—field methods work.[89]

ORGANIZATION

Unruly Ideas is organized into three thematic sections. Part 1, "Beginnings and Destinations," considers the question of origins from multiple directions, calling for particular attention to the creative and dynamic intellectual processes of translation, interpretation, and transmission that have always been central to the history of Kitawala. It also places Kitawala within the long history of healing institutions in Central Africa, paying particular attention to Kitawalist claims that women were and are the arbiters of "secret" knowledge and power within Kitawalist ritual technologies of healing and considering what these claims reveal about the gendered nature of spiritual and therapeutic labor within the church. Part 2, "Violence and Power," picks up the theme of violence, interrogating it from different directions. These chapters consider how Kitawalists themselves imagined and experienced colonial violence—how they sought to wield power in a variety of ways to alleviate the many maladies which it caused them and their communities. But these chapters also consider how colonial violence, and the myriad insecurities it wrought, gave birth to unruliness within the movement itself that manifested in a variety of ways, sometimes compounding that violence in their own communal and intimate spaces. Part 3, "Posts and Presents," enters into the postcolonial history of Kitawala. Its chapters follow Kitawala along multiple trajectories, situating it within "profound" histories of power in postcolonial Congo. It enters into the contentious spaces where new violences have emerge from old violences, continuities have collided with discontinuities, present experiences have shaped past memories, and, through it all, people have continued to reimagine unruly ideas.

PART 1

Beginnings and Destinations

1 ~ Transmissions

IN 1938, three men—Ilunga Jean, Ilunga Levi, and Mutombo Stephan—were busy traveling between villages in the far northern territory of Bosobolo, spreading teachings of Kitawala. All three were influential Kitawalist preachers whom the colonial government had "relegated" to penal displacement and surveillance in the region following their arrest for proselytizing activities in the southern regions of Katanga. According to a report by a territorial administrator named de Valck, the men would "start by browsing the villages, asking here and there for something to drink." After some time, "becoming more audacious," they would "bring out their teachings." Their efforts at "probing the terrain" in this way proved fruitful, and the relegated pastors had very rapidly begun to amass a new community of followers in the areas around their location of forced residence.

De Valck's report also offers a glimpse at some of the teachings the men offered: Jesus had been "born among the whites," but they had killed him and were damned because of it. Jesus would "return among the blacks, who took no part in the murder." The White people were aware of this second coming and were "jealous of the blacks." Because of this, Black people needed to be wary of White people, who offered a false "baptism of the devil" and spoke "the language of the devil" in their attempts to "try to send [Black people] to hell." Happily, Black people could also access the Bible and learn "the whole truth" about baptism and God's teachings. That truth was that "all can become children of God and can go to heaven after their death; whether they are polygamists or monogamists was of little importance, as long as they are baptized." Having learned this truth, "the whole black continent was nearly converted," except a "small area around Bosobolo," so everyone there needed to "hurry while they have a chance, and get baptized."

De Valck fretted that their tactics had been quite successful in the region, and baptisms were happening at all times of the day in the waters of the nearby Bagata and Bwangele Rivers, with "only a small number refusing." During these baptisms, one of the relegated pastors would put a robe on the candidate and take them into the water by hand. They would then submerge the convert and "say some words," after which the convert was free to leave. Some, de Valck noted, were "baptized by surprise and others by force." Many, however, went willingly and became "fervent adepts and active propagandists."[1]

Though de Valck's report myopically focused on the aspects of Kitawalist teachings that the colonial government most feared—namely, the propagation of anti-White ideas—it nonetheless offers a suggestive look at the processes of transmission at work around Bosobolo in 1938. After the colonial government forcibly removed the pastors to a new and unfamiliar territory because of their beliefs, they set out to build a new community. They did so by moving quietly through the surrounding communities, stopping here and there to share a drink with people and strike up a conversation. As they learned about the people they met and found a shared language with which they could discuss their experiences and concerns, these pastors began to introduce the teachings of Kitawala, undoubtedly catering their message to the concerns of the villagers. If de Valck's account is accurate, those teachings were about little more than the duplicitousness and evil of White people and the primacy of the Bible and baptism. But, as this chapter—and indeed this book—argues, transmission was rarely as simple a process as de Valck described, and the concerns, hopes, and desires that drew people into the teachings of Kitawala were myriad. As preachers like Ilunga Jean, Ilunga Levi, and Mutombo Stephan moved through these villages, their conversations would have been shaped by the people they met. No doubt many were concerned about the power of the White people—its origins and moral character—but one can easily imagine that many concerns were more personal, shaped by the contours of individual lives in differing communities. And the ability of Kitawala to address these issues would have been the standard by which those individuals and communities measured its relevance to their lives.

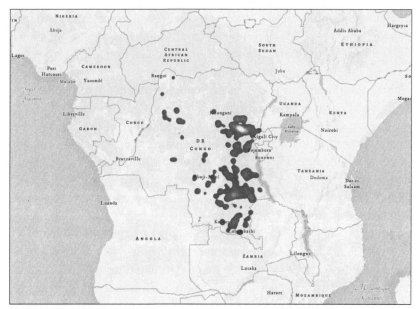

MAP 1.1. Map of Kitawalist arrest records. Created by author using ArcGIS.

This chapter is about these processes of transmission.² It is about the ways that people and ideas move and, in the process, are translated and transformed. But it is also about where those ideas originate and the ways they are received. More specifically, it is about how Kitawala was transmitted across the Copperbelt region of Central Africa, where it was known as the Watchtower movement, and into Congo beginning in the 1920s, where it was greatly transformed as it moved through diverse parts of eastern Congo (see map 1.1). At its core, this chapter asks how we can imagine the processes by which these diverse prophets, preachers, and practitioners—people like Ilunga Jean, Ilunga Levi, Mutombo Stephan, or Paulo Kanumbi (introduction)—transmitted Kitawala into their various cultural and political contexts and made sense of it in their different lives and communities. Understanding their stories and these processes of transmission is crucial to understanding both the intellectual history of Kitawala specifically and the dynamic spiritual, political, and intellectual lives of African men and women living in colonial Congo more broadly.

The chapter is situated in the earliest years of Kitawala's history in Congo, following the lives of early Kitawalist proselytizers and converts as they navigated the first decades of Belgian colonial rule. Although it draws interpretive evidence from later periods of Kitawalist history, most of the cases highlighted in the chapter focus on the era between 1908 and

Transmissions ~ 27

1940, after Belgium annexed the Congo Free State from Leopold II and before World War II. These years were marked not so much by abandonment of the violently extractive capitalist projects of the Congo Free State era as by the refinement and expansion of those projects by the Belgian colonial government, as it sought to render the colony manageable and profitable.[3] Congolese people living in these years witnessed immense economic, political, and social change. Economically, the era brought significant growth in extractive industries ranging from mining to timber and rubber—industries developed by Congo Free State concessionary companies, but expanded with "liberal" state support during this era.[4] It also brought rural agricultural schemes aimed at cultivating particularly labor-intensive crops like cotton and coffee; such projects generally involved the use of force or coercion to secure the labor of rural Congolese producers.[5] Changing industrial development required new infrastructure and involved new patterns of settlement and migration, with significant movement of rural Congolese populations—particularly young men—to urban areas and mining camps, even as it also brought migrant laborers from British-ruled Copperbelt colonies into increasing contact with Congolese people.[6] This movement of people also encouraged the movement of ideas—ideas like Kitawala, among others. And all the while, missionaries, both Catholic and Protestant, sought to expand their influence by building new mission stations and schools in rural and urban areas alike, bringing ever more Congolese people into contact with the ideas of Christianity, and the idiosyncrasies of Christian missionaries—a process highlighted in the case studies below.[7]

At the same time, the era saw the growth of the Belgian administrative state, which sought, with uneven results, to exercise control over all these processes. It attempted to harness "biopolitical" strategies, ranging from eugenics to biomedicalization, and social and political engineering strategies, ranging from administrative reorganization (villagization, creation of chiefdoms, etc.) to reeducation, to establish this control.[8] Its inability to do so effectively in many contexts, particularly as the initial economic growth of the 1910s and 1920s gave way to the Great Depression of the 1930s, fueled the Belgian state's "nervousness," and created precisely the political circumstances in which early Kitawalists were increasingly surveilled, imprisoned, and subject to penal relegation.[9] It is against this backdrop that these early years of Kitawala in Congo must be read, but, as this chapter argues, it is in the more intimate experiences and individual interpretations of their meaning that these processes must be understood.

TRANSMITTING KITAWALA

Transmission has a number of meanings. It can mean circulation or exchange—of ideas, goods, or diseases, for example. It can also mean conveyance, delivery, or broadcast—of a radio signal or a message. And these different kinds of transmission evoke diverse processes. Transmission of an idea often involves translation, whether in written texts or oral discussion. Transmission of a disease involves physical contact and other modes of transference, while transmission of a radio signal involves the materialization of the invisible, of that which is sent from an emitter via unseen pathways and can be accessed by the right receiver. All these meanings convey both a sense of movement and specific modes of reception.

The history of Kitawala in Congo is in many ways about all these kinds of transmission. In the most obvious way, it is about the transmission of an idea—a collection of teachings—at the hands of prophets, preachers, and teachers, who carried their multifaceted and ever-evolving message between villages, cities, and workers' camps across the Copperbelt and into Congo in the 1920s and beyond. Many of them carried Bibles and Watchtower literature, which they circulated and translated within both their own communities and the communities they visited. Many had little access to such literature, and instead exchanged their ideas orally. In most cases, transmission involved a combination of these media.

Transmission undoubtedly involved debate and interpretation. It was not a passive transference of information, but rather a "dynamic and relational" process, similar to Bernault's theory of transactions. Bernault describes transactions as "exchanges, and transfers" that "determined, each day, subtle or major reordering of hierarchies, status, wealth, and knowledge."[10] If "transaction" helps us theorize the process of exchange, the notion of transmission adds to it a sense of motion. It combines transaction with mobility—not only the mobility of people and texts and the ideas that they carried but also the movement of ideas between visible and invisible realms. The history of Kitawala also reminds us that transmission was not always between people. Transmission also took the form of prophecy and mediumship—of divinely emitted messages received by Kitawala converts who, guided by these messages, then further transformed Kitawala, shaping it according to their particular mission. It evokes the image of a medium as an antenna.[11] Like Paulo Kanumbi, whose story began this book, these individuals refracted the meaning of Kitawala through the messages they discerned in various states of ritual and prayer, in powerful spaces like mountains, caves, and prayer chambers.

Meanwhile, the colonial government viewed all these modes of transmission as contagion. And, over the course of Kitawala's history in Congo, they sought at many points to contain, eradicate, and/or "cure" it through policies of imprisonment, relegation, and reeducation. Indeed, the policies the colonial government developed to contain infectious disease and the policies they developed to deal with Kitawala were very similar, as was the language they used to describe the "Kitawala Problem" as they saw it.[12]

But for Kitawalists, transmission was a dynamic process of exchange and (re)interpretation, of divine messages and prophetic inspiration, of translation, debate, and subversive action. It was creative and generative. And it could be unruly and violent. Although it was guided by the movements (sometimes forced), teachings, and actions of particularly charismatic preachers and prophets, it was never entirely controlled by them. For on the other end of transmission there were individuals, families, and communities who came to Kitawala with their own desires, hopes, and expectations. They were people searching for and finding belonging, building what Paul Kollman has called "historically specific relationships of attachment."[13] This was an unruly process in the sense that it gave birth to many diverse and contextually contingent iterations of Kitawala, but also in the sense that many men and women, emboldened by Kitawalist ideas, challenged the legitimacy of colonial rule. They demanded, as one contemporary Kitawalist told me, kujitawala—to rule themselves—in matters both spiritual and political.[14] Thus, different forms of transmission were entangled with each other in a process guided not only by individual personalities—prophets, preachers, and teachers—but also informed by the broader social and political context in which they operated.

This chapter brings together several different strands of the history of transmission. It looks at the early history of transmission of Watchtower across the Copperbelt and into southeastern Congo. Then it looks at the prophetic biographies of several different Kitawalist leaders who emerged from that region. Their stories were connected to the chain of early Watchtower transmission, but they were also shaped at every level by other, sometimes more influential transmissions that found their source not outside of Congo but, like Paulo Kanumbi, in empowered spaces and the ritual of prayer. Such transmissions originated not in Bibles and written tracts, but in the minds of those who heralded visions and messages from the realm of the spiritual and the reputations they garnered. Finally, we will see how transmission was a contingent and generative process, dynamic in its acts of translation and interpretation and malleable in its capacity to speak to a given moment. Together, these different strands of transmission begin to weave a picture of the early history of Kitawala in Congo.

BEGINNINGS

In 1954, the Belgian colonial administrator R. Philippart described the origins of Kitawala thus: "Born in America in 1879, Watch Tower began to grow around 1918, gaining momentum in 1922 as their message was diffused around the world by radio-broadcast. In this way it came to South Africa, where its propaganda was seized on by those agents who would bring it to the Belgian Congo. The movement gained ground in Northern Rhodesia and provoked the Mwana Lesa affair in 1925. In October of 1927, the first converts were discovered in Elizabethville."[15]

Like Philippart, scholars of African history and religion have long situated the history of Kitawala within the history of the Watchtower Bible and Tract Society, more commonly known today as Jehovah's Witnesses. Indeed, as Philippart's historical sketch suggested, Kitawala emerged out of the African variant of Watchtower movement, which started in South Africa in the early twentieth century and made its way to Congo, largely via labor migration routes. The history of the African Watchtower movement was a crucial part of Kitawala's history of transmission. It introduced some of the core discourse of the movement in specific teachings, like those de Velck reported, about the illegitimacy and evil of secular colonial rule and the duplicitousness of White missionaries and administrators. It also emphasized the importance of baptism and biblical scriptures.[16] The African Watchtower movement also helped circulate teachings about the legitimacy and power of Black spiritual knowledge and traditions. Moreover, recognizing Kitawala's connections to Watchtower illustrates how even seemingly remote parts of Congo were connected to important global networks of circulating ideas. Thus, if, as PP2 put it in the introduction to this book, we want to "arrive well to our destination," in many ways it makes sense to begin with Watchtower.

And yet, Watchtower is not where PP2 began his story. PP2 began his story with his father's life history—with the winding paths that led him to learn about Kitawala and, ultimately, to seek divine inspiration for his own interpretation of the movement (the "bible in his mind") in a nearby mountain. And he is not the only Kitawalist who has emphasized other beginnings in narrating the history of their church. In Uvira in 2010, Kibasomba-Wakilongo, a teacher within a variant of Kitawala known as Église du Dieu de nos ancêtres au Congo (EDAC), told me that "the beliefs of EDAC are traditional (ya asili). It was here. It began with our ancestors."[17] Another EDAC leader in the town of Mboko, Ese Ebake, recounted it to me thus:[18] "In short, we can say that EDAC began long ago. Since the time of the Belgians, we have been with this church. The advocate of this church [*mtetezi*] was Mzee Lumumba. During that time, people asked him whether he had a religion. He said he had the religion of this country [*dini ya nchi*]. When they began the struggle to send the Belgians back to their country, many of them said, 'It looks like this guy wants to rule himself [*kujitawala binafsi*].'"[19] Still others identified different beginnings. Further south, in a Kitawalist mission outside of Kalemie, Shindano Masubi Ayubu explained how "Arabs were the first to bring the words of God with Islam. Then they made us slaves. After that, the Europeans came. They came to throw out the Arabs. Then they enslaved us themselves. Then Lobati Ngoma came [with Kitawala] and he told us that we were being enslaved."[20]

None of these versions of Kitawala's history emphasize Watchtower as the beginning of the story. Indeed, Ese Ebake begins his story decades later with Patrice Lumumba, a perhaps surprising narrative choice that I discuss further in chapter 6. Shindano Masubi identifies Lobati Ngoma, who was an early Watchtower convert, as the source of the movement, but does not emphasize his ties to Watchtower. Instead, he explains how Lobati Ngoma came and disrupted a long history of malicious teachings about God's word, which were introduced by those who wanted to exploit the people of Congo. Meanwhile, Kibasomba-Wakilongo roots the history of his faith in tradition (*asili*) with his ancestors.

None of these individuals refuted the connection to Watchtower; rather, in the histories they tell, it did not take center stage. In all cases, when asked, they acknowledged a chain of transmission stretching back to Watchtower as part of their history, but for them the moments when that chain of transmission was disrupted, or redirected, by particular prophetic individuals were often more important. In the case of EDAC, for example, they pinpointed a couple of moments of disruption in the chain of transmission as the most significant. The first was when Patrice Lumumba (according to their telling) became a prophet for their church and all of Congo through his calls for self-rule. Then, in sacrificing himself to the cause of their spiritual and political freedom when he was assassinated in 1961, he transitioned to the world of the ancestors and became, himself, a source of spiritual transmissions, an ancestor whose guidance they could evoke through prayer and ritual. Another came in 2002, when a woman—"just a regular mama" who was not part of their church—came to them "filled with the Holy Spirit," bringing "news from [their] ancestors and [their] mountains" that they should transform their Kitawalist church into EDAC and redirect the focus of their prayers to their own ancestors (including both their specific Bembe ancestors and Lumumba, whom they claimed).[21]

In short, for these church elders, their rupture with the history of Watchtower was as important as—or indeed more important than—their connection to the long train of transmission reaching back to the American Watch Tower Bible and Tract Society. And while this chapter now turns to a discussion of Kitawala's connection to the Watchtower movement, it does so with the acknowledgment that it is but one way to arrive well to our destination.

TRANSMITTING WATCHTOWER

The American Watchtower Bible and Tract Society, out of which the African Watchtower movement emerged, was founded in 1884. In its initial formation, it was a nondenominational society of Bible study groups led by a Pennsylvanian man named Charles Taze Russell. Inspired by the messianic ideas of the Seventh-Day Adventists, Russell preached the imminent return of Christ.[22] Russell taught that Watchtower adherents should oppose themselves to all hierarchy, both religious and governmental, because the world's institutions were the dominion of Satan. Because of this, Witnesses shunned political participation, often including the payment of taxes. They were, and still are, fundamentalists who believe(d) in the literal truth of the Bible, particularly the book of Revelations, and they believe(d) strongly in the immediacy of the apocalypse.

Though, from the viewpoint of the Belgian Congo in 1954, Philippart traced Watchtower's wide reach in Africa to the transmission of Watchtower radio broadcasts on the continent, most scholars have traced Watchtower's earliest success in Africa to the unusual charisma of an English evangelist named Joseph Booth, who preached a relatively progressive interpretation of Christian theology that explicitly tied biblical teachings about the importance of free will to support for free labor.[23] These scholars are correct, to the extent that it was Joseph Booth who first brought Watchtower literature to Africa and who first convinced Russell that the Watchtower Society should focus its missionary efforts on Africans, both in Africa and in the Diaspora.

As a result of Booth's efforts, by 1906 the Watchtower Society began pouring pulp literature into Africa that would make it into the hands of Africans—especially migrant laborers—who then took leading roles in evangelizing the continent. Of those early African Watchtower evangelists, Elliot Kenan Kamwana was by far the most influential. Along with his two childhood friends, Hanoc Sindano and Ngoma Shinkala, Kamwana had, by 1909, baptized more than nine thousand people in Nyasaland.[24] Indeed, it was in light of Kamwana's Watchtower revival that the movement first came into the scope of colonial musings and fears, quickly transforming into a dangerous specter that would haunt the imaginations of colonial authorities from Nyasaland to the Belgian Congo.

Kamwana's Watchtower doctrine was a unique blend of orthodox Watchtower ideas and potent ideas about labor reform, equality, and African liberation that had emerged out of his experience working as a migrant laborer in South Africa. Kamwana baptized followers and preached Watchtower as an ideology of spiritual and cultural equality. In offering baptism and salvation to all Africans, Kamwana freed them from many of the barriers put in place by White missionaries. No longer did converts have to prove that they had undergone a "change of heart" by renouncing polygamy, ceasing alcohol consumption and dancing, renouncing belief in witchcraft, or adopting European language and habits of dress. Accusing the missionaries of withholding God's truth from Africans, Kamwana articulated a theology that, on the one hand, undermined the missionary claims to a monopoly on the path to salvation and, thus, on social and political dominance, and on the other hand, left room for the articulation of culturally relevant interpretations of Christian teachings, particularly about the nature of God's power and His plan for its redistribution in the material world.[25]

Kamwana's influence was so feared by the colonial regime in Nyasaland that, by the end of 1909, they forcibly removed him to South Africa. They allowed him to return to Nyasaland in 1910, but in an effort to curb his influence, they relegated him to a remote district of the country where people did not speak his native language, Chitonga. Despite these efforts, Kamwana continued to spread his Watchtower doctrine until, in 1914, he was accused of "preaching seditiously" of the impending departure of the British and was deported to the Seychelles, where he remained for twenty-three years. Upon his return to Nyasaland in 1937, he found the Watchtower communities that he had left behind still thriving.[26]

KITAWALA INTO CONGO

From Nyasaland the movement spread rapidly along the rail lines into what were then Northern Rhodesia, Southern Rhodesia, and the Belgian Congo. It was Kamwana's friend, Hanoc Sindano, who was at the forefront of the evangelization in northeastern Rhodesia, particularly in the Luapula Valley, along the border with Katanga. There, in one of the most important labor catchments for both Katangan and Rhodesian mining operations, Sindano had, by 1917, established a strong Watchtower presence along the footpaths that laborers used to travel back and forth to the mines. He found a receptive audience; for in the midst of wartime conscription, drought, and outbreaks of Spanish influenza, the region had fallen, in Higginson's words, "below previous levels of subsistence and into the hands of Watchtower prophets and adepts."[27] At one point in 1918, Sindano and his followers even succeeded in driving British magistrates and officers out of the eastern regions of Northern Rhodesia. The exploits of Sindano and his followers have been very effectively recounted by Karen Fields, however, and need not be rehashed here—except for the purpose of pointing out that it was in the context of this Watchtower expansion and the arrest of Sindano that leadership effectively transferred to two emergent leaders in Zambia: Tomo Nyirenda and Jeremiah Gondwe.[28]

Tomo Nyirenda would emerge as the more infamous of the two leaders, when he assumed the title of Mwana Lesa—meaning "Son of God" in the Lala language—and carried Watchtower, which he now called "Kitawala," across the countryside from the northern regions of Northern Rhodesia to southernmost regions of Katanga in the Belgian Congo.[29] Whether Nyirenda was the first to use the name Kitawala is not entirely clear, but, as Higginson has effectively argued, it certainly points to the centrality, within Nyirenda's teachings, of the conviction that "the power to rule" did not rightfully belong to colonial authorities and the chiefs who abetted them.[30] Nyirenda's critiques of immoral exercise of power were not reserved for colonial authorities and wayward chiefs, however. Rather, people across the countryside were invited—and coerced—to cleanse themselves and their communities of impurity, to more effectively practice what might be called "self-rule" of a different kind—the kind that involves assessing one's own morality and that of others as causes or symptoms of larger social, political, and/or spiritual afflictions.

Between February and September 1925, Nyirenda visited villages across the region and left in his wake a spectacular trail of baptisms and witch killings. As word of his powers of witch detection and baptism spread, he was invited to Congo by a chief named Mufumbi, who wanted Nyirenda to "cleanse" his villages.[31] Having run into some trouble in a Northern Rhodesian village, when he was accused of killing an elderly woman whose family (insisting on her innocence) alerted the colonial authorities, Nyirenda accepted the invitation as a fortuitous exit. At Mufumbi's behest, Nyirenda killed accused witches in Katanga at an incredible rate: he and his followers killed upwards of 174 people over the course of two months, from June to July of 1925. Karen Fields notes that at one point, when Nyirenda questioned the scale of the violence and the attention it would draw, Mufumbi allegedly assured him that "killing witches is permissible in the Congo."[32] It was certainly not permissible, however, and by the end of July, the Belgian authorities caught wind of his activities and sent a patrol to arrest him.[33] He evaded the patrol and crossed back into Northern Rhodesia, but British authorities ultimately apprehended him in November and sentenced him, along with fourteen other Kitawalists, to death by hanging in early 1926.

By the time Nyirenda crossed back into Northern Rhodesia, however, the seeds of Kitawala had already taken root in Congo.[34] From this initial area of transmission in southeastern Katanga, Kitawala spread across much of eastern Congo and, ultimately, into parts of western Congo during the era of colonial rule. In the years from Nyirenda's arrival in 1925 to independence in 1960, several major theaters of Kitawalist transmission emerged. These different theaters were at once intimately connected and historically distinct, and can be seen as areas of concentration on map 1.1, which I created using GIS to map over 990 arrest records and other archival documents identifying individuals arrested by the colonial government for various Kitawalist activities. The map gives a sense of who was being arrested for Kitawalist activities and where they were from. However, it is important to note that most of the records identify not where the Kitawalist individuals were arrested for their activities, but rather where their village of origin was located, which, given the history of mobility in the region, were not always the same. The map also lacks data for the years after 1955, when there was significant Kitawalist activity in Equateur. Such are the limits of the archival evidence.[35] Still, most of the individuals do, in fact, appear to have been arrested within fairly close proximity to their village of origin, making this "heat map" a relatively good representation of Kitawala's significant theaters of transmission.

In southern Katanga, the movement continued to amass a following, particularly under the leadership of two men (both baptized by Nyirenda): Lobati Ngoma (Kima) and Mumbwa Napoleon Jacob, who took the movement into new territories.[36] Lobati Ngoma, for example, ultimately made his way to Jadotville, where he continued to baptize and teach Kitawala. From about 1931 to 1936 the movement grew significantly throughout the region. Higginson has argued that Kitawala's deepening influence in Katanga during this era was in many ways related to the series of boycotts and strikes African laborers instigated in the region during the same period as a result of worsening labor conditions, which were exacerbated by the effects of the global Great Depression. Seeing moralistic undertones in African claims that they were receiving unjust prices for their labor, the Belgians assumed that subversive religious ideologies—namely Kitawala—must be behind their grievances. In making and acting on such assumptions (by arresting suspected Kitawalists), Higginson contends that the Belgians in many ways created the Kitawala outbreak they feared.[37] They succeeded not in suppressing it but in sending it underground, where Kitawalist leaders began to gain a reputation for eluding the secret police by using the power to turn themselves White, a claim that only bolstered their reputation as wielders of such forms of miraculous power and brought more converts into the movement.

PROPHETIC BIOGRAPHIES

In the early phases of Watchtower's transmission from the United States to South Africa, across the Copperbelt, and into Congo, it is apparent that particularly charismatic leaders were connected to each other, often through chains of conversion, baptism, and mentorship. But it is also important to note how divergences appeared as Watchtower was transmitted among them. The American Watchtower Bible and Tract Society transformed into the African Watchtower movement. The African Watchtower movement transformed into Kitawala. Particular leaders laid claim to new prophecies and interpretations, with some, like Mwana Lesa, even laying claim to divine authority as the "son of God." Mobility was a crucial part of this history. Sometimes followers went on their own missions, guided by their own desires to proselytize, and sometimes they were sent by their leaders. Sometimes they relocated by invitation; sometimes they moved to evade colonial officials or were forcibly relocated. Finally, we can begin to see how all of this maps onto a regional history of labor migration and connects to intersecting questions about labor rights, wealth accumulation, and the morality of power in the colonial context.

Such accounts are useful to grasp the context and scale of the history and to get a sense of Kitawala as part of an intellectual lineage reaching back to Watchtower. Yet, it is worth pointing out that this way of thinking about the spread of a particular idea—by tracing networks of leaders—also shares much in common with the epidemiological practice of contact tracing, lending itself to an understanding of transmission as contagion. And it is perhaps for this reason that it is the mode of narrating Kitawala's history that dominates in the colonial archives.[38] In virtually every colonial report on Kitawala's history, colonial officials put forth some version of this narrative of transmission.[39] They were convinced that any kind of subversive idea must have been transmitted, like a disease, from outside. Moreover, while this kind of contact tracing can be useful for giving an understanding of how something—like a text or teaching or, indeed, pathogen—can get from point A to point B, it tells us little about how it is absorbed, transformed, and experienced by a particular individual or community. To understand that, one must consider the other dynamics of transmission.

A more robust understanding of the history of Kitawala's transmission requires attention to individual actors—to their distinct biographies and to particular and repeated acts of transmission. It requires stories like the prophetic biography PP2 narrated about his father, which centered not on the history of Watchtower but on the divinely ordained episodes of Paulo Kanumbi's life story that led him to become the leader of a large Kitawalist community around Kabalo. Such stories not only underscore individual experience and agency as a central part of this history but also draw attention to the parts of the history that are emphasized by Kitawalists themselves: the moments when the power of their prophets became apparent, affirming their authority and spiritual insight.

To illustrate this point, this section highlights what I call the "prophetic biographies" of just a few individuals who became highly influential Kitawalist leaders during the colonial era: Mutombo Stephano, Kulu Mupenda, Muyololo Kabila / Ngoie Maria, and Kadiba Ilunga Émile. While not all of these individuals are revered as prophets by contemporary Kitawalists, all were harbingers of messages that profoundly altered the contexts that they touched, and were thus prophetic in that sense. The evidentiary records for understanding the lives of these individuals are uneven. Kadiba Ilunga Émile's biography, which combines archival evidence with oral evidence and "tin trunk," Kitawalist-authored biographies, offers a fairly detailed picture of his life.[40] But I have largely had to excavate the stories of the others from colonial archives—mainly security reports, which are mostly brief and motivated by different concerns than those of the Kitawalist-authored sources. As a result, their stories are more fragmented. Despite this unevenness, taken together their lives paint a more richly textured picture of the intellectual history of Kitawala in Congo than can be gleaned from network-tracing narratives alone.

Mutombo Stephano

Sometime around the turn of the twentieth century, Mutombo Stephano was born to his parents, Kalenga and Ngoie, in the densely populated village of Mulongo, located on the eastern banks of the Lualaba River, in the territory of Mwanza.[41] The archives reveal little information about his early life, although it is clear at some point in his youth he gained access to education, including reading and writing in French—skills that he later employed in his position as a clerk and bailiff to the court at Jadotville.

In the years of his youth, Mutombo Stephano would have witnessed significant changes in Mulongo, including the back-to-back introduction of Protestant and Catholic missions. The Protestant mission was part of the Garenganze Evangelical Mission (GEM), which had originally been founded in Bunkeya, under the permission of Msiri. An Anglo-German missionary named Zentler built the Mulongo mission on the east bank of the Lualaba in 1911, seeing it as a prime location to influence the region. Unsettled by this growing Protestant influence in the region, the Catholic Holy Ghost Fathers built a mission on the west bank of the Lualaba just a year later, in 1912.[42]

It is likely that Mutombo Stephano gained his education at one of these missions, although it is unclear which one. It is possible that it was the GEM mission. As historian David Gerrard has noted, the Catholics would later accuse the GEM mission of facilitating the spread of Kitawala in the region through their teachings about *libre examen*—that is, the free or individual interpretation of the Bible—and their lenience on polygamy and willingness to incorporate the musical instruments and "undisciplined enthusiasm" of indigenous religious practice in their services.[43] Although such accusations are to some extent rooted in Catholic anxieties about Protestant influence, it is possible that Mutombo began to develop an interest in pursuing his own interpretations of the Bible during this era while studying under Protestant tutelage.

In any case, what is clear is that he grew up in a time when the people around him would have been discussing these rival missions and the points of departure between their teachings about Christianity. Indeed, Gerrard even suggests that the rivalries between the two missions became violent at times: they were known to throw stones at each other or even burn each other's books and school desks.[44] It is perhaps not surprising that someone like Mutombo would later grow up to teach about the untrustworthiness of White missionaries.

By the mid-1930s, Mutombo had taken his clerking job in Jadotville. It was almost certainly while he was living in Jadotville that he met and was ultimately baptized by Lobati Ngoma. The circumstances of their meeting and details of their relationship are not apparent in the archive, but Mutombo Stephano was clearly moved by Lobati Ngoma's teachings and began to preach them himself quite fervently. Apparently, he even used work excursions into rural interior regions as opportunities to reach out to people he met and baptize them into Kitawala.[45] One can imagine that this process would have looked very much like the description at the beginning of this chapter—with Mutombo striking up a conversation with local villagers over a drink or food when his clerking duties were through, conversing with them about their desires and concerns.

By the time of Mutombo Stephano's arrest in 1936 in Jadotville, he had begun to focus his proselytizing efforts in the mining camps of the Union Minier in Jadotville. Along with him, some ninety-three people were arrested for preaching such radical ideas as "equality of races" and "equality of salaries."[46] Fourteen of those arrested were non-Congolese and were exiled from the country, seventy of them were subject to natal relegation (relegation to their village of origin), and nine of them—including Mutombo, Ilunga Jean, and Ilunga Levi—were relegated to a remote internment village in Boende, Equateur. Colonial officials hoped that in that far away region, the men, not speaking the language, would have little ability to communicate with the local population and thus no audience for their teachings.

As we know from de Valck's report, within a year of their relegation the authorities in Boende were alarmed when Kitawala began to manifest in that region as well, clearly propagated by Mutombo and the others. By 1942, the authorities decided to relegate them once more to a plantation at Oleka just outside of Lubutu in northern Kivu (today Maniema), in the newly installed "Arab chiefdom," this time thinking that the Muslim population there would be less susceptible to Kitawala. Once again they miscalculated, and Mutombo Stephano very quickly began to make connections in Lubutu.

At that time, the Belgian government was in the midst of war efforts that had precipitated both new forms of resource exploitation and the construction of new roads and infrastructure throughout the region.[47] In this context, Mutombo Stephano and his fellow *relégués* found ample opportunity to share their Kitawalist teachings. Although their own mobility was restricted under the rules of relegation, Lubutu saw a great many people passing through at that time, including laborers who came to work on infrastructure projects like the nearby Libilinga bridge and loggers who came to work in the nearby lumber camps. Also passing through were individuals suffering from leprosy who had themselves been relegated to the leprosarium at Lubutu.[48] Indeed, one of Mutombo's most fervent converts—a man named Boloko—suffered from leprosy and became "their emissary to villages in the region of Wasa and the other mining cités."[49]

Mutombo met, introduced Kitawala to, and ultimately baptized many of these passers-through in the Muyu River, near the very bridge they had been recruited to build. Because his mobility was limited by surveillance, one must assume that many actively sought him out, curious to hear what he had to say, and were instructed in Kitawalist teachings under conditions of secrecy. Of those, many left with his teachings—and some apparently with a copy of a Swahili Bible that he had given them—and took them elsewhere.[50] Some made their way to the work camps of Comité National du Kivu, where Mutombo's teachings ultimately reached a man named Bushiri Lungunda. Bushiri in turn became a powerful prophetic leader in his own right, ultimately leading the infamous Lubutu-Masisi uprising of 1944 (see chapter 3).

For his role in spreading Kitawala to this region, Mutombo Stephano was sentenced to a much stricter form of penal relegation—what in chapter 5 I discuss as *concentrative* relegation—in a camp for "dangerous relégués" known as Ekafera. The last archival mention of him (that I have seen) notes that he was one of a group of prisoners (including Kadiba Ilunga Émile and Muyololo Kabila) who in 1953 joined together to write a letter to the administrators of Ekafera demanding their release from the camp and the freedom to teach Kitawala.[51] It is not clear where Mutombo Stephano went in the later years of his life.

In the end, many of the details of Mutombo's life and work are unknowable. His story shares much in common with the other charismatic prophetic leaders discussed in this chapter. Unlike some of these other leaders, however, it is not clear that Mutombo presented himself to (or was perceived by) those he converted as having any kind of unique prophetic power or knowledge that was divinely revealed to him. We see hints that his popularity as a preacher may have been rooted in rumors of such power, given his appeal to leprosy patients or the suggestion that transient workers sought him out in secret encounters to gain access to new knowledge. But what is also clear is that he did not work alone. Rather, he worked together with his fellow Kitawalists to share and build his knowledge of Kitawala. Ultimately, what emerges is the image of a contemplative, charismatic, and determined man who sought at every turn to inspire people to follow a new path to potential power and wellness.

Kulu Mupenda

Kulu Mapenda[52] was also likely born around the turn of the twentieth century, to his parents Mutombo and Kakuli, in the small village of Kalumbi, located near the confluence of the Lukuga and Niemba Rivers, about sixty kilometers from Albertville (Kalemie). The details of his early life are unclear, although he must have gained at least a basic education, for he was proficient at reading and writing. At some point, he left his home village and made his way to Elizabethville. The nature of his work in Elizabethville is not apparent, but what is clear is that, like Mutombo Stephano, he at some point met, learned from, and was baptized by Lobati Ngoma. Like Mutombo, Kulu became a fervent adept and teacher himself.[53]

The era when Kulu Mapenda was baptized by Lobati Ngoma was a dangerous time for Kitawalists in the southern regions of Katanga. Beginning in the 1930s, the Belgian state, which blamed "subversive sects" like Kitawala for a number of boycotts and labor stoppages in the mining regions of southern Katanga, began to crack down on Kitawalist networks. They did this in part by using the newly formed secret police to hunt down and arrest leaders of the movement.[54] Lobati Ngoma knew that the authorities were in pursuit of him, and in 1936 he fled to Sakania in an ultimately failed attempt to thwart them. But before he fled, he gave Kulu Mapenda a mission: to return to his home territory of Albertville and continue the work of teaching Kitawala.

Just a few months after his arrival in Albertville, however, colonial authorities arrested Kulu Mapenda and sentenced him to relegation in the village of Luseba, not far from his home village, under the authority of a young district chief named Benze.[55] Upon his arrival in Luseba, Kulu found the social climate somewhat unfavorable to the continuation of his mission. In the preceding years, the region from Kalemie to Kongolo had been subject to significant upheaval caused by a different movement called Kibangile, which colonial reports classified as a "hunt for witches" that inspired "abnormal and disquieting" infractions.[56] The reports about Kibangile are intriguing and share much in common with reports on similar movements geared toward cleansing communities of perceived spiritual and "interpersonal malevolence," or witchcraft.[57] In 1934, they described groups of diviners identifying sorcerers in villages across the countryside, from Albertville to Kongolo. People accused of witchcraft went before an inquisitorial tribunal of these diviners, who would force them to confess and relinquish their dawas or face corporal torture.[58] According to one report, diviners designated as many as 164 men and 2,469 women as sorcerers during the episode.[59]

Given the seriousness of the movement, the colonial police pursued and severely punished those involved, and by the end of 1935, the fervor over Kibangile seemed to have subsided. Still, as a result of Kibangile's influence, when Kulu Mapenda arrived at the end of 1936, authorities both customary and colonial in the region remained very mistrustful of any sort of religious innovation.[60] It is perhaps for this reason, as well as his previous arrest, that in the first months after his arrival in Kalemie, Kulu laid low. He waited until the customary chief, Benze, left town for several weeks in mid-February 1937 to begin proselytizing in earnest. Free of "the resistance and the opposition of the customary authorities" in Benze's absence, Kulu declared himself a messenger of God and began teaching and baptizing people into Kitawala, which he called "Dini ya Hoki" or "Dini ya Haki." The names—both of which appear in the archives—evoke different, but potentially related meanings. "Hoki" seems to be an adaptation of the American word *okay* (a possible reference to Watchtower's American roots); while "haki," the Kiswahili word for "justice/rights," may be a reference to Kulu's interest in the human rights language found in documents like the Atlantic Charter (discussed below).[61] Taken together, they suggest that Kulu was doing concept-work around the meaning of Kitawala, teaching that the power of elsewhere (the United States, the Christian God) might be harnessed to bring about wellness (okayness). At the same time, evidence suggests he—and, perhaps more importantly, those he proselytized to—also interpreted those teachings through vernacular theories of power.

Colonial reports indicate that Kulu wielded "an old Bible as talisman" and offered the fact of his relegation as proof that he had power the Belgians feared, underscoring the legitimacy of his teachings. He was aided by several associates who were themselves convicted Kitawalists relegated to the region.[62] Within six weeks he amassed nearly two hundred followers in the territory. Many of them were young people or nonlocal laborers who had come to the region for work in the timber, mining, and cotton industries. But he also converted the chiefs of several villages in the district, who in turn facilitated the conversion of nearly all of their constituents.[63] According to the history Kitawalists themselves keep, Kulu Mapenda was so effective at spreading the news of Kitawala far and wide that he earned the nickname "Kandeke" (or "little bird") to signify the "miraculous" manner in which he moved from place to place.[64]

After learning of Kulu's activities, Benze moved to arrest Kulu, but Kulu's followers attacked and injured the policeman he sent to apprehend him. Apparently convinced that his influence rivaled that of Benze, Kulu went so far as to go to Benze himself and publicly harass him in front of other notables. Kulu had overestimated his position, however, and was arrested shortly thereafter. In his home, the authorities found long lists of converts, and it was those lists that allowed colonial authorities to truly grasp the breadth of his influence.[65]

After his arrest, he was sentenced to concentrative relegation and sent to a penal camp at Malonga, in southwestern Katanga (today Lualaba Province). While imprisoned at Malonga—and ultimately a neighboring camp known as COLAGREL—Kulu gained a reputation as a "dangerous man" because he resisted the camp authorities in myriad ways and continued, at every turn, to preach the power of Kitawala.[66] The policy of relegation and this period of Kulu Mapenda's life are discussed further in chapter 5, but it is worth noting here that the reports about Kulu Mapenda from this era of his life indicate he was a formidable intellectual and teacher who knew long passages of the Bible by heart and would copy many extracts of it into notebooks to circulate among other prisoners. He also recited passages from human rights documents like the Atlantic Charter from memory and used them to accuse his captors of human rights violations.[67]

As with Mutombo Stephano, there is much about Kulu Mapenda's life that is unknowable, in part because the available sources are almost exclusively colonial security reports. But unlike Mutombo Stephano, there is clearer evidence that he presented himself as a prophetic figure who had been sent by God. Or, at the very least, he gained that reputation in the region. As already mentioned, there is his nickname—Kandeke—which signified his reputation for a "miraculous" capacity to move. Additionally, shortly after Kulu's arrest and relegation, authorities discovered another "cell" of Kitawalists between Nyunzu and Kabalo, and among this group, they reported, was practiced a "more mystical" form of Kitawala in which Kulu Mapenda was believed to be a messenger of God. According to their teachings, Kulu had not been sent into relegation after his arrest, but rather had "returned to the Promised Land where the chosen Kitawalists were to come and join him so they could enjoy without further delay all the advantages that the doctrine [of Kitawala] had promised."[68]

These rumors about Kulu Mapenda's fate are interesting on multiple levels. On the one hand, they contain fairly standard millenarian discourse about the "Promised Land" that can be found in a number of comparable religious movements in the history of Africa and elsewhere. On the other hand, they are also situated within the specific history of relegation in Congo, which, in effect, saw people rapidly removed by the colonial state from some contexts and inserted into others. Such forms of forced movement could and did feed rumors that those who were removed from particular contexts—like Kulu Mapenda was from Luseba—were feared by the colonial government for their power and knowledge and/or were moving into a new phase of their faith in which their removal marked them as chosen by God. Such rumors were potent not because they were or are verifiable, but because people discussed and believed them.[69] The people they reached weighed them as a part of Kitawala's potential appeal, rendering them a significant part of the broader economy of power in which they operated.

Muyololo Kabila and Ngoie Maria

In many ways, Muyololo Kabila's story both mirrors and intersects those of Mutombo Stephano and Kulu Mapenda. He was born around the turn of the twentieth century in a village called Kiambi, on the banks of the Luvua River, about sixty-five kilometers (40 mi.) from the town of Manono. At some point, he moved to Kamina, where, in 1935, he met and was baptized by Mutombo Stephano, who had traveled to Kamina to meet with another Kitawalist, Kasongole Kabondo, who colonial authorities had put under house arrest there. After initiating Muyololo, Mutombo returned to Jadotville, where he was arrested shortly thereafter. Muyololo then went to work, traveling through the villages in the territory around Kamina and rapidly converting many people, including a number of chiefs and notables who eagerly invited him into their villages to "preach the good words" of Kitawala.[70]

Because of its similarity to the other two biographies—including eventually ending up at relegation camps, with Mapenda in Malonga and Mutombo in Ekafera—I will not go into Muyololo's story in great detail. But it is worth mentioning because it appears alongside a related story of a woman named Ngoie Maria. In the archive, her story is just a brief footnote to Muyololo's story. But, even in its brevity, that footnote offers important insight into the history of Kitawala's transmission.

Ngoie Maria was apparently the "mistress" and "second" to Muyololo, who had initiated and baptized her while he was preaching in her home village of Kiswa. From there, they moved through the countryside together spreading the teachings of Kitawala. Her job was, in part, to welcome new converts by cooking them meals. More significantly, she also was in charge of teaching the women who were initiated into Kitawala how to sing Kitawalists hymns.[71]

As I will discuss in chapter 2, such activities are an important part of the spiritual labor of women within Kitawala today. Ngoie Maria's story offers evidence that they were in the past as well. This rare acknowledgment of women in a colonial report on Kitawala offers a crucial glimpse into the process of transmission, in which men like Muyololo, Mutombo, and Kulu certainly played a key part but cannot be understood as the only or even the most important actors. Women like Ngoie Maria were also crucial and creative participants in that process. Ngoie Maria moved with Muyololo between villages and endeavored, like him, to spread the news of Kitawala. She also shared her name with another famous Congolese woman—Maria N'koi—who twenty years earlier had built a reputation as a healer and insurgent against colonial rule in Ikanga, and whose connections were known to reach far and wide.[72] It is possible the shared name is a coincidence, for neither name can be considered rare. But is it also possible it is a reference to the history of another powerful woman? It is impossible to know. Regardless, as Nancy Hunt points out in her account of Maria N'koi's life, the name N'koi/Ngoie, which means "leopard," is itself laden with meanings—of chiefly authority, of imperceptibility, of slyness.[73] If it is a coincidence, it is nonetheless suggestive.

The story of Muyololo and Ngoie Maria also reminds us that the history of Kitawala was also a history of intimacy—a story of building "relationships of attachment" not just between men, but between men and women, and among women.[74] In those spaces, people sang, prayed, and communed together over shared meals at which they undoubtedly discussed their hopes and expectations for the future, contemplating and debating the meaning of Kitawalist ideas. Ritual and fellowship are corporal expressions of spirituality that must be understood as breeding intimate connection between participants and "affecting group and individual subjectivities and identities" as participants mutually seek connection and access to divine power.[75] As with Ngoie Maria and Muyololo, such intimate connections undoubtedly took the form of companionship, shared purpose, desire, and even love. However, as is possible with most forms of intimacy, this kind of spiritual intimacy could also take the form of exploitation, coercion, and even violence, a point I will return to in chapter 4.

Kadiba Ilunga Émile

Kadiba Ilunga Émile[76] is revered today as the prophet of the Kitawalist church in much of former Katanga. His followers call their church L'Église de la libération du Saint-Esprit du prophète Kadima Émile Ilunga du Kitawala, and they make up the largest group of Kitawalists in southeastern Congo. Like Muyololo, Kulu, and Mutombo, Ilunga was among the most prominent leaders of Kitawala in Katanga beginning in the 1930s. Of the four men, he is the only one for whom I have substantial evidence outside the colonial archive, including both oral accounts and two biographies—*Histoire de l'Église Kitawala: Prophète Ilunga* (henceforth, the *Histoire*) and *Historia ya Kanisa: Biographie ya Baba Prophete* (henceforth, the *Biographie*)—written by (an) unnamed author(s) from among his followers. These sources detail the story of his life as a preacher, intellectual, prisoner, and prophet.[77]

Kadiba was born to his parents, Mukanya and Mukekwa, in the village of Kitentu, territory of Manono on March 14, 1898. He went to primary school at Lukulu and secondary school at Lubanda Mpala in Moba.[78] In 1919, he moved to Elizabethville, where he took several clerking jobs before landing a position as a clerk at the court around 1921. According to the *Histoire*, he was personally selected for his position at the court by Prince Albert of Belgium because of his superior skills in speaking, reading, and writing French. Given the fact that Prince Albert did not visit Elizabethville until 1926, this story is almost certainly a fabrication, but it nonetheless illustrates an important point: Kadiba was an erudite man who, in the view of his followers, was marked for greatness early, as a young man.[79]

Colonial reports about how Kadiba first learned about Kitawala are murky. Some sources suggest he was baptized by Mutombo Stephano and Kulu Mapenda. Others simply note that the Kitawalist movement in Elizabethville had been started by Lobati Ngoma.[80] All seem to place Kadiba in the chain of transmission meant to illuminate contact tracing between him and other notorious leaders. The *Histoire* offers the following story of his conversion:

> In that torrid atmosphere of the years after the first world war, Kadiba, who had been baptized Catholic Christian in his youth, was touched by the suffering of his black compatriots, who were living in servitude under the colonial yoke. This is why on the 14th of March, 1922, Kadiba, who was a great reader and writer, began his correspondence with Joseph Franklin Rutherford, the living prophet who began to send him various works. The most notable being: *Towards Deliverance, The Harp of God, Who Will Inherit the Earth,* and *The Prophetic Book*.
>
> He learned theological teachings through the works that he received from America, furnished by Rutherford, and from other countries like Switzerland. (The Catholics and the Protestants did not come to Congo in particular and Africa more generally to teach the Blacks about God, but rather to serve the interests of their countries and prevent the blacks from searching for and knowing God.)
>
> He was touched and moved by the doctrines contained in the different works: a) equality of the races, b) the independence of all the people of the world, c) love of the neighbor and the knowledge of the true God.
>
> Kadiba became a loyal apostle of God and his black brothers (1 John 4:7–8; John 10:4–11) from 1923–1935 while he was in correspondence with Rutherford and received his letters via the Boston House Cape Town, an affiliate created in South Africa.

Kadiba matured his faith through personal research through the documents and began to profess them to his compatriots (Galatians, 1:11–12).

In the *Histoire*, then, the kind of transmission his followers emphasized is something quite different: not of direct contact between individuals resulting in contagion/conversion, but of deep contemplation and discernment combined with active pursuit of answers. He was someone who came to his faith through observing the suffering around him and, of his own accord, sought new knowledge about how to alleviate that suffering. He collected works he found "moving" and revelatory (including Watchtower literature) and, according to the *Histoire*, sought correspondences with those who might have further insight—including Watchtower founder Joseph Franklin Rutherford. In using the post this way, he was participating in a broader Congolese history of letter writing as "experimentation" in self- and world-building.[81] Interestingly, there is no mention of Mutombo and Kulu or Lobati Ngoma, and indeed, he is said to have begun his study of Watchtower literature several years before Kitawala came into Congo with Tomo Nyirenda.

This illustrates some important points. Namely, Watchtower literature was circulating outside of formal networks of leaders, and people like Kadiba were encountering, interpreting, and engaging with it on their own. And while the claim that he had direct correspondence with Rutherford in the United States is unverified, archival reports confirm that Kadiba was indeed sending letters to the Watchtower church in South Africa and collecting Watchtower literature. In fact, when he was arrested, officers found thirty pieces of Watchtower literature and a number of letters hidden in the walls and a false table bottom in his home.[82] He also sought out connection to other Kitawalists in Congo. For example, hearing of the imprisonment of Mutombo and a number of other Kitawalists at the prison in Elizabethville in 1936, Kadiba sent a messenger to meet them and ask "*Uko kwa mlango gani?*"—or "What group are you with?"[83] After that it seems that he did indeed build a relationship with Mutombo (though he is not mentioned by name in either Kitawalist biography).[84] But the point is that this process described in the biography was not simply a top-down chain of transmission.

This image of Kadiba as an original thinker and teacher, who always had the welfare of his fellow Africans at forefront of his endeavors and was keenly aware of the selfish intentions of Western missionaries and colonizers, is developed further as the *Histoire* progresses. According to the biography, he exposed the lies of the missionaries and the exploitation of the colonial regime by collecting documents and other accounts proving their duplicitousness. For example, it details how he learned of a "resolution" signed by the White Protestant mission leaders—Methodist (J. M. Springer), Evangelical (James Anton and W. P. F. Burton), Adventist (O. M. Giddings)—at a conference in 1932 in Elizabethville in which they declared that Watchtower was subversive and needed to be suppressed, and denied "the idea that God could reveal himself through a Black."[85]

Furthermore, the *Histoire* recounts that Kadiba kept a copy of a speech given by the governor of Congo in 1930 in which he explained to the White missionaries the goal of evangelization: it was "not to give blacks the knowledge of God, because they have known him since their ancestors." Rather, their task was "essentially to facilitate the work of the administration and the industrial sector." The missionaries were to "detach them [Africans] and discourage them from everything that could give them the means of unifying"—"especially their war fetishes"—to "make sure that the young do not inherit the ideas of their parents." Instead, the speech emphasized, the missionaries should teach lessons about submission and obedience. They should "teach them to read, but not to reason" and "make sure the blacks never become rich." It implored the missionaries to "teach [Africans] that their statues are works of Satan" and "confiscate them to fill our museums in Europe. In this way, they could make the blacks forget their ancestors and worship ours, who do not listen to them: Saint Andrew, Martin, John, and Mary."[86]

This evidence then serves as a foundation for some of the most central teachings Kadiba would ultimately profess—namely, that traditional African spiritual practices were created by God and should be respected and understood as a path forward for African people. According to Kadiba's evidence, one of the most important tactics White missionaries used in trying to oppress Africans was to teach them that their ancestral practices were sinful and had to be abandoned. Through this abandonment, White people could disinherit Africans of the power that God had given them so that it could, in turn, be hoarded by White people, who filled their museums with empowered objects (statues) and benefited from the prayers that went to their own ancestors (Christian saints) instead of the ancestors who truly could hear and respond to the prayers of African peoples.[87] Thus, to achieve freedom from their physical and political slavery, Africans had to seek freedom from this spiritual slavery.

There is a very interesting theory of tradition at work in these teachings, which I explore more in the next chapter. And there is certainly much more to Kadiba's biography beyond this account of his early intellectual and spiritual development and his eventual emergence as a leader in the broader Kitawalist community. Indeed, most of the references to various "miracles" associated with Kadiba come after his arrest in the Kitawalist biographies.[88] For example, the *Biographie* recounts how on the day of Kadiba's arrest, the chief of police, Jean Dubet, fell out of his car and broke his arm. That same day, the wall of the *lycée belge* (a colonial school) fell and many children were injured. Such was Kadiba's power—so great that even the White people recognized, were touched by, and feared it. Meanwhile, "twelve whites accompanied [Kadiba] to [the prison camp at] Malonga, six on each side and him in the middle. Before the boat left, they fired a gunshot. And before he got out at Malonga they fired a gun shot as well. It was a recognition of his power/authority [*ufalme*]."[89] Once in the prison camp at Malonga, Kadiba performed more miracles—including healing a woman in the camp who "had gone insane years earlier"—and continued his work as a Kitawalist teacher in defiance of the camp authorities.[90]

Whether these stories of miracles, formidable repute, and global connections are an empirically "true" part of Kadiba's history is not particularly important. For the Kitawalists who recognize him as a prophet, the stories serve to illustrate his chosenness. Not only was he an empathetic and perceptive intellectual and a translator of God's word who became a charismatic leader, but he possessed a particular kind of strength (power) that came from God—or, more precisely, from God via a renewed connection with the ancestors. To remove these power-laden elements of his history is to remove the most important parts of his biography as his followers tell it. For them, the more empirically verifiable parts of his history—his early career success, his collecting of Watchtower literature, his connections to other Kitawalists, his correspondences—cannot be detached from his spiritual power. Indeed, they were made possible by it.

TRANSMITTING THE WORD

Taken together, these biographies offer a glimpse into the processes of Kitawalist transmission that reveal both the contingency of and connection between their different lives. They help us to see beyond the chains of contagion emphasized in the archive and instead consider the intimate and intellectual lives of Kitawalist leaders as individuals and the contexts in which they lived. Moreover, they implore us to take seriously the "miraculous" parts of their biographies as crucial elements in the story of transmission, rather than dismiss them as fantastical addenda to the more empirical histories of economic exploitation, labor migrancy, and displacement.

However, the biographies also raise further questions about the textual aspects of transmission. Their stories are peppered with references to the many texts these Kitawalist leaders both referenced and produced. How did they use these texts? How did they teach with them and find meaning in their contents? What lessons did they impart with the texts? To what extent did the texts themselves, as physical objects, embody power in the spaces where they were interpreted?[91]

Answering such questions requires thinking of transmission as a process of translation and performance mediated through specific context and audience. The relationship between religious texts, translation, meaning, and performance is certainly a subject many scholars have considered before.[92] As James Bielo writes, "The consensus to be culled from this research is not so much a stability surrounding particular textual meanings as it is a reliability that meaning will be identified, usually in the form of personal application."[93] The meaning of texts is not inherent, but contextually established through processes of acculturation, interpretation, and application. And as Matthew Engelke has argued in his study of the Friday apostolic church in Zimbabwe, "What the written word signifies, and how it does so, cannot be taken for granted."[94] Indeed, for the Friday apostolics, the written texts are "dangerous" because they "take the spirit out of things."[95] While Kitawalists have not historically disavowed written texts in the way the Friday apostolics did and still do, a variety of both archival and oral evidence suggests there is nothing straightforward in how Kitawalist pastors have connected the words in texts to the meanings they transmitted to their congregations—meanings that originated as much from heavenly transmissions as from texts themselves.

To illustrate this final point, I would like to begin by looking at a case of transmission that I witnessed in 2018 during a Kitawalist service in the small town of Kasaji, located in Lualaba Province. I had been invited to the service by the head pastor of the district, Pastor Théophile Mulongo. During his sermon that morning, Pastor Mulongo produced an old copy not of the Bible or of Watchtower literature but of a colonial novel—*Kitawala: Roman*—as the source for his religious lesson. Written by a Belgian named Léon Debertry, the novel is essentially racist colonialist propaganda meant to illustrate the "atavism" of the Congolese people. The actual plot of the novel is rife with colonial tropes. The central character is a formerly "good" subject—a loyal soldier. Unfortunately, he is lured by a woman of Congolese and European heritage into a Kitawalist meeting where he participates in Kitawalist sex rituals with her and falls in love. (The Belgians were convinced that Kitawala was, in addition to being anticolonial, an immoral sex cult, a point I return to in chapter 5.) Much to his dismay, this woman is also the mistress of a powerful colonial settler, so the love-struck soldier uses the chaos of an unrelated mutiny of the soldiers (an event that really did happen in Luluabourg in 1944) as an opportunity to murder his romantic rival. The novel is largely about the unfolding of this criminal case. It also contains an appendix in which the author offers very unflattering explanations of Kitawala's "xenophobic, racist, and immoral" doctrine.[96]

Given the nature of the novel, when Pastor Mulongo pulled it out in the middle of his sermon and began to teach excerpts of it, I was surprised. The section of the text that Pastor Mulongo spent significant time on appears in the midst of a discussion in the appendix highlighting what Debertry considered the "radical and amoral" teachings of Charles Taze Russell, the founder of Watchtower. In the text, Debertry discusses a rather infamous incident from Russell's history in which his wife accused him of adultery. Russell allegedly responded to her accusations by saying that he was "like a jellyfish floating here and there." Debertry uses this incident as evidence of the immorality of Russell, and of Watchtower and Kitawala by association, essentially connecting it to the rumors about Kitawala's sex cult activities as the Belgians imagined them.[97]

Pastor Mulongo discerned a very different meaning from the text, however, and a look at his interpretation offers useful insights. In the original text, Debertry wrote of Russell, "His amorality is remarkable." Pastor Mulongo, having his assistant read the original French text, then translated the meaning for his congregation in Swahili: "It says: That prophet, he had great teachings. If they say that he was 'amoral,' it's because they thought he was bad. But he had very good teachings. They were the teachings that helped us to begin to see and we still have them today." Pastor Mulongo made a subtle shift here: he began to read the incident not as an account of Russell, but of the prophet Kadiba Ilunga Émile. Where Debertry wrote, in judgment of Russell's alleged adultery, that he was an "apostle of free love," Pastor Mulongo translated it as follows: "It says he [Kadiba] was a prophet of love that is free, uncaged. Does he say that no White people could come into our church? . . . It is a national and international mission, and people from Europe/America [*bulaya*] can join. There is nothing barring it."

Pastor Mulongo then asked his reader to continue reading the text: "He proclaims 'I am like a fish who floats here and there. I touch this one and that one and if they don't respond, I float further.'" Pastor Mulongo interpreted this passage as further evidence of Kadiba's acceptance of strangers:

> He said, "Me, Kadiba, when I receive the word, I will proclaim it in front of all of you. You see me here; I am like a fish who goes here and there. Whether to Black or White or whoever. I go to all.

If I come to you to touch you, and you agree. I embrace you. And if someone doesn't acknowledge me, I will move beside them as they work." So, if we are here and have received a guest [*mgeni*], it is our responsibility to welcome them and let them do their work so that tomorrow we won't feel shame. So, we should show love to guests. Kadiba said, "If you accept me, I welcome you. If you don't accept me, I welcome you." We should not forget. It is a sweet lesson.[98]

The entire incident offers an example of how Pastor Mulongo, as a preacher, used the words in this text to remind his congregation of the revelations that the prophet Kadiba Ilunga Émile gave them that could help guide their actions in response to the new situation they found themselves in. That situation was the presence of the rather unusual figure of a White, American, Swahili-speaking woman among them asking them to aid her in learning about their history.[99] The lesson continued, and the gist of what Pastor Mulongo taught his congregation was that it was no accident that I was in their midst. Pastor Mulongo knew that it was, to a large extent, luck of timing that had led me to encounter him in Lubumbashi, where he agreed to bring me back to Kasaji. When I had arrived in Lubumbashi in July of 2018, I had no way of knowing that there was a massive Kitawala meeting taking place there following the death of Ilunga Wesele Joseph (Kadiba's grandson), who had been the leader of the church at the time of his death. My arrival at such a precipitous moment was complete chance—and not for the first time. A similar stroke of luck had unwittingly placed me in Kalemie during a large regional Kitawalist meeting in 2010, which was the first time I met Pastor Mulongo and many of the other elders of the church. Given these circumstances, luck was not how Pastor Mulongo explained my presence. Rather, he taught his congregation that my presence was divinely willed, for I had come to make their story known to the world. He taught them, moreover, that the prophet Kadiba Ilunga Émile foresaw events such as these and offered them guidance on how to receive guests, even a guest who was not necessarily a believer. That guidance could be discerned from the words of Debertry's text.

It was a radical reading of the text. Pastor Mulongo significantly decontextualized the words of the author and interpreted them in such a way that it subverted Debertry's chauvinistic intent. Pastor Mulongo understood the words in the text, but he rejected Debertry's meaning and instead read them in such a way as to render them useful in guiding the actions of his congregation in their present situation. That situation (my presence) was itself read as a kind of transmission from God: a sign that God saw them and

Transmissions ⌒ 53

cared about them. On the one hand, it was a rather uncomfortable reading of the situation for me, as a historian with no such faith in divine explanations and a hefty amount of skepticism that anything about my research or presence was divinely willed. On the other hand, it was and is neither my place nor purpose to refute such an explanation. It is, rather, a reminder that I do not get to dictate the terms by which Kitawalists make sense of either my presence or their own histories. Instead, I am compelled to respect them as a significant way of historical knowing—what I discuss in chapter 6 as "profound history."

Moreover, this incident offers a couple of different insights that are worth considering when thinking about the history of transmission of Kitawala. First, it offers a glimpse into what the process of translating written texts—whether the Bible, a Watchtower pamphlet, or a colonialist novel—into contextually meaningful knowledge might have looked like. It helps to illustrate how traditions of prophetism and revelation that have a very deep history in Central Africa could be reconciled with texts produced in a very different cultural context, often with very different intended meanings. One of the defining characteristics of Kitawala as it moved through different regions of Congo was the diversity of interpretations of the message of the movement—how new converts took ideas that had been taught to them by other Kitawalist proselytizers and brought them home to their own social and political context, altering them to make sense in that context. In many cases, like those of Paulo Kanumbi or Kadiba Ilunga Émile, they did this through divine transmissions that came to them, for example, while in a deep state of prayer in a locally empowered space.

Pastor Mulonga's oral interpretation of the written text also demonstrates the relationship between texts, translation, and oral transmission. It illustrates how orality transforms texts and what the performative aspect of that transformation might look like. Although they do not appear in the exchange above, in the moment, Pastor Mulongo's congregants were invited into the conversation through call and response. They were given opportunities to voice affirmations—"yes," guests are welcome; "no," they should not hide the teachings of Kitawala; "yes," they should help me. For many of the congregants, such statements were perhaps accepted in the moment they were uttered. This also helps to illustrate how orality could transform teachings even more profoundly when further divorced from the text—which was often the case with Kitawala, as many communities lacked easy access to texts.[100] This lack of access is also significant. It points to how the dearth of texts and limited literacy could historically and can today render texts powerful and treasured authorities, even as they are also mediated

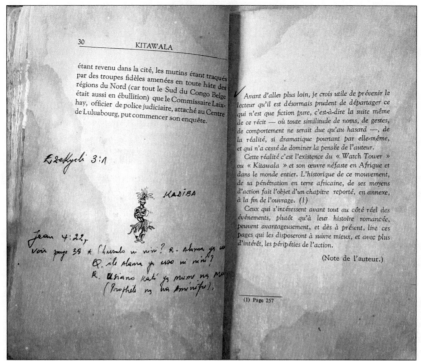

FIGURE 1.1. Marginalia in the pages Pastor Mulongo's copy of *Kitawala: Roman*.

and decontextualized. Debertry's racist colonial novel seems like an unlikely text to treasure, and yet it had clearly been studied closely. Its delicate old pages show all the signs of continued use, including marginalia (see figure 1.1). More than anything, this speaks to the rare access that teachers like Pastor Mulongo have to written accounts of their own history and teachings.[101] These texts become precious and powerful as conduits of God's words, or in this case the words of God's prophet, Kadiba Ilunga.

But Pastor Mulongo's sermon also serves as a reminder that we must not overstate the authority of the text, for the translator or orator also serves as a significant producer and interpreter of knowledge in the process of transmission. This is certainly true in the above case, but archival evidence illustrates that it was also true during the colonial era. In 1954, for example, one of the colonial government's "Kitawala experts," R. Philippart, who we have already encountered, produced a study about the Kitawalist communities in and around Stanleyville in which he included several pages of Bible verses followed by "commentary such as it is made by the Kitawalists."[102] In one example, he explained the Kitawalist interpretation of Matthew 21:1–3. The original verses are as follows: "Go to the village ahead of you, and at

Transmissions ~ 55

once you will find a donkey tied up with her colt. Untie them and bring them to me. If anyone says anything to you, say that the Lord needs them, and he will send them right away." According to Philippart, the Kitawalists, unfamiliar with the Swahili word for "donkey"—*punga*—that was used in their Swahili-language Bible, substituted it with "the blacks." The result was the following interpretation of the verse: "The blacks must not be chained by the Europeans and especially by the priests who lie in order to better keep them enchained."

In another example, Kitawalists interpreted Matthew 7:15–20 as a warning against spies. In the Swahili translation, the verse warns of "false prophets who come in sheep's clothing" and cautions that because "bad trees cannot bear good fruit," they will know the false prophets "by their fruits." Philippart reports the following translation of that verse: "You must pay attention to those who are not just and who come to meetings to spy on us and then go report everything they have heard. They are like bad trees who bear bad fruits and it is necessary to cut them down and throw them in the fire." And in a third example, the Kitawalists interpreted the Swahili word *mamlaka* (power) as *malaka* (a kind cassava). They then read Matthew 28:18—"all the power of heaven and Earth has been given to me"—as a promise from God that they would have all the cassava (i.e., prosperity). They even incorporated this interpretation into their rituals by "putting the stalk of a cassava in the center of a circle as an offering to God."[103]

Philippart went on to describe how most of the pastors did not have Bibles at all, but instead kept notebooks in which they had written down excerpts—like the verses above—with these commentaries given to them by the few who did have Bibles. When they met for their services, the events looked very much like Pastor Mulongo's sermon: the pastor told a reader which verses to read aloud, and then the pastor explained what they meant to the congregation.[104] For Philippart, these commentaries served largely as evidence of how Kitawalists misunderstood and manipulated the Bible. He was, in the study, endeavoring to show that there was no coherence to their beliefs—that it was "only religious in form," and that at its base, they were just preaching politics and xenophobia and "seducing" the "simple adepts" with their "mysterious and secret rites."[105]

And yet, if we leave his obvious prejudice aside, his report nonetheless offers valuable insight into how the process of transmission must have looked during the colonial era. As with Pastor Mulongo, we see a willingness of the pastors to play with the language in order to find meaning. They made substitutions in text—like *Black people* ("the blacks") for *punga* (donkey) that produced useful directives and critiques. They made plays on words—*malafa* for *mamlaka*—that allow them to substitute ritual objects (*cassava* for *power*). Philippart sees this as mistranslation, but this kind of punning in the materials that compose empowered spaces and objects has a very long history in Congo.[106] When read alongside Pastor Mulongo's sermon, these "commentaries" show nothing less than the creative intellectual processes through which Kitawalists in the past and present rendered texts that were never written for them instructive and useful conduits of inspiration and direction.

What all these cases illustrate is that Kitawala's introduction into Congo was facilitated by a variety of kinds of transmissions. Those transmissions were physical (movements of people and texts), spiritual (facilitated by the divine), and oral/aural (involving teaching, listening, and interpretation). Considering these different kinds of transmission allows us to place the spiritual, political, and intellectual lives of diverse African individuals at the center of Kitawala's history. But it also raises questions—questions about reception of these transmissions by the broader Kitawala community. What kinds of hopes and expectations brought people into Kitawala, compelling them to listen to the transmissions of prophets like Kadiba Ilunga Émile or Mutombo Stephan? What theories of power and notions of possibility shaped their understandings of what Kitawala could offer them and their communities? In the next chapter, I consider how thinking about healing as part of the history of Kitawala offers important insights that can begin to answer some these questions.

2 ~ Healing

LIKE THE majority of the Bwari people who live along the shores of Lake Tanganyika in Fizi Territory, Maman Kalema was raised as a Muslim. She joined Kitawala in 1996 and ultimately left the church in 2002 when, at the height of the Secondo Congo war, she was forced to flee to Uvira, where, to her knowledge, there was no Kitawalist church. Around the same time, most of the Kitawalist leaders and many of the followers in Fizi had fled to Tanzania, and as far as she knew, most of them had never returned. If this had not been the case, she asserted, she would still be a member of the church, for she believes that it is a good religion, a religion of truth.

When I first met Maman Kalema in her home in Uvira in 2010, she insisted that we talk in a group made up exclusively of women: Maman Kalema, me, and her daughter. She started off by explaining that Kitawalists do not like to share their secrets. She had been told in the past that people would come looking for the secrets of Kitawala, that they would come searching for its power. Those secrets, she told me, were naturally the domain of women.

When I asked Maman Kalema why she had joined Kitawala, she told me the following story: She had suffered a long, intense illness related to fertility. In her words, she "carried a fetus for seven years," and although she had gone to various healers—biomedical, Muslim, traditional—she could not find relief. She had heard that the Kitawalists healed people for free, so she decided to go to them. When she went to the Kitawalists, they brought her into a prayer chamber, where they prayed over her. They then sent her home with a powder and told her to bathe with it. To procure its healing capacities, the powder had also been prayed over. At long last, Maman Kalema recovered from her illness and she was able to bear a child, a daughter. After her illness was healed, she became a healer herself—a mama of the prayer chamber with a reputation as an *mfumu*.[1]

When I met her in 2010, Maman Kalema was still using the healing practices that she learned from the Kitawalists, though, as noted, she had no official affiliation with the church. She healed a number of maladies. In particular, she helped women who have reproductive problems. But she also offered medicines to help people succeed, whether in a job interview or with a romantic partner. She cited an example of a woman who had gone years without getting married and was getting old. This woman took the medicine Maman Kalema prepared for her and soon enough men started to notice her, and she was married shortly thereafter. In another incident, she presided over a healing ritual that brought prosperity and business success to a family.

Maman Kalema denied accusations that Kitawalists work with *mashetani* (demons or malignant spirits). She insisted they believe in the same Bible as other Christians. They put God and the teachings of the Bible first, but they disagree with those that say the teachings of their ancestors were satanic, and they pray to their ancestors after God.[2]

HEALING

Healing has always been a part of Kitawala's history. Buried within the colonial archives are countless reports of Kitawalists using medicines (dawas), rituals, and empowered objects (*minkisi*) to heal. In many cases, these reports appear in the context of colonial interrogations. When colonial agents managed to uncover a "cell" of Kitawalists, they would often gather lists of alleged adherents and bring them in for questioning as they tried to assess why, how, and by whom the accused individuals had been lured into what they saw as a dangerous and dissident movement. These documents, although impaired by the power dynamics of their production, offer glimpses into the lives of men, women, boys, and girls of Kitawala. In them, these individuals often report being drawn into learning about and joining Kitawala because of various maladies that befell them: epilepsy, infertility, and repeated bouts (for themselves or their children) of various illnesses. In some cases, they reported seeking relief from afflictions related to witchcraft or malignant spirits, experienced both as bodily affliction and generalized misfortune. Sometimes these individuals indicated that they were seeking a way to be empowered in order to find success in hunting, fishing, or in their love lives. And sometimes they simply reported they were searching for a way to once more see and speak with their ancestors, particularly with deceased loved ones such as parents.[3]

It is striking, the extent to which Maman Kalema's story, recorded more than fifty years after these colonial documents, reflects many of the same concerns as these earlier Kitawalists. For this reason, her personal history of faith and conversion and her individual experiences of malady, health, and healing, both within and beyond the Kitawalist community, provide a rich point of entry into the discussions at the heart of this chapter. In her story, some of the major ritual technologies at work in modern Kitawalist healing emerge—in particular, the use of prayer and powder—raising questions about how those ritual technologies operate and the ontological assumptions that guide them.[4] In addition, within her narrative one can begin to see the contours of the epistemological space that Kitawalist healers have inhabited in the therapeutic complex of eastern Congo in recent years: they are possessors and wielders of secret knowledge that makes them powerful (they have nguvu) and that has garnered them a reputation for their abilities to engage with spirits—*wazimu* (ancestral) or mashetani (demonic), depending on the point of view.

Guided by these contours, it is possible to ask a multitude of questions. Why do people go to Kitawalist healers? How do Kitawalists discuss the efficacy of their healing practice? What role does healing play in processes of conversion and proselytization? If, as Maman Kalema insists, it is women who are the arbiters of "secret" Kitawalist knowledge and power, what does this reveal about the gendered nature of spiritual and therapeutic labor within the church? What, in turn, does such attention to gender reveal about how Kitawalists have imagined power and agency in their own history? Finally, to what extent do the answers to these questions differ within and between different Kitawalist communities, and what is at stake in claims of what is and is not proper Kitawalist practice?

I have posed these questions in the present tense. This is because most of the evidence explored in this chapter comes from my own interviews and conversations with contemporary practitioners of Kitawala, conducted over multiple periods of fieldwork from 2008 to 2018, in various locations across Haut Katanga, Lualaba, Tanganyika, and South Kivu Provinces. Many of the discussions we had were about how Kitawala is imagined, practiced, and received today, by people largely born after the colonial era. Thus, the picture these conversations paint is in many ways a picture of the present. And this is valuable in its own right, offering a glimpse of the current spiritual and

FIGURE 2.1. Image of the robe worn by member of EDAC, reading "Follow the god of tradition."

therapeutic landscape of Congo and the niche that Kitawalists have come to occupy within it. But it also offers insight into the ways different communities within that landscape differently imagine and wield the language of tradition, as both signifier and practice. When Kitawalists call their religion and their healing practices "tradition"—*ya bankambo, ya asili*—they are signifying ancestral practices, connecting their own teachings and practices to those of the past (see figure 2.1).[5] They do this knowing full well that their ancestors neither prayed using the Bible nor healed with mass-market talcum powder. Within the tensions created by this paradox lie sophisticated ideas about the nature of tradition, about what it means to embody and respect it while simultaneously embracing its transformation.

Thus, this chapter, like chapter 1, is also about beginnings. It is about historical process, with its tangled roots and unruly branches. It is about recognizing the threads of Kitawala's history that originated in Central Africa and, through processes of transmission, have been translated, innovated, and woven into tapestries of modern relevance. It is about taking seriously Kitawalists' claims that their beliefs and practices are ya bankambo and

Healing ~ 61

considering the politics of authenticity that are at work in claiming and performing tradition in modern contexts with modern materials. And it is about considering the alternative notions of materiality that shape these claims.[6]

RITUAL TECHNOLOGIES

As was the case when Maman Kalema sought healing, Kitawalist healers generally describe working with a minimal number of materials, herbal and otherwise, in their therapeutic practices. Unlike Binti Dadi (the Konde *nganga wa mitishamba* Stacey Langwick worked with in her research on traditional healing in Tanzania) or Kahenga (the Luba *munganga wa miti* interviewed by Johannes Fabian in his ethnographic research in Lubumbashi in 1974),[7] Kitawalist healers do not generally work with a wide array of "roots, bark, leaves, seeds, and flowers" that they have collected themselves in the "bush" and processed by pounding, grinding, mixing, boiling, or grilling.[8] Rather, Kitawalist healing today usually involves just four material elements: powder, candles, oil, and incense. The powder, as I mentioned above, is usually a mass-marketed variety of talcum powder imported from Tanzania.[9] Ideally, the candles, as well as the incense and oil, derive from the *umpafu* tree (*Canarium schweinfurthii*, or African elemi), but are sometimes substituted with mass-market materials. (This is especially true of the candles, but I have also seen canned perfume used in lieu of incense.)

These four materials come together with the performance of "evocations" in "prayer chambers" to constitute what Steve Feierman has called the "ritual technology" of Kitawalists. Looking at herbal healing practices in Ghaambo, Tanzania, Feierman argues that "when the healer addresses the herbs, the words and the herbs are both part of the treatment." For healers in Ghaambo, the words they use to address the herbs "are not mere decoration" for what is ultimately a chemical transaction. Instead, "they are essential for efficacy," and the "ritual transformation of the herbs is an indispensable part of the technology." It is incorrect, Feierman argues, "to treat the herbs as the real source of healing power, and the words as symbolic supplement."[10]

Though he is warning about direct comparisons between herbal healing and biomedicine, Feierman's observations seem particularly important in the context of Kitawalist healing as well. Thinking back to Maman Kalema's experience with Kitawalist healing, it seems obvious that the "herb" she was given was not the real source of healing power. She was taken into a prayer chamber along with the powder that would become her medicine, an "evocation" was performed, and she was sent home to bathe with the powder that ultimately healed her. Talcum powder, however, has very few medicinal properties. In some ways, it seems to suggest the opposite: that the real source of healing power is in the words and that the powder is the symbolic supplement. The powder, then, is simply a kind of container for the real healing properties, which existed in the words and immaterial power (nguvu, puissance) that they evoked. This seems to imply ontics of a different nature, wherein what is effective is the immaterial, and the material is but a vessel.

Yet, a closer look at how Kitawalists describe the ritual technology of their healing suggests that we should not overemphasize the difference. Just as with the Ghaambo healing that Feierman observed, the technology of the immaterial (the words) and the technology of the material (the "herb") are "indissoluble." It is just more complicated, in the case of Kitawalist healing, to explain the technology of the "herbal" in biomedical terms. However, that does not mean there are no terms by which to explain it. In what follows, I present several extended excerpts from discussions I had with Kitawalist leaders about healing within the church. I have reproduced the interviews at some length because I think the details are important if we are to understand the subtleties of Kitawalist thoughts about their ritual technologies.[11]

(IM)MATERIALITY

In 2010, in Kalemie, I conducted a series of interviews with some of the local elders of a branch of Kitawala known as L'Église de la libération du Saint-Esprit du prophète Kadima Émile Ilunga du Kitawala. Our discussion was led by Kabanga Kamalondo, who was the leader of the parish around Kalemie at the time, but was attended by other elders of that parish. When I initially asked Kabanga to explain Kitawalist healing practices to me, he responded as follows:

> The teaching left to us by Mwana Lesa and Ilunga was that Kitawala should not heal with just anything. It should heal with powder and candles. It is the White people [*wazungu*] who make this powder [*shows me a bottle of Vestline talcum / baby powder*]. It is flowers from trees. God told us we will be healed by trees from the wilderness [*pori*].... These trees are an elder sibling to all of us [*mkubwa wetu*]. The first born were the trees, then came the fish and animals, and then we are third. When God made man, he said he was finished with his work. We were created in front of a tree. We do prayers, we do evocations in our church that we were taught by our ancestors. We imbue the powder with that power [pouvoir]. When someone becomes sick, they bring them to us and we blow

the powder at them like this [*demonstrates blowing powder from his palm*]. You blow it over the front of the body and it extracts the spirit [*pepo*] in his/her body. The powder fells the spirit [*inamuangukia;* literally: "forces it to fall down"] and the malady [*malali*] leaves. We take the oil [*mafuta*] from the umpafu tree [*Canarium schweinfurthii*]. We get a candle and we light/burn it. Because a candle is fire/heat [*moto*], it is made from the resin/healing materials [*matunvi*] of the tree.[12] The things we use to heal are trees [*miti*]. We pray to Ilunga and through Jesus we heal. It began with Mwana Lesa in 1925.[13]

When I asked Kabanga whether there were different prayers for different diseases, he responded,

> There is a single prayer, but there are various cures. I told you that this powder is flowers, the candle is the resin/healing materials, and that the oil comes from umpafu tree. That is where the power comes from, because it is our older sibling [*mkubwa yetu*]. When you go there with illness that is circling your head [*malali la kuzunguka kichwa*], you have to say prayers and put the oil on your head, because it is apparent that is where the problem is located, and then you go into the prayer chamber. You tell God that you want to cure a certain malady [*malali*].[14]

At this point, Sermy Nsenga, a colleague at the University of Lubumbashi-Kalemie who accompanied me to several of my interviews, interjected. He seemed unconvinced by parts of Kabanga's answer to my question and insisted on the following clarification:

> So, you are explaining where the power [*nguvu*] of your prayers comes from. You say it is the flowers that come from trees. But it is the prayer that is the power. If you are going to explain how you heal, you need to explain that different prayers heal different diseases or she will think it is all the same.[15]

Following Sermy's interjection, we concluded the discussion of healing for the day, but when we returned to the topic of Kitawalist ritual technologies another day, Kabanga added the following clarification:

> We go into a prayer chamber with you if you are sick. We call the ancestors, and the spirits descend upon us. If they tell us you should go to an herbal healer [*nganga*], you go to an herbal healer. Or if we do not think it is witchcraft [*bulozi*], we may send you

somewhere else.[16] We work with visions. That is to say, we work with shades. We pray to shades to ask for power. What is it, Mama, what is it? She says no, it is this. If we reach three days and there is no change, we call for the ancestors and they descend [*banashuka*]. They say no, don't do that prayer, you must do this prayer, to this shade, and then you heal a person. It is not the Kitawalists, it is God who heals.

That same day, I spent some time speaking with a group of women about healing in the church as well. I will address much of what I discussed with these women in the section below, but the following excerpt from our conversation is particularly pertinent to the topic of ritual technologies. I asked them whether Kitawalists also use various healing materials—herbals and so on—that the ancestors used. Two women, who did not give me their names, together gave me the following answer:

> Yes, we use these things too. We use incense, we use candles, we also use *pembe ya ubabu* [kaolin] and umpafu oil. We also use resin/healing materials from the umpafu, which we put in a form like a candle. You light it and it burns. It gives off light and scent. And *pembe,* it makes powder, which we also use when we are inside our secret prayer chamber. We use incense, pembe, and oil of umpafu.[17]

There is much to be learned from each of these explanations of Kitawalist ritual technologies and practices. Among the most interesting and recurrent themes is the nature of the materials themselves. Kabanga readily acknowledges that the powder they use is not native to Congo. He says that it is made by White people (wazungu)—though it is, in fact, manufactured in and distributed from Tanzania. The provenance of the powder seems of little concern, however. It is rather what the powder is perceived to be made of that matters: according to Kabanga, it is "flowers from trees" (*maua ya miti*)—an understandable connection, given the floral aroma of the talcum powder. On one level, classifying the powder as such allows for it to be incorporated into the same class as other herbs/miti that are used for healing. On another level, it allows for the powder to be perceived through Christian imagery. Kabanga repeatedly insists that the tree is our ancestor, our older sibling, our "*ndugu.*" It preceded us in the creation of the world: "The first born were the trees, then came the fish and animals, and then we are third. When God made man, he said he was finished with his work. We were created in front of a tree."[18] This is an obvious reference to the order of creation

Healing ~ 65

established in the Bible. The tree came before us. It is, in essence, our ancestor and therefore possesses the potential to heal us.

Yet, the fact that Kabanga reads the creation story thus itself seems to be mediated through vernacular imagery and history. In much of sub-Saharan Africa, trees—or "sacred groves"—have historically been important "places of power."[19] As Michael Sheridan argues, such groves "are critical sites in the ideological and material struggles that generate political legitimacy, ethnic and gender identities, and access to resources."[20] They are, thus, critical to the social health of communities. Looking at eastern Congo, Gillian Mathys has written about the significance of ficus trees in the area surrounding Lake Kivu, where even today they serve as an important marker of first-comer status. Looking at the historical significance of the border between Rwanda and Congo, Mathys notes that today Rwandanphone people living in eastern Congo will point to their trees—specifically ficus trees and *Erythrine*—as proof of their claims to land and citizenship. The trees indicate the land that belonged to their ancestors, where their lineage heads first settled. They are revered in annual rituals, generally linked to a specific ancestor.[21] They serve as the vessel through which important ancestors can be addressed.

It is not difficult to see the confluence between these two images—that of the tree as predecessor in the creation story, and that of the tree as ancestral territory marker and node of access to ancestral power. This confluence is only enriched when one thinks about the central role played by the tree of life and the tree of knowledge in Christian thought and imagery related to creation. As something that is simultaneously organic to this world and imbued with significant capacities and knowledge that are beyond this world, the capacities attributed to the tree of life—the knowledge of God—create a somatic overlap between the significance of trees in both readings, offering a prime example of the ways in which Kitawalists regularly read Christianity as "tradition." Viewed through this lens, mass-marketed powder is stripped of its commodity form and essentially incorporated into an imaginary that brings it much closer to other forms of herbal medicine, allowing for its incorporation into a Kitawalist notion of tradition.

Meanwhile, my two female interlocuters made a more direct connection between powder and ancestral healing practices when they indicated the use of pembe ya ubabu, or kaolin. Kaolin is a kind of white clay that has historically been used throughout much of Africa, and more particularly in Central Africa, in contexts where ancestral power is evoked—be it in political, religious, or therapeutic contexts (between which the lines are, of course, blurred). In Central Africa, the color white has historically signified the world the of dead, and kaolin powder has in various contexts been used to adorn objects or individuals in commune with or embodying the spirits: figural minkisi (empowered objects) or spirit mediums, for example. Kaolin has often appeared in ceremonies of purification as well. This is true in religious contexts, but also in healing contexts. For example, during pregnancy women even today often consume kaolin daily as a way of purifying their bodies of toxins.[22] While geophagy is common among pregnant women throughout the world, the particular consumption of kaolin in Central Africa seems likely to be connected to the cultural connotations of power and purity the clay carries.

Within Kitawala, in addition to its use in prayer chambers, as indicated by the women in Kalemie, powder is used by practitioners to ceremonially purify spaces where people engage in prayer or spirit evocation (usually by blowing it into the air to create a cloud of dust). For example, in every Kitawalist religious service I have attended, ceremonial leaders, usually women, used it at various times to purify the space, to open it up to receiving the spirit. They usually blew it throughout the worship space at the beginning of a service. I have also seen the powder blown onto a woman in the midst of a spirit possession (see figure 2.2). Pastor Mulongo, the Kitawalist pastor in charge of the parish in Kasaji, explained to me that the powder (as well as the perfume) quite literally cleanses the bodies of the people present, which are soiled by the sweat and dirt of everyday life. Spirits, he told me, do not want to enter into unclean bodies.[23]

In all these contexts, the mass-market talcum powder and the kaolin appear to be interchangeable. In the past, Pastor Mulongo told me, they would have certainly used kaolin.[24] Kabanga likewise asserted the Kitawalists used powder as a major part of their ritual technology during the time of Mwana Lesa, in the 1920s. This would have presumably been kaolin, since it would have predated easy access to commercial talcum powder. Today, talcum powder can be easier, and likely cheaper, to procure. The point is that in the contexts described above, the material properties of the talcum powder that matter are not the minerals and chemicals that constitute its physical makeup, but rather its visual interchangeability with a symbolically charged material "of the ancestors": kaolin. This, in turn, allows it to be incorporated into their notion of tradition in much the same way that Kabanga incorporated it by viewing it as a product of trees.

The other materials that constitute the matter of Kitawalist healing practices—the oil, incense, and candles of the umpafu—have a more straightforward connection to ancestral healing practices. Umpafu is a tree with essential medicinal properties and a very deep historical relationship

FIGURE 2.2. A woman in midst of a spirit possession during a Kitawalist mass in Kasaji, Lualaba, in August of 2018.

to healing. In English it is known as the African elimi, bush candle tree, gum resin tree, or incense tree. The resin is heavy and sticky, and when it dries it becomes a whiteish solid that is highly flammable. This resin is frequently formed into "bush" candles. When burned, it both provides light and exudes a lavender-like aroma and is often used as incense. It also produces an olive-like fruit that can be pressed to produce oil. The oil and the fruit are both edible. Moreover, the tree has long been a source of medicine to treat a variety of afflictions. Historically, even Europeans exported it for use in pharmaceuticals. It has healing properties that work against certain stomach ailments (dysentery, food poisoning, roundworms, and other intestinal parasites) and can be used as a purgative or diuretic. It is thought to help with certain chest ailments (coughs, chest pains) and has been used to treat skin ailments (eczema, leprosy, ulcers). It can be use both internally and externally.[25]

But again, today the products of the umpafu are also interchangeable with mass-market products—candles and canned perfume from the market, for example. Just as with the powder, the functional interchangeability of the indigenous and mass-market materials suggests that what matters is not so much their matter, but that they have indigenous predecessors with deep symbolic and ritual ties to "tradition" as Kitawalists imagine it. Theirs is a claim to "tradition" that is unconcerned with material authenticity, even as it draws on the memory of authentic materials to signal efficacy. That is, it matters that there are material overlaps between the indigenous and commercial products—that they look similar, that they can fulfill similar ritual functions, and that they can embody immaterial power in similar ways—but it does not matter in any way that would satisfy someone in search of scientific proof of the efficacy of traditional healing within the chemical makeup of the materials.

To further complicate this matter of Kitawalist healing, I offer the response that a leader of the EDAC branch of Kitawala in Fizi gave me when I asked which diseases Kitawalists heal:

> Illness in general. But there are different illnesses. There are illnesses that you can heal with herbs. You can make various herbs into pills. Then it gets complicated.... You need someone who can make the pills and assign dosages. We don't have these resources. So, we use herbs as God directs us. Then there are illnesses you heal by praying without even touching anything. We go into the mountains. We conduct healing ceremonies [*vifungu*].[26] There we do an animal offering: we build alters [*mazabao*], we sacrifice, we pray. "Please help us with this illness... whether it is infertility, you must

help them this year." Whether it is an illness of flow/fertility [*fungu*], witchcraft/power [*anga*], it must not get inside them.[27] There are many illnesses, like cholera, which is so frequent. If it is cholera, we say that we block cholera from entering the body this year, and it is possible. Other illnesses—bothersome spirits [*bazimu*]—we do as usual, and it heals. Epilepsy [*kifafa*], and I don't know what other illnesses. If it is an illness that we get, if you come to us, we will heal you. If we can't, we pray for power [nguvu]. If they [the ancestors] bring us the help of herbs, we use herbs. If they tell us, "No, this person should go to the biomedical hospital and you should go with them," that is what we do. We[28] help each other, that is how it works. Even when we were in the camps, we helped each other. If they could not help someone, they sent them to us. If we were unable to help someone, we would tell them this person needs blood or fluids, or you should test them and give them what they need, and the person heals. But over here they do not understand us, and they do not respond. We do not have any hospitals. If we had one, we would work together with our knowledge and biomedical knowledge, and things would progress. But where we come from [Fizi], there's nothing. We have no one to turn to that can help us. We are alone, we have no guardian [*mlezi*]. We lack anyone to protect us [*kutuleya*].[29]

There are a number of interesting things to be discussed about this particular oral text, and I will come back to them later in this chapter, but for the purposes of the present argument, I would simply like to draw attention to the perceived dearth of viable health care options in the region. This man knows that herbs of various sorts can be made into pills and those pills can be assigned dosages, but he also knows there are no resources for that kind of standardization of healing practices in the region. So, they rely on God and their ancestors to direct them in the use of herbs in contingent ways and depend, ultimately, on the less material aspects of healing. Here again, Feierman's interpretation of ritual technologies—which challenges the notion that the "healing" properties of medicines are inherent to the material and can be separated from the ritual—is useful. But the process I have described above—whereby the materials of healing are substitutable in substance as long as their ritual function and symbolic form is retained—seems to add another layer to the argument. In these cases, it would seem that while it remains true that both the material and the words are significant, they also need not be static and can be understood as more or less alterable, even as they continue to be imagined through the same theories of power. This is why discussing such interpretations as theories—rather than just beliefs—is important: it emphasizes how they are systems of ideas that can be applied experimentally, and revised, in order to make sense of materially different circumstances. Moreover, different groups can and do articulate and reimagine those theories differently, in different contexts. What seems to be at work here is a very different kind of transformation than the biomedicalization of healing described by Langwick, in which the spiritual/immaterial aspects of healing have come to dominate the material aspects, or at the very least alter both the material (by introducing mass-market materials) and immaterial (by introducing Christianity) aspects significantly.

POWER AND PRAXIS

I have spent some time focusing on the material aspects of Kitawalist ritual technologies and the ways that some practitioners have reimagined them in the postcolonial period, but I would like to shift the focus back to other nonmaterial parts of the ritual technology: the words and performances that are essential to the efficacy of that technology. The oral texts presented above have already revealed much about this aspect of Kitawalists ritual technology. Recall Kabanga Kamalondo's account of how the major material element of their technology—the powder—comes to heal people: "We do prayers, we do evocations in our church that we were taught by our ancestors. We invest the powder with that power. When someone becomes sick, they bring them to us and we blow the powder at them like this [demonstrates]. You blow it over the front of the body and it extracts the spirit [pepo] in his/her body."[30]

At the center of this healing is the prayer chamber in which "evocations" are performed as the Kitawalists call on the spirits of their ancestors for the power to heal. That power is then embodied by the powder, which is administered in various ways. Above, it is blown at the person; in Maman Kalema's case, she bathed with it. The candles, oils, and incense of the umpafu are used to facilitate that process by creating the appropriate atmosphere inside the prayer chambers. All these things come together to address the afflictions of the patients.

There is also some variation between different communities of Kitawala. The leader from EDAC, the Bembe man of Fizi cited above, indicated that at times when they want to perform a healing ceremony, they go to the mountains, where they build an alter and make a sacrifice and call upon their ancestors. At other times, however, EDAC healing ceremonies also revolve around prayer chambers. One woman told me the following about EDAC healing: "It comes from our ancestors and our mountains.[31] We have a prayer room. In this room the power [nguvu] of our ancestors and our mountains is shown to us and we use it to heal."[32] Here the description of EDAC healing ceremonies is almost identical to that given by Kitawalists in Katanga. The major difference in this explanation is the invocation of the mountains as a central part of the process. The notion that mountains are sacred places, locations of power, is not necessarily unique to the Bembe followers of EDAC in Fizi. It was also alluded to briefly by one of my Kitawalists interviewees in Kalemie: "This church is a church of this country. The mountains, the trees—they hear our prayers. When God hears our prayers, he answers them through our prayers. This is why people come running to be cured by us."[33]

Yet, in EDAC, the mountains do have a particularly strong significance. In fact, the emphasis that followers of EDAC put on mountains—the sacred homes to their own, Bembe, ancestors—is part of the reason for the schism between the two churches. Oral traditions among the Bembe "trace an ancient origin in the Itombwe Mountains."[34] The mountains are thus understood to be the homes of particularly potent ancestral spirits and feature heavily in the songs and ceremonies within the church. Explaining the reason for the break between the Kitawalist church in Kalemie and EDAC, Kibasomba-Wakilongo, one of the leaders of EDAC, told me the following story:

> During that time [before the split], we called ourselves Kitawala. Now, during that time when Kitawala arrived, there was a lot of uncertainty about laws and procedures. And we said "no." Those people have beliefs like their own ancestors. This religion of Kitawala is Congolese, it's true. They follow the religion of our ancestors. But when we were in Kitawala, if we prayed to even one of our ancestors, just like the White people [wazungu], they would tell us you must stop that, you are praying to *shetani* [demonic spirits/Satan]. They only wanted you to pray to this person: Prophet Kadima Ilunga Mkaja. They told us, no, you mustn't use the name of anyone but this prophet, Ilunga. We said, no, everyone has the right and the freedom to pray to his own ancestors. Because I have my own blood of my ancestors, and they had my blood. And if I am going to pray to God, I am going to do it through them. We know this. So, we said no, we must sever ourselves from them. We left that group and we began this religion.[35]

Kibasomba-Wakilongo's explanation of the reason for the split was one of several explanations—not necessarily contradictory, but of different emphasis—different interlocuters gave for the split between EDAC and Kitawala. When I interviewed the leader of the Kitawalist church in Katanga—Ilunga Wesele Joseph, the grandson of the prophet Kadima Ilunga Émile—he suggested that the reason for the split between the two churches was more political. The leaders of EDAC did not want to be subject to the leadership of the Kitawalist church in Katanga. He seemed to imply that it was not necessarily ideological but was rather a ploy to seize more organizational authority within the church. The implication was that the move was, in part, related to the paying of tithes to the central organization of the church. EDAC, Ilunga argued, was ideologically and theologically no different from Kitawala.[36]

Yet, the story told by the leadership of EDAC consistently related the split to the issues highlighted by Kibasomba-Wakilongo above: it was unequivocally about theology and praxis. There was a theological disagreement between these two groups of Kitawalists relating to orthopraxis—correct conduct—in prayer. It was more than a superficial struggle over authority between church leaders. Indeed, one might argue that it was a struggle over spiritual power—a struggle over the very nature of that power, about who should be able to access it, where they should access it, and from whom it should be accessed. Kitawalists of Katanga did not approve of the way in which Kitawalists in Fizi were calling on their ancestors. In fact, they accused Kitawalists in Fizi of praying to shetani. Given the fact that the emphasis on ancestral mountain spirits during prayer is one of the major differences in praxis between the two sects of Kitawala, it is likely that at the heart of the disagreement between them was the insistence among Kitawalists of Fizi that they would pray to these ancestral mountain spirits (and, as discussed in chapter 6, Patrice Lumumba) above the prophet Ilunga (favored by Kitawalists of Katanga). I emphasize this disagreement here because it is also about healing. It is a disagreement about which words/ancestors should render healing practices effective. It is about which words/ancestors should constitute the other imperative, nonmaterial side of the ritual technology. It is, essentially, a disagreement about who should serve as the intermediary between Kitawalists and God in the procurement of power.

This disagreement highlights a fundamental issue in the history of Kitawala: it has always been defined as much by its heterodoxy as by its orthodoxy, as much by its heteropraxis as by its orthopraxis. In some ways, its orthodoxy is heterodoxy, and its orthopraxis is heteropraxis. If one of the central tenets of Kitawalist belief across Congo has been the notion that prayer to the ancestors is not antithetical to belief in God—that indeed, praying to the ancestors to access God's power is one of the most important spiritual tools God gave to the Congolese people (and to all Africans)—then of course Kitawala would be inherently and historically defined by diversity, for ancestors and modes of praying to ancestors have had highly localized histories. Recall the words of Kibasomba-Wakilongo: "Everyone has the right and the freedom to pray to his own ancestors. Because I have my own blood of my ancestors, and they had my blood. And if I am going to pray to God, I am going to do it through them."

It is for this reason that I have taken such care to emphasize the nature and importance of healing among Kitawalists: it offers a glimpse into some of the contradictory forces that have historically been at the heart of the church, which Wyatt MacGaffey has gone so far as to argue was "not a church at all but a movement loosely identified by certain symbols and myths."[37] As a result of these forces, there are and have historically been multiple Kitawalas. Indeed, it is in some ways inherently problematic to think about *the* history of Kitawala. There are, rather, *histories* of Kitawala. However, these histories are not separate—they exist in dialogue with one another, branching out from one another through the processes of transmission highlighted in chapter 1. That dialogue has historically shared a language—a language of "symbols and myths," as well as a language about the cultural tools that they draw upon in their ritual technologies. But, as the split between Kitawala and EDAC suggests, a shared language does not necessarily imply a shared interpretation. When that shared language emphasizes tradition and ancestral practices in broad terms on the ideological level, it is not surprising that it also facilitates debate and disagreement at the level of praxis. Similarly, this speaks to the core Kitawalist value of self-rule and resistance to hierarchy.

Indeed, I have presented here just one example of divergence between two particular groups of Kitawalists. There are many more. PP2, the leader of Kitawala-Filadelfie in Kabalo, insists that within his church they do not use "prayer chambers" at all, for such practices invite the influence of malevolent spirits. If a person has a problem, he explained to me, they go into the mountains to pray, just as his father did when he first received the teachings of Kitawala-Filadelfie. Those mountains, he explained, are the same mountains his ancestors went to perform evocations and seek out powerful spirits.[38] PP2 insists, though, that they do not go there to access those spirits, but rather God's power. This is an interesting claim, considering that the Kitawalists of the prophet Kadiba Ilunga insist that PP2 and his followers are even more embedded in ancestral practices than themselves, to the point of engaging in witchcraft.[39] The point here is not to doubt one claim over another, but rather to reiterate the argument that this question of power—when, where, how, and by whom it can and should be accessed—is a core question around which Kitawalist identity and history has pivoted. But as Maman Kalema's story illustrates, there is another facet to this question: gender.

GENDERED POWER AND INVISIBLE TRANSCRIPTS

To those familiar with scholarship on charismatic churches in Africa, it will come as little surprise to learn that the healing within the Kitawalist church is often done by women. Many scholars of religion and healing in Africa have noted the prevalence of women in such roles, in both the past and the present.[40] Cynthia Hoeler-Fatton writes that although women rarely occupy official leadership positions in the administrative hierarchies of these churches, they often command "ceremonial leadership," or "leadership entailing the use of mystical talents such as healing and mediumship during specified and limited occasions authorized by men."[41] She notes that ceremonial leadership frequently includes work as midwives, healers, and guardians who are "responsible for the spiritual protection of church members, not only during physical ordeals such as illness and childbirth but also during spiritually dangerous times such as infancy, death, or occasions when the soul of a person in trance leaves her or his body."[42] Moreover, women who do not hold such central roles as healers, midwives, and guardians "exert a great deal of influence over the shape and character of people's collective worship" by their singing, which creates "the atmosphere conducive to trancing." They are also frequently the "primary bearers of prophesies and heavenly messages."[43]

Evidence that women occupy "ceremonial leadership" roles among Kitawalists is abundant. In the narrative that opens this chapter, Maman Kalema indicated as much. She said that women were the guardians of the secrets of Kitawala, of their power, and for that reason, she insisted that we speak in a group composed entirely of women. She assumed I knew this and that this was the reason I, as a woman, had come to ask her about Kitawalist healing practices. And Maman Kalema was not the only one to assume I had knowledge of the power of women. When I asked the leaders of EDAC about the role of women in the church, they made the same assumption. Observe the following conversation, which took place in a meeting with a group of elders in the church of EDAC in the village of Kalonja, in Fizi:

> Me: Is it mostly women or men who do the healing?
> Mama Amisa [*laughs awkwardly and replies in a coy tone*]: Men and women. We help each other.

> Me: Because I've heard that most often it is women.
> [*Lots of laughter from the group*]
> Kibasomba-Wakilongo: Now you know there are difficult things, heavy things. There is milk and there is food. Food is for adults, those with power [nguvu].[44]
> Mama Amisa: And who carries the milk and makes the food? Most often it is the mamas.
> Me: Why is it the mamas?
> [*More laughter*]
> Mama Amisa: It is, of course, the mamas who have all the power [nguvu]. You know this.
> Kibasomba-Wakilongo: You know that if we look at the history of prophecy, the mamas have 80 percent of the power of the heavens. The men have just 20 percent. You don't know that all power is women?
> Mama Amisa: It is the mamas who give birth. Everything is the mamas. The babas (men) are just helpers.
> Kibasomba-Wakilongo: We don't have anything. It is the women.
> Mzee Aliko: It is the mamas who heal/take care [*kutunza*].
> Kibasomba-Wakilongo: Yes, that is how it is, Mama Nicole. Is it not the same where you come from?[45]

Among a group of Kitawalists in a rural Kitawala mission seventy-four kilometers (46 mi.) southwest of Kalemie, my questions evoked a similar reaction with a somewhat different explanation:

> Me: Is it mainly women who do this prayer healing?
> [*Laughter from the group*]
> Sindano [*laughs*]: Yes. You know this.
> Me: Why women?
> Sindano: Because it was women who created original sin. So now they must work as the hand of God. We [men] are simply companions.[46]

In both these exchanges, it is important to understand the role of laughter and assumption in the conversation. Like with Maman Kalema, it was assumed that I already knew about the power of women. In asking about it, I was thought to be performing a form of ignorance in order to coax the interviewees into speaking directly about things that are generally discussed through circumlocution: specifically, the power of women. This performance served as a source of amusement and elicited laughter of the sort one might share over an inside joke. I present it here in this somewhat ethnographic form because I think there are moments in the process of oral research when contextualization is important not only because it highlights the communicative nature of oral text production, but because it can reveal something beyond the language of the text. Laughter here reveals something about what is assumed to be common knowledge and practice among women, and this in turn suggests that these assumptions are deeply rooted in history.[47] After all, common sense is only common in the sense that it is historically and culturally constructed.

In other conversations, the historical depth of women's presence as ceremonial leaders among Kitawalists was addressed more explicitly. In conversation about the role of women in the Kitawalist church in Kalemie, I was told the following:

> Mama Kadima: Our work is to pray. We pray for the world first. The work inside the prayer chambers is the work of women, *wamama*. That's who is involved: we heal, we pray. That's our work.
> Me: Are there illnesses that women heal more and illnesses that men heal more? For example, do women more often heal maladies related to fertility?
> Mama Kadima: Yes.
> Me: And it is just women inside the prayer chamber?
> Mama Kadima: Yes.
> Me: And are there illnesses that men heal?
> Mama Kadima: It is generally women who heal.
> Me: Is there other work that women generally do?
> Mama Kadima: Just to pray.
> Me: Was it like this in the past?
> Mama Kadima: Yes. It was the work of wamama.
> Wamidi: During the time when the men were being arrested, the mamas were praying for them, that they would succeed.
> Kabanga Kamalondo: You recall that during the time of Jesus, it was the mamas who really knew his trials.[48]

Even more explicit was Kabanga Kamalondo's discussion of the role of women in the Kitawalist church during the era when Belgians were arresting Kitawalists:

> Those who were arrested were mostly men, because they were the ones who were in conflict with the Belgians. But the mamas, they were praying in the prayer chambers. When someone was

Healing ~ 77

arrested, the mamas came together to pray that they would find success. So, they created that power within the prayer chambers. They were doing very strong evocations [*kifungo kali*]. They weren't wearing clothes; they were just praying in the prayer chambers. They were doing evocations so that we would defeat the Belgians. A man would go into the chamber, we would get the power to be victorious [*ushindi*], and we would go. When the Belgians came and saw the evocations, they thought, "We need to capture those people." The Belgians then had an evocation so that they could recognize us. Even as we were doing our evocations, so that they couldn't recognize us, they were recognizing us and arresting us. Because they had an evocation in order to recognize. And it was true, they were arresting us everywhere. And we thought, Why are they arresting us? They had this one "lamba," and they saw them with it. And they were just arresting us. Since the beginning, women were in the church, until today. When the men were being sacrificed in the work camps at COLAGREL, they were there doing evocations. When the men were in Kisangani, the women did evocations and that guy[49] went into an evocation.[50]

Kabanga makes it clear that during the colonial period, when men were being arrested, imprisoned, and relegated to internment camps for their involvement with Kitawala, women, as the evokers and arbiters of spiritual power, were working outside of the gaze of colonial administrators to give men the ability to elude and ultimately defeat the Belgians. Drawing on both James C. Scott's ideas of "hidden transcripts" ("discourse that takes place offstage, beyond direct observation by power-holders") and Simon Bockie's work on "invisible powers," I would like to suggest that Kabanga's account of the role of women in the history of the Kitawalist church calls for attention to what I would call "invisible transcripts."[51] In this articulation, invisibility works at multiple levels. The transcripts are invisible in the sense that they are transcripts of spiritual power—a form of power that is material only in the moments in which it is embodied, but the presumed existence of which within a larger economy of power has continually shaped the way that people behave.[52] They are also invisible in the sense that their subject cannot be empirically proven to exist, now or in the past: even if accounts of women in prayer chambers exist in the archive, there is no way to prove that they were, in fact, empowering men to survive relegation in detention camps and to resist the Belgians. Such forms of aid are, in their very essence, invisible. Together, these two forms of invisibility work to cloud our ability as historians to see the importance of women as ceremonial authorities within the Kitawalist church historically, rendering them—and the forms of power they have wielded—invisible.[53]

The oral accounts highlighted in this section certainly should not be read as direct evidence that the roles of women as ceremonial authorities—which seem apparent in the examples given above—were identical in the past. Indeed, even today their role seems to vary between different groups of Kitawalists. Within Kitawala-Filadelfie, for example, PP2 insists that women do not hold any kind of leadership position. But he does suggest that their work within the church is to "pray." Significantly, I was unable to spend any time interviewing groups of exclusively women in Kabalo. This was in part due to the constraints of time—my trip to Kabalo was arduous and rendered short by the vagaries of travel in rural Congo. But I believe it was also due in part to PP2's desire to control the narrative about power within the church, for he repeatedly ignored my requests to speak with a group of women. He did tell me that women, as well as men, go into the mountains to pray when they seek healing. But I cannot know what the women might have told me had the men not been present.

Nor can a few suggestions that women, praying in the prayer chambers, were the arbiters of power that supported men in their public altercations with the colonial government prove that it was so. However, what these oral accounts can and must do is push historians to look for the evidence of invisible transcripts in the archives. Such evidence is inevitably fragmentary and difficult to find. Nonetheless, it can create what Luise White has called a "hologram" image of the past that, "when seen through a single, consistent illumination," can become "vivid and three-dimensional."[54] Oral evidence such as that presented here can and should provide that illumination as, in part 2, I turn back to the colonial history of Kitawala. But, before I do so, there is one final question that emerges out of Maman Kalema's account that must be addressed if we are to have a clear understanding of Kitawalist healing: What was the disease?

WHAT WAS THE DISEASE?
KITAWALIST HEALING IN THE THERAPEUTIC COMPLEX

When Gwyn Prins wrote his 1989 survey of the present state of health and healing in Africa, he posed this central question: "But what was the disease?"[55] He warned against treating disease, its causes and cures, as universally understood categories and argued that it could no longer be assumed that health and healing practices in Africa could be understood independent of the political and economic contexts in which they existed. Nor, he insisted, could the African past or present be understood without serious engagement with the multiple and shifting ways in which Africans have sought to maintain and restore healthy communities. Thus far in this chapter, I have written a great deal about Kitawalists' healing practices—about the ritual technologies, about who is doing the healing, and about the notions of tradition and power that animate them. But I have spent very little time interrogating the nature of the maladies that Kitawalist healers most frequently address. If we are to understand the epistemological space that Kitawalist healers have occupied, today and in the past, in the healing complex of eastern Congo, that is the question to which we must now turn.

To answer this question, I begin once more with Maman Kalema. In the opening narrative, Maman Kalema reveals that she was initially drawn to Kitawala because of an illness of fertility: she had carried a fetus for seven years without bearing a child. Through a biomedical lens, it is difficult to imagine what this illness might be. Maman Kalema did not provide details about the illness beyond noting the extended presence of the fetus in her womb. It is possible, for example, that she may have suffered hyperprolactinemia, an endocrine problem that causes the production of excess prolactin in the pituitary gland, causing lactation and lack of menses. This would have given the impression of prolonged pregnancy, although it is difficult to know how she would have healed without biomedical intervention. Uterine fibroids, if large enough, can also make a woman appear pregnant.[56] Or she may have suffered something similar to the psychiatric condition pseudopregnancy, in which the signs of pregnancy are psychologically induced. However, reading African disease categories that do not map directly onto biomedical disease categories through the language of psychology has a very sensitive imperial history. Westerners have a long history of deeming certain maladies—particularly those attributed to witchcraft—as psychologically induced, challenging the rationality of African etiological categories.[57]

Ultimately, none of these biomedical categories map particularly well onto Maman Kalema's affliction. However, if we think back to the disease categories offered by the leader of EDAC in Fizi, we can begin to see how Kitawalists might have categorized her disease. Kibasomba-Wakilongo stated that Kitawalist healers could cure several major categories of illness: "illness of flow/fertility [fungu]"; illnesses of "witchcraft/power [anga]"; illnesses such as cholera (those identified by John Janzen as "illnesses of God"); and illnesses of spirits (what Stacey Langwick calls "illnesses of mashetani").[58] These categories are not necessarily mutually exclusive, but they can overlap.

Illnesses of flow, for example, can be related to witchcraft or mashetani. It is in fact the category of "illnesses of flow" that is most useful for thinking about Maman Kalema's affliction. Christopher Taylor has studied the significance of blockage and flow in the conceptualization of health in Rwanda specifically, but the symbolic link between flow and health is common in much of Central Africa, including in Fizi.[59] Taylor notes that proper flow—of milk, of menses, of water (i.e., rain)—in the region is closely related to notions of health, wealth, and fertility. Conversely, excessive flow or blockage are symbolically linked with malady, infertility, and death.

Maman Kalema's seven-year pregnancy, although it has no obvious biomedical explanation, fits well into this category of illnesses of flow that Kibasomba-Wakilongo identifies as one of the diseases Kitawalist healers regularly address. One might also fit cholera into this category, for it is a disease of excessive flow. Kibasomba-Wakilongo says that "if it is cholera, we say, 'Block cholera from entering the body this year,' and it is possible."[60] The healers thus create blockage in order to avert excessive flow.

Maman Kalema was hardly the only person to be drawn to Kitawalist healing to address fertility issues. Kilanga Kamikunga, who was himself healed of a "difficult pain in his head," reported, "My wife had a problem with her female parts. She couldn't even walk. Again, the mamas took her into the prayer room. In the middle of the night, the illness peaked. So, I saw that this was the true path. And through the teachings of the Bible, of history, I saw that this was the religion of me, a Black person, and I joined."[61]

Another woman came to Kitawala with a different problem related to reproduction and familial health, but more directly tied to the presence of malevolent spirits than excessive flow: child mortality. She said:

> I was attracted because I was having problems with child mortality. I was always burying. One day I was with my husband and my little baby, and an elder said we should go to that Church over in Kaseka, that church of Kitawala. We were born Muslims. We asked ourselves: Kitawala, those people who wear white? But that child was infected. We said let's just go. We went, and we thought, this religion is a problem. Is this a religion? But we were having such problems with fertility [*tulifungishana sana*]. We searched our souls. And God helped us, and we had faith we'd give birth to a child, and God answered us. They told us just come here and be healed by these mamas and this problem of yours will end here. And our baby did not die, by the love of God, it was true. We went in there with those elders and the mamas began to pray, and God answered. And

Healing

> I thought, this is my life. So now I am here today and until I die. It is the life of my children. I had such troubles. Every year I was burying a child. But since I have converted to this religion, I thank God. It was life, wellness that brought me to this church. It is a church of wellness, of life.[62]

The woman's account is striking in its frank discussion of the horrific realities of child mortality that plague eastern Congo today.[63] But it is also an account that vividly illustrates how people imagine Kitawala within the therapeutic economy. For many, the choice to turn to Kitawalists is not easy, as there are many rumors that circulate about "those people who wear white." Some turn to them when other therapeutic options do not work or are inaccessible. Others turn to them only after they receive a vision from an ancestor, a dream. A final example will help to elucidate this point.

In an account of her own healing abilities, Maman Kalema told a story of a different kind of malady for which people turn to Kitawalists for healing, an illness of misfortune, caused by harmful powers:

> One day I was called to Bujumbura by my brother and his wife who are very religious. They had called me there because they said that the father of our grandfather [*babu*] had used his power to come to them in their sleep. Grandfather said that he saw that they had no luck with their business and had fallen into poverty and that their children were suffering. He told them that they must come to get me in Congo and I must do my prayer healing. They came to retrieve me, and we went to buy the necessary items: the things of our ancestors, the ones they liked to use. And then we ask the ancestors [*wale wazee wa mbele*] to guide us. At noon, we went into the prayer chamber, and I took the herbs. We were at the parcel of our great-grandfather. I began to pray. I prayed and I prayed in order to get [*kukamata*] the power, to call down the spirits that had been plaguing them [*kuwapiga wale watu*]. So, they made a sacrifice, and it was like a miracle [*vitu vya ajabu*]; everything they touched succeeded, whether in Bujumbura or Nairobi.[64]

Maman Kalema's brother and family were plagued by malevolent spirits. It is unclear why—though it seems as if the malevolent spirits had been set on them by others. It was only through Maman Kalema's evocation of these spirits and their appeasement with sacrifice that Maman Kalema's brother and his family were able to be "healed" and to procure the power to be successful.

The incident is interesting, not only because it is a prime example of the point articulated above—that women work as spirit mediums within the Kitawalist church—but also because it highlights an interesting therapeutic specialty of Kitawalists. As I discuss in other chapters, there are numerous rumors about Kitawalists. Some of those rumors revolve around their capacity to help people succeed, whether in love or business. On more than one occasion, the first question I got after I told non-Kitawalists about my research was whether I was hoping to "find gold." Indeed, in South Kivu, where gold mining is a major industry, Kitawalists are rumored to be able to give people the power to mine successfully. These rumors are interesting not only because they shed light on the economy of power in contemporary Congo but also because they bring texture to colonial accounts (see chapter 4) of people who claim they joined Kitawala because it had a "powerful nkisi" and could make them attractive to the opposite sex.[65]

But these stories also highlight the moral ambiguity of Kitawalist healing, which is frequently regarded with suspicion. Indeed, on one occasion the story of Kitawalists' ability to help people find gold was accompanied by a cautionary tale. There was young man who did just that, I was told, and found much gold, only to end up dead in the mines. This was the danger, I was told, of working with mashetani.[66] Kitawalists are known to work with spirits—wazimu, mashetani—and this reputation makes them both appealing for those who are in need of their power and terrifying for those who question its morality.

Thus, the answer to the question of "what was the disease" is varied for each of these cases. Some of them are "diseases of God," such as cholera. Others are diseases of flow. Still others are "diseases of *mashetatani*"—child mortality, or poor luck. These diseases do not fit neatly into biomedical categories, as some seem implausible—seven-year pregnancy—and some seem less like diseases than general forms of misfortune created by the socioeconomic realities of contemporary eastern Congo. But neither does Kitawala fit neatly into biomedical, traditional, or Christian "healing" categories.

Maman Kalema is just one Kitawalist woman with a singular story. But when her story is read in conjunction with those of the many other Kitawalist healers and healed featured in this chapter, together they reveal a vivid picture not only of the nature and significance of healing within Kitawalists communities but also of the nature and significance of Kitawalist healing in the broader therapeutic economy. Their stories push scholars to think about how and why notions of the material and immaterial may have shifted in the postcolonial context. But at the same time, they challenge us to think beyond the postcolonial and, without resorting to characterizations of "tradition" as static, look for ways in which Kitawalist healers today draw upon theories of power that are at once deeply rooted and contextually negotiated. Kitawalists engage in a broader discourse of traditionality in which different actors make varied claims to tradition. Some, such as the healers featured in the work of Langwick, increasingly recognize themselves in, while continuing to distinguish themselves from, the universalizing discourse of biomedicine. Others, like the Kitawalists featured in this chapter, are less interested in recognizing their healing practices in biomedicine than they are in rooting them in tradition even as they draw on the universalizing discourse of Christianity.

Attention to Kitawalist healing practices in the postcolonial era thus raises interesting questions about the process by which Kitawalists have wielded power for purposes that are neither religious nor political. It also paves the way to more readily recognizing the significance of healing and the theories of power it engages in the colonial history of Kitawala. In particular, this account of postcolonial Kitawalist healing raises vital questions about the gendered nature of power within Kitawalist communities today, allowing us to draw out the "invisible transcripts" of the important roles that women might have played in Kitawalist communities in the past. It is toward these questions—and their entanglement with histories of violence—that this study now turns in part 2.

PART 2

Violence and Power

3 ~ Violence

THE YEAR 1944 would prove to be a tumultuous and tragic one for the people in and around Kesese, a small town about 240 kilometers (149 mi.) southeast of Lubutu, in what is today the province of Maniema. There had been a recent history of destabilizing colonial violence in the region. The colonial government had drastically increased labor regimes throughout the colony to meet the demands of the ongoing world war, and in this mining and rubber industry region, people no doubt felt that strain.[1] Additionally, just two years earlier, in 1942, a Belgian territorial administrator named Paul-Ernest Joset—described by his own colleagues as a man "without scruples"—had led an operation to forcibly move an estimated seven hundred families to the region, resettling them to a "deserted" area.[2] It was a process some of his peers considered so controversial that an investigation was launched, the results of which were quickly classified and covered up by his superiors. This had no doubt brought new kinds of insecurity to the lives of people around Kasese, both those who were resettled and those who were already there. That same year, Joset was arrested and spent time in jail for beating a Congolese man so severely with his baton that he "literally scalped" him and put him in the hospital for two and a half months. He nonetheless remained in his position as territorial administrator.[3]

By the beginning of 1944, people in and around Kasese may have already heard rumors about the movement known as Kitawala. And by February of

1944, when a massive Kitawalist revolt broke out just north of them, along the route from Lubutu to Masisi, they would have certainly heard of Kitawala. Some may even have joined the movement, or were interested in learning more. Others were probably afraid—uncertain what the unrest would mean for them, their families, and their livelihoods. By early March, however, the revolt had been violently suppressed by the colonial government and its leaders arrested. Kasese had remained largely calm throughout the ordeal.

For the people of Kasese and surrounding areas, it was not the revolt but its aftermath that would prove most deadly. From March 31 to May 13, a murderous peloton of thirty-seven colonial soldiers came rolling through their villages, terrorizing the population. The leaders of this "military promenade"—a warrant officer named Benzing and an agronomist named Paquay—had been sent there by their superiors as "a simple measure of precaution," in order to "maintain order."[4] Yet, in that six-week window, Benzing and Paquay's bike brigade arrested and brutalized somewhere between one-quarter and one-third of the population in and around Kasese, in the process murdering at least one hundred and gravely injuring hundreds of other individuals.[5] They did so based on unsubstantiated accusations that the victims were a "real threat": Kitawala extremists who were planning to rebel and murder the Europeans in the region.[6]

Reports from the massacre are horrifying. Later, a critical colonial official accused them of having "committed, from village to village, atrocities and brutalities that were nothing less than savage acts."[7] With zero proof beyond the denunciations of a single informant—a captured Kitawalist leader named Mukaba (whose "sincerity" was itself in doubt)—they arrested more than "168 so-called Kitawalists" in Kasese alone. According to an inquest that was performed nearly a year later, they were "whipped to excess and beaten with the butt of a rifle." Of those who survived, most were left with injuries that rendered them unable to work for many months. Between 5 and 10 percent were left with "permanent disabilities," including the following: "disfigurement of limbs," "chronic wasting," and "daze and loss of the ability to articulate words." While Benzing would later insist that they did not order any more than twenty-five to fifty lashes, at least one other European in the area reported hearing them order one hundred lashes, and the soldiers who were ordered to do the whippings reported that "nobody counted"—they just beat the victims "until they were tired of whipping." The rifle butt was used "when they struggled against the whip."[8]

Benzing and Paquay would also later insist that they were merciful to those whom they beat, because they sent anyone with grave injuries to the hospital to be treated. But when they reached the hospital, many died of their injuries, including from infection, concussion, and shock. According to the health agent stationed at Kasese, A. Boivin, their deaths were, in most cases, the result of not receiving medicine to treat infections. While such medicines were available in the area, Boivin fully admitted that he ordered his nurses not to use them on these patients because, in his own words, medicines should be "reserved to treat the transplants and workers" and "to act otherwise would have been wasteful." Medicines used on alleged Kitawalists were, in his view, wasted.[9]

By late April, "alarming rumors" of "murderous engagements" in Kasese were beginning to reach the commander of the colonial troops in the East.[10] When the rumors were ultimately verified, the operation was halted, at which point a new conversation began among colonial administrators about whether and to what extent the massacre should be investigated. Authorities local to the district—and thus directly implicated in the affair—were adamant that an investigation would be "disastrous" and should not be undertaken. Joset, for example, had witnessed the prisoners being "mistreated" but insisted that he could not intervene because "any speech or gesture in public to stop it would have certainly had grave consequences, as the members of the sect would immediately believe they were protected, and it was necessary to avoid such an interpretation at any price." Similarly, if an inquest was done, he insisted, it would appear the colonial government disapproved of the mission, and the Kitawalists "would not hide their joy in sanctions taken against their 'enemies.'" Moreover, he argued, while the actions taken by Benzing and Paquay were "too bad," they were nonetheless considered "just and normal" by the Europeans in the region.[11] Indeed, they considered them "veritable saviors" who protected them from a proliferation of Kitawala that would have been a "true catastrophe for the territory, specifically for mining and rubber producers."[12]

Other officials were less concerned about an inquest causing instability in the region and more concerned that any "publicity of that affair" was undesirable and would "expose grave dangers" to the security of the state.[13] An official named Noirot, for example, worried the Congolese people would "interpret the condemnation poorly and see in it proof that the means of repression taken in hand were illegal." He was particularly concerned about media coverage, arguing that "the newspapers will grab the affair and exploit it to turn the public against the government."[14] Others worried the colonial government would "lose face once more." But some were less convinced by such arguments: the provincial commissaire, Enst R. Preys, for example, argued that the Congolese people must know that "the representatives of authority and all of the Europeans in general are not in solidarity with the criminal acts committed by Benzing."[15]

Ultimately, the calls for an inquest won out and led to charges against Benzing and Paquay. They were even convicted and initially sentenced to two years in detention.[16] Ultimately, however, the defense presented character witnesses who vouched for them and they were pardoned from serving the sentences.[17] And the colonial government worked hard to make sure the details of the story remained largely occluded from the public eye. In the end, there was no real justice for the victims of this massacre, but they are not forgotten. Today the traffic circle at the center of Kasese is remembered as the site where these atrocities took place.[18]

COMPOUNDING VIOLENCES

The Lobutu-Masisi uprising of 1944 began in the village of Magoa, located in the district of Masisi, in the region of Kivu.[19] The leader of the uprising, Bushiri Lungunda, professed himself to be the son of God, charged with the mission of redeeming his African people and relieving them of White rule and oppression. He claimed that his messianic doctrine, a variant of Kitawala he called Mapendo (Love), had been transmitted to him in a vision in December of 1943. As he lay in a nine-day slumber, he was transported by a white airplane to America, where God revealed to him that he was Yesu Mukombozi (Jesus the Redeemer) and that he must "complete the work of the first Jesus" and save the earth.[20] Shortly thereafter, Bushiri began preaching his message and baptizing his earliest followers—most of whom were Bakumu—into the movement. It is these followers who accompanied Bushiri when, on the evening of February 16, 1944, they arrested a local colonial agent named De Schryver at Magoa and forced him to march along wearing nothing but a loin cloth and carrying vines of rubber around his neck. De Schryver's arrest set into motion the events of the revolt, which lasted for more than a month. In that time, Bushiri and his followers arrested two more Europeans, five local agents of the state, and numerous African men and women accused of witchcraft, a number of whom were executed. "Mukombozi" and his followers had plans to capture the three hundred White people living in the area and then to attack the city of Costermansville (Bukavu). Before the revolt was forcefully repressed by the colonial army in mid-March, it had involved upwards of ten thousand men, women, and children and resulted in hundreds of deaths.[21]

The uprising—one of the largest in Congo's history—was an event notable, among other aspects, for the form, function, and level of violence that characterized it. Much of that violence was perpetrated by the colonial state, which reacted with a fear that manifested in massacre and violent excess, both during and after the uprising. Kasese was one example of this, but it was not the only one. In another village, Djembe, colonial soldiers, determined to free two mining managers kidnapped during the uprising, shot into an unarmed crowd of Kitawalists and killed fifty-three men, women, and children and injured many more. They had apparently blocked the road with their "fanatic" dancing and singing.[22]

The violence of these events is a stark reminder that the history of colonial atrocities in Congo did not end with the Congo Free State. By the 1940s, the government of the Belgian Congo preferred to imagine itself as the benevolent benefactor of the Congolese people. Yet, the arbitrariness and brutality with which these colonial officers and their functionaries perpetrated violence was not unusual. Rather, such violence exemplifies the excessive tendencies of what Nancy Hunt has called the "nervous" face of Belgian colonial rule—a face worn not just by the likes of Benzing and Paquay, but by the Josets who were quietly chastised for behaving badly but ultimately left in positions of authority, and by the White settlers who profited from "peace" purchased at the price of Congolese blood.[23] Such realities must be understood as central to the conditions of unease out of which the uprising emerged and as provocation for the kinds of violence that characterized it.

Although the most salient goal of the uprising was to end colonial rule and upend its violent labor regimes, underneath that mantle of anticolonial resistance was a much more unruly amalgam of ambitions: refusals and contestations, but also "reveries" and remedies.[24] Aparicio et al. write that refusal, as a concept, "confounds dominant sensibilities about what constitutes resistance." It "opposes dominant orders; but it is also contestation in ways unthought, or better put, unrecognized—illegible practices and modes of being." Refusal encompasses "projects of existence" that "desert, escape, and abandon," defying clear categorization and upending easy explanations.[25] The Lobutu-Masisi uprising included modes of action that are not entirely legible—not easily accounted for under the ledger of resistance. It involved rebellion, but also creative and sometimes destructive remedies. It was very much an example of what Nancy Hunt has called "therapeutic insurgency," with intentions of both healing and harming, and modes of collective action that could be rehabilitative but also punitive.[26] And the violence of the uprising was not limited to acts perpetrated by or against the colonial government. Bushiri's uprising was internally quite violent as well. It is unclear how many villagers in the region were arrested and beaten by Bushiri's band (many for practicing witchcraft), but a single testimony—that

Violence ~ 91

of Alleloya, Bushiri's right hand—documents a minimum of sixty arrests.[27] They whipped those they arrested (with a *chicotte*) and more than half of them died in captivity. The majority of those they arrested were women, many of whom were subjected, in addition to whipping, to sexual violence and public displays of humiliation.

This chapter sits in the uneasy tensions created by these multiple and compounding registers of violence and asks critical questions about the imaginaries and choreographies of violence at play during the uprising. It does so by locating the uprising, and the forms of violence that characterized it, within the complex theories of power outlined in previous chapters. Arguing for attention to deep histories of violence and vulnerability in central and eastern Africa, David Schoenbrun has written that "histories of violence in Africa that take seriously the challenge of specifying the contexts for potential acts of violence must depict the theories of action that frame imaginary violence, the ever-present double of 'real' violence."[28] The centrality of witchcraft discourse in the uprising and the acts of violence that accompanied that discourse must be understood not as tangential to the larger anticolonial political struggle of Bushiri and his followers, but central to that struggle and the way it manifested in that historical moment.

Bushiri's uprising was clearly an overt challenge to the legitimacy of colonial rule. But, more broadly, it was a challenge to what Bushiri and his followers must have perceived as a dangerously imbalanced economy of power in the region, which posed a grave threat to social and physical health. The fact that the remedy Bushiri and his followers offered frequently took the form of violence—not just against the state and its agents, but also against those (often quite vulnerable) individuals who were presumed to be covetous of, possessors of, and/or (immoral) wielders of power—raises important questions. In particular, it pushes us to interrogate the fraught relationship between healing and violence in the history of both Kitawala and the broader region. It challenges scholars to consider whether the remedy on offer was perhaps not restoration or rehabilitation, but something even more radical and potentially liberatory: destruction, or rupture.[29] But it also reminds us that the unruliness inherent in such ruptures defies easy dichotomies that tend to represent the accompanying violence as either destructive or productive.[30] Bushiri's uprising has been construed as both. The Belgians certainly saw it as destructive violence, but so too did many within the communities the uprising touched. For example, one account describes the mothers of the victims of Bushiri's witchcraft accusations cursing and spitting at him as, in the aftermath of the revolt, he was paraded through villages to prove he had been captured.[31] Yet, in the larger narrative of resistance against the violent and oppressive colonial state and the illness and discord it inflicted, the uprising was geared toward productive ends, toward ending oppressive and extractive colonial economic practices and reinstating self-rule.

It is only in breaking down such dichotomies and highlighting the ambiguous and compounding nature of violence that we begin to see how the relative morality of violent acts committed by Bushiri's band was a contentious and negotiated subject *within* the Congolese communities it most directly affected. Moreover, we begin to see how the ambiguity of the violence was mirrored in the theories of power through which it was articulated. For, like violence, power in Central Africa has long been imagined in dualistic terms—destructive/productive, eating/healing—that have rendered its legitimacy a subject of contention and contestation. It is in "tethering" the history of such contentious notions to the deeper conceptual history in the region that we can begin to more fruitfully interrogate how they were reproduced and reimagined in the colonial context.[32]

MUKOMBOZI AND THE MONGANGA

The arguments articulated above hinge on the understanding that the violence of Bushiri's uprising was predicated on an imbalance in the economy of power in the region. In articulating his messianic vision of Mapendo, Bushiri identified not just the colonial government, its functionaries, and its regimes of labor as the source of the imbalance, but also a broader sort of moral decay signified in the practice of witchcraft. It was this perceived imbalance that inspired and ultimately shaped the uprising, allowing for its rapid spread and rendering Bushiri's claims to the power necessary to correct that imbalance—the power of God, which he embodied as Yesu Mukombozi—at once persuasive and contentious.

Evidence for Bushiri's theories of power—and the actions through which he sought to address imbalance—can be seen in his own testimonies, which are discussed further below. However, some of the richest sources for understanding the uprising come not from Bushiri himself but from those around him. The testimony of Bushiri's second in command, Alleloya, who was a reputed healer, or *monganga*, offers a particularly detailed account of the uprising. Alleloya was a specialist of an herbal medicine (dawa) he called *mataifa* ("nation" or "people" in Swahili), and he and another healer, Albert, were the most powerful figures in the uprising, next to Bushiri. The record of his interrogation by the colonial government after the fact was framed by the circumstances that produced it in some obvious ways. Alleloya had been arrested and was charged with inciting an uprising, and the testimony was his chance to explain his involvement. It is apparent as one reads the source that he was downplaying his own role, insisting he was only a humble healer, unconnected to the violence. Nonetheless, the testimony paints a vivid picture of the uprising from the perspective of one of its leaders. For that reason, I reproduce it at some length here, narrated in the first person, as it was in the interrogation record, although I have edited it for clarity.[33] I have chosen to interrupt my analysis to present Alleloya's testimony in this narrative form because of the immediacy it lends to the events of the revolt, rendering the violence that characterized it and the ideas that animated it real and palpable.[34]

Transcript of Alleloya's Testimony

I had worked for years collecting rubber at Angumu. Sometime before the uprising, I became ill, close to death, and God came to me in a dream. In the dream, God gave me the name Alleloya. He then showed me the medicine of mataifa, and ordained me to heal the people with the dawa produced from the juice of the mataifa plant found in the forest. From that day, I took the name Alleloya, stopped collecting rubber and stayed at my home village in Musimia. Whenever there was a sick child, I was called on to help them with my dawa. In this way, I earned a reputation as a healer.

Around this time, I had also been initiated into Kitawala. For several months before Bushiri's arrival, two men named Nziaka and Ndele had been moving through the area, initiating people into Kitawala. It was Ndele who initiated me, though he was ultimately arrested and beaten by Bushiri.

Before Bushiri came to Wenga, I did not know him. I had seen him when we both worked at Angumu, but we had never spoken. When we first heard news of his arrival, all we knew was that there was a man coming to Hunde from Wenga, preaching that the days of working rubber were over. When Bushiri arrived, someone told him that I practiced the craft of monganga in the region and that I could heal the people with my dawa, mataifa. So Bushiri called on me to be his healer. I just prepared my dawa and I did not beat anyone, but because I was the monganga, I was considered as one of the leaders of the movement.

When Bushiri called on me, I went to him. Then I was called back to my village, so I left Bushiri's band briefly, but he soon called me back. By the time I returned, I found that a local clerk with the rubber collection company, Honoré, had been imprisoned and whipped by Bushiri and his followers. They had burned all of his files, but they kept his rubber meter. [Note: There were rumors about Bushiri having a meter, with which he could detect witchcraft. It was said that the meter was in his arm.][35]

Bushiri decreed that people were no longer to collect rubber. Instead, they should cultivate crops [particularly tobacco]. They could sell their crops to him or to his friend, "Merika" [America]. He said he would destroy the areas inhabited by the whites and take them as his own. His goals were to make war with the Europeans, forbid rubber collection, kill the locals who worked with the whites, and kill the Wanianga and the Bakusu, who had to be "exterminated" because they "practiced abortion."[36] To execute this plan, Bushiri began by imprisoning people accused of witchcraft.

During the uprising, Bushiri took all of the women in the region that pleased him. Their husbands said nothing because they were afraid of being killed and there was no question of *dot* [brideprice]. Bushiri said that he would take one thousand wives to demonstrate that he was the absolute master of the land. He promised each of his adepts one hundred wives. He also decreed that it was necessary for each wife to have ten children. If a woman was not pregnant within three months of marrying, she would be killed. If her husband remarried and there were still no children, he would be killed.

It was at Magoa that Bushiri's men arrested "Bwana Mzuri" [De Schryver]. The band arrested and punished many people. One man was imprisoned for trying to hide his mother, who had been accused of witchcraft. He was whipped twelve times. The wife of one follower was imprisoned for making difficulties for her husband. She was whipped twenty times. Another man who worked as a policeman for the Belgians, Musafiri, was arrested and beaten. Bwana Mzuri was forced to participate in the beating. Musafiri died after receiving more than six hundred lashes with the whip. Before he died, he told Bushiri, "You can kill me, but the state will avenge me." Bushiri told the other prisoners who had worked for the Belgians—Honoré, Léon, and Albert—to renounce the state, but they refused, repeating Musafiri's words.

As we moved between villages, we encountered a number of local notables. Some of them joined us, but others were arrested. We arrested Buhini, successor to the chief of Eliba, and he was whipped to death.

In Wenga, five men were arrested for witchcraft. They fled to the forest, so Bushiri put their wives in prison and they were whipped one hundred times. At least three of them died. In Abunambao, Bushiri arrested four more women and some of them also died after receiving one hundred lashes.

On our way to Maliba, some twenty more people were arrested, many of whom were beaten and killed. An mfumu was denounced and killed. It was also near Maliba that the rubber clerk Honoré was ultimately beaten to death.

At Taweza, many more were arrested and beaten. Three women were whipped, then tied to a tree, with their arms up. Their limbs were broken and they were left to die. At least a dozen people died at Taweza. When Bushiri classified someone as a sorcerer, their children would say nothing. They just let it happen.

Bushiri sent out a series of letters. He sent letters to the villages ahead of us to tell them to prepare to receive him. But he also sent a letter to Bribosia, telling him that he would arrest and imprison him, that he alone was master of the land, and that the rule of the whites was over. Bushiri made Bwana Mzuri watch as he cursed the whites. He showed us on his head where he had a large cross and told us that all of the lands in the four directions of this cross were his and he would not tolerate anyone against him. He said that once he had imprisoned the three white officials in the region, Bribosia, Reiles, and Kiesel, all of the other whites would flee. He would install himself in a place called Bulambo, near the river Bilulu. He would build a road that would allow people to conduct trade there.

When we arrived in Eliba, the same torture as Taweza was applied to another woman, but she did not die. For fun, Bushiri made five elders have sex with five women in the public square of the village of Eliba. They were then whipped. The rest of the victims were whipped to death or killed with blows to the nape of the neck.

It was in Eliba that we learned that the whites were coming. Bushiri told us to throw down our spears, as he would fight the Europeans himself with his words, which he said would be sufficient to kill them all. We went to river and sang the "mataifa" and the "alleloya." The whites did not come that day and we believed that our songs had made it so that the whites could not cross the river.

Then news reached us that Bwana Mzuri had been returned to the whites and Katshaka had been arrested by them. We asked Bushiri why he did not take the battle to the whites. He told us that he could not take the battle to the whites, because all of the villagers would flee. If they were in the way they would also be killed by his words, which were addressed to the whites. But then the whites came and we all fled into the forest, including Bushiri. I took refuge in the forest outside my village in Musimia. The state police camped out in my village. They told everyone that they were only there to arrest me, so I turned myself in.

THE PROPHET, THE HEALERS, AND COMPOSED POWER

Alleloya's testimony is difficult to read. It raises questions about the prevalence of forms of violence that both critiqued and mirrored colonial violence, reflecting that violence back on colonial agents but also directing it toward those deemed dangerous within their own communities. This, in turn, points to the question of women, who emerge at once as wielders of dangerous power, assumed to be the source of "invisible" violence (witches), and vulnerable victims of the movement's violence. But before returning to those questions, I would like to return to the proposition that this Kitawalist uprising was an effort to address the imbalance in the economy of power. In making this argument, I am placing Bushiri's movement within long history of other movements in Central Africa that have struggled to address imbalances within distressed communities, those that have come to be understood as healing movements/associations. These are movements/associations—the Nybingi movement, *kubandwa, lemba, ryangombe*—that historically emerged in central and eastern Africa to address ills both bodily and social, as well as to protect communities from such ills.[37]

Literature on these movements has revealed much that can be of use in thinking about Bushiri and his followers specifically, and Kitawala more broadly, as part of this longer history. In particular, it has highlighted the role that "public healing" has played in the maintaining and restoring of healthy communities. As Neil Kodesh notes in his work about the centrality of kubandwa mediumship in processes of state formation in early Bugandan history, "the semantic histories of words for medicine, different sorts of spirits, and healing techniques" for much of Central Africa reveal that "historical actors thought about health and prosperity together."[38] Thus, public healers, as those charged with creating and maintaining prosperity, were profoundly political leaders. But they did not always imagine or articulate their roles in language that can be translated directly into secular-political or purely "religious" roles without obscuring part of their significance. Moreover, it is precisely this connection between prosperity and health that historically made new healing associations—often in the form of what John Janzen has call "cults of affliction," claiming access to new kinds of spirits, or new means of accessing older spirits—among the primary means through which people sought to address imbalances in the economy of power, in many cases opposing themselves to existing authorities.[39]

There is ample evidence in Alleloya's testimony to suggest that Bushiri's uprising in particular, and Kitawala more broadly, must be understood in the context of such movements and associations. The most obvious evidence is the centrality of Alleloya himself in the movement. We know he was a reputed healer who claimed the knowledge of a medicine called mataifa had been transmitted to him by God in a dream. It is difficult to know what the medicine was composed of, as Alleloya simply states that it came from the "mataifa plant," which could be found in the forest, but it is not clear what sort of plant it was or whether it had any biomedical healing properties. In any case, the name of the medicine is perhaps what is most interesting. *Mataifa* means "nation" or "people" in Swahili. Thus, it seems plausible to read the name of the medicine as a sign that it was, indeed, geared toward curing social ills, the ills of a whole people manifest in the bodies of various individuals, many of whom, Alleloya indicates, were children.[40] It is also unclear whether knowledge of this medicine was specific to Alleloya and the region he lived in or whether it was a medicine more broadly associated with Kitawala.[41] What is clear is that Kitawalists across Congo historically garnered reputations for healing. The prevalence of dawas within Kitawalist communities can be seen in colonial reports about Kitawala from its earliest manifestations in Katanga. And they continued to be central to Kitawala in both the late colonial and postcolonial periods.

While there are few records detailing the concerns of Bushiri's followers, it is clear that healing was a significant part of the movement, as it was Alleloya's reputation as a skilled healer that brought Bushiri to his village in the first place and earned him a position of influence. Although Alleloya represents his role as largely passive in the movement—Bushiri "called him to the movement," he "just prepared his medicine"—there is evidence to support the assertion that he was far more central to the movement than he lets on. Note the following exchange between Alleloya and his interrogator, M. Kiesel, which came at the end of the testimony recounted above:

> Kiesel: Before you joined Bushiri, he had not committed any extravagance, though he had been there [Wenga] for several days. It was only when you arrived that the "danse macabre" began. So, it was you who called Bushiri into the region, or at the very least you knew from the deserters from Semiba that he would arrive soon.

> There were many places he could have gone to find adepts, but he came directly to you. Explain.
>
> Alleloya: All we knew was that there was a man coming to Hunde from Wenga who said that the days of working rubber were done.

Kiesel's question suggests that in the process of their investigation, the colonial authorities had acquired information placing Alleloya in a far more central role than he indicates in his testimony. The accuracy of their information is certainly suspect, but so too is Alleloya's evasive response, as he had every reason to minimize his role. In any case, Alleloya does acknowledge earlier that "it was because [he] was the monganga that he was considered one of the leaders of the movement." What he seems to be denying in this exchange is that he had any formative or functional leadership role, beyond serving as the monganga—a denial that his life depended on in that moment.

Whatever the precise role of Alleloya was in the movement vis-à-vis leadership, it seems clear that he had a reputation for being powerful and that Bushiri sought him out—along with Albert, the other healer (mfumu) who helped lead the uprising—so that he might bring that power into his movement, both strengthening and legitimating it. As historians such as David Schoenbrun have demonstrated, this process—whereby leaders (political/religious/healing) have historically sought to legitimate their own power by creating alliance with or, alternatively, opposing themselves to other powerful figures—has a very deep history in the region.[42] As does the practice of "composing" power through the accumulation of knowledgeable dependents.[43] The centrality of the two healers in the leadership of Bushiri's movement must be read as part of that history. But so too must the fact that the movement was directly opposed to the other figures presumed to be immorally wielding power: practitioners of witchcraft and the colonial state. Let us consider the latter of these two categories first.

THE COLONIAL STATE, YESU MUKOMBOZI, AND THE ECONOMY OF POWER

The idea that the Europeans possessed an immoral amount of power and that the resultant imbalance in the region was the root of social strife was central to the doctrine Bushiri preached and the remedy his rebellion was intended to provide: the redistribution of that power back to the Congolese people.[44] Asked to explain the core of his doctrine during an interrogation, Bushiri highlighted the following three points:

> It is necessary to love God.
> It is necessary to fight the Europeans and kill them because it is they who hold all the power.
> It is necessary to give the power to the blacks.[45]

One could argue that Bushiri here is speaking not of power—in the conceptually and linguistically situated sense outlined in the introduction, with its connotations of spiritual force—but of political authority, economic access, and monopoly on violence. The material grievances of Bushiri and his followers are obvious in the sources. European rule manifested not just as arbitrary acts of violence, like the ones that opened this chapter, but as economic and political dominance. Bushiri quite clearly wanted to bring about the reversal of that dominance. One of the central claims Bushiri made was that he would end the coercive rubber collection in the region and return the people to other forms of cultivation deemed more productive. He suggested, for example, cultivating tobacco and selling it to "Merika"—or America—which was perceived within Kitawalist teachings as an ally to the Congolese in their struggle against European dominance. Recall, as well, from Alleloya's testimony that Bushiri promised his followers that once they had rid themselves of the Europeans, he would create a capital and "build a road that would allow people to conduct trade there." In his interrogation, Bushiri directly claimed that one of the goals of his movement was the redistribution of European property to himself and his followers: "My people and I will take the autos, the trucks, the houses, the wealth, and the women of the Europeans."[46]

Moreover, Bushiri and his followers, and all the people in the region, quite obviously suffered from material forms of violence and social upheaval inflicted on them by the colonial state. In his meticulous reconstruction of the political and economic context of the region touched by the revolt, Mwene-Batende has argued that the Kumu—the ethnic group to which Bushiri and the vast majority of his followers belonged—had, particularly in the ten years preceding the uprising, suffered from the profound and rapid disruption of their "ancestral mode of production."[47] The Kumu had historically been a seminomadic group that subsisted largely on hunting in the forests and some seasonal cultivation. With the arrival of Arab-Swahili traders to the region in the nineteenth century, this had already begun to change, as the Kumu redirected their productive activity from a largely subsistence-based hunting economy to supplying the Arab-Swahili caravans with ivory and food. The presence of Swahili-Arab traders thus led to increased sedentarization in order to facilitate cultivation of enough food to both supply the caravans and account for the redirection of hunting labor toward trade rather than subsistence. Sedentarization also allowed for heightened protection of communities rendered increasingly vulnerable by the presence of the slave trade in the region.

Yet, the social effects of this reorientation toward trade with the Arab-Swahili, which took place largely in that latter half of the nineteenth century, paled in comparison to the profound transformation that came, beginning in the 1930s, with the rapid economic development of the region by the colonial government.[48] Although Congo had been claimed by Leopold in 1885 and transferred into the control of the Belgian state in 1908, the remote region between Lubutu and Masisi remained comparatively unaffected by colonial exploitation until the 1930s. Even in the years that immediately preceded the uprising, European presence in the region was relatively superficial. When, in 1936 (just eight years before the revolt), an engineer named Fournier arrived in the region between Bafwasende, Lubutu, and Walikale—which would be the principal region of the revolt—to start a mine for the Comité National du Kivu, he described the area as "unknown, not penetrated and little peopled."[49] Missionary presence—aside from one Protestant Swedish mission in Lubutu and a few chapel schools in the villages closest to Lubutu—was notably absent from the region as well, even up until the time of the revolt. Reporting from the district of Masisi in 1944, the territorial administrator of Utunda, Bribosia, noted that, for the most part, "the inhabitants have never seen a missionary, nor do they know what is a doctor."[50]

It was in the midst of the financial pressures of world depression and an increasing awareness of the mineral wealth that existed in the region (rich in gold, tin, rubber, and cassiterite) that the colonial government ultimately pressed for the rapid development of the region in the 1930s and 1940s. Between 1938 and 1944, four major mines were opened in the region. And this rapid economic development had been preceded, only five years earlier, in 1933, by the profound political and administrative reorganization of the region, which had upset the existing clan-based political structures by transplanting and regrouping villages into more centralized, and therefore more easily administered, political formations and investing state-appointed chiefs and "sultanis" with political authority in the region. These chiefs and sultanis functioned as representatives of the colonial state, in particular as the implementers of colonial taxation laws, which were used to coerce men, who saw their ancestral hunting grounds rapidly transformed into mines, into working in the very same mines that were destroying their means of subsistence.[51]

The effects these rapid changes had on the well-being of the communities they touched were immense. The dislocation of male, able-bodied workers undoubtedly affected the gendered division of subsistence labor, and most likely led to a poorer diet and, by proxy, poorer health.[52] It seemingly also had deleterious effects on processes of marriage and reproduction, as migratory young men delayed marriage or spent long periods away from their communities. It is significant that during the revolt Bushiri and his followers targeted old men for using witchcraft and taking all the wives while the young men were away working. It is also significant that infertile women were another main target of violence. Indeed, most of the witchcraft victims of the uprising were sterile women and old men who were accused by Bushiri of, among other things, "killing small children."[53] Even the regional colonial administrator De Koster lamented, in a report written in the wake of the revolt, that the people in the region had been "pushed to change in every way: recruitment of all natures, road work, culture, dislocation of customary groups, and displacement of villages" and they "could not digest it all because they had not been prepared."[54] Without reifying the common colonial trope that Africans were too simple to digest modernity, it is possible to acknowledge that the onslaught of economic and political change in the region created significant hardships in people's lives, and those hardships manifested in forms of vulnerability: to disease, to hunger, and to infertility.[55] While it is undoubtedly true that the colonial state offered new and important opportunities for some Congolese, it is also true that, for many more, it had created grave social ills, with tangible, material effects.

Still, to read Bushiri's language exclusively in these materialist and political terms is to miss part of the conceptual field he was almost certainly signaling when he claimed the Europeans "hold all the power." Rumors that colonizers were unethically hoarding or hiding power have a long history in Congo. In some cases, such stories have suggested that they were hiding the power of God. Accusations that priests, in particular, evoked God's power for themselves, and kept the knowledge of how to do so secret, appear often in oral histories.[56] Another rumor of this genre suggests that colonizers stole the ritual objects (statuary, shrines, etc.) of Congolese people so that they could keep their power for themselves.[57] Reading Bushiri's words only through the lens of political oppression and economic exploitation occludes the multivalent inflections of his language, the sense in which he was equally suggesting that the Europeans were hoarding spiritual knowledge and power—and indeed the economic and political dominance were made possible by that hoarding.

The social ills experienced by the people in the region were neither imagined nor articulated in exclusively material, or this-worldly, terms. The uprising was as much a reaction to the "imaginary" violence inflicted by the state (the hoarding of power and the use of it for illegitimate purposes of political and material accumulation) as it was a reaction to the "real" violence inflicted by the state (forced relocation, forced/coerced labor, economic exploitation). Only by acknowledging the realness of that imaginary violence for those who acted against it can we begin to contemplate the "theories of action" that guided them.[58] Emphasizing power as central to those theories draws on a language that can encapsulate both the material and the imaginary aspects of that violence, bringing them together into the same frame of reference, acknowledging their intimate connection. Calling it an "economy" of power emphasizes the fact that the field of power was broad and there was a multitude of actors perceived to be operating within that field, each making claims to legitimacy or illegitimacy, or sometimes being accused of operating within that field independent of their own claims (as with people accused of witchcraft).

Bushiri was just one actor in that economy, but he was offering access to a particularly potent form of power: that of the Christian God, which he laid claim to as Yesu Mukombozi. And those claims—bolstered by the allegiance of healers like Alleloya and Albert—clearly had currency, given the rapidity with which he amassed followers. When the territorial administrator Bribosia visited one of the Catholic missions in the region at the beginning of the uprising, the priests running the mission at Mutongo told him there were rumors of a "*mufalme ngufu* [powerful king/ruler] with 400 warriors." A group of school children were forthcoming in their assessment of Bushiri:

> "He is really the son of God. He is all-powerful. He has the gift of omnipresence. He has a black head, a steel chest, and white legs. He baptizes his followers and is a friend to the missions. He draws his force from himself and his followers and he wants to relieve the poor blacks from rubber collection. He doesn't want to kill the whites, but just to arrest them." The Father Superior informed Bribosia, furthermore, that he had encountered "much trouble convincing his flock that Catholicism and Kitawala [were] not compatible."[59]

This final point suggests that the Father Superior's "flock" saw Kitawala—and Bushiri's movement in particular—as but one potentially potent source of power in the larger economy, not necessarily incompatible with and perhaps even complimentary to others (namely, Catholicism).

Thus, Bushiri tethered his claims to the past not through a bounded set of ancestral practices and beliefs but through the evocation of a dynamic theory of power. And that dynamic theory allowed for innovation:

the embodiment of power from a relatively new source that had proven formidable—the Christian God—in order to correct the imbalance in the community. And when Bushiri entered into that economy claiming he embodied God's power as Yesu Mukombozi and that he could correct the imbalance at the root of their social ills, people believed him and they followed him—whether it was out of fear (because he threatened to kill all those who did not follow him) or out of genuine desire for the social healing he promised (the vanquishing of witches and the overturning of the colonial order) and the hope that he could provide it. Ultimately, as the children Bribosia spoke with so wisely observed, Bushiri drew "his force" from those who followed him. One of Bushiri's captains reportedly echoed this sentiment: "Bushiri was powerful because he was followed."[60] His claims were rendered true because people believed them and followed him. But they followed him because he drew on theories of power they recognized at a time when colonial imposition left them feeling vulnerable. Thus, Bushiri's "imaginary" and "real" power were one and the same. But there was a darker side to Bushiri's power, the violent side of his healing, which remains to be interrogated.

WIVES AND WITCHES? WOMEN, POWER, AND VULNERABILITY

As Alleloya's testimony makes clear, the brunt of the physical violence of Bushiri's uprising was borne by those accused of witchcraft and those who represented the state. Of those who were accused of witchcraft, the majority were women, although men were also accused. As noted above, the accused tended to be old men charged with immoral accumulation—"eating" the resources of the community (particularly of wives)—and sterile women who were charged with harming others out of jealousy, usually by killing their children or hindering their ability to reproduce. As in most of Africa, there is a deep relationship between communal prosperity/health and fertility in Central Africa. And issues related to infertility—high child mortality (often due to malnutrition, which, as noted above, was exacerbated by colonial situation), sterility, and generally poor maternal health—had caused palpable problems within communities in the region of the revolt. Women thus found themselves in a precarious position. They could be accused of being potent wielders of power at the precise moment they were most vulnerable. When witchcraft is thought to be prevalent in communities—which, for the reasons outlined above, is increasingly common in times of deprivation and social upheaval—this fraught relationship is exacerbated. This was the case with Bushiri's uprising, and it remains true in eastern Congo, as in much of Africa, even today.[61]

Yet, I would caution against seeing women only as victims of the uprising. Looking at the archival evidence, this presents a challenge. In Alleloya's testimony, women emerge only as victims of witchcraft accusations, wives of men accused of witchcraft who were punished in the place of their husbands, and women who were coerced into marrying Bushiri and his followers. Bushiri, Alleloya reports, planned to marry one thousand wives and give each of his followers one hundred wives, and over the course of the revolt, he seized numerous women for himself and his followers. De Schryver reported that Bushiri had a "harem of some 20 women."[62] De Schryver also reported at least one rape of a woman who was taken captive, and Alleloya himself reported the incident of the five men and women forced to have sex in the public square. There is also Alleloya's report of the women—accused witches—who were whipped and had their limbs broken and then were tied to trees and left to die. In short, the imagery of women as passive figures and victims in the colonial archive is strong.

Nonetheless, one must try to read against the archival grain, not to minimize the violence experienced by these women but to contextualize it. The numbers that Maurice Lovens presented in his study of the uprising suggest that anywhere from one-half to two-thirds of those involved in the uprising were women and children. In the wake of the massacre at Djembe, noted above, 120 women and children were arrested along with the 160 men arrested. They were integral to the "singing and dancing" that so frightened the colonial soldiers that they opened fire on the unarmed crowd. In short, women were there, and they were not there by force. They were purposefully participating in the movement: singing, dancing, and evoking God's power on the front lines of the rebellion. It is, therefore, unreasonable to assume that they were all coerced into joining or somehow passive victims of the movement. This raises the question of what their role might have been within the movement. There is little evidence in the archives of the revolt that can definitively answer that question, but oral evidence is suggestive.

As we have already seen in the stories of Maman Kalema and Ngoie Maria, women historically have had their own motivations for joining Kitawala. They have proselytized to each other, and they have held central roles in what Benetta Jules-Rosette has called "ceremonial leadership."[63] They are the "mamas of the prayer chambers," and it is they who lead prayer ceremonies in which God and the ancestors are evoked in order to heal people. And as Kabanga Kamalondo pointed out, women have also ritualistically evoked the power that allowed men to resist the Belgians, holding an indispensable role in the church. But such roles were fulfilled in the secrecy of a prayer chamber, not in the public space of a revolt. It is therefore possible to imagine that the women who followed Bushiri exercised a similar function. Moreover, if they did, it should not be entirely surprising that they are not in the archives, for this is how "invisible transcripts" work. Such forms of engagement would undoubtedly have been invisible to colonial officials. Even the Belgian researchers sent to study Kitawala in the wake of the revolt would not necessarily have seen such roles.[64] For as Maman Kalema once told me, "such knowledge is the domain of women."[65]

The purpose here is not to "prove" that women held roles as ceremonial leaders in Bushiri's uprising, but to problematize the colonial archive, which represents them largely as victims, and to suggest that gendered connections to power in that context were not exclusively passive and the gendered experience of the revolt was not singular. Such assertions are based not only on the evidence noted above, but on the significant body of research that highlights the important role of women as wielders of "creative power" in healing movements and independent churches in African history, as well as research that highlights how women have participated in political insurgencies.[66] We know that Bushiri claimed to draw on divine authority to correct the ills caused by both the colonial state and by the witches presumed to be sowing harm within the communities. But we also know that he drew power from his followers as well. Bushiri deemed some men (like the healers Alleloya and Albert) moral wielders of power and went to great lengths to draw them into the movement, while at the same time accusing others of being immoral and punishing them. It is possible to imagine some women may have been drawn into the movement as moral wielders of power that could strengthen Bushiri and his followers by performing evocations in prayer chambers, while other women deemed immoral were violently punished.

Juxtaposing this discussion of women as wielders of creative power and active participants within the uprising with that of women as wielders of immoral power and victims of witchcraft accusations highlights the ambiguous and sometimes duplicitous nature of power—which could be manipulated by particular leaders and communities. It could be used (one might even say manipulated), as Bushiri did, to police boundaries and accumulate authority and influence in the forms of wives and the kinds of alliances and gendered prestige that marriage could bring. It could also be mobilized to justify violent ends, but that violence was often contested and does not encompass the entirety of the ambitions or actions of Bushiri's followers. Overall, the experiences of these different women (both those who were targeted by and those who participated in the spiritual and political work of the rebellion) highlight the gendered edges Kitawalist theories of power, and the extent to which their attempts to apply those theories to their circumstances cannot easily be coded as resistance.

This underscores the reasons why one must think about Bushiri's uprising not just in terms of an anticolonial/political movement, a healing movement, or even a prophetic movement, but as a movement concerned with restoring a balance in the economy of power. It was all those things—prophetic, anticolonial/political, healing—but it was more than each of those things alone. It is particularly important when tethering movements like Bushiri's to the past to not only recognize the language and institutions of healing at work, but to move beyond thinking of that language in terms of "healing," which can have a tendency to create a positive moral valance that obscures the violent side of such movements. But perhaps most importantly, it obscures how ambiguous, volatile, and contested—how unruly—the theories of power that Bushiri and his followers drew on could be.

TETHERING

Thinking back to Alleloya's testimony, I would like to conclude this chapter by considering the choreographies of violence that were at play in the uprising. Given the location of the uprising in the region between Masisi and Lubutu, such an analysis seems particularly necessary. Those familiar with the contemporary political situation in eastern Congo will know that the same area has consistently been at the heart of the ongoing conflict in the region. An area rich in productive tin and gold mines, it was and is the scene of fierce competition between various armed groups over the right to control these resources. It has thus been the scene of some of the most spectacular and devastating incidences of violence—including sexual violence—in the conflict.[67]

This geographic overlap brings to mind questions about place and memory, exposing potential threads that might tie such a past to the present. In an article about red rubber, violence, and historical repetition, Nancy Hunt has argued for attention to the ways in which certain modalities of violence have been reproduced and somatized over time in Congo, "tethering" different eras of colonial violence (the Congo Free State, the Belgian Congo) to each other and to the present.[68] One of the most striking aspects of the violence as described by Alleloya and other witnesses is the extent to which it at once reproduced and overtly critiqued colonial forms of violence. The prevalence of whipping with the chicotte—one of the most wretched icons of colonial dominance—is remarkable. As is the fact that Bushiri claimed that he could detect witches and other deviants with a meter in his arm—an instrument of colonial domination, used by its agents to weigh and process any number of things, including rubber. Bushiri used it to "test" the morality of people. Also notable is the image of De Schryver, the embodiment of the colonial state, stripped naked and forced to porter rubber, bearing a humiliation that had long been borne by Congo's colonial subjects. The choreographies of each of these forms of violence were written by the colonial state long before Bushiri and his followers performed them, and their use during the uprising was a mirror held up to the colonial government, which largely failed to recognize in it the reflection of its own brutality, the choreography that it had written.[69] That the colonial government would then compound this violence with more atrocities in Kasese just further illustrates this process of reproduction. One recalls Jean-Paul Sartre's words in his preface to Fanon's *The Wretched of the Earth:* "For it is not first of all their violence, it is ours, on the rebound, that grows and tears them apart."[70]

It is undoubtedly true that the choreography and the context of the violence performed by Bushiri and his followers was in many ways a reflection of the violence created by the colonial state. But if, as Hunt argues, "it is no longer tenable to imagine that one can write an urgent, effective history about violence and ruination . . . without tethering it to the present," the question remains of how and to what it can be tethered.[71] One might attempt to tether the history of Bushiri's uprising to the present by looking for the reproduction of choreographies of violence first performed by the colonial state. Looking at the ways in which violence against women emerged in Bushiri's uprising—rape, torture, forced public performance of sexual acts—it is possible to see that such choreographies were a repetition of modes of violence condoned and perpetrated by the colonial state and its agents. Hunt has very clearly outlined the prevalence of such forms of violence in Leopold's Congo, a history she quite rightly suggests has for too long been silenced.[72] And it seems fair to suggest that the repetitions of such forms of violence in the present might, indeed, be tethered to the colonial past, where they were first choreographed by the colonial state, only to be mirrored by Bushiri and his followers, and then again in the contemporary conflict.

But if we are going to tether violence in the colonial era to the present, then we must also consider the ways much older imaginaries of violence and power can be tethered both to the colonial context and to the present. One must not give currency to "essentializing notions of Africa's past as one soaked in blood" by suggesting that Central Africa has a "culture of violence."[73] As Didier Gondola points out, violence is never cultural.[74] But neither did Central Africa have a history devoid of violence before colonialism. As this chapter has endeavored to demonstrate, the imaginaries through which violence was articulated prior to colonial occupation did not disappear with the colonial era and nor should we assume they have disappeared since.

In the region of the 1944 Kitawalist uprising, as in most of central and eastern Africa, violence, and its relative legitimacy, has historically been imagined and articulated through the ambiguous and contested language of power. In that language, violence can be healing and healing can be violent, particularly when imbalance in the economy of power has resulted in grave social ills. In a contemporary context where Mai-Mai soldiers make claims to potent powers in the form of various dawa, one cannot help but recall the image of Bushiri's claim to the mataifa medicine of Alleloya. In the image of contemporary armed groups perpetrating violent acts in the name of protecting particular segments of the population, one cannot help but recall Bushiri and his men, claiming to protect the Kumu from the Wanianga, the Bakusu, the Europeans. In the image of a population experiencing grave social ills, but fearful and unconvinced of the legitimacy of emergent leaders perpetrating violence in the name of their protection, one can see the image of mothers of daughters murdered as witches spitting in the face of a captive Bushiri.

It is in the unruliness of such notions of power that the history of Kitawala dwells—in the spaces where malleable ideas and moral ambiguity crash into deadly imperatives borne of colonial violence, producing both precariousness and possibility in the process. Bushiri's uprising exemplifies the compounding nature of that colonial violence. But it also exemplifies the search for a better future—one of health, prosperity, and radical self-love. After all, Bushiri called his doctrine Mapendo and claimed that one of the most important missions God gave him was "to teach people to love themselves."[75] The next chapter explores these themes further by looking to the history of Kitawala in the late colonial era. It illuminates how, in the midst of debate among colonial authorities about the nature of Kitawala, the extent of its threat to the colonial project, and how it could most effectively be combated, Kitawalists continued pursuing and providing individual therapies, building (and disputing the definition of) communities in diverse circumstances, and calling on the power of Kitawala in pursuit of ends that were frequently construed as—and often were—anticolonial, but were also more unruly in their form and function than anticolonialism alone can explain.

4 ~ Unruliness

IN DECEMBER 1955, a group of Kitawalist leaders from the territories around Ponthierville (Ubundu) and Stanleyville (Kisangani) devised a plot to blow up the armory at Camp Prince Charles near Stanleyville. In the previous weeks, the secret police had arrested a number of their leaders around Ponthierville for illegal Kitawalist activity. In response to the arrests, the remaining leaders were outraged, so they held "numerous clandestine meetings" where they decided they must move to regain the trust and confidence of their adepts. It was at these meetings that they made their plan to blow up the armory. The cast of participants involved in the plot was remarkably diverse. There were ex-cons from the Agricultural Colonies for Dangerous Relégués (CARDs), soldiers and officers of the Force Publique, territorial police, prison guards, local chiefs and notables, domestic workers of the colonial personnel, some skilled artisans, and other government service workers. Each had a part to play in the plan. One of the water porters, for example, agreed that he would sink the water barrels when they blew up the armory, ostensibly to prevent firemen from putting out the fire. According to reports after the fact, those who were involved in it even "knew about the Mau movement" in Kenya and "had a tendency to act like them."[1]

Before the plan could be executed, however, the colonial security forces procured intelligence about the plot and called in the police to make numerous arrests. In the wake of the events, the Ponthierville district commissioner, M. Kreutz, reported that "good will was greatly eroded and the arrests were resented," but a relative calm had returned to the region.² Calm did not remain. Less than a year later, in September of 1956, the governor general wrote to the minister of the colonies in Belgium to relay reports coming out of the territory of Basoko, just northwest of Stanleyville, that the Kitawalists in that region had begun a veritable "war against the Europeans to expel them from the territory." They were "violently hostile to the Europeans and Congolese auxiliaries" and were giving "death threats to the police, to Europeans, and to indigenous authorities." There had been "sabotage of work, refusals to work, blows to Europeans who [had] always shown very upstanding behavior, refusals to take the food distributed, difficulties for the bushmen to stock up on the necessities of local production or to receive water and wood, refusals to execute educational work, and abnormal absences in the medical census." As a result, "condemnations for rebellion had tripled" in the past year. They must be firm in their policies of suppression, he warned, because "all time lost today is taken as profit by the fanatics of the movement to render gangrenous ever wider and deeper layers of the population."³

R. Philippart, the district administrator of Stanleyville, likewise fretted that the Kitawalists responsible for the unrest in the region were harbingers of more dangerous things to come. He warned that they were a "nationalist movement of a fatally xenophobic nature that finds its justification in a loose interpretation of the Bible" and insisted that this new manifestation of the movement was far more violent and dangerous than its predecessors. He was particularly disturbed by the fact that the movement involved members of the Topoko-Lokele ethnic group, who, according to his racist assumptions, were of a higher "level of intelligence" than the Walengola-Bakumu, who had brought Kitawala into the region from Lubutu.⁴ For Philippart, the possibility that the Topoko-Lokele could be "seduced" by the "ridiculously infantile credo" of Kitawala was "unbelievable until it happened." The Topoko-Lokele, he fretted, held higher positions—"the famous Mussa was a former clerk!"—and constituted the "petite bourgeoisie natives."⁵ It was for this reason that they constituted a more dangerous threat: they could more easily unite with other groups to become a nationalist movement. Kitawala's unruliness, these colonial officials feared, was getting out of hand.

UNRULINESS

In the aftermath of the 1944 uprising, the colonial government was struggling to make sense of what had been, in their estimation, a disaster. Bushiri's uprising had shocked them, and they would spend the next decade and a half trying to better grasp the nature of Kitawala and develop policies to address it.[6] If Kitawala had been a specter before Bushiri's uprising, it became a veritable colonial paranoia in the years that followed, as administrators and district agents like Philippart feared that Kitawalists would join forces with other religious movements—in particular, Kimbanguism, Ngounzism, and Islam—and would "devolve" into communism or nationalism.[7] In a 1957 memo about Kitawala-related policy, the governor general warned that if proper steps were not taken to prevent it, the varied "secret sects" would unite into "a single vast nationalist movement." He went on to explain that "if today 'Kimbanguism' and 'Kitawala' are a serious threat, tomorrow the unions and cultural associations will constitute a greater threat, if we do not manage to counterbalance their action with the elites and keep the masses with us." The Kitawalists of today, he warned, could and would (and, in the case of the Stanleyville plot, already had) become the nationalists of tomorrow if their communities were left underdeveloped and they remained "uneducated," little aware of the many "improvements" the colonial government had brought them in the past and would continue to bring them.[8]

As this colonial paranoia about Kitawala seemed to escalate in the years following Bushiri's uprising, the colonial government's sense that they could and must do something to alter the situation grew. The immediate reaction was draconian: a colony-wide ban on Kitawala and Watchtower in 1948, supported by the increased use of penal relegation. By the late 1950s, some colonial officials began to advocate for more "soft power" solutions: propaganda and development.[9] In their pursuit of solutions to the "Kitawala Problem," they also commissioned a number of studies, which were intended to clear up the profound "confusion about subversive movements" throughout the colony.[10] In these studies, they worked hard to identify and categorize various "tendencies" of Kitawala: real versus "con," Watchtower versus "purely nationalist and antiwhite," political (dangerous) versus religious (benign).[11] For these "experts," Kitawala was a problem imagined in binaries that could help them to identify and address situations where Kitawala manifested in what was, in their view, its most dangerous and quintessential form of unruliness: nationalist/anti-White/political rebellion against colonial rule.

But Kitawala never fit neatly into such binaries, and its unruliness continued to take a complicated array of forms in this era, not all of which were immediately concerned with colonial rule. Even as the colonial government scrambled to more effectively categorize and address the "Kitawala Problem," ambitious teachers, healers, and prophets facilitated the transmission of Kitawala into new theaters of influence in the years following the revolt, particularly in the districts, both urban and rural, surrounding Stanleyville (Kisangani). As they moved through the region, they often initiated whole villages and clans into the movement at prolonged revivals.[12] They anointed new prophets, introduced new forms of initiation and baptism, developed new interpretations of doctrine, circulated new kinds of remedies, and engaged in new kinds of resistance to both colonial and customary authorities. All the while, the transmission of Kitawalist ideas continued to be a contingent, generative, and multiform process that was guided by individuals with sometimes very diverse agendas and interpretations. For the colonial authorities, the resulting diversity in doctrine and praxis was a perennial source of frustration. But, for Kitawalists, this dynamism was the means by which they endeavored to render different elements of Kitawalist teachings relevant to their individual lives and communities.

This chapter investigates how unruliness continued to be a central characteristic of Kitawala's history in the years after the Lobutu-Masisi uprising. It does so by moving away from discussion of more obvious kinds of unruliness directed at the colonial government—like the Stanleyville plot of 1955 and the "war against Europeans" that followed—and toward the more subtle, less easily categorized kinds of unruliness at work in the period. Plots to blow up government buildings, discussions of nationalism and building a pan-African resistance, labor strikes, and acts of sabotage and civil disobedience were all important parts of Kitawala's history during this era.[13] But unruliness was not always about rebellion or resistance; sometimes it was about forging new kinds of authority from old and new ideas, challenging or reimagining norms, or just searching for unorthodox answers in experimental spaces. And sometimes it was messy.[14]

The cases in this chapter highlight some of the messier ways that Kitawalists challenged, reshaped, and, at times, upended the cultural, political, and religious institutions of their own communities in their efforts "kujitawala," to rule themselves. They did this in ways that could be generative and full of possibility, but also in ways that could be coercive and even predatory. Unruliness as messiness may seem conceptually imprecise, but the imprecision is precisely the point. Sometimes the potency of unruliness was in the very opaqueness of its intents and the improvisation of its implementation. It was in the proximity of its potential for liberation and amelioration to its potential for violence or harm. As this chapter illustrates, Kitawala's unruliness was at times about attempting to build alternate networks of authority outside (or even within) the "customary" rule recognized by the colonial government, but the building of such networks often involved coercion and violence. It was at times about defying or reshaping regimes of moral and reproductive order by engaging bodies as sites of spiritual and reproductive (body/spirit) power, but it could also be about attempts to exploit that power. It was at times about seeking and creating new therapeutic options, but it could also be about the abandonment of those therapies when deemed ineffectual or even harmful. Investigating this messiness is not about making false moral equivalencies between oppressive colonial violence and the violence sometimes inherent in these kinds of unruliness; it is about acknowledging the contingent, multilayered, and entangled nature of those violences in context.[15]

In each of these cases, the messiness is compounded by the myriad violences of the colonial government. This includes the "on the ground" violences of displacement, forced labor, disruption of subsistence production, famine, infertility, surveillance, policing, and other forms of colonial oppression, which often created conditions in which rules and rule makers were in question. But it also includes archival violences of omission, myopia, and misrepresentation rendered through the racist, sexist, and exoticizing gaze of the colonial officers who recorded Kitawalist unruliness from the viewpoint of their own moral and political anxieties.[16] The unruliness of Kitawalists did not happen in a vacuum: it was directed at particular stakeholders, institutions, and circumstances. But the details of which stakeholders, institutions, and circumstances Kitawalists' unruliness targeted can be illusory: fractured and refracted through these colonial violences.[17] Because of this, it is often easier to find evidence, as in the cases below, of converts to Kitawala questioning or breaching norms in their communities and causing upset than it is to grasp the nature of those norms and their upholders in context. This is in part because such norms—of patriarchal, customary authority, of marriage and sexuality, of spiritual practice and healing—are a moving target: they were always already changing.[18] This does not mean that there was nothing at stake in defining or maintaining norms/tradition/order; if anything, it means the stakes were raised. But it does mean that contextual precision can be frustratingly lacking in the cases below, where what Anjali Arondekar has called the colonial archive's "fiction effect" (as a deeply biased system of representation) and its "truth effect" (as both record and coproducer of "real" events) collide to create an often suggestive, but ultimately occluded, image of the past.[19]

In many ways, this chapter is a continuation of the previous chapter, which sought to acknowledge the violence of the colonial government as provocative, while also decentering it as the sole object of Kitawalist imaginaries and ambitions. Like previous chapters, it asks what kind of world different Kitawalists were seeking to build and how those who entered into that world, by choice or coercion, may have made sense of its place in the economy of power. In the end, the diversity of answers to that question—the unruliness of the ideas as wielded by diverse actors—was precisely what made it potent. This is not to say that Kitawala was an empty signifier, for there were aspects of Kitawalist doctrine that were transmitted and retained between different communities, some stretching back to Watchtower. Moreover, many Kitawalists themselves did and do have firm opinions about what constituted proper Kitawala doctrine. It is, rather, to argue for attention to the creative intellectual, political, and therapeutic work Kitawalist individuals and communities engaged in as they moved through the colonial world, along paths that could lead to defiance, rebellion, and healing, but also to danger, disappointment, and harm.

UNRULY AUTHORITIES

In April of 1949, there was a mass Kitawala conversion in the area around Litoko, in the territory of Pontheirville, led by a Walengola man by the name of Malesho Caboboca Lamola, a native of the village of Batiakuanda and a former worker for Cobelmin. The story of Malesho and the community he built among the Bokuma clan is of interest both for what it reveals about the authority of Kitawalist leaders and what it reveals about how one clan chief, a man named Yeni, balanced the competing demands of Kitawala and the Belgian state in his role as a customary authority.[20] Malesho's story illustrates how Kitawalists entered into the field of authority, challenging colonial state-appointed "customary authorities" with forms of authority that were at once novel and, at the same time, "customary" in the sense that they were part of the long history of religious/healing institutions wielding alternative (or complementary) forms of authority in the region.[21] Meanwhile, Yeni's story is an example of how state-appointed customary authorities could also be experimental as they tried to navigate the expectations of both the colonial government and their constituents in order to "compose" effective authority in the midst of colonial insecurity.[22] To so do effectively meant paying attention to new forms of knowledge and potential new sources of power, like Kitawala, and the challenges and opportunities it brought.

The events in question began when Malesho sent his son to the village of Batiamanga, near Litoko, to announce that "God" (Malesho) would be arriving soon. He then came to the village accompanied by an entourage of pastors (also Walengola), as well as a "crowd of adepts and admirers."[23] Following this, there was a week-long revival and Malesho recruited nearly the entire Bokuma clan, including women and children, and saw to the formation of two new Bokuma pastors. At this revival, converts participated in an initiation ceremony that looked similar not only to other colonial accounts of Kitawala conversion but to a number of different kinds of initiations in the region.[24] According to a report by an official named G. M. Neutens, the initiation consisted of first "rubbing the eyes of the initiate with *pilipili* [hot pepper]" in order to allow the initiate to "see the ancestors." The adept then laid on the ground with a baton under their hair and waited until they felt "under the influence" of the pilipili, at which point the pastor applied the juice of sugar cane to their eyes. The pastor then introduced the adept—"barely able to see"—to two "*tokoko*" (termite hills), which had been covered before the ceremony with an American flag, which they said came from their ancestors.[25]

After conversion, adepts were required to follow a number of prescriptions, most of which pertained to modesty and proper comportment in both personal and interpersonal contexts. Neutens listed some examples in his report: They were not allowed to engage in sexual activity while it was raining. They were not to laugh at fellow Kitawalists or look at them twice if they came upon them bathing. They were to refer to wives of other adepts as "madame"—likely to signal equality with Europeans. And they were forbidden from eating aardvark or elephant. The meaning of these later taboos is unclear. But based on ethnographic evidence that comes from the broader Central African region, it is possible that the elephant avoidance may have something to do with avoiding indebtedness in the local hunting/sharing economy, while aardvarks may have carried connotations of medicine or witchcraft and been taboo for that reason.[26] Both seem likely to have something to do with drawing boundaries between Kitawalists and their non-Kitawalist neighbors. Indeed, Malesho told adherents that they must abandon their ancestral customs. In particular, he forbade traditional medicines to members of Kitawala. Instead, he encouraged adherents to use Kitawalist medicines. They used these healing medicines to "coat their bodies" to cure or prevent maladies ranging from a serpent bite to a knife wound. In essence, such medicines rendered Kitawalist converts invulnerable. Examples of Kitawalist medicines reported by Neutens included "the juice of the leaves of an orange tree as well as some other plants (pai-pai, parasoilier, bokosa, matungulu, des herbs, etc.)."[27] While many of these materials could also be found in the very medicines that the Kitawalists were forbidding, it is worth remembering, as Steve Feierman has pointed out, that within many African healing complexes, what rendered a medicine effective was not necessarily its biological properties but the ways that speech was used to transform it and activate its therapeutic properties.[28] It was thus possible for the same materials to be understood as either traditional or Kitawalist, depending on how and in what context they were activated.

Such reports led at least one of Neutens's subordinates in the region, M. Faelens, to dismiss the revival as a "con" that lacked the anti-Belgian ideas that animated Kitawalist thought in other regions. But Neutens questioned that conclusion, noting that even if it was not a subversive movement against the Belgians specifically, it was undoubtedly against the White people. He reported that Malesho was known to use language that was clearly critical of the authority of the White people, implying, much like Bushiri, that they were hiding/hoarding power. In a message to his adepts, Malesho wrote of Kitawalist teachings: "It is a very good message and even if the whites imprison me, I will not abandon my faith. The whites hid the angel Michael from us, and I'm finished consuming the words of those people." Furthermore, Neutens noted, "the adepts are inspired by the absolute conviction that after their death they will become white" and that the quest to see their ancestors was undertaken with intention of confirming this conviction.[29]

Neutens clearly saw this discourse about the duplicitousness of White people and the appropriation of Whiteness as threatening. But more threatening still were the alternative networks of authority set up by the Kitawalists. Part of what Kitawalist leaders did in the region was to set up an alternative system of leadership, with a hierarchy characterized by different ranks: members, pastors, deacons, judges, clerks, and so on. These leaders also organized a system of tithes/taxation to support their immediate communities. Adepts would make small contributions—three francs for men, two for women, and none for children—which were collected and kept within the communities of adepts to serve their needs. Neutens surmised that not only did adepts not find such tithes onerous, but that Malesho probably could have asked them to give ten times that amount "without diminishing the number of adepts." He reported that they also developed a system of courts, which made decisions regarding any number of issues in the community.[30] According to Neutens's subordinate, Faelens, the court was made up of four judges, four Kitawalist pastors, and a clerk who would have "long palavers" about the cases and record the results in notebooks. People convicted of committing infractions against the Kitawalists' community could be fined in francs (one hundred francs, to be precise) or mossolos (goods).[31]

Such appropriation of what David Schoenbrun has called "instrumental power" by emergent Kitawalist leaders is not uncommon in the history of Kitawala.[32] There are a multitude of examples of Kitawalists building alternative or parallel institutions of authority throughout both the colonial and postcolonial eras.[33] If the positions of authority created by the Kitawalists borrowed heavily from Christian and colonial bureaucratic terminology—pastors, deacons, judges, clerks, et cetera—the process of creating such alternative positions and networks of authority within religious/healing networks was firmly rooted within Central African strategies of "groupwork."[34] Indeed, as an institution, the conceptual distance between an organization like Kitawala as it materialized in and around Litoko and one like Nebeli, as discussed by Vicky Van Bockhaven, is not far.[35] Certainly they used different language and rooted their notions of legitimacy in interpretations of power that could—at least from the perspective of most Kitawalists who preached abandonment of "ancestral customs"—put them at odds with each other. But it is precisely the conceptual proximity of Kitawala to such institutions that made them a target of Kitawalist critique.

The similarities between Kitawala and healing institutions such as Nebeli do not end with their propensity to create alternative or parallel nodes of authority. Such institutions also shared in common a tendency to put state-appointed customary authorities in the position of having to "straddle" different fields of authority as they negotiated between the changing demands of their constituent communities and the duties required of them by the colonial state, which included the suppression of "subversive" institutions.[36] The story of the Bokuma clan chief Yeni, the state-appointed customary authority in Litoko at the time of Kitawala's proliferation in the region, highlights very well the processes of negotiation customary authorities engaged in as they struggled to compose their power, revealing a significant facet of the field of authority in the region.

UNRULY ALLEGIANCES

By the beginning of 1948, Yeni seems to have been in contact with Malesho, who was corresponding with him by letter. And when Malesho came for the initiations in 1949, Yeni was "by chance or trick" in Opala to remit his annual receipts—that is, he conveniently absented himself from the region. After that, Neutens suspected, "Yeni began to play a double game." On the one hand, he presented himself publicly as an opponent to Kitawala, sending word to the chiefs of neighboring territories warning that "indigenes of another territory had introduced a bad medicine among the Bokuma." Meanwhile, he was apparently himself a convert to Kitawala, converted by his wife and father-in-law. And back in his own territory he allowed the pursuits of Malesho and his followers to continue unabated. Beyond this, it seems he used his own authority to coerce (or at the very least allowed for the coercion of) other influential figures in his territory into converting. Indeed, Yeni was ultimately suspected of allowing his sons to use violence and torture to intimidate nonconverts.[37]

In one incident, Yeni's sons allegedly went to the home of a nonconvert, a notable named Masumbuku, and pretended they had been on a hunt in the forest and had not eaten, obliging Masumbuku to show them hospitality. Masumbuku suspected, however, that the two had other intentions for coming to his home and attempted to escape. They pursued him, and in the ensuing fight, Masumbuku injured his leg very badly. Ultimately, they allegedly tied Masumbuku and his brothers to a tree and tortured them. Masumbuku died a few weeks later from the injury to his leg. But before he died, he managed to alert territorial authorities in Opala to what had happened, and they discovered Yeni's "game." Colonial authorities then arrested the leaders of Kitawala in the territory of Opala and sentenced those who were accused of the torture to death.[38]

Meanwhile, the authorities detained Yeni for several months in Pontheirville while they deliberated his fate. After the arrest of the Kitawalist leaders, Yeni denounced his affiliation with Kitawala, saying that the only reason he had joined in the first place was because everyone else had joined and because his father-in-law, in particular, had exerted immense pressure on him, demanding that Yeni convert in order to remain married to his daughter. Nonetheless, Yeni managed to maintain an "indisputable prestige" among his constituents, a number of whom migrated to Pontheirville while he was detained there, ostensibly to support him. It was for this reason that colonial authorities were unsure what to do with him. One solution they proposed was to depose him. But if they were to depose him, Neutens argued, he needed to be removed from the territory entirely and sent to a relegation camp. It would come to no good having such a popular former territorial chief living in the vicinity of a chief newly appointed by the state; so, the other solution they proposed was to use him. They could return Yeni's rank and prestige and then keep him under surveillance to guarantee he would henceforth use his influence against Kitawala. Such deliberations—about whether "reformed" chiefs could be used to curb Kitawala's influence—were common among colonial officials charged with addressing "the Kitawala Problem."[39]

It would be easy to read the actions of Yeni, player of the "double game," as purely pragmatic. Facing pressure—to the point of coercion, perhaps—from both his constituents and his family to convert, he did. But he also understood the danger of appearing to support Kitawala to those outside of his community, particularly the colonial government. So, he praised Kitawala out of one side of his mouth and condemned it out of the other. But such a characterization of his actions, as described by Neutens, is perhaps a bit presumptuous. We know nothing about the sincerity of his conversion aside from what he said when under interrogation by the colonial authorities. One might just as easily imagine that, confronted with a new form of knowledge borne by a charismatic figure like Malesho, Yeni was genuinely interested in this new faith and the potential power it could bring to his clan. Yeni's people had, in recent years, struggled with famine—according to Neutens, "hunger reigned" in the region—so it is not unreasonable to imagine that he, like his constituents, was open to innovation.[40] It is difficult to know Yeni's motives, but what seems clear is that he was a well-liked leader who carried "indisputable prestige" in his clan, even after (and perhaps because of) his arrest for involvement in Kitawala. He composed his authority with the tools—spiritual and secular-political—that were at hand, working in tandem with alternative authority figures like Malesho and his pastors to bolster his legitimacy and attend to the health of his community when it made sense to do so, while acquiescing to the demands of the colonial government when pressed.

It is in this way that Yeni's actions could be construed as unruly: messy and hard to pin down. They arose from a desire to ameliorate the circumstances for himself and his community, but also from an understanding of the violence (like that experienced by Masumbuku) borne of such desires. Yeni's endeavors to navigate a changing economy of power were certainly not unique to him, just as Malesho was neither the first nor last Kitawalist leader to upend colonial definitions of customary authority by joining the long history of alternative religious/therapeutic authorities in the region. Such forms of unruliness, although perhaps less spectacular than Bushiri's uprising or the Stanleyville plots, offer a window into a crucial part of Kitawala's history. They force us to imagine transmission and conversion as a multilayered process in which people like Malesho and Yeni had decisions to make. They had to pursue their personal well-being and the well-being of their families and communities within the ever-present context of colonialism's spiritual and physical violence, from which they both sought, in their own ways, respite or deliverance. To do so, they drew on their own (historically and culturally informed) interpretations of how power could and should function in the world in order to forge a path forward.

But such paths—which all Kitawalists chose, in their own way, to travel—were winding, and could lead to potentially dark places. In those places, radical interpretations of Kitawala sometimes collided with colonial prejudice in ways that are both uncomfortable and important to investigate. The next section considers how Kitawalists may have defied and/or reshaped regimes (both colonial and traditional) of moral and reproductive order by engaging bodies as sites of spiritual and reproductive, or body/

spirit, power. But it also considers how desires for such power could potentially turn violent.

UNRULY BODIES

In the colonial archives, references to Kitawala as, essentially, a lurid sex cult are abundant. It was a rumor that circulated widely in colonial circles. So common was it in the colonialist popular imagination, that it featured as a central element in the plot of Léon Debertry's 1953 novel, *Kitawala: Roman*, which we already encountered in chapter 1. Largely a work of anti-Kitawala propaganda, the novel tells the story of a loyal Congolese soldier who is lured into Kitawala by a biracial woman with whom he falls in love after she takes him to a Kitawalist "orgy."[41] As a work of fiction, it is a monument to the sexual-racial anxieties and desires of colonizers that have been so effectively discussed in the works of Ann Stoler, Anne McClintock, and numerous other scholars of colonialism and sexuality.[42]

But the novel is just one of countless references to erotic practice that populate the colonial record on Kitawala. Sometimes such references appear in the margins of larger reports of Kitawalist activities; at other times they appear at the center of colonialist claims about the moral degeneracy of Kitawala and all who adhered to it. In particular, the colonial officers were drawn to reports of erotic practices they considered outside their established norms, such as polyamory, orgies, incest, or ritual sex. Practicing "communism of wives" and engaging in other forms of "sexual promiscuity" were perhaps the most common accusations.[43] Building on a robust body of queer and indigenous studies theory, T. J. Tallie has argued that the "queering" of indigenous customs, practices, and bodies in this way was central to the exercise of colonial domination and state-making. Even when such customs/practices/bodies remained "ostensibly heterosexual in their orientation," Tallie writes, "their existence constantly undermine[d] the desired order" of colonial states.[44] For the Belgian colonial administration, Kitawalists were queer, not just in the ideas and beliefs they adhered to, but in the very ways they existed in their bodies. They imagined Kitawalist bodies as unruly bodies that refused to conform to colonial ideals of "civilized" monogamous sexual practices, and that nonconformity served as further justification for their oppression.[45]

When it comes to marriage, sex, and family, however, the Belgians certainly would not have been the sole enforcers of order and conformity. Such intimate matters were also the concern of various stakeholders within African communities—from heads of family and kinship groups, to chiefs and councils of elders, to spiritual and therapeutic authorities—and had long been at the center of "efforts to gain material resources and fulfill moral ambitions."[46] Indeed, under Belgian colonial law, such matters were legally the concern of indigenous courts.[47] In Congo, as elsewhere in Africa, particularly since the 1930s, debates over such matters often put patriarchal authorities into conflict with defiant juniors and dependents in search of answers to their concerns about production and reproduction—or just in search of intimacy and pleasure.[48]

In the context of Kitawala's history during this era, the concerns of such locally embedded stakeholders are difficult to disentangle from those of the colonial government, both because their interests sometimes aligned and because it is the colonial officials who wrote the reports on these matters, and they generally said very little about the concerns or identities of local stakeholders. It is rare in general to find a direct reference to the concerns customary authorities had about Kitawala, and sources written by such authorities themselves are even rarer.[49] I have only seen one such document. In 1953, the "Sultanis of Opienge" wrote a short letter to their territorial administrator complaining that nearly all their constituents had converted to Kitawala and "no longer [did] work like before." They warned that it would be worse than 1944 if the colonial government did not do something about it and that they "should not be surprised when they start killing people."[50] And while Amandine Lauro's work has quite clearly illustrated that Congolese men, in particular, did regularly write letters of complaint to the colonial government about issues concerning "matrimonial problems" (namely, unruly wives), I have not seen any such letters related to Kitawala directly.[51] Thus, any concerns they may have had about how Kitawala was challenging norms or eroding their patriarchal authority in regions like Lowa, discussed below, can only be discerned analogically, by considering how such authorities reacted in other contexts to those who refused "to abide by socially validated standards of etiquette" and thereby "endangered civil order."[52]

This is further complicated by the question of whether reports of Kitawalist erotic practices did, indeed, chronicle "real" phenomena or whether they are entirely fictions of the colonial imagination. While sensationalism and outright fabrication must be considered possible—and even probable—in some cases, recent studies in colonialism and sexuality suggest that taking seriously colonial reports of erotic practices, preferences, and desires as more than fictions can offer an important window into the intimate lives of colonized peoples.[53] Certainly, the reports are tainted by the colonial gaze, but when read critically they can potentially offer important insight into the history of what might be called "body-spirit practices" within

Congolese communities: practices that center the body as a site where spiritual power manifests and can be accessed.[54] Such practices, particularly when exercised by women, might have possessed the capacity to challenge both European and indigenous norms, in the process threatening the order of things on multiple levels. By challenging customary, patriarchal authority over both male and female bodies, they could have further thwarted colonialist attempts to maintain order through customary authorities. In connecting spiritual practice with sexuality, they could have threatened the disciplined order of missionary Christianity with its "preoccupation with controlling and restricting sex."[55] And, in centering intimacy and the body in their spiritual practice, they could have challenged any notion of an orderly separation between the physical and spiritual realms.

"COMMUNISM OF WIVES," UNRULY WOMEN, AND RITUAL SEX

To illustrate these points, it is necessary to first consider the kinds of references to Kitawalist erotic practices that exist in the archive. In his 1954 study of Kitawala, R. Philippart (one of the "Kitawala experts" in colonial circles) noted that colonial administrators, missionaries, and settlers alike "talked a lot" about Kitawala erotic practices, including accusations of "incest, nocturnal saturnalias, orgies, and communism of wives."[56] In 1942, for example, a district administrator from Lubutu reported rumors that "scenes of sexual promiscuity would take place" among Kitawalists, including "communism of wives and spouses belonging to all of the adepts."[57] In 1949, Catholic missionaries in the area of the Lubutu-Masisi revolt reported a revival of Kitawala that was "characterized by nocturnal meetings, followed by orgies."[58] In 1957, one of the administrators of the Kitawalist prison camp COLAGREL (see chapter 5) described Kitawala as a "a physical dictatorship for the women" in which they were forced to participate in "communism of wives" and other ritual sex acts.[59] The source of his information, he claimed, was a group of spies and indigenous personnel who had been secretly employed by the camp administrators. Reports of exchanging wives also emerge in the interrogation records, fueling the opinion among colonial officials that "communism of wives is certainly practiced" among Kitawalists. During an inquest in Lubutu in 1944, for example, two different men claimed, while under interrogation, that when they joined Kitawala, they were told that their wives would need to "live with a comrade" for a period of time or "sleep with the brothers."[60] That is, they would be expected to share their wives with other Kitawalists.[61]

Reports like these are certainly dubious in their resemblance to some widely circulating colonial stereotypes about uncontrolled African sexuality and must be read skeptically for that reason alone. And they can also be read as evidence of accusations of *coercive* erotic practice, in which the consent of participants (particularly of the women) is in question. However, such evidence of polyamory, practiced by both men and women in a given ritual community, need not be read through the colonial moral lens, and coercion need not be assumed (though it should be considered possible). Instead, it might be read as evidence that there was more than one "sexual regime" at play in these contexts. If indeed it existed, this particular polyamorous regime, which encouraged both men and women to have multiple sexual partners, would have likely been at odds with expectations (both colonial and "customary") about "ideal/typical family relations": namely, marriage (whether monogamous or polygamous) in which sexual access to wives was reserved for individual male husbands.[62] But the existence of such ideals (as spoken or unspoken "rules") has never precluded their transgression. It is also possible to imagine that in these spaces, these particular communities of Kitawalists engaged in "experimental intimacies" that made a connection between polyamory and their body/spirit well-being.[63] Although our understanding of the nature of that connection is severely limited by the sources, it could potentially be related to ideas about ritual fluid exchange and health, discussed below. Finally, it is possible to imagine that within some Kitawalist communities, people engaged in intimate ritual relationships outside of their marriages that were not sexual at all, but were coded that way by outsiders with no insider knowledge.

Still other reports proffer accusations of what might be called *seductive* erotic practice within Kitawala. For example, another common claim was that Kitawalists "only permitted relations within the movement" and would "no longer have sexual relations with the profane," or non-Kitawalists.[64] And it was often women who were accused of having seduced men into Kitawala by withholding—or in the case of Debertry's novel, offering—sex. For example, in a 1956 colonial study of Kitawala, Paul-Ernest Joset (of Kasese infamy) wrote that "often the women were baptized first. And the men would follow if they wanted to have sexual relations with their spouse."[65] This also correlates with the customary chief Yeni's claim that it was his wife who seduced him into joining Kitawala.[66] The claim also appears in a 1947 interrogation record from Lubutu, in which an accused Kitawalist, when asked whether a baptized Kitawalist can have "intercourse" with her husband, replied, "No. Both must be baptized."[67]

Of all the rumors that circulated about Kitawalist erotic practices, this is among the most interesting and, perhaps, plausible. For the male colonial officers writing about these rumors, such reports were a source of anxiety about unruly women.[68] Yet, if we once again cast their moral judgments aside, it is worth noting that such claims place women and their spiritual and bodily concerns at the center of Kitawala's history and transmission—a characterization that shares much in common with stories like that of Maman Kalema and the other contemporary Kitawalist women discussed in chapter 2. While none of those women discussed sexual intimacy explicitly, they did make it clear that many of them were drawn to Kitawala out of concerns about their body/spirit welfare, often with fertility and family welfare at the center. That such concerns could enter into the politics of sex and intimacy within their relationships should not be surprising. Moreover, as numerous studies of women, gender, and power in Africa and elsewhere have demonstrated, women have used sex and intimacy as tools of gendered power and influence throughout history.[69]

Another frequent rumor about Kitawalist women contended that there was a position within the Kitawalist church, second only to the head pastor, held by "free women and young girls" called the "Mama Losiya," whose job was to "prepare meals" and serve as a "prostitute" to male adepts. Philippart, for example, wrote that this was a "primordial role" for women who were meant to "satisfy, during their meetings, the sexual appetites of the adepts."[70] Another colonial Kitawala "expert," Jacques Gérard, doubted this claim. Betraying his own prejudices, he contended that role of a prostitute within the community would not be necessary, especially among the Bakumu, where the "general immorality of the population rendered the existence of prostitutes useless."[71] Meanwhile, Joset suggested that the reality was somewhere in the middle, comparing the role of the Mama Losiya to the customary female role of the *amampombo*, which was allegedly common in the areas northeast of Lubutu. The existence of this role, Joset explained, was originally reported by a territorial administrator in the region named Ledin, who claimed that the amampombo were "customary prostitutes." This claim was then "repeated by numerous territorial administers" until the "legend was formally established."[72] This is an uncommonly candid acknowledgment of the echo chamber of colonial reports, which frequently established "facts" about indigenous cultural practice largely through repetition.

In contrast, Joset suggested that describing the amampombo as "customary prostitutes" was a poor characterization. Rather, he wrote, in the northeastern part of the territory of Lubutu, the amampombo were mostly married women and "exclusively healers." While Joset conceded that some of these women lived "outside the family"—that is, as "free women"—this was not "their function." He continued: "Likewise, many Kitawalist women will render some sexual service to another Kitawalist, and primarily to the pastor in authority. But we should see in it only signs of sympathy and not the performance of a compulsory function. The only difference between the non-Kitawalist Bakumu and the Kitawalist Bakumu, from this point of view: the former can only afford relations of this kind within the movement."[73]

In Joset's opinion, then, while it was possible that the Mama Losiya had sexual relations with other men in the community—and especially with the pastor—this was certainly not the "function" of this position any more than it was the "function" of women who held the title amampombo within the traditional religious/healing complex of the region. He allowed for the possibility that sexual intimacy could be part of the relationship between the Mama Losiya and the men in the community, but argued that, instead of being compulsory, such relations could simply be about affection or sympathy. Here Joset came to a surprisingly nuanced conclusion. Although the language he used betrays significant racism and misogyny, he also allowed for agency and individual desire on the part of women to exist at the center of both the role of the amampombo and that of the Mama Losiya.

Still, there is every reason to doubt that sex entered into the role of the Mama Losiya—or indeed of the amampombo—at all, just as there is good reason to doubt any of the claims made in colonial reports about Kitawalist or other indigenous erotic and intimate practices. As the works of Yolanda Covington-Ward and many others illustrate, colonizers were prepared to see what they considered sin, immorality, and obscenity in most any indigenous cultural practices, particularly when they involved drumming and dancing, as in religious or healing practices.[74] Moreover, as the above exchange makes clear, the colonial officials themselves debated and doubted these claims even at the time, acknowledging that they were, at the very least, "difficult to prove."[75] A number of them expressed concern that these rumors about Kitawalist erotic practices were just that: rumors that had been perpetuated by Kitawalists themselves to distract the officials from their true purpose of undermining the colonial government. Philippart, for example, noted that during interrogations, "pastors and adepts deny the communism of wives." One pastor he quoted said, "The whites believe that we practice communism of wives, but it is false. When we were arrested and interrogated, in order to not reveal our doctrine and our rites, we made up the sexual practices."[76] Indeed, many pastors disavowed such rumors when interrogated. In the same series of 1944 Lubutu interrogations that produced claims about adepts being told they would need to share their wives with their comrades/brothers, a different pastor, when confronted with these same claims, rebuked them: "Not at all . . . it goes against our teachings."[77] An important difference here is that while the two men who affirmed the claims were denying continued affiliation with Kitawala, the pastor proudly proclaimed it: the former had more reason to defame Kitawala than the latter, but the latter had more reason to minimize aspects of Kitawalist practice the colonial interrogator might find concerning. This brings up important questions about power, performance, and truth in the context of a colonial interrogation—questions that I will address further below.

SEX, POWER, AND LIFE

In short, it is necessary to problematize the undoubtedly racist and patriarchal gaze of the colonial archive and allow for the possibility that deception of the colonial authorities on this matter may have actually been a strategy on the part of Kitawalists. And yet, it is also important to avoid *queering* Kitawalist erotic or intimate practices—if, indeed, such practices were a part of their history in some regions—by reproducing colonial moral anxiety about the subject. Instead, it is useful to consider how they might be read through the lens of ideas about sex, fluid exchange, and health that appear in the historical record of many parts of the central and interlacustrine regions of Africa. Sarah Watkins, for example, has written about the significance of ritual sex in the history of the Rwandan royal court. Such forms of intercourse played an important role in annual rites of renewal that assured fertility and health within the kingdom by assuring the "flow" of life and wellness.[78] Meanwhile, Schoenbrun has described how "sex symbolism and activity are common features of songs sung during initiation into healing groups" and ritually controlled sexual activity was a critical part of assuring the "good powers of fertility."[79]

In eastern Congo, reports of ritual forms of sex were not limited to the Kitawala archives. Writing about the political organization of the Nyanga chiefdom in 1956, for example, colonial ethnographer Daniel Biebuyck discussed the important role of ritual sex in the enthronement of a new Nyanga chief. Specifically, he described the role of a woman known as the *mumbo/nyamumbo* who, during the enthronement, had "sexual relations" with the ascendent chief "in the presence of certain initiators and high dignitaries." After this ceremony, a mumbo "acquired the stature of a man" and could "marry other women."[80] Ritual intercourse and the controlled exchange of sexual fluids, then, have historically had a significant role to play in assuring communal wellness throughout the region. They have likewise provided pathways through which women could attain important forms of prestige or "stature" typically reserved for men.[81] Such pathways need not be read as a dismantling of patriarchal authority, but they certainly highlight infrequently recognized textures in the performance of gender in the African context: neither masculinity nor femininity were homogenous categories.[82]

When read against the description of the Mama Losiya as "second only to the pastor" or the story of Ngoie Maria from chapter 1, who was the "mistress" and "second" to the influential pastor Muyololo, such evidence is suggestive. On the one hand, it may simply be evidence that intimate relationships could and did emerge from desire or intimacy borne of shared spiritual experiences and ambitions.[83] That is, Kitawalist men and women, who shared ideas and ritual spaces, may have simply come to love and desire each other. On the other hand, it suggests that it is plausible that, in some communities, Kitawalists may have developed a ritual position for women in Kitawalist leadership that involved a sexual—or otherwise ritually intimate—relationship with influential Kitawalist men. Or to put it differently, men's power and authority in some Kitawalist communities may have been mediated and sustained through proximity to the intimate ritual power of women, which assured the wellness of the community. Colonial officials found the possibility of such ideas threatening because they did not fit neatly into hierarchies of patriarchal customary authority that they depended on to maintain colonial order. It is less clear from the sources what Congolese authorities and observers outside of Kitawala might have thought about such rituals, but it can easily be imagined that they would have also found them troubling, not necessarily because the ideas evoked were unprecedented, but because they were not under their control.

At the time same time, the accounts of women seducing the men in their lives into Kitawala compel us to consider how women's desires for power—especially reproductive power, which connects sex and fertility to public prestige—may have led them to consider Kitawala as a potential new pathway to their desired ends, namely motherhood or other kinds of female authority (including as a healer). Moreover, it may have led them there in defiance of those men (fathers, brothers, husbands, etc.), some of whom may have then joined at the behest of these women, while others (like the colonial officials fretting about "free women") would have likely considered them unruly as they challenged gendered hierarchies of authority through control of their bodies.[84]

In the end, the picture these sources paint remains murky, irredeemably muddled by the colonial gaze, but nonetheless suggestive. At the risk of entering into the troubled waters of empiricism, it is worth entertaining the possibility that these reports offer glimpses of "real" (if distorted) phenomena, the historical existence of which matter to our understanding of gender, intimacy, and sexuality in Central African history. On the one hand, it shows us potential pathways through which women in these times and spaces may have sought and gained significant forms of power and authority.[85] It also hints at some of the creative ways Kitawalist men and women may have navigated the intersection of their existing knowledge about body/spirit power with the teachings of Kitawala circulating in the region. On the other hand, it challenges easy narratives of creativity, resistance, and women's empowerment by raising questions about coercion and consent, as well as agency and oppression. Such binaries offer neat heuristics through which particular actions or practices are often assessed as positive or negative, moral or immoral, liberating or oppressive, but they also often belie the messiness of history, particularly as it relates to gender and sexuality in colonial contexts.[86] This becomes even more apparent when discussing some of the more troubling and—in the context of Congo's too-often-sensationalized history—analytically fraught accounts of erotic transgression and body/spirit power that exist in the colonial Kitawala archives: those that report sexual violence.

CONFRONTING SEXUAL VIOLENCE

Sexual violence has already appeared in this history of Kitawala, in the context of the Lobutu-Masisi uprising discussed in chapter 3. In that context, evidence for sexual violence emerged mostly as punitive action—as punishment for witchcraft practice or for refusing to support the movement. But there are other stories of sexual violence that appear in the colonial archive. In a 1945 Pontheirville case that took place outside of Pontheirville, for example, the accused initiate, Okete, allegedly "had sexual relations with his sister, Mina, a native girl who had not yet reached the age of puberty." As a result, the government ultimately charged him with "the infraction of rape" under Article 175 of the penal code, which forbade "public outrages against good morals."[87] And while it is important to note that colonial officials themselves regularly ignored such laws and abused young African girls, it is nonetheless true that the colonial legal code converges with modern legal code in considering the situation above, if indeed it did happen as described, a form of sexual violence or rape committed against the young girl in question. It is not the only such example in the colonial Kitawala archives.

In 1947 in Lowa, a territorial administrator named Buysschaert conducted a series of fifty-three interrogations after uncovering a "cell" of Kitawalists in region. Located not far from Walikale, an important site in the 1944 uprising, Lowa and the region around it had been under scrutiny by the colonial government since a report in 1946 indicated a significant Kitawalist following in the region—perhaps as many as four thousand adult men in the towns between Lowa and Lubutu.[88] The report does not mention women or children, though, as the interrogations reveal, women and children were certainly involved. The vast majority of people Buysschaert interrogated were young boys and girls, between the ages of ten and eighteen, whom he questioned about their initiation into Kitawala. Most of the questions he asked these young people were about (a) the reasons they joined Kitawala and (b) the process of their initiation into Kitawala. In the latter category, one of his most common questions was whether and/or with whom they had had sexual relations during their initiation: for example, "With whom did you have sexual relations?" or "Did you have sexual relations with X?"[89] To make this uncomfortable scene perfectly clear, an adult male colonial administrator forced a series of young girls into an interrogation room with him and asked them directly whether and with whom they had had sexual intercourse.

The power dynamics of these exchanges must be kept in mind. Like the interrogations about "communism of wives" above, the "truth" of what these young girls said must be assessed in light of these situational power dynamics. Indeed, they ultimately cannot be disentangled from them. It is possible, for example, that in asking these questions to frightened young girls, he fabricated the very evidence that he went in expecting to find. And given that it was often the very first question he asked, he clearly did expect to find it. And that expectation must be rooted in the broader echo chamber of colonial rumors about Kitawalist sexual practices that no doubt informed it.

And yet, like Abina, the protagonist in Trevor Getz's *Abina and the Important Men,* the young girls in these interrogation records implore us to listen to their voices, even when they have potentially been distorted by the work of "important men" like Buysschaert.[90] Consider, for example, this exchange between a young (about fifteen years old) girl named Beyaya-Aliso and her interrogator (content note: explicit descriptions of sexual violence):

> Q: With which man did you have sexual intercourse?
> R: Ongombi-Gabriel.
> Q: Who initiated you?
> R: Johanne-Beyaya.
> Q: What did he do?
> R: He cut me, then he told me that when my parents died, I would be able to see them.
> Q: When did you have sexual relations with Ongombi?

R: Before the meeting in the forest. Ongombi came through the village and called me and he grabbed me to sleep with me on the ground, then he put a hand over my mouth and opened my legs with the other hand, this happened in the woods.
Q: At what time of day?
R: The evening, it was already dark.
Q: Why did your father not claim the customary dot [brideprice]?
R: Because that day the Chef du Secteur had come to apprehend the Kitawalists.
Q: Then it was at the meeting and in the forest that you had intercourse?
R: No.
Q: Where were you cut [inciseé]?
R: In the house of Beyaya (du Pere).
Q: Who else was there?
R: Just Beyaya and me.
Q: Who entered before you?
R: I know nothing.
Q: Why were you initiated?
R: To be loved by men and to have lots of fish and to have the power of the whites.

Beyaya-Aliso's voice jumps out of the archive and commands us to confront the sexual violence in her testimony: Ongombi raped her. Johanne-Beyaya told her that if she joined Kitawala, she would be able to see her parents after their death and that she would be loved by men, have lots of fish, and have the power of the White people. Instead, she was taken to a secluded area by Ongombi and assaulted. In his own interrogation a week later, Ongombi revealed that he had, himself, joined Kitawala because he had been told that he would gain the "power to have intercourse with all of the initiates, to see deceased parents, and to have the power of the whites." He insisted, however, that the coupling had been consensual, arguing that it could not have happened the way Beyaya-Aliso claimed because "everyone would have heard." And yet, as a large body of scholarship has very well established, rape accusations are rarely fabricated, because there is little to be gained for the woman making the accusation and much to be lost. And the fact that many of the other girls said they refused sex because it would be "bad," because their "brideprice had not been paid," makes it clear that there were possible moral and social consequences for girls like Beyaya-Aliso.[91]

Unruliness ⁓ 131

Moreover, Beyaya-Aliso clearly did not consider the encounter with Ongombi consensual or acceptable. Nor would her family have considered it so. Indeed, they would have insisted that they be compensated with dot/brideprice had the colonial government not already intervened. Her willingness to say as much in what must have been a very uncomfortable context is a testament to her courage and her discontent. Moreover, she was not the only girl to make such an accusation against the male leadership of this particular community of Kitawalists.[92] And while other young girls—as young as thirteen—did claim to consent, their capacity to do so at that age is clearly in question.[93]

In short, there is significant evidence that there was an interpretation of Kitawalist doctrine at work in this particular Kitawalist community in Lowa that transgressed into the realm of sexual violence. That interpretation would have undoubtedly been considered illegitimate not only by the families of these young people and other authority figures in Lowa but also by other Kitawalists. Like the sexual violence within the Lobutu-Masisi uprising, it cannot be ignored, but it must also be contextualized. Kitawala was a set of ideas that guided people's thoughts and actions. They combined it with other sets of ideas—be they regionally embedded ideas about the power of sex and sexual fluids or other "new" ideas like nationalism and Kimbanguism—in ways that rendered it relevant to their own conditions and ambitions. This was an inherently messy process, and one that makes it very difficult to pin down "Kitawala doctrine." It was a process that both challenged customary authorities in the ways outlined above and perpetually unnerved colonial officials, who were constantly trying to assess whether a newly discovered community was the "real" Kitawala.[94]

Such unruliness has historically left space for some interpretations of Kitawala to enter into the realm of violence and predation. It is possible to acknowledge this without reaffirming the colonial opinion that it serves as damning evidence of general Kitawalist depravity. Most Kitawalists would have condemned such interpretations themselves, and sexual violence certainly cannot be considered a kind of core principle or practice in Kitawala. As Didier Gondola has argued, "Not all practices and behaviors within a given culture or subculture should be viewed as 'cultural,' and rape, even when it becomes systemic within a group, should by no means qualify as 'culture.'"[95] But neither can it be considered extraneous to the history of Kitawala. Rather, it must be considered a part of that history: an example of the volatility of unruly ideas about body/spirit power in the wrong circumstances. Such ideas held within them the capacity for experimentation and even liberation, but also the possibility of exploitation and violence. As with

Lobutu-Masisi, this is where attention to the larger context that created the conditions of violence in Lowa becomes necessary. Importantly, the same interrogations that revealed that violence also offer ample evidence for understanding the context of colonially imposed violence and insecurity that shaped the actions and intentions of both Ongombi and Beyaya-Alisa. They were searching for healing—for wellness—and exploring Kitawala as a possible remedy. The remedies they devised under the umbrella of Kitawala could be become violent themselves, as in the cases above. But in other cases, they offered possibilities for people who, under the unrelenting violence of colonial rule, sought alternative therapies for persistent and emergent problems.

UNRULY REMEDIES

For the most part, colonial officials rarely described Kitawalist healing practices in any depth. And yet, they were and are at the center of Kitawala's history. Most colonial agents referred to such practices only with disparaging terms like *superstitions*. One sees references, for example, to itinerate Kitawalists "posing as ngangas" peddling their dawas, or to communities of Kitawalists refusing colonial medicine in favor of their own healing, which "came from God."[96] Some of the most interesting material on Kitawalist healing comes not from administrative reports but from the secret service records, like the 1944 Lowa interrogation records. Like Beyaya-Aliso, nearly every single Kitawalist in the Lowa records described how they had been initiated into the movement because they wanted (1) to see their dead parents, (2) to become attractive to the opposite sex and/or be married, (3) to be successful in the hunt/fishing and have plenty of meat to eat (and "never die of hunger"), and/or (4) to have the power of the White people, which they were "promised" by their initiators. The process they describe to acquire such power was nearly identical in each case. The initiator made incisions on their chests, which were then rubbed with ash. Then they rubbed a mixture of pilipili (hot peppers), water, and sexual fluids (semen for women and vaginal fluid for men) into their eyes.[97] For those who wanted to see their dead parents, "mannequins" were made out of kaolin and/or the dirt from a termite hill. And, as we have seen, several of the girls report engaging in, or being asked to engage in, sexual intercourse (forced or consensually).

There are a number of interesting things to consider in these records. First, the report that they were all asking to see their deceased parents seems peculiar. One questions whether their responses were appropriately translated into French and whether the term was not more likely a less specific name for "ancestors," such as *wababu*. Unfortunately, it is impossible to know. The fact that they were nearly all teenagers is also curious. If they were, in fact, all teenagers with deceased parents, it would indicate that Kitawala in that region, at that time, had a particular appeal to certain, similarly afflicted populations. It would tie Kitawala to the regional history of affliction-based therapeutic institutions—or "drums of affliction," as John Janzen has termed them.[98] At the very least, the similar ages of the converts point to larger social processes—concerns about resource access, courting, and reproduction, compounded by concerns about the colonial government—affecting young people.

The therapies themselves are also interesting. There are notable material congruences between historically rooted Central Africa ideas about how to access and wield power and those described by the young Kitawalists. The use of termite hill dirt is a good example. In her work on the early history of the Batwa, Kairn Klieman has noted that in much of west-central Africa—indeed much of the Bantu-speaking world—termite hills have historically been employed in various ritual contexts, where they served as "receptacles for ancestral first-comer spirits who control the fecundity and fertility of people and land."[99] This connection between the ancestors and termite hills seems far from coincidental in a context where the young Kitawalists were using the dirt of termite hills to summon their deceased parents/ancestors. The ritual use of hot peppers, which also appeared in the rituals of Malesho's community, is likewise historically common in the region.

Interrogation records containing such rich and interesting details are far from common in the colonial archives, although another series of interrogations—by an agent named Émile Bastin, near Stanleyville—is also enlightening. A man named Yailo reported to Bastin that he "entered Kitawala because they healed him" by rubbing him with oil. Another Kitawalist, Gilbert, reported that within the church, dawas (medicines) were prepared by the *zikonis* and the *bouwesi*, whom he compares to nurses (bouwesi) and nurses' assistants (zikoni). Quick to deflect any criticism of their healing practices, Gilbert pointed out to Bastin that "among the whites it is the same thing." Another man, Akaluko, also reported that he had fallen ill and the Kitawalists healed him using "plants of the forest" that were boiled in water and inhaled as a vapor. He claimed that he rested for two days with the Kitawalists and returned to the village healed. Another man described a medicine called *sango* that was "put on the body" when one became ill. He noted that "if [the patient] is healed, they were in a good relationship with God." Another—a Kitawalist healer—indicated that the dawa he carried in his pouch was palm oil. One man reported going to Kitawala in search of a cure for his daughter's epilepsy. Yet another told Bastin that he was baptized very quickly into the movement because he was told they had "a nkisi that heals people" and he had been sick.[100]

As with the previous interrogations, these interviews strongly indicate that Kitawala was interpreted and received as a new and potent therapeutic option in the regional economy of power. Even some colonial "experts" realized as much. Jacques Gérard, for example, argued that Europeans had introduced a cycle of the destruction, followed by reintroduction, of various forms of empowered objects/medicines, or bwanga. In his 1969 ethnography of Kitawala, he described how, when the Europeans arrived, the "*féticheurs*" (healers) thought they could "adapt by imposing new bwanga." But their new bwanga (i.e., practices/objects geared toward procuring power) proved ineffectual against the influence of the strangers. So, they turned away from these bwanga and burned their fetishes. Then a new bwanga would come that could vanquish the others. But then this new bwanga would once more prove unsatisfactory. It would be vanquished and the old bwanga would return. Then the "iconoclasts" would "make a clean sweep of all of the bwanga," and the cycle would continue. Through all the waves of different bwanga—by which, one could posit, he meant various healing movements—certain ancestral bwanga were presumed to retain their efficacy. Among the Bakumu, he explained, this bwanga was tied to the spirits of *esumba* (the initiation rites tied to local territorial spirits), and it was embodied in a shrine kept in each village. The esumba was the supreme bwanga, but it did not suppress the other bwanga. What made Kitawala different from all the other bwanga that preceded it was that it represented "the most powerful bwanga," because it could also suppress the bwanga of esumba. Kitawala's currency in the economy of power, then, was that it was a veritable superpower—not different in kind or conceptualization, but in potency: its bwanga—which came from the Christian God—was more effective than even the most powerful bwanga that preceded it.[101]

Gérard gave this explanation in trying to make sense of the fact that Kitawalists regularly built a reputation for renouncing "fetishes," while at the same time retaining the use of "dawas." He offered an example of a Kitawalist preacher who denounced "fetishes" but honored his clan's taboos and kept the medicine horn he procured at his esumba initiation close at hand. Gérard was, in essence, trying to make sense of what he and his contemporaries—and many who have followed them—referred to as the "syncretism" of Kitawala. For most colonial commentators, particularly missionaries, "syncretism" had a distinctly negative connotation. It implied that Kitawalists used "loose interpretations of the Bible" to justify their "fatally xenophobic" movement, and that its leaders "seduced" and created "tyranny" over the masses with the use of "magic and superstitious techniques."[102] Moreover, it implied that there were two distinct spheres of influence—"Christian" and "traditional"—that Kitawalists inexpertly mixed together to create something new (and dangerous).

If Gérard largely avoided overly simplistic interpretations of transmission, his work nonetheless remained mired in colonial prejudice. Although his observations on how Kitawala fit into a longer history of waxing and waning sources of bwanga were insightful and, indeed, supported by the work of many other historians of the region, where Gérard failed was in his insistence (in the vein of Placid Tempels) that bwanga was a philosophy of power innate to the "Bantu race."[103] It was not a historically, culturally, and linguistically situated discourse of power that could be and, as the evidence presented above suggests, was mobilized and rearticulated by individuals in their interactions with and interpretations of Kitawala in the colonial context, but something essential to "the Bantu mind." Gérard failed when he brought Kitawala, and bwanga more broadly, out of the realm of history and into the realm of racial essentialism.

But what Gérard did manage to pinpoint precisely was the context of insecurity that shaped the events in Lowa. The violence of colonialism was an onslaught that took many forms and bred many kinds of insecurity in the lives of people like Beyaya-Aliso. And the search for protection from that violence could itself breed new kinds of risk, including the risk involved in seeking unruly remedies: remedies rumored to be powerful, but marginal, and even hostile to the existing therapeutic complex. To acknowledge this is not to concede the diagnosis of "cultural schizophrenia" that so many colonial commentators bemoaned. Such diagnoses were rooted in the fear that colonial subjects, bereft of cultural rules and disloyal to customary authorities, would be impossible to control. Rather, it is to acknowledge experimentation and innovation as generative facets of unruliness. And what it generated could be beneficial to individuals and communities, in the form of soothing medicines and new forms of belonging, but it could also become violent. The key is to acknowledge that the root of that violence—what drove young men to violate young girls in search of power—was the insecurity and violence created by colonialism itself.[104] Acknowledging this, in turn, need not mean that we ignore individual agency of people—be they the young men and girls of Lowa or customary authorities like Yeni—who assessed, and then reassessed, the value of Kitawala to their lives and communities. It is, rather, to concede to the layered and often entangled nature of such violences, which shaped both the possibilities and limits of the remedies that Kitawala could offer. And certainly, many who came to Kitawala searching for remedies did ultimately find its purported remedies disappointingly—even dangerously—limited.

UNRULY CONVERTS

If, for many initiates, Kitawala served as a means by which to access much-needed power in their lives—whether to ameliorate their own social and physical ailments or those of their families and communities—for others, it proved ineffectual. The danger of focusing on what brought people into Kitawalist communities is that it obscures the experiences of those who perhaps joined and found it insufficient for their needs, those who refused to join in the first place, or those, like Beyaya-Aliso, who were abused by Kitawalists. As Gérard pointed out, there were any number of religious/healing institutions that preceded Kitawala and many of them were, at some point, found wanting, and they were abandoned for new options in the changing economy of power.

While many of those who went to Kitawala looking for healing found it and stayed, many did not. The same man who went to Kitawala hoping that his daughter would be cured of epilepsy reported that she was not cured and he had left the religion. Six of the people interviewed by Bastin told him that they had "learned nothing from the religion" and "would not stay." These reports must be read in the context of interrogation: they may have felt it was in their best interest to disparage Kitawala. But they may also be sincere. One of the young girls interviewed in Pontheirville in 1947 likewise reported that she did not stay in Kitawala once she was initiated because she "suffered too much." She felt she had been lied to by the leader who baptized her because she had been promised she would be "loved by all men" and was not.[105]

The point is that not everyone found what they were looking for when they joined. Still others reported that joining Kitawala had adverse effects on their social lives and positions within their communities. One man reported that he was a Kitawalist for a time but ultimately decided to renounce it. He was then installed as a police captain in his village, but the villagers "refused to obey" him because he was a Kitawalist. He ultimately decided that because he was still considered an adherent, regardless of his renouncement, he would just return to Kitawala.[106] There are also numerous reports of unwilling, or coerced, baptism. In 1956, in the village of Yalikombo, just up river from Stanleyville (Kisangani), a local notable reported that his nephew came to him to tell him he had "a medicine" to give him. When he asked which medicine, the nephew said, "Come and I will show you." He walked him through the woods and through a swamp and then said, "Voilà, you are now baptized Kitawalist." The man said he did not want to be baptized and would alert the *chef du post,* but his nephew told him that "there was nothing he could do, because he was already baptized." He also told people that if they were not baptized Kitawalist and given the "dawa," they would be dead in two days.[107] Cases like these illustrate the extent to which Kitawala was contested within many of the very same communities it had become influential. As was also the case during the Lobutu-Masisi uprising, unruly remedies were not always welcome in the communities where they appeared.

Even within the Kitawalist communities there was contestation and disagreement about what the "moral project" of Kitawala should be and how it should be achieved.[108] It is striking, for example, that in his report about how the Topoko-Lokele near Stanleyville had become *kitawalisé,* Philippart noted that after they had been "seduced by the mysterious and secret character" of Kitawala, they could not tolerate being under the "domination" of the Walengola for very long. As a result, schism very quickly took root. Philippart explained that the two tendencies "despised each other"— "*Wanapita pembeni wa njia—watoto wa shetani*" ("They do not follow the way, they are children of Satan")—and spoke with repugnance about the pastors in the other group. The language here is strikingly similar to that used in the more recent break between EDAC and Kitawala of Katanga discussed in chapter 2. As with the two groups in South Kivu and Katanga decades later, it is not unreasonable to suggest that the Walengola and the Topoko-Lokele were disagreeing about how one should access and wield power, and to what ends.

Still others who had initially been attracted to and believed vehemently in Kitawala as a viable means of procuring power left the church, no longer convinced of its viability. In a 1958 report, Philippart wrote about what he labeled the "Lotika Jean Affaire." Philippart had come across a notebook that belonged to Lotika Jean, who was one of the original leaders arrested in Katanga with Mutombo Stephan and relegated to Lubutu. The notebook detailed the story of how Lotika had abandoned Kitawala after his arrest, deciding that it was a bad religion, full of hate. In 1957, he was approached by present Kitawalist leaders who asked him to take his place at the head of the church, since the different wings were feuding. They wanted him to reunite them. He refused, telling them he would give them spiritual guidance instead. He wrote that he became a Kitawalist because he believed that one must be baptized before God and abandon idols because they are not good. He also said that one must respect the "rod of authority" on earth because God made it that way. He cited the Belgians as an example: if they were ruling, he said, it was because God put them there. Philippart was shocked by what he found in the notebook, writing that he had never encountered such sentiments from a Kitawalist. He questioned whether it was Kitawala at all. Lotika Jean also named a successor to himself, but Philippart doubted that all the factions would agree with the choice. In his report on the notebook, Philippart was almost gloating that this major founder of Kitawala had turned away from it and left the remaining factions feuding.[109] Some Kitawala converts, it would seem, ultimately found the movement too unruly.

Unruliness took many forms in the history of Kitawala. It came in the form of rebellions—both enacted (Lobutu-Masisi) and merely plotted (Stanleyville)—and in other forms of overt subversive action. But it also came in more subtle forms that were less directly confrontational with the colonial government and more concerned with questions of authority, mortality, and wellness internal to Congolese communities. It came in the form of authority figures like Malesho and Yeni, who used the tools they had at hand to try crafting a future for themselves and their communities that made sense in the context of the challenges colonialism brought, in the process reshaping and reimagining traditions as they navigated a changing economy of power. It may have come in the form of polyamorous communities or the Mama Losiya, whose unruly bodies thwarted some traditions of patriarchal control, even as they drew on other traditions about the body/spirit power of those same bodies to assure communal well-being. But it also may have come in the form of unruly interpretations like those of the young men in Lowa who used those same ideas about embodied power as a rationale for sexual violence, although as I have argued, the occurrence of such violence must be contextualized within the insecurity colonialism wrought. Such insecurity in turn heightened the demand for unruly remedies, which reimagined the tools and materials of traditional healing to address it. But it also left room for the doubts of unruly converts, some of whom decided that Kitawala could not remedy their ills and indeed may have caused new ills.

Yet, even as Philippart gloated that one great Kitawalist, Lotika Jean, had lost faith in the power of Kitawala, others reaffirmed and reimagined connections within and between their communities. As we will see in the next chapter, some Kitawalists in the relegation camps saw in their detention the realization of a community rich with the power of Kitawala and a chance to create a moral monopoly, to dominate the economy of power, and to reaffirm their beliefs that they were feared by the Belgians because of their power.

5 ~ Relegation

IN 1952, Pastor Théophile Mulongo was born in COLAGREL—a penal colony for relegated Kitawalists located outside the small town of Kasaji, in what is today the province of Lualaba. His father, Mulongo Paul, had been sent to COLAGREL in 1947 after his arrest for proselytizing Kitawala in his home territory. Per Belgian relegation policy at the time, his mother and siblings were also forced to accompany his father to the penal colony. Although he was a young child when the prisoners in the camp were liberated in 1960, after the departure of the Belgians, Pastor Mulongo knows many stories about life in the penal colony. Some are his own stories, based in his own memories. Others were passed down to him by his father and the other men and women in his community who spent years—sometimes decades—of their lives imprisoned in COLAGREL and its predecessor (a smaller camp in nearby Malonga). As we walked the deteriorating grounds of COLAGREL together in the summer of 2018, Pastor Mulongo shared many of these stories with me.[1]

One of the stories Pastor Mulongo told featured a large grove of mango trees, located on the northern side of the camp. As we walked through the grove, on our way to visit the graves of Kitawalists buried at the camp, he stopped to tell me its origin story. It was the prisoners themselves, he explained, who planted the trees during the period when COLAGREL was under construction. According to his community's oral tradition, the guards brought a large quantity of mangoes over from Malonga. They gave each of the prisoners five mangoes. They then ordered them to eat the mangoes and plant the seeds. For each seed that did not germinate and grow into a sapling, guards whipped the prisoners with one stroke of the chicotte.[2]

Another story featured the scare tactics the prison guards used to try to get the prisoners to abandon their Kitawalist faith. One day, Pastor Mulongo told me, the guards dug a number of empty graves. They then brought the prisoners over to look at them and said, "You! Do you love Kitawala? Because if you love Kitawala, we will bury you here." Then they slaughtered a goat and let its blood run into the grave. And when the prisoners saw the blood, Pastor Mulongo explained, they believed it was true. The guards would bury them in such graves.

Pastor Mulongo also told me a story about the prison building located in the center of COLAGREL. Camp authorities would send the Kitawalists to this prison for disorderly conduct, or if they caught them practicing or preaching Kitawala in secret. It contained two rows of tiny solitary cells, with their walls painted black to maximize the darkness for those locked inside (see figures 5.1 and 5.2). If you spent just a few hours in these cells, Pastor Mulongo explained to me, you would come out dizzy and confused. Some men spent days in them, leaving only for meals. Others were allowed to leave during the day to work in the fields, only to return to the darkness at night.

As we stood inside the crumbling walls of this building, a memory came flooding back to Pastor Mulongo. When he was a young boy—maybe six years old—his father was sent to this prison for a period of time. One day, he went to visit his father after working hours. When the prison guards indicated it was time for his father to go back inside, young Mulongo defiantly told the guard, "I'm not going home, I'm staying here with Papa." So, the guard decided it would be amusing to lock the child in the cell with his father. As soon as he locked the door, young Mulongo, predictably, became terrified. He started bawling until the guard came and opened the door, at which point he was too scared to go anywhere, and he again told the guard, "No, I will stay here with Papa." So, they shut him back into the pitch-black cell, again causing him to cry. Grown weary of their cruel joke, the guards then grabbed him and threw him out.

Finally, Pastor Mulongo told of when news of impending independence reached the prisoners. The Belgian prison director at the time called them all into a meeting. He said, "We have fought a war with you. We told you to

FIGURE 5.1. The prison inside of COLAGREL.

FIGURE 5.2. Entry to a "special cell" in COLAGREL.

abandon Kitawala and you told us you wouldn't abandon it. We've been here a long time. But our time is over. We are leaving. Be well." And then he gave them the keys to the buildings. The leader of the Kitawalists looked at him and said, "Since you tell us that you are leaving, these things are ours now." According to the Kitawalists, this comment disturbed the director so much, he went directly to Kasaji and hired an engineer to go to COLAGREL and demolish his house so that no one else could live in it.

Descendants of the prison director remember the incident differently. By their account, the building had apparent structural weaknesses and needed to be demolished for safety.[3] And indeed, a large crack can be seen in images of the building prior to demolition (see figures 5.3 and 5.4). The demolition also happened in 1956, four years before independence. But none of this negates the Kitawalist memory of the incident; for although it predated the actual date of independence, it did not predate decolonization as a serious topic of discussion in the colony. By 1956, nationalist activists, including Lumumba, were building political momentum—including in Kisangani, where Kitawalists had just been arrested for the Stanleyville plot, after which many of them had been relegated to Kasaji. It is entirely possible that a conversation of the sort Pastor Mulongo recounted happened at this time, conspicuously overlapping with the demolition. Moreover, that they would remember the demolition as a malicious act on the part of colonial

FIGURE 5.3. The prison director's office. The building, which also served as the Matton's home initially, was modeled after the town hall in Dendermonde, Belgium. From the personal archive of Karel Van den Eynde (1926–2008).

144 ∽ *Violence and Power*

FIGURE 5.4. COLAGREL guards stationed outside the prison director's office. On the far left of the photo, a large crack can be seen in the brick. From the personal archive of Karel Van den Eynde (1926–2008).

officials, whose purpose in that space was to deny their freedom, should not be surprising; acts of colonial sabotage and looting (including of archives) were common at the moment of decolonization. Rather, it offers a telling glimpse at how the events were experienced and interpreted very differently from opposite sides.

CARCERAL SPACES, POWERFUL PLACES

Most of Pastor Mulongo's stories do not exist in the colonial archive. They are, rather, the memories of a community, guarded and passed on by individuals like Pastor Mulongo. Some circulate more widely within the community, appearing, for example, in sermons where they carry moral lessons for parishioners about faith tested and retained. Others, like that of young Théophile Mulongo, tormented by prison guards, seem more tethered to the space itself. They are what Tamara Giles-Vernick has called "body memories" that emerge in the moments where body, space, and memory meet.[4] And, as this chapter will argue, COLAGREL was and is a potent symbolic space—one that can evoke past traumas, even as it remains home, to this day, to many descendants of those who were once detained within its confines. The small concrete barracks in which they live were once the prisoners' quarters of their parents and grandparents. The mango trees growing behind their houses were planted in the blood of their ancestors. The streets

Relegation ~ 145

they walk are lined with buildings designed to facilitate their surveillance and ensure their domination.

Taken together, the stories Pastor Mulongo tells reveal how the Belgian colonial state used various forms of intimidation and torture for purposes of forcing submission and extracting labor. Indeed, they are a prime illustration of the violence of what Nancy Hunt has called the "nervous" face of the state.[5] It was a nervous face that, as Hunt rightly points out, was prone not just to violence but also to related "moods" of paranoia, tension, edginess, and volatility as it "policed and securitized" unruly ideas.[6] All these moods animated the history of relegation, and they profoundly shaped the experiences of the camp guards, administrators, and prisoners alike. Yet, few studies of those experiences exist—and none that center on the stories of the hundreds of Kitawalist men, women, and children who were detained at COLAGREL.[7]

Pastor Mulongo's stories call on us to investigate those experiences and contextualize them in the little-explored history of relegation as policy and practice. Although it constituted a major component of carceral practice in colonial Congo, particularly during and after World War II, there are few published accounts of the history of relegation.[8] And yet, thousands of people were compelled to live in these camps for periods of five, ten, twenty, and even upwards of twenty-five years. They were subject to surveillance, harsh physical punishment, and psychological trauma, and compelled to do manual labor by the state. It is a long-overlooked history of state excess and violence in a colonial state that had no shortage of such histories.

Yet, the history of relegation also reveals the limits of the colonial state. If the archives and oral traditions tell a story of oppression born of colonial paranoia and insecurity, of people displaced, of lives disrupted, and of years and bodies sacrificed to these penal colonies, they also tell a story of oppression thwarted, communities built anew, and faith maintained and even strengthened in times of tribulation. If we consider the stories of oppression and violence alongside other Kitawalist stories about the same period—in which they recount how they mobilized spiritual forms of power to protect their communities and further their work in freeing the Congolese people of "spiritual and physical slavery"—a more nuanced picture begins to emerge.[9] Ultimately, the Belgian colonial government was severely limited in its capacity to control and shape Kitawalist communities and dictate what the camp and the experience of relegation should mean to them.

The history of Kitawalist relegation pushes us beyond reiterating points that many scholars have noted before: namely, that colonial states could be fragile and often inept, and that colonial prisons and prison camps were almost invariably sites of resistance.[10] It does so by reminding us that carceral spaces must be interpreted through multiple lenses, and that the notions of power circulating in and around such spaces were not singular.[11] Indeed, meaningful histories of such spaces must take into account imaginaries and narratives articulated by the imprisoned themselves. And as this chapter will argue, in the case of the Kitawalist relegation camps, such narratives and imaginaries often emphasized the role of faith and spiritual power in the experience and memory of colonial incarceration. If the colonial government intended COLAGREL as a space where they could exercise totalitarian, regimented control over the bodies and minds of Kitawalist prisoners, the prisoners themselves, in turn, imagined it as a space where, strengthened by their forbidden faith, they might be empowered by the transformative experience of their greatest tribulation.

RELEGATION AS POLICY

To understand how relegation was experienced, one must first understand how the policy worked. From 1910 until independence in 1960, thousands of Congolese people were subject to relegation. The exact number of people who ended up in relegation camps like COLAGREL is difficult to know. In 1957, when the Belgian official Paul Joset conducted an investigation of the state of the camps, he found that there were around five thousand people (including prisoners and their families) living in just the four largest camps: Ekafera, Kasaji, Belingo, and Oshwe. While Joset's number included people relegated for participation in other "subversive movements," like Kimbanguism, many of those prisoners were Kitawalists. In that same year, COLAGREL alone—which housed exclusively Kitawalists—reported a population of nearly seven hundred.[12] But, as illustrated by map 5.1, Kitawalists were relegated to a number of other locations throughout the colony. Ekafera camp, in particular, housed a large population of Kitawalists, including many of those convicted after the Lobutu-Masisi uprising.

The legal justification for the policy of relegation derived from a series of decrees issued by the colonial government, beginning in the era of the Congo Free State with a 1906 decree that forbade any activity that threatened "public order and peace." In 1910, the Belgian colonial government issued another decree that gave the state the ability to detain and relegate all "natives," whether Congolese or migrant, whose activities violated the decree of 1906.[13] These were followed by further decrees in 1936 and 1943 that together rendered relegation the primary form of

Relegation ~ 147

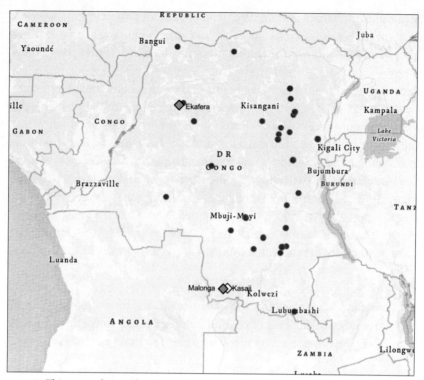

MAP 5.1. This map shows the sites of relegation listed for 207 Kitawalist prisoners between 1936 and 1953. Most were sent to the camps at Ekafera, Malonga, and Kasaji.

punishment applied to those arrested for religious dissidence, including Kitawalists.[14]

In its earliest iterations, relegation did not mean incarceration in a formal penal colony. Rather, early relégués (the term colonial officials used for people sentenced to this form of punishment) were generally subject to less organized forms of relegation. Some were subject to what I will call *dispersive* relegation, in which they were relegated outside of the defined area where colonial officials believed that they could cause trouble.[15] This could mean relegation beyond a city perimeter, or perhaps outside of a particular linguistic zone. The idea behind the latter was that if influential leaders were relegated to regions where they did not speak the local language, they would not be able to continue proselytization. As we saw with the case of Mutombo Stephan in chapter 1, this was a faulty assumption.

Within this category of dispersive relegation was another subcategory of relegation that I will call *natal* relegation.[16] Individuals subject to this kind of relegation were sent to their "milieu of origin" (i.e., village or territory of origin), where colonial officials hoped customary authorities would help to control them. As with other forms of dispersive relegation, their guiding assumptions proved to be ill-conceived, and this form of relegation greatly contributed to the proliferation of Kitawalist teachings into rural areas. As we have seen, for example, it allowed Kulu Mapenda to build a large following of converts in and around his ancestral village of Luseba, where he was relegated in 1936.[17] There are many other cases like his.[18]

While neither of these forms of relegation entailed the use of formal penal colonies, individuals sentenced to either of these kinds of relegation were subject to what one official described as "discreet but effective" surveillance and were often settled in a "fixed residence," separated from the rest of the population.[19] Until about 1936, for example, many Kitawalists subject to this form of punishment—particularly those arrested in Katanga—were relegated to labor encampments in areas around Lubutu and Ankoro.[20] In these locations, they lived separately from the other "free" laborers but were allowed to circulate freely for their work within a defined area, making it relatively easy for them to proselytize.[21]

Ultimately, both of these dispersive forms of relegation failed to contain unruly ideas. By the mid-1930s, colonial officials were beginning to recognize some of the weaknesses in their dispersive approach to relegation, particularly as it pertained to the leaders whom they considered the most dangerous.[22] Thus, they moved to build more formal penal colonies, ushering in a new form of *concentrative* relegation. In the early days of these camps, colonial officials often referred to them as "concentration camps."[23] Ultimately, after *concentration camp* became a loaded term, following the World War II, they began referring to them as CARDs, an acronym that translates to Agricultural Camps for Dangerous Relégués.

Among the earliest of these concentration camps was the Malonga camp, which was completed in 1936 and received its first prisoners that year. Between 1936 and 1947, Malonga served as the site of internment for most major Kitawalist leaders arrested in the province of Katanga. Kadiba Ilunga Émile, Kabila Muyololo, and Kulu Mapenda all spent time in Malonga and became influential leaders within the camp itself.[24] (The sometimes-contentious relationship between these different leaders and their followers will be considered in greater depth below.)

By 1943, the close proximity of Malonga camp to the road, to the Angolan border (which might allow for cross-border Watchtower communication), and to the rest of the population in Malonga convinced the colonial authorities that they needed to relocate the camp to somewhere more remote. After a prolonged search in which they struggled to find a customary authority willing to cede land for the new camp, a customary chief named Tshisangama finally agreed to allow the colonial government to build the new camp, which would become COLAGREL, in a remote part of his district, about eighteen kilometers (11 mi.) outside the town of Kasaji.[25]

In the same period, the colonial government moved to build another concentrative relegation camp at the remote location of Ekafera in the province of Equateur. They intended Ekafera to serve as penal colony for the most dangerous leaders of subversive religious movements, including Kitawala and Kimbanguism, among others. Plans to build Ekafera were underway by 1939, and its first prisoners arrived in 1944.[26] Many of them were transfers, who had previously been relegated elsewhere but were ultimately deemed too dangerous for their initial sites of relegation.

Overall, the impression that one gets from colonial correspondences about the policy of relegation, from the mid-1930s up until independence in 1960, is one of improvisation, hand-wringing, and often futile reduplication. In 1957, colonial officials were, themselves, fretting that relegation laws were poorly defined in the legal code, unevenly applied, and "arbitrarily enforced," and that, moreover, relegation was a "grave measure that deprives liberty without limit of time and with no possible recourse."[27] And yet, they had continued to implement the policy for decades, even though it consistently failed to achieve its intended goals of suppressing Kitawala and reeducating its leaders—goals that were always already undermined by the racist assumptions at the core of their design. Of course, it is important to remember that what was perceived as failure from the perspective of the colonial government was perceived as evidence of their power by many Kitawalists—a point which I pick up below.

One can certainly see major shifts in relegation policy over these years—shifts that were accompanied by resource allocation (to build the camps, for example) and real-time effects on the lives of relégués, who were increasingly concentrated in camps. But these policy shifts were never total, and there was constant disagreement within administrative circles on how best to implement them. And while there was a discernible move toward concentrative relegation by the late 1930s, dispersive relegation—particularly natal relegation—continued to be a major component of relegation policy. Moreover, who should be subject to which kind of relegation and how it should be organized and administered was a constant subject of debate among colonial authorities. Was it dangerous for Kitawalists to be mixed into camps with relégués from other religious movements?[28] Kimbanguists—with whom they feared Kitawalists would unite—were a particular concern.[29] Should "simple adepts" be relegated with "dangerous leaders," risking their radicalization?[30] What about those who claimed to have repented in the relegation camps: Were they faking their contrition?[31] If not, could they be released into natal relegation?[32] Could they be used as plants back in their villages to preach the futility of Kitawala?[33]

Equally contentious was the question of what to do about the apparent failure of the policy to reform and reeducate most individuals who were subject to it.[34] In fact, by the 1950s, this was such a concern that the colonial government sent an investigative team, led by Joset, to Kenya to learn more about how the British had managed reeducation in the Mau Mau detention camps. Joset returned from Kenya with reports about the "brilliant" success that the reeducation policy of "screening" had achieved with former Mau Mau dissidents in British detention camps, suggesting that Belgium should follow their example.[35] However, as the work of historians like Caroline Elkins and David Anderson has demonstrated, the results of British reeducation efforts were far from "brilliant," and their camps were notoriously violent.[36] One wonders to what extent this was a cross-border exchange of misinformation meant to hide the failures of one colonial regime from another. Indeed, in 1957, the current director of CO-LAGREL, frustrated that he was being blamed for the failure of his camp to live up to such expectations, wrote of the report that it is "easier for a different country to sell you their successes than it is for them to admit their failures that they are hiding."[37]

In any case, the result of this frequent improvisation and constant debate was that many relégués experienced multiple forms of relegation, often moving over the course of their internment toward increasingly more restrictive forms of relegation. The cases of Mutombo Stephan and Kadiba Ilunga Émile will help illustrate this point.

Mutombo Stephan was arrested in Jadotville and initially relegated (dispersive, but not natal) to Bosobolo in 1936. Then, in 1937, after organizing a group of Kitawalists while in relegation at Bosobolo, he was sent to prison briefly in Stanleyville before being re-relegated (dispersive, but not natal) to Lubutu. After once again—famously—precipitating another major conversion of Kitawalists in Lubutu, he was arrested in 1942 and imprisoned at Stanleyville until 1944, when he was relegated (concentrative) to Ekafera. In 1950 he was incarcerated in the prison inside Ekafera. In 1953, while in the prison in Ekafera, he apparently joined with Kadiba Ilunga Émile and Kabila Muyololo (who ultimately ended up in Ekafera as well) in writing a letter to colonial authorities demanding they be released so that they could further propagate their faith. A bold move, to be sure, which his prison record cites as proof of the continued fanaticism of these relégués.[38]

Kadiba Ilunga Émile was likewise moved around during his relegation. He was initially relegated to Malonga in 1937. As mentioned earlier, there he became an important leader for a major faction of Kitawalists imprisoned in the camp. But the camp authorities feared his influence over the other relégués. According to the history kept by his descendants, he got into trouble with camp authorities on multiple occasions. Within months of his arrival in the camp, Kadiba created a clandestine school in which he taught other prisoners about literacy, the French language (reading and writing), the law, the penal code, human rights, geography, history, and God's love, among other subjects. When administrators learned about it, they were "very discontent and alarmed to see what these people who they considered low class were learning, so they arrested them and submitted them to tortures."[39] He spent two years in prison for these activities, from 1938 to 1940, before being reintroduced to the camp. Ultimately, for his continued recalcitrance, Kadiba was moved to Ekafera in late 1945, not long after it opened.[40] There, he was again arrested and, in 1949, detained in the prison at Ekafera, where, as we have already learned, he joined together with Mutombo Stephano, Kabila Muyololo, and others in 1953 in making demands for his freedom.[41] It is not clear how long he remained in the prison within Ekafera, but he was not released from the Ekafera CARD until independence in 1960.

These are just two cases of many. In a 1955 list of 967 Kitawalist arrest records, at least seventy Kitawalists appear to have been relegated to more than one location, with most being moved to the more secure camps of Ekafera and Kasaji.[42] These cases certainly illustrate the contingency and constant revision that was involved in the application of the policy of relegation. Still, as a policy it had clear contours, which shaped the experiences of those who endured it in very real ways. Sometimes relegation succeeded in intimidating and exhausting those who were its targets. Sometimes it convinced them to doubt and renounce their faith. As Pastor Mulongo plainly put it, "The Belgians were afraid of the Kitawalists. So, they tried to scare them. And it worked on some, and they left. Others said, 'No we will die here.' And they stayed."[43] For many of those who stayed, insisting at all costs on the sacrality and truth of their beliefs and refusing to submit to colonial authority, the price was indeed very high, paid in corporal punishment, isolation, and years of their lives. But it was not necessarily without meaning. It was in many ways, for many Kitawalists, a powerful experience. To understand this latter point, I turn now to the case of COLAGREL.

BUILDING COLAGREL

The official order to create COLAGREL came in 1943, but work on the camp did not begin in earnest until 1947.[44] Early sketches of the camp reveal that the officials involved in designing it envisioned it as a *cité jardin*—a kind of idyllic "garden city," which was a popular concept in urban planning in Brussels in the early twentieth century (see figure 5.5).[45] Part of the turn toward developmentalism as colonial policy more broadly in the postwar years—and specifically as a tactic for trying to stop the spread of Kitawala—the sketches reveal something about the hopes of some colonial officials that relegation camps like COLAGREL could serve as spaces that would convince recalcitrant Kitawalists of the many benefits of living peacefully within the colonial state.[46] The legacies of the cité jardin plan can be seen in the tree-lined central road of COLAGREL, as well as the lush mango forests that abut the back end of the camp (see figure 5.6). These are the same mango groves that feature in Pastor Mulongo's story—a cruel irony that effectively illustrates the gulf between the developmentalist rhetoric of the colonial state and the violent reality of COLAGREL's history.

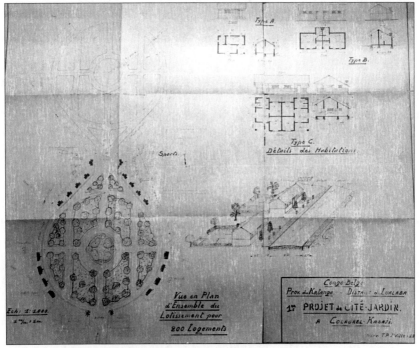

FIGURE 5.5. Original planning sketch for COLAGREL, designed as a "*cité Jardin*." From the Archives Africaines at Ministry of Foreign Affairs in Brussels.

Relegation ~ 153

FIGURE 5.6. The tree-lined road between the prisoners' barracks in COLAGREL in 2018.

On the ground, it was Maurice Matton who would ultimately serve as the first (and most infamous) director of the camp and was in charge of its construction. Matton was by all accounts a violent man. His own peers described him as someone who "easily becomes violent in his speech and attitudes" and was "ferocious" when criticized. After just two years of service at COLAGREL, they expressed concerns that he was engaged in a "war of nerves" with the Kitawalists that would cause him to "loose his sanity or 'nervous balance.'"[47] Despite these concerns, he continued to serve as director of the camp until 1956.

Both because of the long duration of his service in the position, and because of his long-enduring reputation as a *mukali sana* (hard/mean/strict man) within the Kitawalist communities around Kasaji, he serves as the "Prison Director" archetype in most Kitawalist stories of the camp. For example, when Pastor Mulongo told me the story of the prison director blowing up his own home so that the Kitawalists could not have it, he named Maurice Matton as the director. Although Matton built the house, he was no longer the director at that time. In other words, Matton's name has become synonymous with stories of oppression in the camp.

154 ⁓ *Violence and Power*

To build the permanent infrastructure of the camp, which included the prison, the guard tower, and the housing for the prisoners, guards, and other colonial officers and employees, Matton enlisted a number of single, young, male prisoners from Malonga camp. Initially, Matton tried to press a number of local inhabitants of Tshisangama's district into the uncompensated labor of building provisional housing for these prisoner-laborers. This he attempted to do at the peak of the planting season in what was and is a largely agricultural zone. Predictably, the result was a growing resentment for the penal colony among the local population, who felt they were being forced to "abandon their own fields to help criminals," and Matton was very quickly advised by his superior officers to change his tactics.[48] After that, he forced the prisoners from Malonga to build their own provisional mud-brick residences.

Once the provisional housing was complete, the prisoners were put to work building the permanent structures of the camp. Matton's superiors envisioned this labor as a kind of moral and vocational training for the prisoners. It was "a means of training the kinds of workers that are necessary to the colony: builders, masons." Through such work, they believed, the prisoners might be redeemed as productive colonial subjects. As such, they endeavored to pay the prisoners wages similar to those of other free laborers in the region. For the colonial authorities, the purpose of paying wages was twofold. On the one hand, earning wages could serve as a kind of moral lesson about the fruits of hard work. On the other hand, wages offered an answer to the question of how to get provisions to the prisoners until the colony's fields could produce enough food for them to feed themselves: they could use their wages to purchase food from the local market vendors, who might periodically hold a small market in the camp.

But the colonial officials were also concerned about the plan's potential risks. In their correspondences about the project, they worried about allowing local vendors to interact with the prisoners. The Kitawalists, after all, had been relegated to the camp for spreading dangerous "propaganda." Was there a risk of contamination?[49] This debate and others like it reveal important tensions around the creation of the camp. Such tensions manifested as concerns about the relationship between the camp officials and the local population outside the camp, as well as concerns about the relationship between the local population and the prisoners themselves: how they interacted, but also how they perceived each other. One official, for example, warned that while the prisoners should be able to live "normal lives," they needed to be careful about giving the surrounding villagers "the impression that these individuals in revolt [were] treated better by [the colonial government] than the honest farmer of the interior."[50]

Whatever the debates and concerns of the planning officials, the reality on the ground was that the prisoners, despite being paid wages, were also exposed to a very grueling regime of labor under Maurice Matton's guardianship. Their work in the camp began with a roll call at 6:30 a.m. and did not end until sundown at 6:30 p.m. If they were late for the roll call or did not show, they were punished. While working in the fields or on their assigned project in the camp, they were subject to surveillance from camp guards and were given just two brief breaks. This strict regime was required six days a week. Sundays were free, unless the guards deemed that they had completed a task poorly, in which case they were required to redo that task on Sunday. In other cases, they were forced to do corvée labor on Sundays as punishment for various infractions, such as a late arrival to roll call.[51]

While many aspects of this labor regime resembled that of other forced/coerced laborers in colonial Congo, it in no way resembled a "normal life" for the prisoners. And yet, as noted above, colonial officials spent significant time trying to engineer the ideal "normal life" for the prisoners as they saw it. In fact, it was in pursuit of this "normal life" that they introduced the policy of forcing the wives and children of the prisoners to move into the camps. Camp administrators hoped that bringing in the prisoners' families would ease the "discomfort" of their internment and better facilitate their rehabilitation.[52] Thus, after the construction of the permanent camp was completed in 1951, camp officials moved to force all the wives of the relegated men to move to COLAGREL to live with their husbands, along with their nonadult children. I will consider the experiences of these women and children further below. But first I would like to turn to a different set of questions: Who were these prisoners? What kinds of communities did they build within the confines of the camp?

COMMUNITY AND CONFLICT

The men and women detained at COLAGREL originated from many parts of Congo, but nearly all of them came from the eastern provinces of Katanga, Kivu, and Orientale. Map 5.2—which illustrates the villages of origin of 250 of the prisoners who ended up at Malonga (and then ultimately COLAGREL) between 1936 and 1952—gives a sense of the diverse identities of these prisoners. Many of them came from the areas around a handful of major nodes of transmission (what the Belgians often referred to as "cells" of Kitawalists). Some of these nodes, like the node around Mwanza/Mulongo/

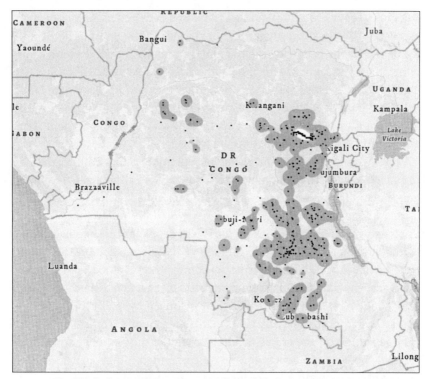

MAP 5.2. The black dots indicate unique villages of origin. The shading indicates "hot spots" where many of the dots signify multiple individuals. The map was created by the author using ArcGIS and archival arrest records.

Manono, are clearly visible on the map. Others, like the group of Kitawalists who arrived from the Kisangani node in 1956 (whose story features in chapter 4), do not appear on the map because the list of 990 arrest records from which I constructed the map unfortunately ends with 1955. Still others came from smaller nodes of transmission.

These diverse prisoners arrived at different times, often after a particular "incident," or series of incidents, that precipitated multiple arrests. This, in turn, shaped the kinds of communities the prisoners built inside the camps. An example of one series of incidents centered around Manono can illustrate how this process often worked.

In 1940, a man named Edward Thomas, who had come to Congo from Cape Town, was arrested along with several of his followers in Manono for spreading Kitawalist doctrine among the miners at Géomines. In the wake of his arrest, the Kitawalist community around Manono continued to grow, unbeknownst to the authorities, who realized its growing influence only in September 1941, when they intercepted a letter between leaders in Manono

Relegation ～ 157

and a relégué named Loisa Mulongo, who was detained at Malonga. Upon discovering this link, they arrested a man named Kiwele Abusolome and two of his adepts. Following their arrest, a number of other converts came to the prison in Manono, where the authorities had detained them, and demanded to be arrested with them, declaring "they would also die for God" and threatening that if they were not also arrested, they would call one hundred more Kitawalists from the worker camps. Twenty-one of them were arrested and sent to prison in Albertville.[53]

Just two months after the events of September 1941, another group of Kitawalists centered at Géomines decided to protest the arrest of one of their leaders. Their plan, after freeing their imprisoned leader, was to march to the Malonga, where they believed they would be free to practice their beliefs and no longer have to work for White people or the colonial state.[54] By midday, some two thousand Kitawalists had descended on the center of the town, surrounding the territorial administrators office in an attempt to replace "the blue flag of Belgium with the black flag of Kitawala."[55] They were "baptizing openly" and "singing and wearing crowns of thorns" as they protested in front of their flag.[56] The guards in front of the office "panicked" and opened fire on the crowd, killing fourteen of the demonstrators, who had made no violent provocation and were unarmed.[57] They then arrested a number of the protestors and order was briefly restored.

Order did not last, however, as a second group of Kitawalists arrived the next day, once again unarmed, and surrounded the office of the territorial administrator. Colonial accounts indicate that "with an attitude of aggression, they mocked and injured the representatives of the state."[58] The soldiers of the Garde Territoriale Volontaire, a volunteer corps of White settlers, arrived, and a fight broke out. The soldiers managed to overcome the demonstrators and put them in prison. Several more groups arrived in succession, at least one of them throwing stones and attempting to take the weapons of the soldiers, but they too were arrested. At that point, unrest also broke out within the prison as the detained Kitawalists decided they would try to destroy the building by burning it down. Ultimately, a platoon of government soldiers arrived from Elizabethville to reestablish order by force, and that was the end of the unrest.

All told, the unrest at Monono lasted for six days, resulting in fourteen deaths and the arrests of 925 Kitawalists,[59] 103 of whom were condemned and sent to prison in Elizabethville. Of those arrested, records show that at least 13 of them were sent to Malonga in November 1941.[60] While the fate of the others is unclear, it is very likely that many were subject to forms of dispersive relegation.

This series of incidents at Monono offers a number of important insights into the nature of Kitawalist communities both within and outside the camps. For one, it makes it clear that there were connections between those inside and outside the camps. Particularly in the years at Malonga, the boundaries of the camp were porous, and leaders inside and outside of its confines did communicate with each other secretly.[61] This was part of the justification for moving the camp. Yet, even at Malonga it was dangerous and difficult and, like Loisa Mulongo and his correspondents, they often got caught and punished. But the prisoners continued to try. In later years at COLAGREL, the camp's guards had to regularly inspect the paths around the camp that led to the river or hunting traps, to make sure the prisoners were not communicating with the outside.[62] Even then, they sometimes found ways, but it was not easy; and many went years without news of their families or their fellow Kitawalists who had been sent to other camps. For example, Pastor Mulongo told me that after Kadiba was sent to Ekafera, his followers who remained in Kasaji did not get news about him for years, and some feared he was dead. Not until several years after independence did they finally get news about him, after they managed to convince a White man named La Planche (whose identity beyond his name is unclear) to inquire about him, and he returned with news that Kadiba was alive and well, which "gave them strength again."[63]

The Manono incidents also reveal how the prisoners coming into the camp often shared particular experiences before their arrest. Most of those coming from Manono, for example, had worked for the mining company Géomines. They had been part of the same node of transmission and undoubtedly shared particular interpretations of Kitawalist teachings, imparted to them initially through Edward Thomas and then transmitted through those he converted. Eight years after their arrest, Matton identified one of these Manono prisoners, Monga Djoni, as one of seven "spiritual leaders" in the camp.[64] Each of these leaders seems to have represented a particular tendency in Kitawalist practice, and Monga Djioni's appearance in the report as one of them suggests that the prisoners from the Manono node may have maintained ties with each other, perhaps constituting a particular faction or tendency within the camp.

Evidence that there were factions within the camp is abundant. And these factions did not always get along. One infamous example of this involved Kadiba Ilunga Émile and Kabila Muyololo. It occurred in 1938, while the prisoners were still at Malonga. Both men were rising Kitawalist leaders before relegation, and both became influential leaders in the camp, each with his own group of followers. According to the version of this history kept by the descendants of Kadiba and his followers, disagreement between the two groups escalated to the point of violence in 1938, when four of Muyololo's followers—Mutumba Paul, Ilunga Ezone, Ngoie Belge, and Kazadi Bilato—tried to burn down Kadiba's house while he and his son were still inside. They escaped the fire, but two books that Kadiba had managed to hide in his quarters were destroyed—a loss so substantial in the context of the prison camp that Kadiba's descendants remember it as one of the few details of the fire.[65]

The reasons for the violence are not entirely clear, but according to the *Biographie*, the prisoners in the camp at that time "saw many miracles [*miudiza mingi*]," and then "broke into two sides." They write that "jealousy came between the prisoners," and that is what led Muyololo's followers to burn the house down.[66] The *Histoire* further elaborates on the nature of these miracles, reporting that Kadiba "miraculously healed the wife of Ngoie Belge, who had gone mad." This is in contrast to Muyololo and his followers, who are described in much more disparaging terms as "semi-literate and féticheurs."[67] Such accounts of the incident, although one-sided and relatively vague, are nonetheless very suggestive of the kinds of rifts that developed within the prisoner community.[68] Kadiba's followers label Muyololo and his followers as "jealous" and "féticheurs"—language that directly evokes Central African discourses of witchcraft and interpersonal malevolence.[69] Meanwhile, from their drastic actions, Muyololo and his followers appear to have likewise considered Kadiba and his purported miracles as dangerous and threatening. Indeed, the very man whose wife Kadiba healed was also named as one of the arsonists! Such details can be puzzling and highlight the opaqueness of these accounts, pointing to ultimately unknowable interpersonal tensions lurking below the surface of the story. But they also place questions of power and morality at the center of this account of intracommunal conflict. The accusation of "semi-literacy" is also interesting, and points to the significance of literacy and the capacity for proper textual interpretation (and thus proper and morally sound transmission) within Kitawalist hierarchies of authority. Importantly, the two things appear to be connected: improper textual interpretation is dangerous and can lead down the immoral path of the "féticheur," while proper textual interpretation gives access to miraculous powers.

These rifts were not necessarily permanent, and interpersonal and communal relations shifted over time as prisoners came and went and, perhaps more importantly, debated and discussed the nature and possibility of their Kitawalist beliefs within the confines of their incarcerated lives. While the relationship between Muyololo and Kadiba was fractured enough to elicit violence in 1938, we have already learned above that a decade and a half later, in 1953, these men allied with each other to demand their freedom in a letter written from the prison inside Ekafera. Whatever disagreements had led them to violent confrontation years earlier had seemingly dissipated.

In short, there is ample evidence indicating that there were particular factions within the camps, which, for a variety of reasons (whether because they came from shared nodes of transmission, or simply because they grew into communities of shared ideas and experiences within the camps), coalesced under different leaders. And the prison administrators were constantly trying to grasp the internal dynamics of the prisoner community so that they could identify which groups were more or less "fanatic" and posed the biggest threat to order in the camp.[70] Matton even tried to use leaders from the ten different regions of origin represented in the camp as "advisors," who would lead the prisoners in their work and maintain the peace.[71]

However, not only were these leaders not necessarily always in conflict with each other, but, much to the dismay of the administrators, ample evidence suggests that they regularly acted in solidarity with each other.[72] Take, for example, an incident that happened in 1949. Four of the "strong leaders" in the camp—Ngoie Belge,[73] Kasadi, Levy, and Mulongo André—arranged a work stoppage among the prisoners. As punishment, Matton held these men responsible as a group and forced them to finish the work themselves, hoping that their capitulation to his authority would diminish their reputations within the camp. Two years later, however, Ngoie Belge showed up in a monthly report from October 1951 for, once again, leading collective action. This time, Ngoie and his collaborators refused to pay their taxes or accept the seeds for the peanuts, tobacco, and cotton that Matton insisted they plant. Two of them were imprisoned for it.[74]

When I asked Pastor Mulongo about the relationship between different factions of Kitawalists in the camp, who had come from different regions at different times, he told me that they welcomed each other as "family." Of course, families fight. They do not always see eye to eye on matters of grave importance. But they also recognize their connection to one other, connection that can manifest as solidarity in times of hardship. The camps put people from different regions and different eras of transmission together. At COLAGREL, there were those who had been arrested in the 1930s and early 1940s and were the original relégués of Malonga. Then there were those who came later, after COLAGREL was in operation, many from regions much farther north—Kisangani, for example—whose version of Kitawala was separated from the Malonga prisoners by hundreds of kilometers and decades of transmission. But if divergence was a central characteristic of Kitawala's

Relegation ~ 161

transmission over time and space, convergence—the coming together of different communities of Kitawalists to exchange ideas and find common cause—was also an important characteristic. Indeed, it was one that colonial officials often fretted about, fearing that the convergence of different Kitawala tendencies would result in unification and threaten colonial order.[75]

In the camps, such forms of convergence and solidarity were a constant source of both annoyance and fear on the part of the camp administrators. And they were part of a bigger problem the administrators faced over the course of the camp's operation: passive and active forms of resistance.

REPERTOIRES OF RESISTANCE

Resistance took a variety of forms in the camps, including the kinds of collective action that one might expect: work stoppages, sabotage, and even riots. Such forms of collective action are common to both the history of Kitawala specifically and in colonial contexts more broadly.[76] They are also common to contexts of imprisonment. And as we have learned from the Manono incidents and the other incidents from the history of Kitawala discussed in previous chapters, many of the individuals imprisoned in COLAGREL had been arrested and relegated for very similar kinds of unruly activities outside the camp. But to see resistance in only these easily visible forms is to ignore the broader economy of power within which relegated Kitawalists operated. Kitawalists did engage in these common forms of resistance, but they also engaged in less visible—and necessarily secret—kinds of resistance that took forms like prayer, devotion, and ritual. These forms of resistance not only thwarted the reformative mission of the camp but also called on the power of the spiritual realm to strengthen them in their time of tribulation.

Already in this chapter, we have seen at least two examples of collective resistance to the labor regime of COLAGREL. There was the work stoppage organized by the different "strong leaders"—who Matton referred to as "malignant"—in 1949. And then there was the movement against planting crops or paying taxes, led by Ngoie Belge in 1951. There were many similar instances. Six months before Ngoie Belge's move to refuse planting, Matton reported that the prisoners were refusing to sell their manioc harvest (and thereby frustrating the agrobusiness schemes of the camp authorities), arguing that it was against their religion. In the report, Matton complains that "next they will be asking to practice their cult if one isn't on guard."[77] Indeed, the prisoners had already asked "to be able to continue their proselytizing activities" on at least one previous occasion and would continue to do so throughout the existence of the camp.[78]

Other reports suggest that sabotage of the agricultural labor regime was common. Such reports appear early on in the records for COLAGREL, including a 1948 report that noted prisoners were becoming more and more tense and giving "themselves over to sabotage (awaiting perhaps an open revolt)."[79] And these reports continued throughout its operation. Reporting in 1957, Matton's successor, Dullier, wrote that the prisoners would "take every opportunity to sabotage" and complained that they would "boil the seeds and then carefully sow them in front of the guard."[80] Matton once argued that the reason they engaged in passive resistance and hated working in the fields was because they had all been employed in the mines before their arrest.[81] It was a convenient excuse that implied their obstinance was about the kind of work, rather than the injustice of having to perform forced labor for an illegitimate regime under conditions of imprisonment.

There are also reports about the repeated acts of resistance by particular prisoners. Kulu Mapenda was sent to Malonga in 1937, after his arrest in Luseba earlier that year. Over the course of his incarceration in the camp, he gained a reputation among camp authorities as a "dangerous man" who liked to "play the martyr" and seemed to "welcome it if a measure of discipline is taken against him." Apparently, when the administration moved to transfer the prisoners to COLAGREL in 1947, he "incited" a group of relégués under his leadership into refusing to move to the new camp. He was repeatedly locked up in the camp prison and whipped for charges like "refusing work," "arrogance toward the prison guard," and "manifest laziness in his chores." In March 1948, he faced fifteen days of detention for "instigating his team to refuse the ration" (i.e., the cash ration that the prisoners were given to buy food in the canteen when they first moved to COLAGREL and had not yet produced any of their own crops).[82]

Kulu Mapenda also refused to back away from his role as a teacher of both Kitawala and human rights. In October of 1948, he faced seven days in the "dungeon" for "teaching the doctrine of Kitawala." Matton described him as a "fanatic and active" instructor who copied many extracts of the Bible into notebooks from memory and then distributed them to the other prisoners. Apparently, he regularly spoke to the other prisoners of the "Atlantic Charter" and human rights, reciting passages he memorized ("poorly," Matton claimed disparagingly) by heart. In 1948, he told Matton he would "accuse him in front of the Watchtower of South Africa."[83] Just as Kadiba Ilunga Émile did with his clandestine classes, Kulu Mapenda used his familiarity with international discourses of human rights to both threaten the colonial regime and educate the other prisoners and encourage them not to accept the terms of their incarceration. The tools of resistance Kulu

Mapenda and other prisoners used were physical, intellectual, and, as I will highlight shortly, spiritual.

But first, it is worth noting there were also moments when resistance in the camp turned into outright insurrection. One such incident took place in 1958. It happened at a moment when there was a transition in the camp's leadership. The previous director, Karel Van den Eynde, who had taken the position in 1956, had recently been replaced by a new director named Carpentier. According to reports after the event, Carpentier's demeanor was comparatively "firm," and he possessed none of the "politic of the good father of the family" that his predecessor had, which brought about an "attitude of non-collaboration, indeed hostility on the part of the relégués." Tensions over this transition came to a head when, on November 14, a group of twenty-three prisoners dropped their tools and refused to work after being chastised by the guards for showing up late. For their insolence, seven of the purported leaders were sentenced to fifteen days of detention with hard labor in the camp prison. But when the guards came to their barracks to try and escort them to the prison, a brawl broke out between the prisoners and the guards. The prisoners began throwing bricks at the guards, who were attempting to fight the prisoners with batons.[84] "Seeing their husbands under attack," the wives of prisoners also joined in the fight.[85]

Meanwhile, Van den Eynde, who was still residing at the camp, went to his house to get a Sten machine gun and fired two rounds into the air in an attempt to stop them.[86] He ordered the men into the prison, but they refused, and instead, together with their wives, "moved as a group" toward the entrance of the camp, all the while singing a religious hymn. There they remained into the night, with their own lookouts posted. Aware that he did not have enough soldiers to surround them, Van den Eynde posted guards at all entrances. He then called on the leaders of the other prisoner factions and got them to agree that they would not get involved in any further altercation and to announce to their communities that they did not approve of the actions of the "rioters."[87] In the meantime, he sent someone to call the chief of police in Kolwezi, who deployed a squad of soldiers on bicycles to ride all night to COLAGREL.[88]

The incident ended in the early hours of the next morning, when Van den Eynde called a meeting with the leader of the "recalcitrants," Kulu Cyprien, who agreed to meet him accompanied by two men. Kulu asked Van den Eynde to give a letter to the district commissioner and then finally agreed, under threat of the impending military intervention, to go to the prison.[89] In the end, six leaders of the "rebellion" were sent to prison in Kolwezi. Carpentier's superiors also reprimanded him for being too quick to implement his new, stricter rules and advised him to introduce future changes to his predecessor's policies more slowly and justifiably. Notably, the district commissioner, Warnier, nonetheless believed that "a stricter approach can also produce good results."[90] Harsh policies were fine, so long as they did not create disorder.

While this level of insurrection appears to be singular in the history of the camp, it was clearly part of a larger pattern of resistance that included actions like late arrivals, work stoppages, and appeals to authorities outside the camp who might recognize the violation of the inmates' rights. In this case, the prisoners appealed to the district commissioner to hear their case. In the case of Kulu Mapenda, he hoped to appeal to the South African Watchtower church. Kadiba Ilunga Émile's descendants say that in 1945 he went so far as to write to the president of the United States in hopes that he would intervene on their behalf:

> Baba Émile then went into the desert with his son and they did a *kifungo* [fast] of two weeks without eating or drinking. When he returned, he wrote another Declaration to America in 1945.[91] Mr. Truman got his letter and gave it to Mr. Roosevelt and he sent it to King Leopold II in Belgium. He contacted the Governor of Katanga and asked: how did this letter get to America? This is when Mr. Kyesar, Mr. Parent Émile, and Mr. Joseph Willemus went to Malonga to ask how Baba Émile sent the letter. [Kadiba] responded: By post. They then asked him: Why are you accusing us at the UN? He responded: I didn't accuse you, but it was to show them what is happening here in Congo.

While the claim that Roosevelt wrote to Leopold II on the behalf of Kitawalists is dubious, it nonetheless illustrates a point that is also clear in the colonial archives from the camp: the prisoners in this camp were wielding the discourse of human rights as a tool of resistance. They were also using letter writing as a "strategy of extraversion," which could offer "deliverance from colonial enclosure."[92] More importantly, they were doing so as part of a larger repertoire of resistance that went hand in hand with the spiritual tools of resistance: Kitawalist teachings, evocations, prayer, and the rebellious singing of religious hymns. If Baba Émile was able to write to the president of the United States, it was because he had evoked the power to do so during his kifungo. This recalls a similar account, already discussed in chapter 2, which the leader of the Kitawalist community in Kalemie told me in 2010, that "when the men were being sacrificed in the work camps at COLAGREL, [the women] were there doing evocations."[93] These evocations empowered the men to continue their fight against the camp authorities.

In the face of immense pressure from camp authorities, who wielded every tool in their own repertoire—imprisonment, psychological torture, physical punishment, espionage, coercion, and propaganda—to try and get Kitawalists to abandon their faith, the men and women incarcerated in the camp persisted in their beliefs. And evidence of their continued faith is scattered throughout the camp records. In 1950, for example, a guard discovered a group of five men conducting a Kitawalists meeting in the night. Upon discovering them, the guard grabbed their illegal Bible and threw it in the fire. Immediately, two of them men jumped on the guard while a third grabbed the Bible out of the fire and ran. That same month, another group was nearly discovered holding a service in the middle of the forest at night, but a Kitawalist woman—probably on watch duty—sounded the alarm and the guards were unable to apprehend anyone. According to the report, it was a recent relégué named Manase, who had come with "encouraging news from outside," leading these prayer meetings. Following these events, he was put under special surveillance, but the report warns that "with fanatics like him it is necessary to understand that being relegated is a point of honor."[94] Colonial authorities were not unaware of how their containment schemes were backfiring.

In another instance, in 1949, the (unnamed) wife of one of the Kitawalist leaders, Goy Simbi, was caught attempting to smuggle Bibles and other Kitawalist writings into the camp. Apparently, she had wrapped them in banana leaves and hid them within a suitcase full of chikwanga![95] Such incidents reveal not only the lengths to which the prisoners were willing to go to maintain their faith but also how central they considered their faith—and the power it gave them—to their very ability to endure life in the camp. The figures of the chikwanga-smuggling wife, the women who joined their husbands in rising up against the camp authorities in 1958, and the watchwoman sounding the alarm for clandestine worshippers draw attention to another important facet of the camp's history: the forced migration of the wives and children of relegated Kitawalists to the camp.

WOMEN AND CHILDREN

Women were in the camps since they were first built. A small number of them had been sentenced to relegation themselves, while others, like Goy Simbi's wife, had come to live with their husbands at the camps, seemingly of their own volition. By 1951, however, the colonial authorities had decided to make it official policy that the wives and young children of all male prisoners were to be brought to COLAGREL in order to create "normalcy" for the male inmates and relieve their "discomfort."[96] This policy ultimately proved to be quite controversial, eliciting a number of different reactions from both the women themselves and the camp administrators.

While some of these wives were no doubt happy to be reunited with their husbands and went willingly to the camps—even, as in the case of Goy Simbi's wife, attempting to smuggle forbidden goods into the camp—many were reluctant to be uprooted from their lives in their home territories and forced to move with their children to the relegation camps. Indeed, a number of them attempted to divorce their husbands in their absence rather than move to the camps. Frustrated by their unwillingness to comply, the colonial government threatened such women with thirty days in prison if they did not go to join their husbands. Many still refused to go, preferring the thirty-day prison sentence to an unspecified amount of time in the relegation camp. Ultimately, many were forced to go to the camps.[97]

It is difficult to discern from the archives either the motives of these women who refused to join their husbands or their impressions and experiences once they got to COLAGREL. To do so would require making unverifiable assumptions about their intimate lives and experiences. The truth is that we cannot know how these women, as individuals, felt about their husbands. Perhaps some did not care to be reunited with their Kitawalist husbands. Perhaps they did not approve of its teachings. Perhaps they were just afraid, for themselves and their children, about going to an unknown place. Or perhaps, like the mamas in the prayer chambers praying for their men in the camps, they simply felt that their labors—both physical and spiritual—were more productive outside the camp.

In 1957, one territorial administrator, Franz Cannon, reported that the women in the camp did not want to live with their husbands because "Kitawalism, which is for men a physical dictatorship, is also a physical dictatorship for the women (that is to say a practice of communism of wives)."[98] The source of his information was a group of spies and indigenous personnel who had been secretly employed by the camp administrators. These women, he argued, simply did not want to live under the "dictatorship" of their Kitawalist husbands who might force them to participate in the ritual sex acts he and other colonial officials believed happened within Kitawalist communities. For Cannon, the wives' resistance to join their husbands in the camp was just another piece of evidence illustrating the depravity of the Kitawalist men in the camps.

But other evidence contradicts such reports. Consider, for example, Matton's 1951 report of a woman who was sent to COLAGREL two months before the arrival of her husband (who was still in prison at Elizabethville). In the report, he describes her as "resistant from the start," regularly arriving late to the morning call and returning from the field before others. He complains that she "pretends to be sick but won't go to the dispensary," choosing instead to face punishment. The reason for her recalcitrance? She "wanted to be reunited with her husband."[99]

Similarly, when R. Philippart, a member of the colonial government's "team" of Kitawala experts, visited the camp as part of a special investigation of Kitawala 1956, he noted a phenomenon quite the opposite of that described by Cannon.[100] In many cases, he observed, it was the women who were exercising negative influence on their husbands. He reported that "through their mockery and their sarcasm, they have recast their husbands into the fatal orbit of active Kitawala." He quoted one woman's mockery of her husband as follows: "You are afraid. Are you not a man? I was married to a great pastor, but now I'm married to nobody. Everyone mocks me and I am ashamed."[101] Incidents like these—combined with reports of women joining their husbands in numerous other acts of resistance—really challenge the portrayal of women in the camps as all disgruntled to be there and passively under the thumbs of their "dictator" husbands. Instead, what emerges is a picture of women who were instrumental in "keeping the faith" for their absent or wavering husbands.

The children in the camps were likewise a concern for administrators like Philippart, who fretted that the children of Kitawalists, who had been relegated to the camp for five, ten, fifteen or more years, would leave the colonies having known nothing other than their family's relegation. Philippart warned that it was the sole experience animating their regard for the Belgians: "The most violent, the most profound, the most irreducible xenophobia inevitably animates them." He believed that the camps were "the best school of revolts and revolutionaries that one can possibly conceive."[102] And while the camp authorities had hoped that they would be able to use the school they built in the camp to indoctrinate children to abandon Kitawala, many of the Kitawalist parents, including Pastor Mulongo's father, refused to let their children go to the schools, knowing full well that the schools were a force of colonial propaganda.[103]

When I shared these stories from the archives with Pastor Mulongo and the Kitawalist women living in Kalemie and COLAGREL in 2018, they really resonated with them. Pastor Mulongo told me that, after I showed him the document in which the camp authorities described how they would use the schools to indoctrinate the children, he went home that night and found he could not sleep—not until he prayed to his father for forgiveness for having ever doubted his judgment in keeping him from the school. Apparently, he had harbored some resentment into his adult life about being kept from school, feeling like he had fallen behind. But the archives confirmed that his father was right to be suspicious of the motives of the camp authorities.

As for the account of the women "keeping the faith," Pastor Mulongo said, "You know it's true what you say. It is often the women who come to church and are most devoted to their faith. I think that power of the church really is in their hands."[104] Women in the camps exerted their own agency, for their own reasons. Undoubtedly, some of them did not want to be in the camps and resented being forced into them, most for reasons we will never truly know. But their presence in the camp was also powerful. And it was not defined exclusively by their relationships to their husbands: they also showed strength and solidarity in their relationships with each other. In one instance, for example, when four women were sentenced to detention in the prison for disobeying orders and refusing their work, the entire group of women working with them insisted that they too would go to prison.[105]

The sacrifices that women made in the camp are inextricable from the memory of the place—so much so that the most important annual religious event at the camp today is a ritual commemoration of the first woman to die at COLAGREL, Mama Saint Nkulu Kwamwanya Adolphine. Mama Adolphine, who had been arrested along with Kulu Mapenda's followers in Luseba, was among the first prisoners incarcerated at Malonga in 1936. In 1947, she was moved with the other prisoners to COLAGREL. She died there a year later, on March 22, 1948, of malaria. She was the first Kitawalist to die in the camp. According to Kitawalist tradition, she was given a "mission" at the time of her

FIGURE 5.7. The grave of Mama Saint Nkulu Kwamwanya Adolphine.

Relegation ⁓ 169

death to protect the people in the camp in her afterlife. Because of this, she is considered a saint within the church, and the day of her death is an important holy day—the Day of the Mamas.[106] On that day each year, Kitawalists throughout the region who have the means of transport come to COLAGREL to celebrate her memory. They have a service, feast, and sing and pray together. On the night between March 22 and 23, they sleep outside in the cemetery where she is buried, on the edge of the camp, to mourn and show reverence to her (see figure 5.7). There they bathe, eat, and have a special service where they read her biography. At this service the women in particular are given time to sing and pray and evoke her spirit so that she might bring their prayers to the other saints. They also use this occasion to clean and tend to the graves in the cemetery, which hold the bodies of all who perished in the camp.[107]

PAIN AND POWER

The annual veneration of Mama Adolphine speaks clearly to the history and memory of COLAGREL as a powerful space. Her grave is a sacred place where Kitawalist women and men can evoke the spirit of one of their ancestors, a saint who can carry their prayers to God. But evocation of COLAGREL as a powerful place has been part of its history since the beginning—since the prisoners were located at Malonga. That Kitawalists understood it as such is apparent in the rumors they circulated about it and the reputation it carried among them. When, for example, the protestors at Manono in 1940 declared that their ultimate plan was to march to Malonga, where they would rejoin their leaders and be free to practice their beliefs and freed from having to work for the colonizers, they were evoking an understanding of that space as imbued with precisely the kind of power the colonial government hoped to suppress with its creation.

And such understandings of relegation camps were not limited to Manono. Rumors about the power of the camp circulated throughout the region of eastern Congo. For example, another report from the northeastern territory of Bafwasende in 1948 indicates that Kitawalists in the region believed that "it is only when one goes to relegation that life begins." They preached that in the forests by the camps "a book will fall from heaven" which, once burned, will "turn blacks into whites."[108] Another report came from a colonial official named Marmitte, who, during an inspection of COLAGREL in 1949, found that Kitawalists living there had "retained their spirit of fanaticism and saw in the creation of the [camp] the material realization of their 'Kitawala Church' and did not ever want to leave."[109] He suggested that even the very nature of the buildings undermined the purpose of the camp, for the surveillance tower built on the grounds of the camp resembled

170 ~ *Violence and Power*

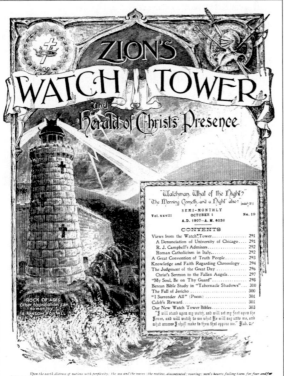

FIGURES 5.8 AND 5.9. A Watchtower pamphlet next to an image of the watch tower at COLAGREL.

the tower pictured on the front of Watchtower publications, further fueling the notion that the camp was destined to be a Kitawalist colony (see figures 5.8 and 5.9).

Each of these reports suggests that the camp took on a spiritual significance as a place of power, out of which a liberated or transformed Kitawalist community would emerge. Matton himself notes that for many it was a "point of honor" to be relegated to the camp.[110] Such signification was beyond the ability of colonial authorities to predict or control. Yet, as this chapter illustrates, they nonetheless tried in a myriad of ways, using both violence and coercion. And in some instances it worked: numerous prisoners did renounce Kitawala. At one point they even created a separate wing of the camp where "reformed" Kitawalists could live. Some were even sent home, after much hand-wringing among the officials about the truth of their renunciation.[111] Moreover, camp authorities were able to find prisoners within the camp willing to spy and report on their fellow Kitawalists. Not everyone in the camp retained their faith.

COLAGREL is a place that embodies pain and trauma—a phenomenon that is both inherent in Pastor Mulongo's stories and scattered throughout the archive. It is the kind of pain that brought an elderly man (one of the few remaining Kitawalist elders born in the camp) to stand before his fellow congregants, me, and his God nearly sixty years after the camp closed and testify that "the Belgians treated us like we were animals" in a voice heavy with the sorrow of that memory.[112] It is the kind of trauma that led many of the prisoners to remain living with each other even after their release, initially in a separate village they built nearby, but ultimately once again in the concrete and iron camp buildings their parents had been forced to build.[113] On the one hand, they had spent so long inside the camp that they had no other life to which they could return. On the other hand, they had forged a community in the context of their relegation. In the end, it was precisely the very oppressive nature of the camp—as the place where Kitawalists would undergo their most significant spiritual trials—that rendered it powerful to them. And the notion that something important and transformational happened there certainly endures in the moments when people meet there to recall and evoke its memory.

PART 3

Posts and Presents

6 ~ Posts

IN A fascinating study published in 1976, Congolese sociologist Mwene-Batende tells the story of the Belukela group of Kitawalists who, at that time, lived in a village known as Lubunga, on the outskirts of Kisangani. From 1959 to 1961, as Congo made its tumultuous transition to independence, the Belukela Kitawalists had become intimately involved in MNC-Lumumba party activism. They had joined the nationalist cause, Mwene-Batende explains, "in the hope to one day see the realization of the promises of total liberation and the arrival of the 'golden age' long awaited, when Kitawala would be officially recognized as the grand religion of the Blacks and adopted into the national agenda."[1] However, following the death of Lumumba, amid rising disillusionment with the results of independence, the Belukela followers decided to withdraw from mainstream society. Forswearing the amenities of the "modern world," in 1961 they created their enclave community in Lubunga. The move came after the leader of the group, Belukela Ismael, had a dream in which he was "called to effectively lead his group" into the new era, where they would be "entirely purged of the stains of this world." But, Mwene-Batende explains, Belukela was "uncertain" about the dream, so he "went the next day around midnight to the cemetery at Lubunga to interrogate his ancestors on the foundations of his vocation." The ancestral spirits "confirmed his dream and instructed him to first die spiritually and then be reborn in the new Kitawala." So, according to Belukela Kitawalist tradition, "he executed himself," was entombed for thirty minutes, and upon his resurrection was reborn with a "new spiritual force." After this rebirth, Belukela also proclaimed that Lumumba was a deity, "the super-human leader of all the Blacks."[2] Henceforth, Lumumba became the most important figure in the Belukela Kitawalist trinity, the subordinate two figures being Belukela and his wife, Marie.[3] They were not the only Kitawalists to elevate Lumumba in this way.

Around the same time, far to the southeast in the remote village of Muhanga, Paulo Kanumbi and his family (including PP2) began their journey back to their home in Kabalo. For five years they had been relegated to the village where they lived in a single-room house and tried, with much difficulty, to survive off fishing and farming. At the time of independence, they decided to return home, but it was an arduous journey. The government offered them no resources to make the trip and they had to walk the entire way along difficult roads. In the course of their journey, one of PP2's sisters, Elizabeth, died. They did not make it back home until 1961. Like Belukela and his community, they no doubt had hopes for a new, better future once they were freed from Belgian rule, but independence did not bring them the kind of freedom they desired. According to PP2, "the real time of being beaten was when [they] returned." By 1966, Paulo Kanumbi, his brother, and a number of leaders in their community were "arrested by Mobutu's officers" and "beaten from morning to night." Their crime: they had refused to participate in the census because his "father said that taking part in the census is forbidden by the Bible. Only God knows the number of people who live at any time."[4] This was not their last run-in with the Mobutu government.

Meanwhile, up in the northwestern province of Equateur, Kadiba Ilunga Émile left the prison at Ekafera on June 16, 1960. After his release he went to Kinshasa, where he began to rebuild his life and followers and founded a small *cité*. At the same time, 1,300 kilometers (800 mi.) away in COLAGREL, the newly freed prisoners began to leave the camp. Many of those whose homes were close enough returned to those homes. Others either lived too far away to return or felt their community was now at COLAGREL. But those who stayed did not remain in the prison camp. Instead, Pastor Mulongo explained, they built a new village of mud-brick houses nearby because the prison barracks were "a reminder of the time of colonialism."[5] They waited in their new village for eight years for Kadiba to find them there. Then, in 1968, Kadiba finally made his way back to the camp, where he found they had built him a house. He did not remain in the house but returned for long visits in 1972 and 1974. According to the tradition of his followers, during his visit in 1974, the Holy Spirit descended upon him with a prophecy. Then, in 1975, he was killed in a car crash and "went to heaven to complete his prophecy."[6] He was not the only Kitawalist leader to receive spiritual transmissions after independence.

POSTCOLONIAL ENTANGLEMENTS AND PROFOUND HISTORIES

In the years after independence, Kitawalists, like all former colonial subjects, endeavored to make sense of their place in a postcolonial world. The final decades of colonial rule had upended their lives and altered their families and communities in ways both large and small. As Mwene-Batende pointed out, for many Kitawalists, independence signaled the possible arrival of their prophesied "golden age," when they would be free to pursue their moral projects unencumbered. But as the three cases that opened this chapter make clear, there was nothing straightforward about navigating the turbulent social, political, and spiritual waters of the Congolese postcolony. Instead, Kitawalists were faced with difficult questions to answer about what their path forward could or should be and forced to contend with the relevance of their teachings in the aftermath of colonial rule. Yet, as the preceding chapters have demonstrated, the moral projects of Kitawalists were never limited to ending colonial rule. They were always at once broader and more intimate in their intended outcomes, and Kitawalist communities found many new—and not so new—avenues of spiritual and social action to pursue after independence. They also found some recognizable barriers to their pursuits.

The personal and communal histories that Kitawalists tell about the years since independence speak to important continuities and entanglements between the colonial and postcolonial eras. That such continuities and entanglements existed is hardly a novel observation about postcolonial history.[7] But it is a part of Kitawala's history that has been little explored in scholarship, and it encompasses stories that have been little heard outside of Kitawalist communities themselves. Their stories are valuable for these reasons alone. They are also valuable, however, for what they can teach us about what historian Wamba dia Wamba has called the "profound" history of Congo—that is, the register of history in which "spirits, ancestors and God intervene in human actions." Writing about the teachings of the religious movement Bundu dia Kongo, Wamba dia Wamba described the profound register of history—as explained to him by the Bundu dia Kongo prophet, Ne Muanda Nsemi—as one in which the "inspired and intuitive" historian "is capable of grasping and revealing the invisible and profound causes of events."[8] In this register of history, politicians both embody and come to fear prophetic power, spirits hand off empowered objects in jail cells, and the events of the material/secular world are inextricably tied to—and indeed given meaning through—the spiritual world.

For Kitawalists, and many other religious individuals and communities in Congo, this profound history is not an addendum to real history—it *is* history. Profound history is a theory of history in which the past lives in the present not just as memory but in forms of agentive spiritual power.[9] Such histories do not always respect chronological timelines. Instead, multiple pasts, exhibiting multiple kinds of agency, exist in dialectical relationship to the present and the future. Through these dialectics, Kitawalists, like other crafters of profound histories, "critically assesses the past in order to address the predicaments of the present."[10] They are everyday theorists of history and the nature of power within it. And it is for this reason that attention to the profound history of Kitawala in the postcolony is at the center of this chapter, where it exposes new facets of continuity and entanglement in Congolese history.

On another level, this chapter is about what happened to communities of Kitawalists during the transition to independence and the decades that followed. It touches on how they contended with the question of the morality of the state in the postcolonial context, drawing out important continuities they identified as they contended with the loss of Lumumba and the rise of Mobutu. It highlights some of the violence they faced under Mobutu and the consequences of that violence, bringing to light stories of an era of Congolese history that remains understudied. And it considers how such stories, when compared with the history of the Church of Simon Kimbangu during the same era, highlight the unevenness of the historiography of this era of Congolese history—an unevenness that is itself entangled in profound histories.

PRAYING TO LUMUMBA

On June 30, 2010, while most people in Congo were convening in city streets and squares to celebrate the fiftieth anniversary of Congo's independence with parades, speeches, and other festivities, I traveled to a remote little town called Swima, in the Fizi territory of South Kivu. I went there to meet with a group of contemporary Kitawalists. For reasons already discussed in chapter 1, this particular group of Kitawalists had, in the 1990s, changed its name to EDAC, or the Église du Dieu de nos ancêtres au Congo (the Church of the God of Our Ancestors in Congo). Within EDAC, June 30 is considered the most important day on the religious calendar. This is because they believe that it was for Congolese independence—indeed for the independence of all Black Africa—that Lumumba made the ultimate sacrifice with his life.

Coincidentally, the second most important day in their religious calendar is January 17, the day of Patrice Lumumba's assassination.

The celebration in Swima in 2010 was a three-day affair that gathered followers from throughout the region to celebrate services dedicated to Lumumba. Hundreds of them gathered, despite reports circulating that the militias hiding in the highlands were planning to descend upon the main road through the region. During those three days, people sang songs to Lumumba, gave sermons about his life, wore robes with "Praise Prophet Lumumba" printed on the back, and built altars and made sacrifices in his name.

For members of EDAC, like the members of Belukela Kitawalists in Kisangani, Lumumba is an unequivocally important sacred figure. He is not just a prophet; he is *the* prophet. As the leaders of EDAC explained it to me, Lumumba was the prophet of all "Black Africans"—in the same way that Jesus was the prophet of the White people, Moses was the prophet of the Israelites, and Mohammed was the prophet of the Muslims. He was sent to Africans by God to fight for their freedom from oppression, and it was through God that he was able to succeed; although just like Jesus, he ultimately had to sacrifice himself to do so. Indeed, it was precisely that sacrifice—his assassination—which played out in a Christlike drama of betrayal and martyrdom that rendered him newly powerful, and thus newly accessible through prayer and evocation. Lumumba's assassination delivered him into the realm of the ancestors, and in so doing, made him accessible to the people, like the members of EDAC, who would seek to call on his divine guidance to heal their communities of the various spiritual, economic, and political afflictions plaguing them.

The use of the image and name of Patrice Lumumba in contexts that portray him as a prophet and/or Christlike figure is by no means unique to EDAC. It is, in fact, a recurring theme in much of Congolese popular thought and culture, and one that has been discussed and explored by a number of scholars of the region. Looking at depictions of Lumumba in different regions of Congo, Bogumil Jewsiewicki has discussed how both Christian and local "cultural imaginations" offer the building blocks and "paradigm which enables the Lumumba of collective memory to be thought of as the Moses of the Congolese people, as an Anamongo cultural hero and as Christ."[11] Isabelle de Rezende has discussed the image of Patrice Lumumba as a charismatic religious icon, inspiring devotion, reappropriation, and reassembling.[12] Filip De Boeck has discussed the beliefs of Bundu dia Kongo, another Congolese religious group that reveres Lumumba as a prophet.[13] And Katrien Pype has noted that today the International Association of Young Lumumbists uses Christ metaphors when speaking about Lumumba. Its members believe that Lumumba's nationalist message needs to be consumed just like Christ's body.[14]

Perhaps most famously, the Christly figure of Lumumba is also a theme in Tshibumba Kanda Matululu's painted history of the DRC.[15] Bogumil Jewsiewicki has also written about the widespread popularity of Tshibumba's work throughout Congo, and the vision of Lumumba as a Christlike martyr it represents.[16] He writes that such "representation of Lumumba results from an effort to think of the collective self as a part of humanity that matters."[17] Congolese people accept the Christly image of Lumumba as a martyr because it renders them historically visible. As Jewsiewicki puts it, "Memory of Lumumba allows such a group to conceptualize itself as being, at a given time and in a given space, on a stage on which they have a central role to play."[18]

However, those who believe Patrice Lumumba was a prophet—and who pray for his spiritual agency in their lives—are not just claiming that they are important on the stage of history but also that the stage of history is bigger and more multifaceted than academic historians have traditionally acknowledged. It is a stage that includes profound history. And to pray to Lumumba is to seek to engage with power and the possibility inherent in a profound history in which Patrice Lumumba's assassination and transition to the ancestral plane marks a pivotal moment: the closing of one door in Lumumba's history and the opening of another. In that moment, Lumumba's power in the past became accessible in infinite presents through ritual evocation so that it might guide people successfully into the future.

Interestingly, in their own profound histories, it is not only after Lumumba's death that many Kitawalists consider invisible forms of agency to be central to his story and significance. Consider this history of Lumumba's efforts to secure Congo's independence as narrated to me by one of the leaders of EDAC, Amani Simbi, in 2010:

> You know, during the time of independence, Lumumba was asking for total independence. He asked for freedom of the body [*uhuru wa kimwili*], then he asked for freedom of the spirit [*uhuru wa kiroho*]. He also asked for economic freedom [*uhuru wa uchumi*]. The children of the country should enjoy the fruits of their labor themselves. Now, when he went [to Belgium], he did not want to practice the politics of secrecy and deception [*kuwa mfanya siasa wa kujificha*]. He said things openly. He went with ancestral things [*vitu vya asili*]; he went there with the religious things [*vitu vya dini*] his elders told him about. So, we believe that we must spread the

news of this church, for it is founded in his name, and in his actions before his death he implored us to do so. Now we have gradually come to see him as our prophet and savior. Even though he worked as a minister in the government, his true orientation was toward spiritual leadership: religion.[19]

According to EDAC, Lumumba's work was not just about political and economic liberation; it was about spiritual liberation. And he secured it not just through his political work but with the aid of "ancestral things" and "religious things" that came from the elders. To use Wamba dia Wamba's words, his "human actions" were made possible by "spirits, ancestors, and God."[20] And although he worked as a minister in the government, the true meaning of his work went much deeper than that, into the realm of the profound or the spiritual.

In another interview, Kabanga Kamalondo, who was head of the Kitawalist church further south in Kalemie in 2010 and a follower of prophet Kadiba Ilunga Émile, narrated a similar profound history of Lumumba:

> Lumumba was a Kitawalist. That power that he used to ask for independence came from Kitawala. To even desire to get rid of White people it was necessary for Lumumba to perform a miracle [*kufanya ajabu*]. You see, we have all learned about Lumumba since primary school. He was the one that got the Belgians out of Congo. But, if he had these words that could get rid of the Belgians, where did they come from? The others were at the Roundtable and they were not succeeding. Lumumba stayed back because he was finishing an evocation that would give him that power [*kifungo cha ile pouvoir*]. They said, "Lumumba is still back there, we must wait for him." And when he arrived, he arrived with that power [pouvoir] that came from the Kitawalists. That is when he asked for total independence. When he spoke over the radio, his voice emanated from bottles. Imagine: it was as if we were sitting here, and there was a bottle there, and his voice was coming out of it. It was that kind of power [pouvoir]. The White people were baffled and said, "We should go." And when they ran away to Brazzaville, many of them were dying, because the Congolese threw them out without pity [*waliwafukuza mubaya*].[21]

According to this history, Lumumba was not only a Kitawalist, but his very capacity to demand independence—a feat so implausible that it required "a miracle"—came from Kitawalists. In a ritual evocation, they transferred that power to him, and it gave him "the words" he needed to get rid of the Belgians. Here we have a story about Lumumba's success as a nationalist leader that suggests he could not have secured independence without the power that was quite literally given to him by the Kitawalists in a ritual evocation, in which they themselves would have called upon God and their ancestors to support him. And, in their telling, Lumumba came away from that exchange so empowered that his voice was emanating from bottles across Congo.

Stories like this are not empirically verifiable. There is certainly archival evidence demonstrating that in the final years of colonial rule Kitawalists did act in support of Lumumba's MNC party. In December 1959, for example, a Belgian settler in a rural district of Orientale reported that the region was "infested with Kitawalists" who held Lumumba as "their grand liberator" and were pressuring others into supporting his party.[22] However, I have seen no evidence that suggests Lumumba was, himself, in contact with Kitawalists. Although it is not impossible; as we know, Kitawalists were plotting against the colonial government in Kisangani in 1956. Yet, as with Luise White's vampire stories, verifiability is not really the point.[23] The point is that at the profound level of history, as explained by these different Kitawalists, Lumumba was and is embedded in a world infused with what Kabanga Kamalondo called "that kind of power." His life and death are given meaning by it, and the present and future are transformed through it. And taken together, these stories of praying to and for Lumumba challenge scholars to take seriously the epistemologies and profound histories of those to whom he was most beholden, and most beloved.

POWER UNDER MOBUTU

Stories about the Kitawalist affinity for Lumumba also raise questions about their place in postcolonial Congo after Mobutu seized control. Joseph-Désiré Mobutu was the military officer cum politician who served as president of Congo (Zaire) from 1965 to 1997. It was his Belgian- and American-backed coup that ultimately overturned Lumumba's democratically elected government. Mobutu was a complicated figure who endeavored to be both populist and autocrat. Drawing on Achille Mbembe's work, Emery Kalema has recently described Mobutu's political philosophy and mode of governance as a "politics of enmity," in which neutralization and annihilation of perceived enemies animated his attempts to "become the sole and undisputed master of the Congo."[24] Kalema contrasts this with Lumumba's "politics of life," which called for "peace, prosperity, and grandeur" for all the people of Congo. Kalema explains that Mobutu at once feared the legacy of Lumumba's nationalist "politics of life"—which could not effectively coexist with his politics of enmity—and tried to lay claim to it in the form of public monuments and rituals of remembrance. This precarious position left little room for profound histories of Lumumba's continued influence and other unruly ideas about the immorality of the secular state. As such, a number of different Kitawalist communities had a contentious, sometimes violent relationship with Mobutu's government. It was a relationship which was, itself, animated by rumors about profound sources of power.

Kitawalist animosity toward Mobutu's regime—and devotion to Lumumbist ideals—manifested early in his political career. Oral evidence suggests that many Kitawalists in northern Katanga joined the rebels in the Mulelist uprising of 1963. For example, the father of Kabanga Kamalondo, who was the head of the Kitawalist church in Kalemie, was a commander in Laurent Kabila's army.[25] While Kabanga was quick to point out that Kitawalists were not necessarily involved in the rebellion as a group—"church is church and politics is politics"—as individuals, many joined the rebellion, and they were rumored in some cases to have provided power to the rebels through prayer and ritual evocations.[26]

Interestingly, there are also examples to contradict Kabanga's assertion that Kitawalists did not join the rebellion as groups. In another part of northern Katanga, Kitawalists allied with rebel forces in a concerted effort to "regenerate society and purify it of elements, foreign and national, of westernization."[27] Writing of these Kitawalists, Guy Bernard suggests that their objectives "diverged profoundly from those of the political leaders of the rebellion," and the Kitawalists soon entered into conflict with them because of it. Ultimately, the Kitawalist leaders were massacred by the rebels and their followers dispersed as a result. Bernard concludes that "the liaison, though temporary, of Kitawala and the rebels demonstrates well that political and prophetic protest can unite in the postcolonial situation."[28]

Other Kitawalist communities exhibited their disapproval of Mobutu's rule in other ways. One common tactic was, like the Belukela group, to remove themselves from society and build enclave communities, where they endeavored to live outside of the state. In the 1970s in Equateur, for example, some Kitawalist communities withdrew deep into the forest, where they lived in isolation from Mobutu's state.[29] The few existing reports of such communities indicate that they lived in their forest communities in "excellent health" under their own authority and that they showed a particular attraction to the portrait of Patrice Lumumba.[30] Indeed, they refused to accept any national currency other than the old twenty-makuta notes that bore the likeness of Patrice Lumumba. Elsewhere, political scientist Michael Schatzberg has hypothesized that their "refusal to accept currency with Mobutu's portrait indicated a fear of exposing themselves to the magical powers of surveillance that the currency imparted to Mobutu."[31] This interpretation of Mobutu's portrait on the currency seems plausible, given Mobutu's infamous reputation for mixing spiritual power and state politics.[32] As Ellis and ter Haar document well, rumors that "Mobutu was in close contact with the most evil forces of the spirit world" were widespread during his rule, sometimes fed by his own ministers.[33] Moreover, the idea that money—like other objects—is "porous" and can be "a potential carrier of evil forces" that render it "unproductive, counter-productive, and eventually destructive" is not unique to Kitawalists, and is widespread in Central Africa.[34]

What is interesting about the Equateur example, when considered alongside histories of praying to and for Lumumba, is that the two cases seem to address the question of the relationship between the politically powerful and the profound source of their power from different directions. While Kitawalist claims about the origins of Lumumba's power suggest they see their own power, which was given to their ancestors by God, as central to the political history of Congo and the liberation of the Congolese people, their refusal of Mobutu currency suggests that they understood Mobutu's self-serving use of power and his politics of enmity as morally and politically reprehensible, not to mention dangerous to their prosperity. Yet both imply that the stage of history has a profound level, in which power has invisible facets that can be wielded toward political ends.

Mobutu was not unaware of Kitawalist animosity toward his regime. In fact, rumor had it that he was himself wary of their power, as well as that of the numerous other independent churches in newly independent Zaire. Over the course of my fieldwork in 2010, I heard rumors both of Mobutu imprisoning Kitawalists "because he knew they had power" and of Mobutu actively seeking to acquire their power.[35] Upon learning the topic of my research, the mother of a friend told me that she had known of the Kitawalists when she lived in Maniema. They were known to be powerful, she told me, and they had come into trouble with Mobutu. She remembered that in the 1980s, Mobutu had come to Maniema with the purpose of gathering sources of spiritual power—something he was rumored to do regularly in all the provinces—and the Kitawalists were one of the groups he had tried to consult.[36] The fact that, in 1971, Mobutu passed an ordinance under which seven hundred independent churches were denied civil status—leaving only the Catholic Church, the Greek Orthodox Church, and a handful of Protestant churches consolidated into a single organization, the Église du Christ au

Zaïre, with legal rights to exist—at the very least confirms he was concerned about his inability to control such groups. Under the politics of enmity, such avenues of dissent could not be tolerated. And in the profound version of that history told by my friend's mother, the unruliness of Kitawalists was defined, in part, by the power they possessed that Mobutu coveted for political ends.[37]

Nor did Kitawalists make a secret of their animosity toward Mobutu and his politics of enmity. For example, in one incident in 1979, a Kitawalist group in Manono reacted to Mobutuist incursions into their community by attacking the state's administrative offices and killing two soldiers.[38] Such accounts of Kitawalist violence against the state are rare, however. Much more common are reports of Kitawalists facing backlash from local representatives of the Mobutu government after refusing to follow laws that required them to show allegiance to the state through activities like participating in the census, paying taxes, or saluting the flag of Zaire.[39] Paulo Kanumbi's community was one such case. Recall that he and other leaders of Kitawala-Filadelfie were arrested after their refusal to participate in the census in 1966. They were also brutally beaten and kept in prison for at least two months. They faced subsequent arrests in 1970, '71, '72, and '73—each time for refusing, in various ways, to participate in the apparatus of state (refusing, for example, to attain identity cards).[40]

In our oral interviews, PP2 described how each time they were arrested the leaders of Kitawala-Filadelfie were subject to corporal punishment and torture, which led to the deaths of several members of their community. In one incident, PP2 explained how his father had his genitalia slammed in a door while under arrest. Among the most harrowing accounts of state excess told by PP2 is one that happened in 1980, when, according to him, the territorial administrators burned all their Kitawalist villages to the ground and then left them to live in them, with little access to food, shelter, or clothing, for two months. If they preferred to live without the conveniences of the modern world, they were told, then they could live like animals. PP2 described having to walk around naked during that time, with hardly a leaf to cover up. They began to wear raffia and animal skins. Ultimately, they were allowed to rebuild their communities when a priest—who PP2 described looking upon their community with tears streaming down his face—intervened on their behalf. PP2 did not mention any major incidents after 1980, but he did say it was only when Mobutu was finally ousted from office and replaced with Kabila, who "knew them," that they "could breathe."[41] To this day, PP2 and his community wear "raffia clothing" on special occasions as a reminder of this history.[42]

Kitawalist attempts at flight were not always successful, and the intense violence with which they were met by the Mobutu state—including arrest, torture, and death—reveals important continuities between the colonial and postcolonial eras in both the language people used to critique state authority and the state's use of violence to suppress challenges to its legitimacy. PP2 told Kitawala-Filadelfie's history of harassment under Mobutu with a mixture of regret and indignation for the troubles he, his family, and his community faced but also pride in the strength of their faith. Like the prisoners in COLAGREL, their endurance through violence—born not from aggression toward the state but from their decision to abstain from it—was believed to be a sign of the power of their community and the truth of the revelations his father had on the mountain in 1949. It is, itself, a kind of profound history in which the malevolent/eating power of the state, as embodied and exercised by Mobutu, is countered by the strengthening/healing power of God, as embodied and exercised by the Kitawalists.

The relationship between Kitawalist communities and the state in the postcolonial era, especially under Mobutu, has had consequences beyond their withdrawal from the larger Congolese social and political body and their periodic experiences of violence and harassment by the state. It has also shaped their relationship to public memory. That is, their estrangement from the state has largely placed them outside the institutions of public recognition and memorialization. The best way to illustrate this is to consider the postcolonial history of Kitawala in comparison to the postcolonial history of Kimbanguism. For some Kitawalists—and perhaps for Kimbanguists as well—this history also has a profound level.

KITAWALA, KIMBANGUISM, AND PUBLIC MEMORY

During the colonial era, the histories of Kimbanguism and Kitawala were entangled in a variety of ways, and shared much in common, including the history of their surveillance, detainment, and relegation under colonial law. For the colonial government, Kitawala and Kimbanguism were the two biggest pillars of the "subversive sect" problem, as they saw it. Moreover, as we have seen, it was a major fear of the colonial government, particularly in the postwar era as dispersive and penal relegation became more standard policy, that the two movements would, along with communism, unite into "a single vast nationalist movement."[43]

Their fears were not unfounded. As Ngoy Kyunga wa Nsungu established in his 2001 comparative study of the two movements, they shared much in common in both their doctrine and goals, particularly during the colonial era.[44] And Kitawalists did in some instances merge their teachings with those of Kimbanguism, and vice versa, finding clear affinities between them. This was particularly true among the relegated prisoners of Equateur, Orientale, and Kivu. Kitawalists and Kimbanguists often ended up relegated to the same penal camps—Ekafera, for example—or were placed in work camps in close proximity. This inevitably fueled cross-transmission. Even in COLAGREL, there was a faction of Kitawalist prisoners in the camp who identified with Kimbanguism.[45]

Simon Kimbangu, as a prophet, also often appeared in Kitawalist teachings, and entire new communities sprung out of profound histories about the connections between them. In Stanleyville, in 1958, for example, a movement called the Kintuadists emerged under the leadership of a woman named Sarah Ngeuketwa, who was the wife of a Protestant Baptist Missionary Society pastor and the daughter of a relégué stationed at Lowa named Kuyoka Antoine. These Kintuadists believed that Mutombo Stephan—the Katangese Kitawalist leader who sparked the massive wave of conversion in Lobutu between 1942 and 1944—had, in fact, been baptized and empowered by Simon Kimbangu while they were both prisoners at Elizabethville. They also believed that Kimbangu had appeared to the relégué community at Lowa in 1952 and spent a week with them, performing a number of miracles during his visit. Under the leadership of Sarah Ngeuketwa, they began to garner a reputation for healing—so much so that the colonial government fretted that they were "spreading medical contra-propaganda." The colonial officials in the region complained that "too many women" were "leaving their homes and their duties there to help at meetings" and "asking for divorces."[46]

The report is remarkable for a number of reasons, not least as evidence of a female-led religious community with ties to Kitawala and connections to Lowa—the very place where, just a decade earlier, young girls had reported abuse by Kitawalist pastors. The gaps in that history are tantalizing to be sure, if ultimately unknowable from the available sources. But it is not the only example of Kitawalists claiming that Simon Kimbangu appeared to them under miraculous circumstances. In 2018, PP2 told me a story about the connections between Kimbanguism and Kitawala. It is a fascinating account and worth reproducing at some length:

> At that time [colonial era] we prayed in the same place. When it reached 1950, Kimbangu died in prison in Katanga. In 1959, he was resurrected in Kisangani. He began to appear in the countryside. The government said, if you're really Kimbangu then show us your grave, so he left with guards and traveled by train to show them his

grave. Along the way, if they needed food, he would make it appear. He was always praying in the train car. When they left Kongolo, my father was in prison. When they got to Kabalo, Kimbangu disappeared from the train car. He appeared to my father in prison and gave him a "small thing" [*kakitu*]. Then he returned to the train car. Then he appeared in the countryside [outside Kabalo] and he walked on water for 25 meters. He washed himself. He applied oil. He prayed. But when the train started to leave the station, the guards went to check on him and he was there. When he arrived in Lubumbashi, the government began to follow him. He went to his grave [to show them it was empty] and there he disappeared and hasn't been seen again. When he left my father that thing, we [Kitawalists and Kimbanguists] were all praying in the same place. Where we differ from Kimbanguists is that when he disappeared, the Belgians had a "*politique nguvu*" [powerful politics] and they took one of his children to America. They made another the governor of a bank. And they put another child who had not gone to school in charge of their church. The one who had gone to Bulaya (the West), he came back in 1963/4 and said there is no more praying in the wilderness and that is when we split. Kimbangu left his children a tree and said when it falls, the power will be in Katanga. That is to say, the power is in Katanga. He was no longer the Simon Kimbangu of the Bakongo, he was now the Simon Kimbangu of the Baluba. In 1966, the tree fell. They tried to prop it up with ropes, but ultimately the power fell to Katanga. Why are the Kimbanguists known so much by the state? Because after the Belgians, they decided to get authorization from the state in the time of Mobutu. They no longer followed the doctrine of their father. They began a different doctrine.[47]

What becomes clear from PP2's account is that he understood Kimbanguism and Kitawala as movements that were connected from early on. In fact, later in the same interview he said that Simon Kimbangu had actually been baptized by Eliot Kamwana, arguing for a direct line of transmission, not unlike the Kintuadist story that Simon Kimbangu had baptized Mutombo Stephan. Simon Kimbangu is part of a profound history of eastern Congo and his history is entangled with that of Kitawala. He appeared in miraculous contexts, healing the sick in the case of Lowa and offering a powerful "thing" to PP2's imprisoned father in Kabalo. When I asked PP2 what the "thing" Kimbangu gave his father was, he said, "Dada Nicole, you are trying to test me. It wasn't a thing like an object, like this phone here. It was a word he gave him that gave him power." According to PP2, not only had he appeared to his father at a difficult time to give him that power, but he had, after his death, promised that a time would come when his power would transfer to Katanga—no longer Simon Kimbangu of the Bakongo, but henceforth Simon Kimbangu of the Baluba.

PP2 insisted that the Kimbanguists are aware of this history—indeed they tried to prevent it from coming to pass—and that they even invited him to meetings. But he did not go, because he saw the Kimbanguist church as too tied up in the politics of the what he called DEMONcratic Republic of Congo—his scathing moniker for the Congolese state. They were deceived by the Belgians with their "*politique nguvu*" and lost the way of their father, Kimbangu. The latter point matters as a reminder that, for PP2, it was ultimately the Belgian politics of trying to keep the two movements apart that caused the rift between them. If the Kimbanguists lost their way, it was because the Belgians coerced them into taking the wrong path—the path that would ultimately lead them to affiliation with the Mobutuist state.

PP2's profound history of the relationship between Kimbanguism, Kitawala, and the state also points to a possible answer to another question: Why is it that the history of Kimbanguism as an anticolonial and "authentically African" religious movement remains prevalent in the popular memory in Congo and widely published upon in academic circles, while Kitawala has mostly receded to the margins? PP2 seems to suggest that the reality stems in part from their different relationships with the Mobutuist state, which led them down alternate paths after independence. There is other evidence to support this suggestion.

That some of the leaders of the Kimbanguist Church had a cozy relationship with the Mobutuist state is well-known.[48] In *Dialectics of Oppression*, political scientist Michael Schatzberg suggested that the warm public relationship between the Kimbanguist Church and the Mobutuist state was mutually beneficial. It helped the Kimbanguist Church because it legitimized them as a religious institution at the same time it delegitimized other religious groups, with whom they were competing for influence. As discussed above, Mobutu's 1971 ordinance officially recognized only three major religions—Catholicism, Protestantism, and Kimbanguism—thereby rendering all other religious groups extralegal under the law. Schatzberg noted that "to gain official recognition, sects had to deposit Z 100,000 with the state, a condition that few could meet." Kimbanguists were pleased by this "because many sects were offshoots of [the Kimbanguist Church] and when they were banned, membership in the official Kimbanguist church rose markedly." Mobutu benefited from this close relationship with the Kimbanguist Church both because it bolstered his program of *authenticité* (by publicly supporting an indigenous church) and because supporting the Kimbanguist Church gave him a counterbalance to the influence of the Catholic Church, which by the early 1970s had an increasingly conflicted relationship with the regime. So close was the connection between the state and the Kimbanguist church that when Schatzberg published his study in 1988, he wrote that "the Kimbanguist Church has become, for the most part, a Mobutiste mouthpiece and one of the state's main ideological supports."[49]

To acknowledge this close relationship between the Kimbanguist Church and the Mobutiste state is not to somehow implicate the entire church in supporting the most devastating aspects of his dictatorial regime. Seeking recognition by Mobutu's government must be understood, in part, as an administrative expediency. They had similarly sought—and been granted in 1959—recognition by the colonial government to practice their faith and publicly organize their church. And Kimbanguists are not defined by the historical relationship between some of their leadership and the Mobutiste state. As with most religions, there is and has historically been a diversity of sometimes contradictory opinions and ideas about doctrine, praxis, and administration within the church. And as numerous scholars of Kimbanguism have pointed out, at the grassroots level (particularly in rural areas), it has often looked much different from the image promoted by official church doctrine.[50]

Moreover, as Pedro Monaville has demonstrated in his work on Congolese student activists in the era of decolonization, this kind of maneuver—in which different, but not wholly incompatible, visions for the future of Congo (Zaire) were counterpoised against each other by elevating one and suppressing another—was part of Mobutu's playbook. He was, as Monaville astutely observes, always trying to "neutralize subversive ideologies" and bring the Congolese "back within mental enclosures policed by religious institutions and the nation state."[51] He did this by playing with the language of revolution, authenticity, and cultural decolonization. His initiatives could be seductive, offering a vision of "authentic nationalism" that could elevate a "new African discourse about the world." And Congolese intellectuals and cultural leaders—from students and university faculty to Kimbanguist leaders—could and did mobilize Mobutu's initiatives to their own ends, using the "plasticity" of such concepts to make space for interpretations of authenticity that were not wholly in line with "immediate propaganda needs of the party state."[52] But on the flipside of that process was the violent repression of interpretations the state deemed incompatible with its projects. And Kitawala, with its critical interpretations of what self-rule meant and what it should look like, was not compatible.

There are also other possible reasons for Kimbanguism's larger growth and elevated public profile in comparison to Kitawala. For example, the regions in which Kitawala gained popularity have also not historically shared the kind of political, ethnic, and linguistic unity seen in Kikongo-speaking regions. The East is historically more fragmented. The Bakongo followers of Kimbangu are also geographically closer to what became the geopolitical center of the state: Kinshasa. Thus, there are what one might call differences in political and social infrastructure between the regions where each developed that made unity within the Kimbanguist Church more achievable. Similarly, since very early in its history, Kimbanguism has had a centralized holy city at Nkamba, which became the seat of church activity in 1956 and has contributed to the development of its orthodoxy and sense of shared identity.[53] No such unifying "holy city" exists for Kitawalists. And finally, there is the unifying figure of Kimbangu himself, who has been connected by many (and not just Kimbanguists) to a long line of Bakongo prophets dating back to the Kingdom of Kongo. One can imagine that for Kimbanguists—for whom Kimbangu's prophecies and teachings are truth—this is perhaps the most important explanation. Indeed, one might consider it a profound history in which Kimbanguism has grown into one of the largest independent churches on the continent of Africa because Kimbangu's prophecy was and is real.

Certainly, these are all important points to consider in comparing the postcolonial histories of Kitawala and Kimbanguism. Still, it is also true that institutional recognition by Mobutu's government mattered. It allowed Kimbanguism to exist and grow in a very public, and ultimately international, way. This allowed for significant growth within the church and made its social and political influence much more visible, allowing Kimbanguists, to some extent, to dominate the national narrative of religious oppression under colonial rule.[54] Mobutu did not give Kitawalists the same opportunity for official recognition. It is arguably in part for these reasons that Kimbanguism has come to dominate both public memory and scholarship about religious movements in Congolese history. There is a confluence between postcolonial politics and postcolonial memory at work, and whereas it has facilitated recognition and remembrance of Kimbanguism, it has done quite the opposite for Kitawala.

The end result of all the tension between Kitawalists and Mobutu was that they were pushed to the margins of the state. They were denied the institutional legitimacy and the public acceptance and visibility that

Kimbanguist leaders had cultivated. This had consequences for organization within the movement. On the eve of independence, both Kitawala and Kimbanguism were fractured movements—the result of years of illegality under the colonial government—and the varied local interpretations of each movement's teachings had made heterodoxy one of their defining features. As I have suggested above, institutional and political legitimacy allowed Kimbanguism to unify, at least to some extent, under one body of leadership.[55] While there was potential for Kitawalists to unify as well—perhaps under the leadership of the prophet Kadima Ilunga Émile in Katanga—they were never very successful in doing so. This is in part because of the very heterodoxy that has become apparent in this book: the unruliness of Kitawalist doctrine. But it must also be understood as partially a result of the politics I have just recounted: both of Mobutu, who appears to have considered them a threat and marginalized and harassed them accordingly, and of Kitawalists themselves, who rejected Mobutu's politics of enmity as evil. This, in turn, has obscured visibility of the postcolonial history of Kitawala and led to its comparative neglect in the historiography.

The study of the postcolonial history of religious groups such as Kitawala has something to teach us about the experience of living in eastern Congo under Mobutu. Mobutu took a number of measures to increase his legitimacy and create national unity early on in his presidency, including implementing populist policies like authenticité, trying to reappropriate Lumumba's legacy by declaring him a national hero, and nationalizing the mining industry. While he had some success, Mobutu's control of much of the country was, as Emizet Kisangani put it, "more apparent than real," and "the state had no control in eastern Congo."[56] From the time of the Simba Rebellion of 1964–66 to the Shaba Wars of 1977–78 and the First Congo War of 1996, which ultimately ousted Mobutu from office, the region had been a problem for him. Although he tried to use patronage politics to gain control of the region, his efforts were more successful at exacerbating ethnic rifts in regions like North and South Kivu (in ways that would have dire consequences in the recent conflicts in the region) than at securing any real control. The result was a state that was, as a consequence of its own fragility, highly intolerant of dissent and quick to use violence over seemingly minor infractions (like the refusal to salute the flag, participate in the census, or procure government IDs) because they undermined its authority in symbolically important ways. The stories of communities like Kitawalists add important texture to narratives of the region, which have tended to focus less on how people on the margins experienced and made sense of the state's intolerance of dissent and more on how Mobutu's shifting politics of ethnic inclusion and exclusion (namely of Rwandaphone peoples) during this era had long-term consequences for the peace and stability of the region. They remind us that there are many more stories to tell from the region.[57]

Though it was institutionally disfavored and disorganized under Mobutu, that did not ultimately deter the spread of Kitawala, which, when it was not in conflict with the state, continued to exist and grow just outside the state's view. Indeed, Kitawala grew notably in the 1970s and 1980s in some regions. It was, in fact, during this time that Kitawala first moved into South Kivu, one of the regions where I have worked closely with Kitawalists. But this raises the question that is at the heart of this chapter: Why did this religious movement, whose most widely recognized feature was its anticolonialism, continue to grow in the postcolonial period? Writing about Kalemie in 2007, the journalist Coleen Braeckman argued that the proliferation of Kitawalist churches in the region in recent years was a reflection of the "fundamental social breakdown as a result of the years of war."[58] Philip DeBoeck attributed it to a "synthetic nostalgia" for a time when such movements held a vision for a future that had not yet withered in the "grave of the post-colony."[59] Undoubtedly, such interpretations touch upon elements of the truth. It is, after all, true that religious groups have proliferated in moments when the state has shown the least capacity to create meaningful order, when it has willfully neglected that responsibility, or when conflict has created personal insecurity. Yet, these interpretations fail to move beyond the most functionalist explanations for this proliferation, and more importantly, they ignore the profound historical explanations that Kitawalists themselves value.

In the case of Kitawala, underneath this functionalist facade lies a profound history of power: how it has been transmitted, acquired, and, in some cases, abused; how it might be used to protect and heal; and how it has animated major events in Congolese history. It is a theory of history that weaves the past and present together in ways that are insightful, highlighting both the hope inherent in past visions for the future and the weight of their loss in the present. At the time of independence, Kitawalists prayed for Lumumba to imbue him with the life-giving, liberatory power of God and their ancestors, and today many of them pray to Lumumba in hopes of drawing on the power of his "politics of life." During the era of Mobutu, many of them endeavored to withdraw from the influence of the state, which they continued to experience as invasive, predatory, and evil. This era also led to Kitawala's estrangement from Kimbanguism after independence, as, in both the political and profound histories of the period, they took different paths.

This, in turn, has had long-term consequences for their position within public memory and, ultimately, historiography. It has positioned Kitawalists on the margins, but even from the margins, they offer important insights about the continuities between the colonial and postcolonial eras, as experienced by those who, for reasons based in both their faith and experience, remain unconvinced of the morality of the state. It is to the question of the morality of the state in the post-Mobutu era that the next chapter turns.

7 ~ Presents

ON APRIL 26, 2020, I received a disturbing piece of news: government soldiers had opened fire on PP2's Kitawalist community in Kabalo.[1] A vehicle full of soldiers had driven past their church and shot into an unarmed crowd of worshippers, injuring nine people.[2] In addition, soldiers beat and arrested other members of their community, including PP2 himself. The reason for this attack? They had refused to follow the Congolese government's recent COVID-19 ban on public gatherings.

That PP2 and his community refused to follow the COVID-19 guidelines was hardly surprising. As this book has made clear, PP2 and his community have had a long, tumultuous, and at times violent history with state authority—from the colonial era, through Mobutu's rule, and even into the 2010s, when (as this chapter will discuss) UNICEF and the Congolese state targeted them for intervention as polio vaccine refusers. As a result, they do not trust the state or its agents. But more than that, they believe it to be corrupt, immoral, and spiritually impure. PP2 often quipped that the country's name reveals it all: the "DEMONcratic" Republic of Congo.

In some ways, one can sympathize with the challenge that communities like PP2's pose to the government of the DRC, which struggles to assert legitimacy among many segments of its population.[3] To see such struggles as the failure of the Congolese state alone is to ignore the long and complicated history of colonialism, neoimperialism, and neoliberal capitalist extraction that has undermined the project of state-building in Congo. Nonetheless, the result is a fragile and disorganized state that has, too frequently, resorted to what Achille Mbembe has called the "necropolitics" of "state terror" in attempts to assert authority.[4] For examples of this, one need look no further than the 2018 election cycle, the lead-up to which was characterized by multiple incidents of state violence toward the electorate, and toward the opposition to the ruling party in particular, in the name of maintaining peace and order.[5]

Faced with the challenge of COVID-19, implementing public health measures to prevent the spread of such a terrible disease was a logical course of action. In a country where the health system was already overburdened and underfunded, a wide-scale outbreak threatened to leave many without care.[6] But such public health measures have also proven to be potentially risky, even deadly, when handled poorly.[7] In Congo—and many other parts of the world—such measures exacerbated the precarious economic position of much of the population, for whom stay-at-home orders and market speculation created new forms of insecurity, in particular by disrupting food supply chains and creating inflation.[8] But an equally great risk, and one which the incident with PP2's community exemplified, was that in their endeavors to prevent the disease, the Congolese government might "tether" itself to a long history of the state—in its varied iterations, from the colonial period to present—using violence to impose its will on populations perceived as troublesome or uncooperative.[9]

Given the history of their treatment by the government and the nature of their beliefs, PP2 and his community were never going to comply unquestioningly with COVID-19 restrictions on public gatherings. Moreover, COVID-19, although deadly and dangerous, was hardly the only or even most significant public health threat in the region at the time. PP2 and his community understood this. When I spoke with PP2 after the COVID-19 incident, he told me that the real risk for his community at that time was food insecurity, after recent flooding of the Lualaba River around Kabalo had destroyed many of their crops.[10] For PP2 and his community, the risk of not praying together for protection from these more immediate and tangible forms of hardship and insecurity was much higher than the risk of contracting COVID-19.

To point out all of this is not to suggest that if public health institutions, both national and international, could not immediately solve existing public health crises like flood damage or the endemic tropical disease burden, they should not have bothered trying to combat COVID-19. But it is a reminder that people like PP2 and his community were operating within matrixes of vulnerability that put them in the position of making difficult choices about which risks were more imminent threats to their own lives and livelihoods. And those lives and livelihoods have been unevenly shaped by their historical proximity to state power. Not everyone believes—nor have they been given reason to believe—in the good intentions of the state's interventions in their lives. This is as true in the United States as it is in Congo.[11] The continuously reiterative presents of such marginal communities are both haunted by and given profound meaning through their pasts.

REITERATIONS

This chapter is about reiterations and refusals. It is about how repetitive patterns have created compounding presents in which modes of violence are reproduced, fear and doubt are reinforced, and inequalities are perpetuated. But it is also about how marginalized communities, like that of PP2's, discern and interpret such patterns, contemplating their significance and considering how they should inform moral action in particular circumstances. More broadly, it is about the continued centrality of religion, religious institutions, and religious leadership to the sociopolitical landscape of Congo. Not only do such individuals, institutions, and ideologies wield significant moral authority, but they play a profound role in shaping and exposing relationships between the people and the state.[12]

Numerous scholars of Congo have observed the "enormously important role" religious networks, institutions, and leaders have had in the past and continue to play today in the region, particularly during and after the chaotic years of the First and Second Congo Wars.[13] Ayo Whetho and Ufo Okeke Uzodike, for example, have argued the influence of religious networks in Congo "may rival (or even surpass) that of the state."[14] Often such observations focus on the role of religious communities, especially the Catholic Church, in civil society, particularly as mediators in peace-building efforts or conflict transformation and as agents of development.[15] And others have pointed out that religious groups have served as networks through which disenchanted populations have challenged the legitimacy of the state, which in turn has led the "troubled" state to reveal its own weakness through the excessive use of violence to suppress their criticism.[16]

Such works have very clearly demonstrated that religious institutions, networks, and leaders have constituted a significant sociopolitical force in modern Congo. Building on these works, this chapter looks at how members of communities like PP2's, who purposely live on the margins, have articulated their notions of power and authority in relation to the post-Mobutu, neoliberal state. It argues for greater attention to how they center the spiritual in their conceptions of morality, peace, and power, and how such conceptions, in turn, have oriented and complicated their relationship not only to the state but to those outside their communities.

Though there are exceptions, most Kitawalist communities live in peace with the government today. If they do protest the state, they do it not through direct engagement with its representatives and policies but through disengagement with the state altogether. So, even if they are at peace with the government, they also endeavor to live largely outside its authority. They refuse the legitimacy of the state and its relevance and jurisdiction in their lives not by assembling in public spaces to express their discontent but by withdrawing from the state into remote, avowedly apolitical enclave communities and refusing to acknowledge mandates they find unjustified.[17] Their choice to live on the margins has sometimes led observers—whether scholars, journalists, or just other Congolese people—to consider Kitawalists and other marginal religious communities as "eccentric" anachronisms, mired in incomprehensible "traditions," and/or as largely irrelevant to the Congolese social and political landscape. Contrasted with the Catholic Church or Protestant churches, which often draw on international aid networks to offer social services, they are sometimes even regarded as predatory.[18]

However, as this book has endeavored to illustrate, Kitawalists are neither incomprehensible nor negligible. Like members of numerous other marginal religious groups in Congo, Kitawalists are rooted in particular histories and they have been shaped by—and have shaped—their political, social, and spiritual contexts in a myriad of ways. Although they may not wield the same influence as mainstream religious institutions like the Catholic Church, in aggregate such independent religious communities command an important place in Congolese society—both in the moments when they confront the state and in the moments when they attempt to avoid it. In many ways, they are no different from other religious communities. They grapple with the same questions of authority and morality, where they must decide how to reconcile the material and spiritual worlds and what actions such reconciliation demands. But they do so from a position of marginality—a position that has to some extent been dictated by the more unruly ideas about the relationship between religion and politics that they espouse: ideas that seek to subvert, transform, or escape the prevailing status quo.[19] And this position has historically left them particularly vulnerable to state violence.

By focusing on the kinds of protest Kitawalists and other marginal religious communities have engaged in during the post-Mobutu era of Congolese history, this chapter necessarily offers some insight into the current state of the state in Congo. But the critiques of the Congolese state articulated by such religious communities are not just about its weakness under a particular regime. They raise broader questions about the morality of the state's authority—about whether and in what form the state should exist and what it means to exercise authority in a moral way. They are about the nature and the spirit of authority: what it is, what it should be, and whether it is possible to build institutions of authority rooted in imaginaries other than the neoliberal capitalist state. They are theories of power and such theories are rooted in history, even as those who articulate them wield history as tool. This chapter, then, is about recognizing the history and continued significance of unruly forms of religious and political thought in Congo in the twenty-first century and contemplating both the nature of their appeal and its limits.

RELIGION, PROTEST, AND STATE VIOLENCE

In many ways, the experiences and actions of PP2 and his community in 2020 are not unique. As this book has endeavored to illustrate, religion broadly—and Kitawala specifically—has long served as a vehicle through which Congolese people have both interpreted and addressed the morality and actions of the government (both colonial and postcolonial), and the government has long sought ways to either harness or repress it. In recent years, there have been other high-profile cases of protest against the state led by religious groups, some of which have also resulted in state-sanctioned violence.

Bundu dia Kongo (BDK), a self-described politico-religious community that emerged in the far-western province of Bas-Kongo in the 1980s and has had a series of very violent encounters, is a good example. In their first violent encounter with the Congolese government in 2002, fourteen members of the BDK community were gunned down by government soldiers for demonstrating in favor of provincial autonomy for Bas-Congo. This was followed by another clash in June of 2006, in the lead-up to provincial elections, between BDK members and the state police that left thirteen BDK members dead. But the most violent incident happened in 2007, when members of BDK organized protests following alleged election fraud and the arrest of their leader, Ne Muanda Nsemi. The protests rapidly turned violent when government soldiers armed with rifles clashed with BDK members armed largely with sticks, stones, and other rudimentary weapons (if at all). In the course of the demonstration, perhaps a dozen government police officers were killed, but at least 104 members of BDK and bystanders were killed and many more were wounded. A clear case of excessive reactionary force, the state's handling of the protest was widely criticized in reports issued by human rights groups.[20]

In the wake of this deadly clash, the BDK responded with a "campaign of state defiance," in which they moved to effectively challenge state authority in the region, beginning with their strongholds in the districts of Luozi and Seke-Banza.[21] They set up roadblocks, took over government buildings, freed other BDK members from prison, and used threats and acts of violence to intimidate state officials. They even set up their own tribunals in which citizens accused of offenses to the Bakongo community and culture—including theft, witchcraft, and adultery—were subject to punishment for their crimes, including death in some cases. All of this would ultimately build up to another incredibly violent clash between BDK adherents and the state in early 2008. In this case, the initial confrontation (sparked when BDK protested the arrests of two of their members) led to only five deaths—one security officer and four BDK members. But in the weeks that followed, the government would label BDK a "terrorist organization," outlaw it, and deploy hundreds of security police to the region in what appeared to be an effort to systematically destroy the movement. Human Rights Watch estimated that these security forces killed over two hundred BDK members, summarily executing many and dumping their bodies in the Congo River. They also injured, arbitrarily arrested, and/or tortured hundreds, perhaps thousands, of other suspected dissidents and systematically destroyed BDK meeting and worship spaces known as *zikua*.[22] Given permission by the Kabila government to use state-sanctioned violence in the name of restoring security, these poorly monitored security forces committed massacres.

In another example, in December of 2013, followers of another popular Katangese prophet and politician named Mukungubila carried out a series of short-lived attacks in Kinshasa on the national airport, the national television station, and the military camp at Tshatshi. The purpose of the coup was, according to its executors, to free the Congolese people "from the slavery of the Rwandan" (i.e., then president Joseph Kabila).[23] Mukungubila and his followers believed that Kabila was secretly a Rwandan working against the interests of the Congolese people in favor of his Rwanda allies (a belief many of Kabila's detractors espoused). They saw Kabila's willingness to negotiate with the recently subdued M23 militia in North Kivu as proof of this alleged masquerade, and it sparked the attacks. In the wake of the attacks, the government arrested numerous followers of Mukungubila in Kinshasa and Lubumbashi, and Mukungubila himself fled to South Africa. Official government reports claim 103 deaths in the incident, but human rights reports place the death toll much higher, with perhaps as many as 250 more civilian deaths from retributive killings executed by the government in Katanga.[24]

Finally, in late 2017, religion again became the focal point of political struggle in Congo when, with the support of local bishops and Catholic priests, an organization of Congolese Catholic intellectuals known as the Lay Coordination Committee (CLC) organized a series of protests intended to pressure the government into respecting the constitution and organizing free and credible elections. At that time, the Kabila administration had already delayed elections for more than a year, and rumors were circulating that the president was investigating the possibility of changing the constitution in order to run for a third term. In the days leading up to the first protest, dozens of people—including Catholic priests, CLC members, opposition leaders, and other prodemocracy activists—were arrested by security forces in an attempt to stifle the growing support for the protest movement. On December 31, 2017, as thousands gathered peacefully to protest in front of Catholic churches across the country, they were greeted by the state police, who fired live bullets and tear gas into the crowds. Eight people were killed and dozens were injured. This protest was followed by two more on January 21 and February 25, 2018, which similarly resulted in violent suppression and at least ten more civilian deaths and many more injuries and arrests.[25]

There are some obvious differences between these cases in both scale and intent. The Catholic Church has been entwined with the politics of the state in Congo since its earliest appearance on the continent in the fifteenth century, and perhaps most notoriously so in the colonial era, when its collusion with Leopold and later the Belgian regime earned it a place within the "colonial trinity" of the state, the church, and the private business sector.[26] The Catholic Church likewise took a central role in the building of an independent Congo/Zaire, as the state leaned on its institutions (such as schools) to provide some stability in the midst of Congo's turbulent process of decolonization. But the church has also (reluctantly) risked its privileged position within the state to voice opposition to state corruption and oppression before. For example, protests similar to those of 2017 had been organized by the church in 1992, in the midst of calls for democratization and reform of Mobutu's deteriorating regime.[27] These protests similarly resulted in violent suppression by state police.

But the Catholic Church and its lay organizers have never denied the legitimacy of the state in the same manner as more marginal groups like BDK, Mukungubila and his followers, or Kitawalists. Mukungubila and his followers, for example, believe that the independence granted to the Congolese in 1960 by "Whites" was not a real independence and that Mukungubila, as a prophet and politician, must usher in a new, "real" independence. Their vision for remaking Congo involves a much more radical change in the established order than the CLC's calls for constitutional fidelity and electoral transparency.

Ne Muanda Nsemi and the BDK have likewise articulated a much more radical vision for reordering the state. The core objectives of their movement are as follows: (1) reuniting the Kongo Kingdom as a sovereign state built on Bakongo principles of power, authority, and governance; (2) training a new, more moral political class that would recognize and respect the spiritual dimension of their calling to serve the Kongo people; and (3) abandoning Western values (language, religion/Christianity, political culture) that have (in the opinion of BDK) served only to subordinate and enslave Bakongo/African people and revitalizing traditional Bakongo values and practices (religious, political, and scientific) in their place.[28] In practice, these objectives have manifested as a variety of attempts—both from within (through the formation of a political party) and outside (through protests like those of 2008) the democratic systems of Congo—to secure political representation and ultimately independence for Bakongo people from a Congolese state they believe has failed on multiple levels.

The failure of the state as the BDK see it is not an exclusively secular-political failure. Instead, they have imagined state failure on multiple levels that are connected to each other and rooted in a history of not only wrong political action but wrong spiritual action—particularly in the abandonment of ancestral spiritual traditions in favor of Christianity. Such understandings of the illegitimacy of the state are significant not only for how these groups perceive themselves but, for better or worse, how they are perceived by others. Their views are often considered quite controversial not just by the government but by the broader population of Congo, the overwhelming majority of whom identify with more mainstream forms of Christianity. For example, Ne Muanda Nsemi's assertion that Christianity is a religion of the colonizer that has been used to oppress Africans is not acceptable to many. In fact, the political scientist Denis Tull suggests that it hinders the group's appeal and drives away other potential allies from their political projects.[29]

Yet, the spiritual agendas of such groups are neither secondary to nor extricable from their political agendas. This is, arguably, an important part of their appeal. In his research on the role of churches in peace building and conflict resolution in eastern Congo, religious studies scholar Roger Alfani writes about how when people discuss what it means to achieve peace, they consistently express the view that in order for real peace to exist in the material world, it must also be secured in the spiritual world.[30] The one cannot exist without the other, for the two worlds are intertwined. This understanding of the relationship between the spiritual and the political has a very deep history within Congolese political and religious thought. If people do not always agree with every aspect of the views of figures like Ne Muanda Nsemi or Mukungubila on how to achieve such balance, many nonetheless seem to recognize and value the questions he asks, which consider the profound meaning behind events and processes in the material world. Although they may not agree with every aspect of their teachings, those teachings nonetheless push people to imagine what more radical change might look like. And they speak to a deep sense of loss at the cultural destruction perpetrated by colonialism and its political descendants.

Taken together these cases highlight the high stakes that such critiques of the moral character of the state in Congo continue to have, both in their capacity to inspire radical actions on the part of believers and in the fear and violent reaction they continue to evoke from a state that struggles to assert its moral legitimacy. It is a struggle that is only compounded by the high profile of such incidents, the reiterative patterns of which only further confirm the government's untrustworthiness to many who already doubted it. The consequences of these reiterations can be seen not only in moments of crisis, like in the above examples, but also in the reactions of these marginal communities to the more mundane public projects the government tries to implement, including in the domain of public health.

THE DEMONCRATIC REPUBLIC OF CONGO

In 2011, the government of the Democratic Republic of Congo decided, with the support of UNICEF, to push for universal vaccination against polio. In some parts of the country, particularly in what is today Tanganyika Province, government health workers encountered serious pushback from these efforts, as numerous local communities exhibited deep mistrust of their intentions. PP2 and his community, Kitawala-Filadelphie, were among them. In an article and short documentary produced by UNICEF detailing the story of PP2 (who they introduce as the "Elephant King") and his community in their interactions with health officials dealing with the vaccine, they present PP2 as a brave but cautious modernizer. PP2 is portrayed as UNICEF's great hope in a place where the road to universal vaccination is "strewn with magical pitfalls and biblical challenges" and "people act based on tradition and faith." "The Filadelphie process of reform may show potential," the UNICEF reporter wrote, "but it relies completely on the strength of the Elephant King; and he, in turn, risks permanently weakening his authority or even being thrown out of his role as leader." This is so, they tell their audience, because PP2 lives in a community divided, where the "Civilian Kitawala" are "more open to modernization," but the "Armed Kitawala" are "fundamentalists" who are "more likely to wear clothes made of raffia and to carry bows and arrows."[31]

This juxtaposition of "Civilian" and "Armed" Kitawalists recalls a much older juxtaposition, one that dates back to the colonial history of Kitawala: "Religious Kitawala" versus "Political Kitawala." Sixty years earlier, Belgian officials were also convinced that there were two kinds of Kitawala—a relatively benign "religious" Kitawala that might, with the appropriate use of development and propaganda, be rendered compatible with the state, and a more dangerous, "xenophobic" and "political" Kitawala that used "magic and superstition" to turn the Congolese against them and posed a grave threat to the colonial project.[32] The two contexts are decidedly different, but there are parallels. As a solution to vaccine hesitancy, the health workers with UNICEF proposed a much more nuanced approach than any the Belgian colonial government had ever managed. They emphasized dialogue with the community (led by Congolese health officials) and training community members to educate their peers (what they call the "Trojan Horse Strategy").[33] Yet, the shared principles of social engineering in the two contexts are notable.

It is hardly a novel observation that development projects today share an ideological and political heritage with those of the colonial period.[34] More pertinent to this chapter is the question of enduring representations and of histories articulated, but not addressed. Woven into UNICEF's account of triumph over "tradition and faith" are the layers of an unacknowledged history of state-sanctioned oppression and coercion—a history that has informed the interactions between Kitawalists and the state health officials at every level. Clearly exasperated by the constant incursion of the health officials, PP2 sardonically told them: "If they [the community] refuse you and you cannot agree with that, then you might as well take us all into a plane and throw us into the ocean. All your problems will be gone."[35] That PP2 imagined the endgame of state interference as violence is significant; for in that moment, he was evoking a long history in which that had been the case.

Guided by these experiences, the members of PP2's community expressed reservations about the intentions of the polio vaccine campaign, which they saw as suspiciously irrelevant in its aims: "These cases of polio you're talking about. Look around. You won't see even one. You could pass through five more villages and you still wouldn't see one. . . . But [the vaccine] won't stop our children's fevers. And they die."[36] Why was the government mounting an entire campaign to vaccinate for a disease their community was not experiencing, while the health challenges they *were* experiencing were ignored? The UNICEF reporter dismissed their attitude as a preference for "home brews and prayer," but it can more accurately be read as critical refusal.[37]

Such refusal is rooted in a communal ethic that has, since its earliest formation, cautioned its members against the moral intentions of the state. Recall the central teachings of Kitawala-Filadelfie that were revealed to PP2's father, Paulo Kanumbi, by the Holy Spirit in 1949: (1) from today, it is forbidden to enter into a political party, (2) it is forbidden to get vaccines, and (3) it is forbidden to pay taxes. Each of these restrictions was supported by a justifying Bible verse. As guiding teachings, these directives implored members of the community to live outside the regulation of the state in three key realms: politics, health, and wealth. They also undergirded the imperative for Kitawala-Filadelfie members to live in rural enclaves, removed from easy access or surveillance by the government. Members of the community were and are implored to abandon *mambo ya politiques* (political things) for *mambo ya mungu* (godly things). Kanumbi's revelations, as interpreted by him and his followers, called for a rural, agrarian life of peace.

Yet, the revelations are much more complicated than just three prohibitions. Members of Kitawala-Filadelfie have interpreted and reinterpreted these seemingly straightforward directives as guiding principles in a variety of circumstances. For example, when I met them in 2018, they were continuing to refuse government-issued IDs or to participate in any way in elections. They did not run for political offices and generally avoided interaction with government bureaucracy, choosing instead to live under their own system of authority. They also refused most development projects, emphasizing instead an imperative to do work within their own communities, without unsolicited aid from the outside. PP2 insisted that they were perfectly happy to learn about and adopt new technologies that may be useful, but that they had no interest in having NGOs do work for them.

UNICEF portrayed their community as one mired in "tradition and faith."[38] Yet, the irony is that the entire polio vaccine affair demonstrates that no such place exists. Instead, what the story revealed was an example of the creativity and discernment with which PP2 and his community debated and reinterpreted the meaning of his father's prophesies in the context of contemporary issues confronting them. There is space in their theology for exceptions, but the guiding principles push them to ask incisive and probing questions about the intentions and priorities of projects run by the government or NGOs.

The people I met at Kitawala-Filadelfie were not anticommunity. They emphasized the importance of living and working together in their teachings, and they lived these teachings by doing important works of charity in the surrounding communities. In particular, they made an effort to feed the prisoners, widows, and those in the hospitals who could not feed themselves. Their attention to prisoners was, in part, a kind of tithe meant to recall their own imprisonment by the state. They were also not anarchists. They believed in laws, particularly biblical laws that also guide the state: do not steal, do not murder/harm others, and so forth. And they even conceded jurisdiction to the state police in some serious matters such as murder. But they did have a particular ethics of power. And the state—which, as they saw it, ignored the spiritual imperatives of the moral exercise of power—was antithetical to it. PP2 named it the "République DEMONcratic du Congo" because the politics of the state were, in his view, extractive and abusive, revealing its evil and immorality.

REFUSALS

PP2's community is in some ways particular—a somewhat radical manifestation of Kitawala in the twenty-first century. Other Kitawalist communities, like those that trace their teachings to the prophet Kadiba Ilunga Émile, do participate in most basic civic functions, such as getting government IDs and registering their churches with the government. But the tendency to create nonstate enclaves of authority is not unique to Kitawala-Filadelfie. There are, for example, other Kitawalists living illegally in the forests of Equateur.[39] In a 2004 study of bonobos in Salonga National Park, researchers encountered a five- to seven-thousand-inhabitant village called Kitawala. At some point during the bonobo research project, the researchers had to abandon the bonobo survey because they were "threatened" by the Kitawalists.[40]

In 2016, a group of activists described as "Bitawala" (Kitawalists) allegedly held a protest on June 30—the anniversary of Congo's independence—in which they "unequivocally declared the end of the power of alias Joseph Kabila." According to the report—which was, itself, issued by followers of Mukungubila—these Kitawalists lowered the state flag, chanting, "The independence celebrated today is a false independence because it was granted in a malignant way by the White people. We are waiting for the true independence that will come to us from the Black man!" They then promised to come back to "demolish the office." In response, the government allegedly sent a "colonel" and "some soldiers" from Manono to investigate the incident. But the colonel "did not dare to come to the village of the so-called 'Bitawalas,' certainly out of fear." Two weeks later the Kitawalists allegedly came back to Ankoro to continue their protest, but were apprehended and whipped before being put in prison.[41]

The events described above are difficult to verify without further on-the-ground investigation in Ankoro, but they are certainly plausible. Kitawalists have lived in Ankoro since the colonial era, and it is not the first time Kitawalists in the regions around Manono have come into conflict with the government since independence.[42] The story also shares much in common with stories told by PP2 and other marginal religious communities in Congo.[43] Moreover, the fact that the events were reported by a different religious community—Mukungubila's followers—itself speaks, at the very least, to the reputation that the Kitawalists around Ankoro carried: they lived in an enclave "village," they were "feared" by government representatives, and they did not recognize the authority of the Congolese state (at the time governed by Kabila) as legitimate. It also speaks to the expectations that communities like the Kitawalists and Mukungubila's followers have about how the government will behave when confronted by such "truths": with fear, arrests, and violence.

For Mukungubila, the "prophecy" pronounced by these Kitawalists about the false independence served as evidence that his own similar teachings were truth—a truth recognized even by those outside his community. Regardless of whether one believes that "truth" or the account, the entire incident is an example of how reiterations (of state violence and negligence) have rendered such stories familiar to many people in Congo. This, in turn, functions to justify refusals—refusals to acknowledge the legitimacy of the state and refusals to participate. It also illustrates how the reiterations and refusals themselves become part of profound histories: histories that question not just the legitimacy or illegitimacy of the state as a political entity, but the very source of its power, which is presumed to have been procured in a malignant way from White people and not in a way predicted by God's prophets. Moreover, it seems to replay the recurring dialectic with the state, under colonial control or Mobutu, in which the government's crackdown on Kitawalists reveals the authorities' fear of the power legitimately derived from their faith and their leaders (via ancestors and ultimately from God).

Though these are perhaps marginal examples, one could argue that this form of protest—by abstention from state politics and/or by physically distancing communities from state oversight, to varying degrees—is quite common in Congolese history, and not just for Kitawalist communities. There are certainly other communities who choose to live in enclaves largely under the authority of their religious leaders, if not going to the same extreme of withdrawing entirely from the state. The Wamalkia wa Ubembe community[44] and the Bundu dia Kongo movement are two clear examples.[45]

Presents ~ 207

For Kitawalists, as for most of these communities, the decision to withdraw from state authority was and is spiritual. Peace and prosperity—balance—in this world can be achieved only through attention to the proper order in the spiritual realm. When this balance and proper order in the material and spiritual world is clearly not being assured by existing authorities, whether colonial, postcolonial, or customary, people in Central Africa have historically drawn on traditions of community-building and authority that do not necessarily center the state, but rather the restoration of balance through spiritual leadership.[46]

The state seeks, by its very nature, to place itself at the center of people's worlds—to monopolize authority and violence. It insists that abstention is a challenge to that authority. And it is. But for communities like that of PP2, and many other marginal religious communities, challenging the state's authority is a consequence of seeking to build a different, more spiritually attuned and balanced world, not the guiding motivation for their action. In most cases, such groups have sought to build enclaves of authority outside the state—or in a reimagined state—not necessarily to protest or challenge the existing state but to build a world free from its inefficiency and excess that recognizes and values the interconnectivity of the political and spiritual worlds and acknowledges that such a system of values has deep roots in tradition as they imagine it. In the process of doing so, they have often found themselves counterpoised to existing authorities.

Considering their histories gives us a more robust set of categories through which to interpret and understand Congo in the present. It helps us not only to make sense of how the actions and expectations of PP2 and his community were shaped by historical experiences and reiterations but also to recognize the perspectives of those in Congo who find figures like PP2 unsettling—whether because they see them as an impediment to development in Congo, and/or because they find their beliefs are un-Christian, backward-looking, evil, or just perplexing. To imagine such opinions to be solely the perspective of UNICEF reporters and colonizers is to ignore the opinions of many non-Kitawalists in Congo, both today and in the past. As I have traveled through Congo conducting research about Kitawala for the better part of decade, I have encountered a diversity of Congolese people harboring such notions of Kitawalists—as a nuisance, as naive "village" people clinging to an outdated nationalist politics (*wafanya wanationalistes*), as *walozi* (practitioners of witchcraft), or as just another of the burgeoning number of "cults" in Congo.

Kitawalists, like many of the other groups discussed in this chapter, have asked profound and relevant questions about the nature of authority—about what a world that refuses the domination of secularized Western institutions, and is built on values of spirituality attentive to Congolese culture as they define it, might look like. For many—perhaps even most—in Congo today, their answers are perhaps impractical: either too radical, too militant or conducive to conflict/violence, or too particular, unable to accommodate the diversity of lived experiences in Congo in the twenty-first century. Whatever one thinks of their vision, Kitawalists are not necessarily wrong about the state's failure to accommodate that same diversity. Thus, for many others, their questions are evocative, even appealing, and the answers they provide do at least acknowledge the pernicious problem of spiritual insecurity and its sources. As Wamba dia Wamba has argued, the philosophies of power and the "theories and practices of cultural change" articulated by these marginal communities constitute a sophisticated realm of Congolese knowledge production.[47] Radicalism, reform, refusal, prophesy—these are core aspects of Congolese history; and although they may often emerge and reside in the margins, from these very margins they ask people to consider what it might look like to make radical changes at the center or to build a community based in an ethic other than the neoliberal state.

Conclusion

Our Destination

AT ITS core, this study has endeavored to tell the stories of the people who have practiced, preached, transmitted, and transformed Kitawala. It has, above all, tried to center their profound histories—their ways of knowing and their theories of power, in both the past and present, situating them as thinkers and everyday theorists within Congo's intellectual history. What it has revealed in the process is the multiplicity—and the unruliness—of those histories, which defy easy categorization and illuminate varied and intersecting themes. It is a history of violence and healing, transmission and translation, tradition and Christianity, religion and politics, gender and sexuality, refusal and resistance. It is a history of all these things and what lies between. It sits in the uneasy tensions that their confluence has created at various moments in Congo's past.

In many ways, what emerges from these confluences is a history of how people have tried to parse similarity across space and time, not because the contexts they lived in were not changing but precisely because they were. In parsing similarities—between Christianity and asili, between bulozi and God's power, between demonic powers and the state, between violence and healing, between Kimbanguism and Kitawala, between Lumumba and Christ, across ethnic and linguistic lines, and so on—Kitawalists were seeking to make sense of precisely the changing social, political, economic, and spiritual forces they were encountering in their lives. Indeed, they were seeking to make sense of how Kitawala, as a set of ideas, might help them navigate those changes. And through the process of transmission, they were altering that set of ideas. They proposed visions of the future that grew out of their interpretations of the past and the presents they found themselves in, and in the process disturbed many who had alternate visions (and were often willing to use violence to impose those visions). This includes figures ranging from colonial authorities to customary patriarchal authorities to Mobutu to twenty-first-century public health officials. Situated within these dynamics, their stories reveal facets of eastern Congo's history that have been too little explored.

A SHRUNKEN HISTORIOGRAPHY

One of the consequences of a conflict as long, protracted, and devastating as that in eastern Congo is that it has had a way of becoming the refracting lens for scholarship about the region. The desire to understand and explain what went wrong becomes a kind of necessary teleology: conflict emerged in eastern Congo because a series of complex historical circumstances set it on that trajectory. A long history of regional migration; Belgian colonial policies of extraction coupled with its politics of division; Mobutu's shifting politics of ethnic patronage; global forces of colonialism and extractive capitalism; Cold War politics and the economic and political liberalization it left in its wake; and long a history of disputes over land tenure and resource access: these are just a few of the entangled circumstances frequently evoked to understand the conflict.[1] And they undoubtedly matter deeply because a nuanced understanding of the historical dynamics of the conflict is of immediate and dire consequence for the region. It does the important work of denaturalizing conflict—making it clear that there were multiple complex processes at work that have led eastern Congo down this path, and that those processes must be acknowledged and addressed to end the conflict. But it has also resulted in what might be called a shrunken historiography for the region: a narrowing of the kinds of stories that get told. It is a historiography that spends more time on exploring ways that people have parsed difference than it does on considering how they have parsed similarity.[2]

In his work on religious peace building in eastern Congo, Roger Alfani astutely observes that religious community constitutes an important space where people in eastern Congo try—not always successfully—to cultivate a perception of self and others beyond the confines of ethnicity. In doing so, they attempt to transcend conflict by imagining community broadly.[3] Mwene-Batende argued similarly that, prior to and during the 1944 uprising, one of the factors that made Kitawala appealing to many who became involved was that it proposed a mechanism of shared identity for people living in a region where immense economic and political upheaval—including migration and isolation from family and community—had left them searching for understandings of self and community that at once connected to and transcended the local.[4] This does not mean that their efforts at these kinds of "groupwork" were necessarily always successful.[5] As we have seen, in their attempts to enact new visions of community, Kitawalists faced multiple impediments. Some of those impediments came from sources like the colonial government, which found their attempts to parse similarity and solidarity across ethnic, linguistic, religious, and political lines threatening. But Kitawalists also faced impediments from other Congolese people, including not just those who were invested in maintaining existing orders of community and identity but also those who found the tactics Kitawalists sometimes used—including violence, sometimes directed toward vulnerable people—unsupportable. But it is precisely the complexity of this narrative that makes it a necessary addition to the historiography. It changes not just our understanding of the kinds of groupwork people have engaged in, in eastern Congo, but also our understanding of where and when Congolese people have engaged in concept-work—that is, the embodied, agentive work of conceptualization.

The history of Kitawala compels us to pay close attention to the processes by which people and ideas move and are transmitted, received, and transformed. Congo's intellectual history—and intellectual history in Africa more broadly—has tended to focus on the ideas and experiences of elite, urban, educated actors, whose "cosmopolitan imaginaries" and transnational connections shaped the visions of both the past and future that they crafted for themselves and their communities.[6] Sometimes those elite intellectuals conceived their communities narrowly (in ethnic, gendered, or classed terms) and sometimes they conceived them more broadly (in nationalist or Pan-Africanist terms).[7] Mostly, their histories have exposed the many ways that these different understandings of identity and "imagined community" have intersected and changed over time.[8] Together, such histories have revealed much about the mediums and mechanisms through which these elites and aspiring elites sought to transform both their selves and the worlds they lived in—whether they were *évolués* in inter- and postwar colonial capitals,[9] activist students at African universities from the 1950s to the 1970s,[10] or postcolonial African thinkers on subjects ranging from political theory, to theology, to history.[11]

Centering such forms of elite-making intellectual history and the urban spaces where it most often played out has revealed much about the "high political" history of Congo, deepening our understanding of the formation of

Congo's shifting political elites and their critics. It has also as made clear the importance of cosmopolitanism—or "worldedness"—as a category of African experience and aspiration.[12] Thinking about Kitawalists as intellectuals only broadens this historiography, by considering a community of thinkers who have historically been less urban, less elite, and less physically proximate to the centers of power in the colonial and the postcolonial states and the access to global networks such proximity facilitated.[13] Proximity to these centers and the media and institutions they granted access to must not be understood as the sole entry point to the cosmopolitan imagination, however. And neither should the cosmopolitan imagination and transnational impact be considered the most important markers of historical significance. Rather, we must make space for the histories of people who troubled such strategies of worldmaking, at once adopting some of their discourses and tactics and refusing some of their premises. We must look to histories of people who did not fit neatly into most commonly invoked identity binaries—peasant/évolué, radical/conservative, Christian/traditional.

Writing in a 1956 colonial report about the "political character of Kitawala," Jacques Gérard summarized the lives and aspirations of several Kitawalist men. He described the first, a man named Salamu, as "strong and intelligent and admired by all." But he was also illiterate; so, the "doors to power available to clerks" were "forever closed to him." Although he had tried working in the mines, he did not "possess the servile nature" to do that kind of work. The position of a chief or notable, which required "a certain level of ascendency," was likewise unavailable to him. Thus, "in the humble bush," Salamu became "a great pastor"—"a chief" who ran the group "with great strength" and represented well "a strong man with power." But, Gérard lamented, "in other circumstances, had he been more educated," he might have been "distinguished" in some manner: "able to command, to impose himself, to emerge from the masses." Instead, "Kitawala was the only lever within his reach." A second man, Asumani, was similarly intelligent—someone who ruled "by language and argument" and "beat the record in female conversion." He was literate and could give "good sermons" and "could fool even the 'experienced' functionary with his bag of tricks." But because he was not born into a powerful family, he could "never be an important notable."[14]

The tone of the short biographies is condescending—painting a picture of the men as "victims of modernity."[15] Bereft of the family prestige that could land them a position as a customary authority, or the access to education that could make them into évolués, their "remarkable" capacities—their "political spirits"—were wasted on Kitawala.[16] Unable to "emerge from the masses," they grasped at the "only lever" of authority within their reach. Gérard's underlying assumption was that such forms of authority—or indeed, power—could never, themselves, be the object of aspiration. He clearly struggled with the space they inhabited: they embodied forms of authority that were neither "customary" (chiefs and notables) nor colonial (educated, clerks): they were at once "remarkable" and also part of "the masses"; they were both illiterate "strong men" and readers/writers, guided "by language and argument"; and they recruited women into their ranks. From the colonial perspective, the existence of such an unruly space and those who inhabited it had to be pathologized.[17]

It is imperative that historians avoid reproducing that pathologization. Without minimizing the fact that the Belgian colonial government created systems of authority and prestige that purposely excluded individuals like Salamu and Asumani, we can nonetheless question the appeal of those systems. We can instead read Salamu's and Asumani's choices as a politics of refusal—of disinterest in participating in those systems and desire to dismantle them. Similarly, we can avoid assuming their aspirations and interpretations are either variations on ideas from elsewhere or forms of atavism. Rather, we can take their lead and refuse the binary. This is where the work of conceptual history comes in to play. Conceptual history implores us to observe not just the fact that the meanings of concepts shift over time, but that people shift them. They reconceptualize meanings in conversation with their understandings of the past, their observations about the present, and their imaginaries of the future. Older meanings are not fully dissolved, but neither are they fully replaced, and the space where that concept-work happens is itself often contested.

From that space, Kitawalists have imagined the world as they wanted to remake it: both universal and particular, global and vernacular. It is in that space where they have experimented with modes of action ranging from writing to ritual evocation to rebellion. As the histories of Kadima Émile Ilunga writing letters to Joseph Rutherford and President Roosevelt or Muyololo citing the Atlantic Charter in a prison camp reveal, Kitawalists have looked outward in their communications and aspirations. And they have cited texts—the Bible, Watchtower literature, human rights documents, colonial novels, and so on. But their aspirations have also been tethered to deeper histories and vernacular concepts. They have found answers to their moral and ethical queries by reading their ancestral theories of power against biblical theories of power and against their historical experiences. Without ever reading Foucault, they have developed theories about how the state functions as a conduit of power—and its limits. Without referencing

Marx, they have found language to critique neoliberal capitalist exploitation. Their theories have mobilized knowledge—about spiritual agency, about modes of transmission, about healing and violence, about body-spirit power, and about profound history—that come out of an intellectual tradition that was no less dynamic for being historically oral. They must not be treated with "epistemological 'disregard.'"[18]

Kitawalists sought to break with the past even as they sought to preserve and draw from it; they applied and adapted anew theories and practices of power they discerned from tradition and brought them into conversation with those they drew from elsewhere. The contradiction between being ya asili and Christian is only a contradiction if both are imagined as static and contained. As a recent Kitawalist email bulletin put it, Kitawala is both "an authentically African religion" and "derived from the Watchtower," constituting "a religious community in the DRC that is faithful to African culture."[19] The notion that scholars must choose between casting people like Kitawalists either as cosmopolitans looking toward the outside, dreaming of universalism and a break with the past, or as neotraditionalists, wittingly or unwittingly reproducing tradition in new clothes, is a false dichotomy. They theorized a world in which universalism and traditionalism were not considered opposites, where the universalism of Watchtower Christianity and the traditionalism of "African culture" as they interpreted it did not need to be in conflict. In the process, they were also redefining both. And it is in that process—and the kinds of intellectual, political, and spiritual work it entailed—that one finds the history of Kitawalist agency and knowledge production.

CENTERING CONCEPT-WORK

The lives of prophetic figures like Kadiba Ilunga Émile, Mutombo Stephan, Paulo Kanumbi, Kulu Mupenda, and Muyololo Kabila offer insight into concept-work as a central feature of Kitawala's history. As young men, educated at missions, disillusioned with colonial inequalities and searching for answers, they measured Kitawala's ideas against the world in which they lived, received divine transmission about how to teach their beliefs, and translated, debated, and shared their interpretations with those around them. But the history of Kitawala's transmission cannot be reduced to the activities of these men. It also involved Ngoie Marias, Maman Kalemas, and thousands of other unnamed women who sang, prayed, communed, and otherwise engaged Kitawala's ideas, enacting its relevance in the day-to-day lives of their families and communities, exploring its possibilities as a source of body-spirit power. Such women "trafficked in history, in boundary work, and in cultural products" in ways just as significant as men.[20] Like Kitawalist men, these women participated in acts of translation that brought Kitawala more fully into their conceptual world, altering that world in the process. They were at times the arbiters of "secret" knowledge and power within Kitawalist ritual technologies of healing, and it is important to consider what their claims to such knowledge reveal about the gendered nature of spiritual and therapeutic labor within the church. Paying attention to their ideas about the gendered nature of power offers crucial insights into the conceptual world through which Kitawalists have imagined agency in their own history.

That conceptual world involved theories of power rooted in a long history of healing practices and institutions in Central Africa. Some scholars have questioned whether healing remains a useful category for thinking about the African past, out of concern that the concept has been expanded so far as to encompass "the whole social field," occluding the possibility that "not everybody wants to be healed."[21] But such critiques minimize the nuance with which scholars of health and healing have endeavored to root the language of healing in specific linguistic and historical worlds, using methods like historical linguistics, archaeology, and oral history to reconstruct entire semantic and cultural fields around it, and revealing both continuities and innovations—and innovation as a continuity.[22] It is not that everything is healing; it is, rather, that health is rooted in a multidimensional field of human experience that includes religion, politics, natural environment, economy, and all the crises (human and natural) that can touch those fields.[23] In Central Africa, in particular, people developed conceptual vernaculars that linked those things, without necessarily dissolving them into each other. The interplay between them is the stuff of history.

Kitawalists engaged in concept-work in which the vernaculars they employed were rooted in idioms rich with the language of healing: the materials (minkisi and other power objects, powders and other miti, bodily fluids), the titles (*monganga,* mfumu), the ritual technologies (bathing, cutting, prayer chambers), and other semiotics of therapeutic power (dreams, prophecy, mountains).[24] Many did seek departure—to build the world anew, not to reconstruct what had been. But that does not mean the tools with which they sought to build it were entirely new as well. Such a read ignores the fact that many Kitawalists explicitly sought to recover powerful traditions they felt had been stolen from them, even as they sought departure, conversion, or transformation. More importantly, it minimizes the intellectual work that Kitawalists engaged in as they, themselves, debated and disagreed on these very issues.

Moreover, healing is just one conceptual pathway to understanding Kitawalist theories of power—one that has tendency to evoke a positive moral valence. As the history of the Lobutu-Masisi uprising illustrates, violence was just as much a part of their theories as healing.[25] While that violence was at times directed toward the colonial government, the colonial government was never the sole target of their moral judgments. Kitawalist violence was also put to work creating and enforcing boundaries within Congolese communities, creating a reality in which colonial violence was compounded. This was not only true in the case of the Lobutu-Masisi uprising but also in much less spectacular moments of Kitawala's history. Kitawala's unruliness was about anticolonial insurgency, but it was also about more subtle forms of Kitawalist innovation, revision, and subversion. It challenged, shaped, and sometimes violently transgressed norms in many communities that it touched. It brought some Congolese healing, but others harm. Its moral projects always had discontents.

Kitawala's history also exposes the little-known history of the system of penal—or "relegation"—camps that was built across Congo to detain and (attempt to) reeducate thousands of "religious dissidents" during the colonial era—particularly Kitawalists. In COLAGREL, Kitawalists employed repertoires of resistance and evoked theories of power the Belgian government could neither control nor suppress. They experienced and thought about their incarceration not just in terms of oppression, but in terms of transformation. Today the children of COLAGREL's prisoners live with both the traumatic memories of that history and the pride of having endured through it. Their community is forged in the memories of that period but not defined by them—even as they continue to live in the same camp where their parents were imprisoned.

Their history, like that of other contemporary Kitawalists, speaks to a history of continuities between the colonial and postcolonial eras. Such entanglements are defined by patterns of repetition—reiterations—that compound presents. In the face of such continuities, many Kitawalists have sought refuge in refusal—in enclave communities where they have attempted, with varying degrees of success, to evade the government. And they have kept profound histories that call on a past out of which a better future might be built. This book is not suggesting such strategies are solutions. Rather, it has sought to situate those strategies within the intellectual history of the region—to understand the desires that drive, the contingencies that frame, the violences that reverberate. As a history, it resides in the messiness, the unruliness of all these processes.

Notes

INTRODUCTION

1. The opening narrative that follows is a direct translation of Pastor Paul II's (hereafter PP2) words in parts, and a summary/paraphrase in other parts. PP2, interview with author, digital recording, Kabalo, August 28, 2018.
2. Throughout this study, I have capitalized both *Black* and *White* in all instances where they refer to the historically, politically, and socially constructed categories of racial identity, excepting when I quote documentary sources. On this issue, see Kwame Anthony Appiah, "The Case for Capitalizing the *B* in Black," *Atlantic*, June 18, 2020, https://www.theatlantic.com/ideas/archive/2020/06/time-to-capitalize-blackand-white/613159/; Nell Irvin Painter, "Why 'White' Should Be Capitalized, Too," *Washington Post*, July 22, 2020, https://www.washingtonpost.com/opinions/2020/07/22/why-white-should-be-capitalized/.
3. Most of the available studies are in French: Mwene-Batende, *Mouvements messianiques et protestation sociale: Le cas du Kitawala chez les Kumu du Zaïre* (Kinshasa: Faculté de théologie catholique, 1982); Mwene-Batende, "Le Kitawala dans l'évolution socio-politique récente: Cas du group Bulukela dans la ville de Kisangani," *Cahiers des religions africaines* 10, no. 19 (1976): 81–105; Maurice Lovens, *La révolte de Masisi-Lubutu: Congo belge, janvier–mai 1944* (Brussels: CEDAF, 1974); Gaston Mwene-Batende, "La sorcellerie comme pratique sociale des Kumu et l'opposition au Kitawala," 1979 (3111), in *Turner Collection on Religious Movements*, 5-04-007 (Birmingham, UK: Sely Oak Colleges Library, Study Centre for New Religious Movements in Primitive Societies, 1983), fiche 155; Jacques E. Gérard, *Les fondements syncrétiques du Kitawala* (Brussels: Centre de recherche et d'information socio-politiques, 1969); Jean-Pierre Paulus, "Le Kitawala au Congo belge (mouvement indigène à caractère politico-religieux)," 1956 (3213), in *Turner Collection on Religious Movements*, 5-04-007, fiche 173; Marc Spindler, "Le mouvement Kitawala en Afrique centrale," 1968 (1470), in *Turner Collection on Religious Movements*, 5-06-000, fiche 227; Jacques-Oscar Anyenyola Welo, "Le mouvement Kitawala en Republique du Zaire," 1972 (3104), in *Turner Collection on Religious Movements*, 5-04-007, fiche 153; Daniel Biebuyck, "La

société Kumu face au Kitawala," 1957 (3117), in *Turner Collection on Religious Movements*, 5-04-007, fiche 156; and Kikasa Kabazo, *Le début du mouvement Kitawala au Katanga-Shaba, 1923–1937* (Lubumbashi: Université nationale du Zaire, Faculté des lettres, 1972). There is also a novel about Kitawala, written by a Belgian colonizer: Léon Debertry, *Kitawala: Roman* (Elisabethville: Éditions essor du Congo, 1953). In Anglophone literature, see John Higginson, "Liberating the Captives: Independent Watchtower as an Avatar of Colonial Revolt in Southern Africa and Katanga, 1908–1941," *Journal of Social History* 26, no. 1 (1992): 55–80; and Dominic Pistor, "Developmental Colonialism and Kitawala Policy in 1950s Belgian Congo," in *Religion, Colonization and Decolonization in Congo, 1885–1960*, ed. Vincent Viaene, Bram Cleys, and Jan De Maeyer (Leuven: Leuven University Press, 2020), 261–84. Kitawala emerges in, but is not the focus of, several studies: Michael Schatzberg, *The Dialectics of Oppression in Zaire* (Bloomington: Indiana University Press, 1988); Terence Ranger, "Connexions between 'Primary Resistance' Movements and Modern Mass Nationalism in East and Central Africa," pt. 1, *Journal of African History* 9, no. 3 (1968): 437–53; Ranger, "Connexions," pt. 2, *Journal of African History* 9, no. 4 (1968): 631–41; and Nancy Rose Hunt, *A Nervous State: Violence, Remedies, and Reverie in Colonial Congo* (Durham, NC: Duke University Press, 2016). There is also one study in German: Hans-Jürgen Greschat, *Kitawala: Ursprung, Ausbreitung und Religion der Watch-Tower-Bewegung in Zentralafrika* (Marburg, Germany: N. G. Elwert, 1967).

4. Mwene-Batende, *Mouvements*.

5. Karen Fields, *Revival and Rebellion in Colonial Central Africa* (Princeton, NJ: Princeton University Press, 1985). See also David Gordon, *Invisible Agents: Spirits in Central African History* (Athens: Ohio University Press, 2012); and Sholto Cross, "The Watch Tower Movement in South Central Africa, 1908–1945" (PhD diss., University of Oxford, 1973).

6. Higginson, "Liberating the Captives."

7. Ese Ebake, interview with author, digital recording, Mboko, South Kivu, June 17, 2010. The other explanation for the name Kitawala holds that it was a derivation of Watchtower: *ki + tower*. See Higginson, "Liberating the Captives," 64. In fact, both of these explanations of its root meaning can be understood as "true." In a personal communication, Joshua Castillo offered a very interesting linguistic explanation: "This linguistic distinction in naming the movement likely had a class component; IIRC [if I recall correctly], Kitawala began as an africanization of ki + tower from watch tower. In terms of sociolinguistics, modifying sounds when borrowing from a high prestige language like English in Zambia is associated with lower education levels (basilectal variation), whereas maintaining sounds is associated with higher education levels and higher social class (acrolectal borrowing). This would make sense given what Higginson describes as the two groups' relationship to colonial rule, with the Kitower group more targeting (educated)

industrial workers, and the kitawala group aiming more for rural dwellers/ having a more radical, anti-government edge" (Castillo, personal communication, August 1, 2020). In fact, I am not convinced that the distinction between the two groups was ever so clear, but this explanation does help to illuminate why both "histories" of the name are significant and "true" for those who maintained them. The questions of transmission discussed in chapter 1 are relevant here. The naming of Kitawala is discussed further below.

8. Examples of people citing dawas or nkisi as central to their understanding of and attraction to Kitawala are numerous and are discussed at length in chapters 2 and 4.
9. See, for example, Pascal Boyer, *Religion Explained: The Evolutionary Origins of Religious Thought* (New York: Basic Books, 2001), 268. For a good summary of this debate within the field of religious studies, see the general introduction to Anita Maria Leopold and Jeppe Sinding Jensen, eds., *Syncretism in Religion: A Reader* (London: Routledge, 2004), 2–13. Like Roger Alfani, I also do not use the pejorative term *sect*. See Roger Alfani, *Religious Peacebuilding in the Democratic Republic of Congo* (New York: Peter Lang, 2019), 11.
10. Birgit Meyer, *Translating the Devil: Religion and Modernity among the Ewe in Ghana* (Trenton, NJ: Africa World Press, 1999). On the process of translating Christian concepts into the vernacular, see also Paul S. Landau, *The Realm of the Word: Language, Gender, and Christianity in a Southern African Kingdom* (Portsmouth, NH: Heinemann, 1995); Paul S. Landau, *Popular Politics in the History of South Africa, 1400–1948* (Cambridge: Cambridge University Press, 2010); and Walima Kalusa, "Christian Medical Discourse and Praxis on the Imperial Frontier: Explaining the Popularity of Missionary Medicine in Mwinilunga District, Zambia, 1906–1935," in *The Spiritual in the Secular: Missionaries and Knowledge about Africa*, ed. Patrick Harries and David Maxwell (Grand Rapids, MI: Eerdmans, 2007), 245–66.
11. On this, see Vicky Van Bockhaven, "Anioto: Leopard Men Killings and Institutional Dynamism in Northeast Congo, c. 1890–1940," *Journal of African History* 59, no. 1 (2018): 21–44.
12. Steven Feierman, "Colonizers, Colonized, and the Creation of Invisible Histories," in *Beyond the Cultural Turn: New Directions in the Study of Society and Culture*, ed. Victoria E. Bonnell and Lynn Hunt (Berkeley: University of California Press, 1999), 184–85, 208–9.
13. Florence Bernault, *Colonial Transactions: Imaginaries, Bodies, and Histories in Gabon* (Durham, NC: Duke University Press, 2019).
14. Higginson "Liberating the Captives," 60.
15. For a useful (if imperfect) discussion of Kitawalist beliefs vis-à-vis customary authority, see Gérard, *Les fondements syncrétiques*, 93–103.
16. The differences between Watchtower as practiced in Zambia and Kitawala in Congo are certainly discussed in this study, but they are not a central

theme. My inclination is to argue—given what is known about the history of Mwana Lesa in Zambia (discussed in chapter 2)—that the differences between Watchtower and Kitawala, particularly during the early years of its influence in the Copperbelt, should not be overexaggerated. The policy of legalization in the late colonial era in Rhodesia, which brought more direct influence from American Watchtower, led to more marked differences between the two movements/churches in the late colonial and postcolonial years. But even in that context, the works of Meyer, *Translating the Devil*, and Landau, *Realm of the Word*, suggest that a more nuanced understanding of translation of Watchtower concepts would dismantle any notion that Zambian Watchtower was somehow a more genuine conversion than Kitawala, or indeed that such terms are a useful way to think about conversion. As I have not done the fieldwork in Zambia necessary to do a more direct comparison, this is not an argument that is highlighted in this study.

17. Ilunga Wesele Joseph, interview with author, digital recording, Kitawala Mission, eighteen kilometers (11 mi.) outside of Kalemie, Katanga, DRC, November 11, 2010.
18. On the importance of performance and gesture in expression, see Yolanda Covington-Ward, *Gesture and Power: Religion, Nationalism, and Everyday Performance in Congo* (Durham, NC: Duke University Press, 2016), 4–17.
19. Kabanga Kamalondo, interview with author, digital recording, Kalemie, Katanga, DRC, October 18, 2010. The italics here signify the emphasis used in the original spoken word.
20. I refer here to Bernault's notion of "transaction." See Bernault, *Colonial Transactions*.
21. John Janzen explores this relationship between physicality and metaphor in the history of minkisi in Western Congo. See John M. Janzen, "Ideologies and Institutions in Precolonial Western Equatorial African Therapeutics," in *The Social Basis of Health and Healing*, ed. Steven Feierman and John M. Janzen (Berkeley: University of California Press, 1992), 203.
22. The major exceptions here are the instances where I am discussing the work other scholars have done around the concept of power, in which case I retain their terminology.
23. Axel Fleisch and Rhiannon Stephens, "Introduction: Theories and Methods of African Conceptual History," in *Doing Conceptual History in Africa*, ed. Axel Fleisch and Rhiannon Stephens (New York: Berghahn Books, 2016), 2–5.
24. Fleisch and Stephens, 3–5.
25. Fleisch and Stephens, 3–5.
26. Here I am building on a recent trend in historical scholarship in which "work" signals everyday forms of critical agency. See, for example, David L. Schoenbrun, *The Names of the Python: Belonging in East Africa, 900 to 1930* (Madison: University of Wisconsin Press, 2021), 3–13. Gillian Mathys has also recently begun an ERC project on the subject of "violence work" in the history of Congo.

27. The existence of a Central African tradition, rooted in a shared conceptual world but characterized throughout history by the dynamism of its institutions, has been established by numerous scholars of the region. See, for example, Jan Vansina, *Paths in the Rainforests: Toward a History of Political Tradition in Equatorial Africa* (Madison: University of Wisconsin Press, 1990); Gordon, *Invisible Agents,* 9; and Van Bockhaven, "Anioto."
28. David Lee Schoenbrun, *A Green Place, a Good Place: Agrarian Change, Gender, and Social Identity in the Great Lakes Region to the 15th Century* (Portsmouth, NH: Heinemann, 1998), 12.
29. Schoenbrun, 13.
30. See Feierman, "Colonizers, Colonized," 190; Iris Berger, *Religion and Resistance: East African Kingdoms in the Precolonial Period* (Tervuren, Belgium: Musée royal de l'Afrique centrale, 1981), 22–24; and Neil Kodesh, *Beyond the Royal Gaze: Clanship and Public Healing in Buganda* (Charlottesville: University of Virginia Press, 2010).
31. Schoenbrun, *Names of the Python,* 3–13.
32. See Vansina, *Paths in the Rainforests.*
33. Schoenbrun, *Names of the Python.*
34. Kabanga Kamalondo, interview with author, digital recording, Kalemie, Katanga, DRC, October 18, 2010. See chapter 2.
35. Wyatt MacGaffey, *Kongo Political Culture: The Conceptual Challenge of the Particular* (Bloomington: Indiana University Press, 2000), 2; Simon Bockie, *Death and the Invisible Powers: The World of Kongo Belief* (Bloomington: Indiana University Press, 1993), 47. Bernault also makes this point. See Florence Bernault, "Body, Power and Sacrifice in Equatorial Africa," *Journal of African History* 47, no. 2 (2006): 208.
36. For an in-depth linguistic discussion of *-bwanga,* as it is defined in Kilbua, see E. Van Avermaet and Benoit Mbuya, *Dictionnaire kiluba-français* (Tervuren, Belgium: Museé royal du Congo belge, 1954), 24–27. See also Gérard, *Les fondements syncrétiques.*
37. MacGaffey, *Kongo Political Culture,* 12.
38. Michael G. Schatzberg, *Political Legitimacy in Middle Africa: Father, Family, Food* (Bloomington: Indiana University Press, 2001); Stephen Ellis and Gerrie ter Haar, *Worlds of Power: Religious Thought and Political Practice in Africa* (New York: Oxford University Press, 2004).
39. Joseph Tonda, *Le souverain modern: Le corps du pouvoir en Afrique centrale (Congo, Gabon)* (Paris: Karthala, 2005); Joseph Tonda, *L'impérialisme postcolonial: Critique de la société des éblouissements* (Paris: Karthala, 2015); Peter Geschiere, *Witchcraft, Intimacy and Trust: Africa in Comparison* (Chicago: University of Chicago Press, 2013); Peter Geschiere, *The Modernity of Witchcraft: Politics and the Occult in Postcolonial Africa* (Charlottesville: University of Virginia Press, 1997).
40. Gordon, *Invisible Agents,* 4.
41. Janzen, "Ideologies and Institutions."

42. Florence Bernault, "Aesthetics of Acquisition: Notes on the Transactional Life of Persons and Things in Gabon," *Comparative Studies in Society and History* 57, no. 3 (2015): 753–79.
43. Bernault, *Colonial Transactions.* See also Bernault, "Aesthetics of Acquisition."
44. See the introduction in Osumaka Likaka, *Naming Colonialism: History and Collective Memory in the Congo 1870–1960* (Madison: University of Wisconsin Press, 2009), 3–20.
45. *Dictionnaire Cilubà-Française,* Ciyèm, Research Center for African Languages and Cultures, University of Gent, https://ciyem.ugent.be/index.php?qi=10813.
46. Daniel R. Magaziner, *The Law and the Prophets: Black Consciousness in South Africa, 1968–1977* (Athens: Ohio University Press, 2010), 6.
47. Derek R. Peterson, *Ethnic Patriotism and the East African Revival: A History of Dissent, c. 1935–1972* (Cambridge: Cambridge University Press, 2012), 281.
48. Sadaf Jaffer, "Women's Autobiography in Islamic Societies: Towards a Feminist Intellectual History," *Journal of Women's History* 25, no. 2 (2013): 159.
49. Wyatt MacGaffey once described Kitawala as "not a church at all but a movement loosely identified by certain symbols and myths." Wyatt MacGaffey, "Religion, Class, and Social Pluralism in Zaire," *Canadian Journal of African Studies* 24, no. 2 (1990): 262.
50. Steven Feierman, *Peasant Intellectuals: Anthropology and History in Tanzania* (Madison: University of Wisconsin Press, 1990), 18.
51. On the "shrunken milieu," see Hunt, *Nervous State,* 2.
52. Adam Hochschild, *King Leopold's Ghost: A Story of Greed, Terror, and Heroism in Colonial Africa* (Boston: Houghton Mifflin, 1999); Hunt, *Nervous State.*
53. As a wide body of literature has illustrated, the instability in eastern Congo can by no means be reduced to a story of "mineral conflict." It is a highly complicated history of disputes over political representation, land tenure, migration, autochthony and citizenship, and a number of other issues. But it is also situated in a long history of both colonial and postcolonial extraction from the region and competition over mineral wealth—and other resources—is deeply entangled with those other issues. For good accounts of the history of the conflict in eastern Congo, see, for example, Emizet F. Kisangani, *Civil Wars in the Democratic Republic of Congo 1960–2010* (Boulder, CO: Lynne Rienner, 2012); Thomas Turner, *The Congo Wars: Conflict, Myth and Reality* (London: Zed Books, 2007); Filip Reyntjens, *The Great African War: Congo and Regional Geopolitics, 1996–2006* (Cambridge: Cambridge University Press, 2009); Gérard Prunier, *Africa's World War: Congo, the Rwandan Genocide, and the Making of a Continental Catastrophe* (Oxford: Oxford University Press, 2009); Séverine Autesserre, *The Trouble with the Congo: Local Violence and the Failure of International Peacebuilding* (Cambridge: Cambridge University Press, 2010); and Jason Stearns, *Dancing in the Glory of Monsters: The Collapse of the Congo and the Great War of Africa* (New York: PublicAffairs, 2011).

54. Kisangani, *Civil Wars*.
55. Hunt, *Nervous State*, 3.
56. A notable attempt to move beyond this narrative is Gillian Mathys' forthcoming book on histories of connection across the Congo-Rwanda border. Mathys, *Conflict and Connection: Making Histories in the Lake Kivu Region* (Oxford University Press, forthcoming).
57. Hunt, *Nervous State*, 4.
58. On refusal, see Ana Aparicio et al., introduction to *Ethnographic Refusals, Unruly Latinidades*, ed. Alex E. Chavéz and Gina Pérez (Albuquerque: University of New Mexico Press, 2022).
59. Steve Biko, *I Write What I Like: A Selection of His Writings*, ed. Aelred Stubbs (New York: Harper & Row, 1978); Frantz Fanon, *The Wretched of the Earth* (New York: Grove Press, 1965).
60. Aparicio et al., introduction, xx.
61. Some classic examples of this are Terence Ranger, "Connexions," pts. 1 and 2; and Robert I. Rotberg, *The Rise of Nationalism in Central Africa: The Making of Malawi and Zambia, 1873–1964* (Cambridge, MA: Harvard University Press, 1965), 56. See also Cross, "Watchtower Movement." Ranger later revised his stance on whether movements like Kitawala constituted "protonationalist" resistance movements, but the general impression of Kitawala as "resistance" endures. Terence O. Ranger, "Religious Movements and Politics in Sub-Saharan Africa," *African Studies Review* 29, no. 2 (1986): 3.
62. R. Philippart, "Contributions à l'étude du Kitawala," 1954, dossier no. 4737, 26, Affaires indigènes Series, Archives africaines, Ministère belge d'affaires étrangères, Brussels; "September 9, 1956," trans. Albert Van den Eynde, Archief Karel Van den Eynde (1926–2008). On Belgian debates about this subject, see Pistor, "Developmental Colonialism."
63. I borrow the term *moral projects* here from Derek R. Peterson, "The Intellectual Lives of Mau Mau Detainees," *Journal of African History* 49, no. 1 (2008): 75.
64. Aparicio et al., introduction, xxvii.
65. I use quotes around "ethnographic" because I employ the term cautiously, with an eye to self-reflection (below). The "ethnographic" work I did in Congo—by which I mean general observation and interaction, beyond oral interviews, within the communities where I worked—was far less systematic and theoretically grounded than the word perhaps implies. Nancy Hunt makes the distinction between "ethnography proper" and "parachute ethnography," where one moves in and out of a context. Out of unfortunate necessity—rooted in the many challenges of travel in eastern Congo—my fieldwork more often resembled the latter. Hunt, *Nervous State*, 238.
66. I was also able to fruitfully consult the personal archive of at least one colonial official—Karel Van den Eynde—thanks to the proactive work of his son, Albert Van den Eynde, who contacted me after reading a blogpost I wrote about the COLAGREL prison camp featured in chapter 5. The

entire incident is an important reminder that public history writing is a worthwhile endeavor that can and does lead to important research connections. Thanks also to Miles Larmer for inviting me to write the blog post as part of the *Comparing the Copperbelt* project: Nicole Eggers, "Remembering COLAGREL: Space, Memory, and Oral History," *Comparing the Copperbelt* (blog), November 19, 2019, https://copperbelt.history.ox.ac.uk/2019/11/19/remembering-colagrel-space-memory-and-oral-history-nicole-eggers/.

67. The iconic example of this is the Mau Mau files in Britain. David M. Anderson, "Mau Mau in the High Court and the 'Lost' British Empire Archives: Colonial Conspiracy or Bureaucratic Bungle?," *Journal of Imperial and Commonwealth History* 39, no. 5 (2011): 699–716.

68. Between 2011 and 2016 (the two longest periods of archival work for this project), at the Archives africaines, I went from only being able to take handwritten notes on a particular (and particularly crucial) collection of files—known as the Gouvernement Générale (GG) files—to being able to take photo copies only of permitted files (the basis of permission was unclear). Although decidedly more (highly critical) GG files were made available to me in 2016, other files continued to be off limits altogether. The cost of copies in the archive, it should be noted, was high enough at thirty (euro) cents per page to be prohibitive for me as a grad student / new professor. This prohibitiveness is surely only compounded for historians coming from institutions—namely in Congo—with fewer resources.

It should also be noted that since I worked in the archives in 2016, a number of previously classified files have been released, some of which undoubtedly pertain to the history of Kitawala. I regret being unable to consult them. On this issue in Belgium in particular, see Gillian Mathys and Sarah van Beurden, "II.—Archives," in Chambre des représentants de belgique, DOC 55 1462/002, October 2021, pp. 356–58, https://www.dekamer.be/FLWB/PDF/55/1462/55K1462002.pdf.

69. Michel-Rolph Trouillot, *Silencing the Past: Power and the Production of History* (Boston: Beacon Press, 2015).

70. Marisa J. Fuentes, *Dispossessed Lives: Enslaved Women, Violence, and the Archive* (Philadelphia: University of Pennsylvania Press, 2016).

71. Bernault, *Colonial Transactions*, 18–20.

72. Many have rightly pointed out that Europeans and Africans were not discrete categories of actors operating in separate spheres. Hunt, for example, has highlighted the "nearness" of the colonial state. And Bernault has emphasized how, in the colonial context, Africans and Europeans "transacted" with each other in shared spaces with "congruent imaginaries." Such points are important and build on the work of scholars like Anna Stoler who insist it is also important to read "along the archival grain." This book does not refute these arguments; it is simply more interested in centering Kitawalist actors and interpretations. Hunt, *Nervous State;* Ann Laura Stoler, *Along the*

Archival Grain (Princeton, NJ: Princeton University Press, 2010); Bernault, *Colonial Transactions*.

73. Karin Barber, "Introduction: Hidden Innovators in Africa," in *Africa's Hidden Histories: Everyday Literacy and Making the Self*, ed. Karin Barber (Bloomington: Indiana University Press, 2006), 1.

74. A plan for a 2016 period of fieldwork was thwarted by the politics of visa allocation. The United States and Congo were in the midst of a moment of tension—related to upcoming elections in Congo—that put the allocation of Congolese visas to Americans on hold for several months at the precise moment I needed one. Such visa politics, it should be noted, are an obstacle that researchers coming from Africa to the United States or Europe are infinitely more likely to face.

75. The latter three provinces were still collectively part of Katanga Province in earlier periods of research. I also spent time in Kinshasa, but did not do oral research there.

76. On this earlier notion of oral history, see Jan Vansina, *Oral Tradition: A Study in Historical Methodology*, trans. H. M. Wright (London: Routledge and Kegan Paul, 1965). Vansina later revised this method in *Oral Tradition as History* (Madison: University of Wisconsin Press, 1985).

77. See Luise White, Stephen F. Miescher, and David William Cohen, eds., *African Words, African Voices: Critical Practices in Oral History* (Bloomington: Indiana University Press, 2001).

78. Luise White, *Speaking with Vampires: Rumor and History in Colonial Africa* (Berkeley: University of California Press, 2000), 93.

79. I use the term *culture space* here reservedly. Hunt has pointed out the problem with always associating the "oral" with Africans and the "archival" with Europeans when, in fact, both groups produced both kinds of text. In the context of the history of Kitawala, however, there are very few archival sources written by Congolese available, so the notion of "cultural space" is arguably applicable. Nancy Rose Hunt, *A Colonial Lexicon of Birth Ritual, Medicalization, and Mobility in the Congo* (Durham, NC: Duke University Press, 1999), 23.

80. For a good overview of this scholarship, see Andriaan van Klinken, *Kenyan, Christian, Queer* (University Park: Pennsylvania State University Press, 2019), 23–27.

81. Van Klinken, 24.

82. It is worth noting here that all the interviews featured in this study were conducted in Swahili by me and have likewise been translated from their original Swahili by me. While Swahili is not the maternal language of any of the people I spoke with, it is regularly spoken in everyday interactions, particularly in larger towns and cities in the Kivus and in Haut Katanga, Tanganyika, and Lulalaba. The dialect spoken in South Kivu and Tanganyika, in particular, is far closer to standard Tanzanian Swahili—Sanifu—than that spoken in other parts of eastern Congo, although it is most certainly a dialect that borrows heavily from local languages and uses far less of the Arabic

vocabulary found in coastal Swahili. Congolese people in Lubumbashi regularly refer to the Swahili of these regions as "Swahili Bora"—Better/High Swahili—because it is so much closer to Standard Swahili than the Kingwana dialect of Swahili highlighted in Johannes Fabian, *Language and Colonial Power: The Appropriation of Swahili in the Former Belgian Congo, 1880–1938* (Berkeley: University of California Press, 1991). I suspect that the reason for this—and for the high level of fluency among people in this region—has much to do with the recent conflict, which forced many Congolese in this region into Tanzanian refugee camps for extended periods of time. I also suspect it is related to increased mobility related to trade in East Africa, but further linguistic research on this subject is necessary. In any case, although the choice of Swahili as the language of expression was dictated in large part by my own limitations in local languages, the people I interviewed were entirely comfortable expressing themselves in Swahili and would clarify with local words or with French when articulating complex ideas. While I often traveled with research companions—namely, Michael Ahuka, Amisi Mas, and Sermy Nsenga—when conducting interviews, and they regularly participated in and shaped our conversations in important ways, I did not work with a translator.

83. Ernest Wamba dia Wamba, "Bundu dia Kongo: A Kongolese Self-Styled Fundamentalist Religious Movement," in *East African Expressions of Christianity*, ed. Thomas Spear and Isaria N. Kimambo (Oxford: James Currey, 1999), 222.
84. Aparicio et al., introduction, xxix.
85. Aparicio et al., xxvi. Here the authors are drawing on the work of Paul Farmer. See Michael Griffin and Jennie Weiss Block, eds., *In the Company of the Poor: Conversations with Dr. Paul Farmer and Fr. Gustavo Gutiérrez* (Maryknoll, NY: Orbis Books, 2013), 127.
86. I am grateful to Aliko Songolo, (now) emeritus professor of African Literature at UW–Madison, for helping me to connect to them.
87. It is worth noting here that Amisi and Marceline insisted that I not pay them. Amisi, in particular, was adamant (despite my insistence that I pay him for his labor) that he was not a "research assistant." He had his own work through their NGO— SOS Femmes en Danger—and was more interested in the currency of "connections" that I could provide him in my position as an American researcher. Networks of connection and obligation remain a powerful currency in the political economy of region. Sermy Nsenga, likewise, cannot be considered a "research assistant." He was and is, rather, a more senior scholar whose expertise in Congolese history exceeds my own, but who has graciously shown interest in my project and my safety on multiple occasions. He likewise has refused payment. Michael, on the other hand, has accepted payment for his work.
88. While I generally did not require a translator—I speak Swahili, the lingua franca of the region, quite well—they nonetheless frequently helped me to grasp deeper levels of meaning behind certain words and concepts.

89. Aymar Nyenyezi et al., eds., *The Bukavu Series: Toward a Decolonization of Research* (Leuven: Presses universitaires de Louvain, 2020).

CHAPTER 1: TRANSMISSIONS

1. "Kitawala en région Stanleyville," 1938, dossier no. 17714, Gouvernement générale Series, Archives africaines, Ministère belge d'affaires étrangères, Brussels (hereafter cited as AA/GG, followed by the dossier no.).
2. I am grateful to my colleagues at the University of Tennessee, Knoxville, particularly Charles Sanft and Allison Vacca, for first inspiring me to think about the events and processes in this chapter in terms of "transmissions." From the fall of 2017 through spring of 2019, they organized a UTK Humanities Center Faculty Seminar on the topic of transmissions, which I was able to take part in. Parts of this chapter were first presented during that seminar.
3. Georges Nzongola-Ntalaja, *The Congo from Leopold to Kabila: A People's History* (London: Zed Books, 2002), 26–27. See also Gillian Mathys, "Travail et capital: Quelques aspects de l'économie colonial," in Chambre des représentants de belgique, DOC 55 1462/002, October 2021, 356–58, https://www.dekamer.be/FLWB/PDF/55/1462/55K1462002.pdf.
4. Benjamin Rubbers, "Mining Towns, Enclaves and Spaces: A Genealogy of Worker Camps in the Congolese Copperbelt," *Geoforum* 98 (January 2019): 90.
5. Osumaka Likaka, *Naming Colonialism: History and Collective Memory in the Congo, 1870–1960* (Madison: University of Wisconsin Press, 2009), 32–36.
6. Didier Gondola, *Tropical Cowboys: Westerns, Violence, and Masculinity in Kinshasa* (Bloomington: Indiana University Press, 2016), 35–41; Bogumil Jewsiewicki, "The Great Depression and the Making of the Colonial Economic System in the Belgian Congo," *African Economic History*, no. 4 (1977): 153–76.
7. Reuben Loffman, *Church, State and Colonialism in Southeastern Congo, 1890–1962* (Cham, Switzerland: Palgrave Macmillan, 2019).
8. Nancy Hunt, *A Nervous State: Violence, Remedies, and Reverie in Colonial Congo* (Durham, NC: Duke University Press, 2016), 1–26; Mwene-Batende, *Mouvements messianiques et protestation sociale: Le cas du Kitawala chez les Kumu du Zaïre* (Kinshasa: Faculté de théologie catholique, 1982), 101–12; Gillian Mathys, *Conflict and Connection: Making the Histories of the Lake Kivu Region* (Oxford University Press, forthcoming).
9. Hunt, *Nervous State*, 8.
10. Florence Bernault, *Colonial Transactions: Imaginaries, Bodies, and Histories in Gabon* (Durham, NC: Duke University Press, 2019), 8–10.
11. I have seen this image explicitly evoked in Congo, in particular by the members of another religious movement known as "Wamalkia wa Ubembe," who refer to their mediums as "anntenne." On Wamalkia wa Ubembe, see Nicole Eggers, "Prophètes, politiciens et légitimité politique: Discours locaux du

pouvoir et transformation religieuse dans le conflit congolais," *Politique africaine* 129 (March 2013): 73–91.

12. Nancy Hunt made a similar observation in her chapter on the Ekafera prison camp in Equateur that detained a number of Kitawalist prisoners. Hunt, *Nervous State*, 167–206.
13. Paul Kollman, "Classifying African Christianities, Part Two: The Anthropology of Christianity and Generations of African Christians," *Journal of Religion in Africa* 40, no. 2 (2010): 135.
14. Ese Ebake, interview with author, digital recording, Mboko, South Kivu, June 17, 2010.
15. R. Philippart, "Contributions à l'étude du Kitawala," 1954, dossier no. 4737, Affaires indigènes series, Archives affricaines, Ministère belge d'affaires étrangères, Brussels (hereafter cited as AA/AI, followed by dossier no.).
16. There are numerous sources, both colonial and scholarly, that highlight these major themes in Watchtower discourse. See, for example, Karen Fields, *Revival and Rebellion in Colonial Central Africa* (Princeton, NJ: Princeton University Press, 1985), 91–127; and David Gordon, *Invisible Agents: Spirits in Central African History* (Athens: Ohio University Press, 2012), 69–78.
17. Kibasomba-Wakilongo, interview with author, digital recording, September 4, 2010.
18. Ese Ebake is a pseudonym. As a rule, when citing interviews, I have used the real names only for public figures in the Kitawalist community who indicated that I should use their real names. PP2, Théophile Mulongo, and Ilunga Wesele, for example, are real names, as are all names that come out of archival documents. All others have been altered.
19. Ese Ebake, interview with author, digital recording, Mboko, South Kivu, June 17, 2010.
20. Shindano Masubi Ayubu, interview with author, digital recording, Mission Kitawaliste, seventy-four kilometers (46 mi.) from Kalemie, Katanga, 2010.
21. Elders of EDAC, interview with author, digital recording, Kalonja, South Kivu, December 12, 2010.
22. For a more in-depth discussion of the American roots of Watchtower, see Fields, *Revival and Rebellion*, 92.
23. Very early in Booth's career, he made a name for himself when he wrote what John Higginson has called "a broadside on behalf of a group of African workers who had organized a strike against several large farms run by the Presbyterian mission in Nyasaland." John Higginson, "Liberating the Captives: Independent Watchtower as an Avatar of Colonial Revolt in Southern Africa and Katanga, 1908–1941," *Journal of Social History* 26, no. 1 (1992): 59. See also George Shepperson and Thomas Price, *Independent African: John Chilembwe and the Origins, Setting and Significance of the Nyasaland Native Rising of 1915* (Edinburgh: Edinburgh University Press, 1958), 397–400; and Fields, *Revival and Rebellion*, 105.

24. Higginson, "Liberating the Captives," 61.
25. Fields, *Revival and Rebellion* 117–123.
26. Robert I. Rotberg, *The Rise of Nationalism in Central Africa: The Making of Malawi and Zambia, 1873-1964* (Cambridge, MA: Harvard University Press, 1965), 68–69.
27. Higginson, "Liberating the Captives," 64.
28. On Sindano, see Fields, *Revival and Rebellion*, 144.
29. Higginson, "Liberating the Captives," 64.
30. Higginson, 64.
31. Fields, *Revival and Rebellion*, 170. Fields is citing an archival account. See Fields, 306n39.
32. Fields, 171. Here Fields is citing an archival source: a witness to the events in Katanga.
33. Efraim Andersson, *Messianic Popular Movements in the Lower Congo* (Uppsala, Sweden: Almqvist & Wiksells, 1958), 248.
34. There were Watchtower converts preaching in Congo before Nyirenda's arrival, as early as 1923, but it was not until the flourishing of Kitawalist activity during Nyirenda's sojourn in Congo that the movement really gained momentum in the region. Higginson, "Liberating the Captives," 65.
35. Judicial records that could further improve this map have become available in recent years, but I was unable to consult them for this project.
36. "Lobati Ngoma" is the name that he is remembered by in oral histories. Kabanga Kamalondo, interview with author, digital recording, Kalemie, DRC, October 15, 2010; Shindano Masubi Aiubu, November 10, 2010; Kibasomba-Wakilongo, November 4, 2010. "Lobati Kima" is an alias and is the name that Higginson uses to refer to him. See Higginson, "Liberating the Captives," 68.
37. Higginson, "Liberating the Captives," 66–67. The secret police were formed in 1932, in part to deal with what the Belgians saw as a proliferation of subversive sects.
38. The colonial tendency to view ideas they considered deviant through the lens of contagious pathology is widespread in the history of Africa. See, for example, Ibrahima Thioub, "Juvenile Marginality and Incarceration during the Colonial Period: The First Penitentiary Schools in Senegal, 1888–1927," in *A History of Prison and Confinement*, ed. Florence Bernault (Portsmouth, NH: Heinemann, 2003), 84.
39. See, for example, Philippart, "Contributions à l'étude," 1954, AA/AI 4737; "Synthèse du mouvement subversif Kitawala," 1955/56, AA/AI 1621.
40. Karin Barber, "Introduction: Hidden Innovators in Africa," in *Africa's Hidden Histories: Everyday Literacy and Making the Self*, ed. Karin Barber (Bloomington: Indiana University Press, 2006), 1.
41. I have no record of his birthdate, but by the 1930s he was an adult, working as a clerk within the colonial court system, so this is an estimation based on that fact.

42. David John Garrard, *The History of the Congo Evangelistic Mission / Communiauté Pentecôtiste au Zaïre from 1915–1982*, vol. 1, *The Colonial Years, 1915–1959* (Mattersey, UK: Mattersey Hall, 2008), 17–18.
43. Garrard, 111–12.
44. Garrard, 134.
45. "Synthèse du mouvement," 1955/56, AA/AI 1621, 143.
46. "Synthèse du mouvement," 166.
47. Mwene-Batende, *Mouvements messianiques*, 99–125.
48. "Rapport no 2 sur les agissements des relégués de la secte 'Kitawala' en Lubutu," box 7, folder 1, Maurice Martin de Ryck Congo Papers (hereafter MMRC), Michigan State University, Lansing.
49. "Le Kitawala en province du Kivu," n.d., dossier no. 5483, Divers, Archives affricaines, Ministère belge d'affaires étrangères, Brussels (hereafter cited as AA/D, followed by dossier no.).
50. Colinet, the territorial administrator of Lubutu who reported on these activities in 1942, notes that Mutombo Stephano was circulating copies of a 1938 Swahili edition of the King James Bible published by the London British and Foreign Bible Society. "Rapport no 2 sur les agissements," MMRC.
51. "Synthèse du mouvement," AA/AI 1621, 124.
52. For Kulu Mapenda's biography, I borrow significant content and language from a previously published article that discusses Kulu Mapenda's case: Nicole Eggers, "Authority That Is Customary: Kitawala, Customary Chiefs, and the Plurality of Power in Congolese History," *Journal of East African History* 14, no. 1 (2020): 24–42.
53. "Synthèse du mouvement," AA/AI 1621, 56
54. Higginson, "Liberating the Captives," 66–67.
55. "Synthèse du mouvement," AA/AI 1621, 149–55. See also Higginson, "Liberating the Captives," 69.
56. "Synthèse du mouvement," AA/AI 1621, 146.
57. On Kibangile, see Reuben Loffman, "'An Interesting Experiment': Kibangile and the Quest for Chiefly Legitimacy in Kongolo, Northern Katanga, 1923–1934," *International Journal of African Historical Studies* 50, no. 3 (2018): 461–77. On other witch-finding movements in Central Africa, see Gordon, *Invisible Agents*, 50–68; and Fields, *Revival and Rebellion*, 163–93.
58. See "Synthèse du mouvement," AA/AI 1621, 146–47; "Letter Regarding Indigenous Superstitions," 1936, dossier no. 1613 9138, Service AIMO Gouvernement général, Archives affricaines, Ministère belge d'affaires étrangères, Brussels (hereafter cited as AA/AIMO, followed by dossier no.).
59. "Synthèse du mouvement," AA/AI 1621, 146.
60. "Rapport sur les assignements," 1937, MMRC.
61. "Rapport sur les assignements," 1937. Mwene-Batende notes the name of Kulu's group as Dini ya Haki (or "Religion of Justice"). Mwene-Batende, "Le Kitawala dans l'évolution socio-politique récente: Cas du groupe Belukela dans la ville de Kisangani," *Cahiers des religions africaines* 10, no. 19 (1976): 85.

62. "Synthèse du mouvement," AA/AI 1621, 150; "Rapport sur les assigments," 1937, MMRC.
63. "Synthèse du movement," AA/AI 1621, 150.
64. *Histoire de l'Église Kitawala: Prophète Ilunga*, p. 8, Archive of l'Église de la libération du Saint-Esprit du prophète Kadima Émile Ilunga du Kitawala. This source, henceforth cited as "the *Histoire*," is a written history of the prophet Kadiba Ilunga Émile that is kept in the archive of l'Église de la libération du Saint-Esprit du prophète Kadima Émile Ilunga du Kitawala. The copy that I photographed was shared with me in Lubumbashi in the summer of 2018. It is available in my personal archive.
65. "Synthèse du mouvement," AA/AI 1621, 150.
66. "Fiche de punitions et fiche de renseignements, Kulu Mupenda Kandeke," September 1949, AA/GG 17502.
67. "Rapport mois de novembre 1948," November 1948, AA/GG 17502.
68. "Synthèse du mouvement," AA/AI 1621, 158.
69. Luise White, *Speaking with Vampires: Rumor and History in Colonial Africa* (Berkeley: University of California Press, 2000).
70. "Synthèse du mouvement," AA/AI 1621, 160–63.
71. "Synthèse du mouvement," 161.
72. N'koi was known to have connections as far away as Monkoto, 640 kilometers (400 mi.) miles from Ikanga. Kamina, where Ngoie Maria lived, is around 970 kilometers (600 mi.) from Ikanga. Hunt, *Nervous State*, 63.
73. Hunt, 62.
74. Kollman, "Classifying African Christianities," 135. On religious communities as spaces of intimacy, see also Natasha Erlank, *Convening Black Intimacy: Christianity, Gender, and Tradition in Early Twentieth-Century South Africa* (Athens: Ohio University Press, 2022).
75. See Yolanda Covington-Ward, *Gesture and Power: Religion, Nationalism, and Everyday Performance in Congo* (Durham, NC: Duke University Press, 2016), 9–12.
76. Like many named Kitawalists, there is some variation in how Kadiba's name appears in the archives and other sources. Sometimes he is named Kadima instead of Kadiba (a reflection of how close the "b" and "m" sounds are in the pronunciation of the name). Sometimes his name is written Illunga Kadima Émile. I choose Kadiba Ilunga Émile—shortened to Kadiba—because it is how his name in written in the *Histoire*. In fact, his full name was Kadiba Ilunga Mukanya Émile.
77. *Historia ya Kanisa: Biographie ya Baba Prophet*. As with the *Histoire*, neither authorship nor date is listed on this account. This Swahili-language document was given to me by the leadership of Kitawala in Lubumbashi in 2019. They photographed it and shared it with me via a WhatsApp message. I have a copy of this document in my personal archive as well.
78. *Historia ya Kanisa*.
79. *Histoire*, 1–3.

80. Joset Files, AA/D 483.
81. Pedro Monaville, *Students of the World: Global 1968 and Decolonization in the Congo* (Durham, NC: Duke University Press, 2022), 39–40.
82. "Synthèse du mouvement," AA/AI 1621, 145.
83. *Historia ya Kanisa*. Confirmation that the prisoners were communicating with Kadiba can be found in the colonial archives as well: "Synthèse du mouvement," AA/AI 1621, 145.
84. "Synthèse du mouvement," AA/AI 1621, 145.
85. *Histoire*, 5. I am unsure whether there was a conference of this nature in 1932, but there certainly was a Protestant conference in Katanga in 1934, at which Watchtower was declared "one of the most subversive influences militating against the maintenance of amicable race relations." J. R. Hooker, "Witnesses and Watchtower in the Rhodesias and Nyasaland," *Journal of African History* 6, no. 1 (1965): 101n23.
86. *Histoire*, 5.
87. This teaching came up often in discussions with contemporary Kitawalists as well. For example, Kadiba's grandson Ilunga Wesele Joseph mentioned it in an interview I conducted with him in 2010. Interview with author, Kitawala Mission, seventeen kilometers (11 mi.) from Kalemie, November 11, 2010.
88. Discussion of Kadiba performing miracles also came up in the oral interviews. Interview with author, Kitawala Mission, November 11, 2010.
89. The word *ufalme* has this semantic field: it means more than rule and implies an inherent capacity for authority that comes from the ancestors/God. Its use here evokes that meaning.
90. The woman Kadiba healed was the wife of Ngoie Belge, a member of a group of Kitawalists in Malonga camp who stood "in opposition" to Kadiba's group. *Histoire*, 8.
91. David Gordon similarly writes about how Watchtower adherents in Zambia in the early twentieth century believed books themselves to contain "sacred and divinatory power." Gordon, *Invisible Agents*, 77–78.
92. Kollman, "Classifying African Christianities," 135; Paul S. Landau, *The Realm of the Word: Language, Gender, and Christianity in a Southern African Kingdom* (Portsmouth, NH: Heinemann, 1995); Lamin Sanneh, *Translating the Message: The Missionary Impact on Culture*, 2nd ed. (Maryknoll, NY: Orbis, 2009); Birgit Meyer, *Translating the Devil: Religion and Modernity among the Ewe in Ghana* (Trenton, NJ: Africa World Press, 1999); Susan Harding, *The Book of Jerry Falwell: Fundamentalist Language and Politics* (Princeton, NJ: Princeton University Press, 2000); James S. Bielo, "On the Failure of 'Meaning': Bible Reading in the Anthropology of Christianity," *Culture and Religion* 9, no. 1 (2008): 1–21; Matthew Engelke, *A Problem of Presence: Beyond Scripture in an African Church* (Berkeley: University of California Press, 2007); Eva Keller, *The Road to Clarity: Seventh Day Adventism in Madagascar* (New York: Palgrave Macmillan, 2005); Thomas G. Kirsch, *Spirits and Letters:*

Reading, Writing and Charisma in African Christianity (New York: Berghahn, 2008).
93. Bielo, "On the Failure of 'Meaning,'" 5.
94. Engelke, *Problem of Presence*, 18.
95. Engelke, 8.
96. Léon Debertry, *Kitawala: Roman* (Elisabethville: Éditions essor du Congo, 1953).
97. Debertry, 261.
98. For ease of reading, I have cut some of the repetition out of this sermon, which was delivered in a much more "call and response" manner than is apparent in this transcription. Kitawalist Mass, digital recording, Kasaji, Lualaba, August 11, 2018.
99. This is not to imply that White people studying African history are uncommon. This is not the case in an academic field that remains concerningly White in its demographics. But my appearance in this church in the rather remote and difficult-to-reach town of Kasaji, my Americanness (which is relevant for its connection to Watchtower), and my femaleness were certainly unusual and unprecedented.
100. Engelke, *Problem of Presence*.
101. In a similar case, I was first given a copy of a 1956 colonial report on Kitawala (*sureté*) when a Kitawalist leader in Kalemie, Kabanga Kamalondo, brought it out for me to photograph when I met with him to discuss their history. The book was similarly worn, missing the entire front section of the study. It took me several years to find a full copy because the only information I had about its production was that "some Belgian" had written it. But it was clearly quite valuable to them despite the fact that it was, like the novel, quite critical of Kitawala.
102. Philippart, "Contributions à l'étude," 1954, AA/AI 4737, 17–26.
103. Philippart, 17–26.
104. Philippart, 25.
105. Philippart, 26.
106. John M. Janzen, "Ideologies and Institutions in Precolonial Western Equatorial African Therapeutics," in *The Social Basis of Health and Healing*, ed. Steven Feierman and John M. Janzen (Berkeley: University of California Press, 1992), 203.

CHAPTER 2: HEALING

1. *M(u)fumu* is commonly used as a synonym for *(mu)nganga* (healer) in the Swahili of South Kivu and Northern Katanga. In its usage, in contemporary Congo, *mfumu* tends to carry a connotation of witchcraft or the use of mashetani (evil spirits) in healing practices. But not always. Johannes Fabian has noted the usage of the word in the same manner in Lubumbashi. See Fabian, *Ethnography as Commentary: Writing from the Virtual Archive* (Durham, NC: Duke University Press, 2008), e-book, loc. 891. Interestingly,

mfumu is defined in Kiluba as "important person" and was historically a title given to a chief and his councilors. E. Van Avermaet and Benoit Mbuya, *Dictionnaire kiluba-français* (Tervuren, Belgium: Museé royal du Congo belge, 1954), 153–52. At the same time, in his work on the early Great Lakes region, David Schoenbrun has suggested that *bafumu* (pl.) came to be recognized as "highly versatile experts with ties to ancestral knowledge" that gave them "power over life, death, and nature." Schoenbrun, *A Green Place, a Good Place: Agrarian Change, Gender, and Social Identity in the Great Lakes Region to the 15th Century* (Portsmouth, NH: Heinemann, 1998), 110. This draws out the ambiguities in the exercise and conceptualization of "creative" and "instrumental" power that I emphasized in the introduction (see Schoenbrun, *Green Place*, 12–15).

2. Maman Kalema's story, as I have presented it here, is compiled from both my field notes from the first interview that I conducted with her and direct quotes from my second interview with her, which was recorded. I have rearranged some of her words for the sake of narrative ease and have chosen not to indicate which moments (drawn from the recorded interview) I am quoting her directly and which are drawn from the initial, notated interview. In essence, these are all Maman Kalema's words; I am simply quoting them directly at times and paraphrasing at other times. Maman Kalema, interviews with author: field notes, Uvira, South Kivu, DRC, April 18, 2010; and digital recording, Uvira, South Kivu, DRC, April 21, 2010.

3. There are many documents that include such accounts. They are discussed at length in chapter 4.

4. Steven Feierman, "Explanation and Uncertainty in the Medical World of the Ghaambo," *Bulletin of the History of Medicine* 74, no. 2 (2000): 326.

5. The translation of *asili* as "tradition" is imperfect but justifiable. Looking at usage in southern Tanzania, Stacey Langwick glosses the semantic field of asili as "derivation-transformation from one state to another, the process of reasoning out, explaining, or following a train of logic." She notes that it is "most often used in relation to medicine and efforts to scientifically investigate plants." She contrasts this with two other words that are frequently translated as "tradition": *Jadi* and *kinyeji*. Jadi "captures development through generations," while kinyeji "implies the growth of (and the growth out of) a place." Kinyeji "reflects the importance of specificity and the acts of specifying that are at the root of some forms of healing." Langwick, *Bodies, Politics, and African Healing: The Matter of Maladies in Tanzania* (Bloomington: Indiana University Press, 2011), 88. The way that asili is used in eastern Congo, however, does not precisely match any of these definitions. In John Whitehead's 1928 dictionary of Kingwana (Congolese, especially Katangan, Swahili), asili is defined as "origin, source, aboriginal, rudiment." Whitehead, *Manuel de Kingwana: Le dialecte occidental de Swahili* (Le Lualaba, Congo: La Mission de et à Wayika, 1928). When Kitawalists

use it, they frequently qualify it with "ya bankambo," which Fabian notes refers to "'ancestors' generally, not specific relatives" (Fabian, *Ethnography,* loc. 1037). As such, I think a fair translation here is "of the ancestral tradition," although I use "tradition" as shorthand.
6. *Alternative materialities* is a term I borrow from Langwick, who uses it to discuss how Tanzanian healers differ from biomedical doctors in their conceptions of "what objects are central to life and the relations that sustain them." See Langwick, *Bodies,* 232.
7. *Wanganga za mitishamba* and *Munganga za miti* can both be translated as "herbal healer"—*nganga,* being the root word for "healer," and *miti,* referring to "a tree but also to plant or vegetal matter in general." Fabian, *Ethnography,* loc. 824.
8. Fabian, loc. 1309. Fabian's study is an "experiment in ethnographic writing" (loc. 19) based on the textual and contextual translation of a single interview with a healer, Kahenga Mukonkwa Michel, that he conducted in Lubumbashi in 1974. While his interview must be located in a different historical context than my own interviews with Kitawalists, it is one among very few examples of an in-depth interview with an herbal healer in the region where Kitawalists have historically been present. Indeed, Kahenga is from the northern regions of Katanga, where a good portion of my own interviews with Kitawalists took place. As part of Fabian's experiment in ethnography with "virtual archives," the entire text of the interview, in both Swahili and English, is available to read online: Johannes Fabian, "'Magic and Modernity': A Conversation with an Herbalist and Practitioner of Magic," *Archives of Popular Swahili,* vol. 7 (July 8, 2005), http://www.lpca.socsci.uva.nl/aps/vol7/kahengatext.html.
9. Vestline talcum / baby powder. A brief internet search reveals that it is produced by Tanga Pharmaceutical and Plastics Ltd. in Tanga, Tanzania.
10. Feierman, "Explanation and Uncertainty," 326.
11. I root my approach here in Fabian's ideas about commentary and close (con)textual analysis as an important genre in the field of ethnography. Fabian, *Ethnography,* loc. 144.
12. The term he uses here is *matunvi ya mti.* I have been unable to find a reference to the specific term in a dictionary, but it likely derives from the Kiswahili root *-tunza,* "to care for." In Congolese Kiswahili, it is common to say of someone who has gone to the doctor, "*walimtunza,*" with the connotation not just of being cared for but of being healed. Thus, "healing materials" seems to be a good translation here. Contextual information indicates that, more specifically, he is referring to the resin of the tree here, since the resin of umpafu trees is used to make candles.
13. Kabanga Kamalondo, interview with author, digital recording, Kalemi, Katanga, DRC, October 18, 2010. I have chosen to remove most of the repetition from the original transcript for ease of reading.
14. Kamalondo, 2010.

15. Sermy Nsenga, interview with author, digital recording, October 18, 2010.
16. The implied meaning here is to biomedical doctors.
17. Group interview with author, digital recording, Kalemie, Katanga, DRC, October 19, 2010.
18. Kabanga Kamalondo, interview with author, digital recording, Kalemie, Katanga, DRC, October 18, 2010.
19. Elizabeth Colson, "Places of Power and Shrines of the Land," *Paideuma* 43 (1997): 47–57.
20. Michael J. Sheridan, "The Environmental and Social History of African Sacred Groves: A Tanzanian Case Study," *African Studies Review* 52, no. 1 (2009): 74.
21. Gillian Mathys, "People on the Move: Frontiers, Borders, Mobility and History in the Lake Kivu Region, 19th–20th Century" (PhD diss., University of Ghent, 2014), see especially chapter 10. Reuben Loffman has also noted that "sacred groves, or *hatas*," were crucial sites of authority-building among the Songye, to the west of the Lualaba in Katanga. Loffman, *Church, State and Colonialism in Southeastern Congo, 1890–1962* (Cham, Switzerland: Palgrave Macmillan, 2019), 95–96.
22. There has been some very recent research done on the prevalence (and effects) of this practice in Africa more broadly and in Congo specifically, where estimates suggest that as much as 29–56 percent of pregnant women engage in the practice. Claudia Gundacker et al., "Geophagy during Pregnancy: Is There a Health Risk for Infants?," *Environmental Research* 156 (July 2017): 145.
23. Pastor Mulongo, interview with author, digital recording, Kasaji, DRC, September 12, 2018.
24. I have also seen references to kaolin in archival materials. As I discuss in chapter 5, kaolin was one of the materials—along with the dirt of a termite hill—used by Kitawalists to fashion "mannequins" meant to give converts the ability to "see their dead parents." "Kitawala Lowa," 1947, dossier no. 13939 Gouvernement générale Series, Archives africaines, Ministère belge d'affaires étrangères, Archives africaines, Brussels (hereafter cited as AA/GG, followed by dossier no.).
25. "*Canarium schweinfurthii*," AgroForestry Tree Database, ver. 4.0, Center for International Forestry Research, World Agroforestry (CIFOR-ICRAF), accessed January 12, 2023, http://apps.worldagroforestry.org/treedb2/speciesprofile.php?Spid=1765.
26. *Vifungu* derives from the root *-fung-*, which relates to "flow/closure." The verb *kufunga*, for example, means to "close/block" and *kufungua* is to "open/unlock." It is used in eastern Congo to refer to ceremonies, or evocations, in a religious/healing context.
27. I translate "illnesses of fungu" here as "illnesses of flow/blockage," including fertility issues. On the significance of blockage and flow in the conceptualization of health in the region, see Christopher Taylor, *Milk, Honey, and*

Money: Changing Concepts in Rwandan Healing (Washington, DC: Smithsonian Institution Press, 1992). Illnesses of *anga* is translated as "witchcraft/power" because it is the root of *bwanga*, which in Kiluba—as well as numerous other Congolese languages—means, essentially, "puissance/pouvoir/force." For an in-depth linguistic discussion of *-bwanga*, see Van Avermaet, *Dictionnaire*, 24–27.

28. "We," here, means Kitawalists and biomedical providers.
29. Kibasomba-Wakilongo, interview with author, digital recording, Uvira, South Kivu, DRC, September 4, 2010.
30. Kabanga Kamalondo, interview with author, digital recording, Kalemie, Katanga, DRC, October 18, 2010.
31. It is interesting to note that as soon as the topic of healing comes up, a woman takes over the position of interlocuter.
32. Mama Senwa, interview with author, digital recording, Kalonja, Fizi, South Kivu, DRC, December 12, 2010. Mama Senwa is an alias that I have given this woman, whose real name was not given.
33. Anonymous, interview with author, digital recording, Kitawala Mission, seventeen kilometers (11 mi.) outside of Kalemie, Katanga, DRC, November 11, 2010.
34. Daniel Beibyuck, *Lega Culture: Art, Initiation, and Moral Philosophy among a Central African People* (Berkeley: University of California Press, 1973), 71.
35. Kibasomba-Wakilongo, interview with author, digital recording, Kalemie, Katanga, DRC, September 4, 2010.
36. Ilunga Wesele Joseph, interview with author, digital recording, Kitawala Mission, seventeen kilometers (11 mi.) outside of Kalemie, Katanga, DRC, November 11, 2010.
37. Wyatt MacGaffey, "Religion, Class, and Social Pluralism in Zaire," *Canadian Journal of African Studies* 24, no. 2 (1990): 262.
38. PP2, interview with author, digital recording, Kabalo, August 29, 2018.
39. Pastor Mulongo, interview with author, digital recording, Kasaji, August 12, 2018.
40. See, for example, Iris Berger, *Religion and Resistance: East African Kingdoms in the Precolonial Period* (Tervuren, Belgium: Musée royal de l'Afrique centrale, 1981); Iris Berger, "Rebels or Status Seekers? Women as Spirit Mediums in East Africa," in *Women in Africa: Studies in Economic and Social Change*, ed. Nancy J. Hafkin and Edna G. Bay (Palo Alto, CA: Stanford University Press, 1976), 157–82; Marie-Claude Dupré, "Les femmes mukisi des Téké Tsaayi rituel de possession et culte anti-sorcier (République populaire du Congo)," *Journal de la Société des africanistes* 44, no. 1 (1974): 53–69; and Phyllis M. Martin, *Catholic Women of Congo-Brazzaville: Mothers and Sisters in Troubled Times* (Bloomington: Indiana University Press, 2009), 18–41.
41. Cynthia Hoehler-Fatton, *Women of Spirit and Fire: History, Faith, and Gender in Roho Religion in Western Kenya* (New York: Oxford University Press, 1996), 99. Hoehler-Fatton draws the term *ceremonial leadership* from Bennetta

Jules-Rosette, "Women as Ceremonial Leaders in an African Church: The Apostles of John Maranke," in *The New Religions of Africa*, ed. Jules-Rosette (Norwood, NJ: Ablex, 1979), 127.
42. Hoehler-Fatton, *Women*, 100.
43. Hoehler-Fatton, 101.
44. "Kuna ya maziwa na chakula. Chakula ni kwa watu, wale wa nguvu." The implication here is there are things that helpers (i.e., men) can do, but that most of the ceremonial weight is carried by those with the power (nguvu): women.
45. Elders of EDAC, interview with author, digital recording, Kalonja, South Kivu, DRC, December 12, 2010. Mama Amisa and Mzee Aliko are pseudonyms.
46. Shindano Masubi Aiubu, interview with author, digital recording, Kitawala Mission, seventy-four kilometers (46 mi.) from Kalemie, Katanga, DRC, November 10, 2010.
47. Nancy Hunt has likewise written about the important role of laughter as a sign of nervousness. Certainly nervousness, or, perhaps more accurately, awkwardness, could be read into this moment, but it was not the overwhelming mood of the exchange. Recounting it here nonetheless serves as an "instructive thread" in writing about the exchange. Nacy Rose Hunt, *A Nervous State: Violence, Remedies, and Reverie in Colonial Congo* (Durham, NC: Duke University Press, 2016), 31, 39–41, 249.
48. Kitawala church elders, interview with author, digital recording, Kalemie, Katanga, DRC, October 19, 2010.
49. The referent here is unclear, although it is possible he is talking about Lumumba, given the context of the interview.
50. Kitawala church elders, interview with author, digital recording, Kalemie, Katanga, DRC, October 19, 2010.
51. James C. Scott, *Domination and Arts of Resistance: Hidden Transcripts* (New Haven, CT: Yale University Press, 1990), 2; Simon Bockie, *Death and the Invisible Powers: The World of Kongo Belief* (Bloomington: Indiana University Press, 1993).
52. David Gordon, *Invisible Agents: Spirits in Central African History* (Athens: Ohio University Press, 2012), 3–8.
53. Steve Feierman makes a similar argument in Feierman, "Colonizers, Colonized, and the Creation of Invisible Histories," in *Beyond the Cultural Turn: New Directions in the Study of Society and Culture*, ed. Victoria E. Bonnell and Lynn Hunt (Berkeley: University of California Press, 1999), 182–216.
54. Luise White, *Speaking with Vampires: Rumor and History in Colonial Africa* (Berkeley: University of California Press, 2000), 273.
55. Gwyn Prins, "But What Was the Disease? The Present State of Health and Healing in African Studies," *Past & Present* 124, no. 1 (1989): 165.
56. Personal communication with Sara Champlin, MD, of Health Partners, Bloomington, MN, August 21, 2012.

57. See, for example, Langwick, *Bodies;* and Lynette Jackson, *Surfacing Up: Psychiatry and Social Order in Colonial Zimbabwe, 1908–1968* (Ithaca, NY: Cornell University Press, 2005).
58. Kibasomba-Wakilongo, interview with author, digital recording, Uvira, South Kivu, DRC, September 4, 2010; John M. Janzen, *Lemba, 1650–1930: A Drum of Affliction in Africa and the New World* (New York: Garland, 1982); Langwick, *Bodies,* 157.
59. Taylor, *Milk.* See also Wauthier de Mahieu, *Qui a obstrué la cascade? Analyse sémantique du ritual de la circoncision chez les Komo du Zaïre* (Cambridge: Cambridge University Press, 1985).
60. Kibasomba-Wakilongo, interview with author, digital recording, Uvira, South Kivu, DRC, September 4, 2010.
61. Kilanga Kamikunga, interview with author, digital recording, Kalemie, Katanga, DRC, October 19, 2010.
62. Anonymous, interview with author, digital recording, Kitawala Mission, seventeen kilometers (11 mi.) outside Kalemie, Katanga, DRC, October 19, 2010. The woman did not give a name in the interview.
63. The World Bank reports that in 2011 infant mortality rates in Congo were at 174/1,000. By regional comparison, the infant mortality rate in Tanzania was 68; and Uganda was 90. "Mortality Rate, under-5 (per 1,000 Live Births)," World Bank, http://data.worldbank.org/indicator/SH.DYN.MORT.
64. Maman Kalema, interview with author, digital recording, Uvira, South Kivu, DRC, April 21, 2010.
65. "Kitawala Lowa," 1947, AA/GG 13939.
66. This story comes from a chance conversation with a young man named Amisi in Kalemie. As the conversation was informal, I do not have his full name, nor was it recorded. The date was November 5, 2010, field notes.

CHAPTER 3: VIOLENCE

1. Mwene-Batende, *Mouvements messianiques et protestation sociale: Le cas du Kitawala chez les Kumu du Zaïre* (Kinshasa: Faculté de théologie catholique, 1982), 99–125.
2. H. de Raeck, "Note pour Monsieur le Gouverneur de la Province," November 23, 1944, dossier no. 1638, Service AIMO Gouvernement générale, Archives africaines, Ministère belge d'affaires étrangères, Brussels (hereafter cited as AA/AIMO, followed by the dossier no.); V. Devaux, "Dossier Joset Paul," December 14, 1944, AA/AIMO 1638.
3. H. de Raeck, "Note pour Monsieur."
4. Peigneux, "Promenade militaire région de Kasese," June 4, 1945, AA/AIMO 1638.
5. Yogolelo Tambwe ya Kasimba and Hangi Shamamba suggest the number was in the hundreds. Yogolelo Tambwe ya Kasimba and Hangi Shamamba, "Lungundu, Bushiri," *Dictionary of African Christian Biography,* accessed

June 25, 2021, https://dacb.org/stories/democratic-republic-of-congo/bushiri-lungundu/.
6. Declerck, "Affaire Benzing et Paquay," January 6, 1945, AA/AIMO 1638; Enst R. Preys, "Affaire Benzing—Opération militaire Masisi," November 18, 1944, AA/AIMO 1638.
7. Peigneux, "Promenade militaire."
8. Declerck, "Affaire Benzing et Paquay."
9. A. Boivin, "Décès kitawaliste en région Kasese," August 25, 1944, AA/AIMO 1638. In a separate report, the state inspector criticized Boivin because he "preferred to leave the dying without care than to go beyond his instructions and claim the medicines of the Director of Mines." "Note pour Monsieur le Gouverneur Général," August 18, 1945, AA/AIMO 1638.
10. De Ryck, "Promenade militaire de Kasese," April 27, 1945, AA/AIMO 1638.
11. Paul-Ernest Joset, "Kitawala en région Kasese," June 14, 1944, AA/AIMO 1638.
12. Joset, "Kitawala en région Kasese"; Declerck, "Affaire Benzing et Paquay."
13. Preys, "Affaire Benzing."
14. Preys, "Affaire Benzing." Here, Preys is quoting Noirot in his letter.
15. "Avis de l'Administrateur Territorial de Bribosia," January 15, 1945, AA/AIMO 1638.
16. Peigneux, "Affaire Benzing-Paquay," July 16, 1945, AA/AIMO 1638.
17. Maurice Lovens, *La révolte de Masisi-Lubutu: Congo belge, janvier–mai 1944* (Brussels: CEDAF, 1974), 126–38.
18. Yogolelo Tambwe ya Kasimba and Hangi Shamamba, "Lungundu, Bushiri," *Dictionary of African Christian Biography*, https://dacb.org/stories/democratic-republic-of-congo/bushiri-lungundu/.
19. Large sections of this chapter also appear in my doctoral dissertation: Eggers, "Kitawala in the Congo: Religion, Politics and Healing in Central Africa" (PhD diss., University of Wisconsin–Madison, 2013).
20. "Comptes-rendus d'audience," Iterbo, August 7, 1944, 213, cited in Lovens, *La révolte*, 46.
21. Numbers are debatable. The estimate of 10,000 is somewhere in the middle of the range given by Lovens, who estimates the number of "insurgents" to be somewhere between 4,426 (1,885 men) and 15,000 (4,700 men), based on desertion reports from Comité National du Kivu posts in the region and reports collected from witnesses after the revolt. For an in-depth discussion of the matter, see Lovens, *La révolte*, 23.
22. They later reported that they shot into the crowd because the Kitawalists were dancing and singing like "fanatics" and had "blocked the road." "Déposition de Monsieur De Schryver," 1944, dossier no. 4737, Affaires indigènes Series, Archives africains, Ministère belge d'affaires étrangères, Brussels (hereafter cited as AA/AI, followed by the dossier no.).
23. Nancy Rose Hunt, *A Nervous State: Violence, Remedies, and Reverie in Colonial Congo* (Durham, NC: Duke University Press, 2016), 5–8.
24. Hunt, 19–21.

25. Aparicio et al., introduction to *Ethnographic Refusals, Unruly Latinidades*, ed. Alex E. Chávez and Gina M. Pérez (Albuquerque: University of New Mexico Press, 2022), xxviii.
26. Hunt, *Nervous State*, 11–12. I made a similar argument in the 2013 article on which this chapter is based. See Eggers, "Mukombozi and the Monganga: The Violence of Healing in the 1944 Kitawalist Uprising," *Africa: Journal of the International African Institute* 85, no. 3 (2015): 417–36.
27. See "P.V. d'arrestation: Mpunzu Mikaeli," April 30, 1944, AA/AI 4737. Given the breadth of the uprising, these are likely only a fraction of the total number of witchcraft arrests and deaths. I have no account of the number of people arrested in the other major theaters of the revolt. This is simply an account of the number of people arrested and punished by the core group in the Masisi theater of the uprising.
28. David Schoenbrun, "Violence and Vulnerability in East Africa before 1800 CE: An Agenda for Research," *History Compass* 4, no. 5 (2006): 743.
29. Derek R. Peterson, "The Politics of Transcendence in Colonial Uganda," *Past & Present* 230, no. 1 (2016): 203.
30. Florence Bernault and Jan-Georg Deutsch, "Introduction: Control and Excess; Histories of Violence in Africa," *Africa: Journal of the International African Institute* 85, no. 3 (2015): 385–94.
31. Lovens, *La révolte*, 116.
32. Nancy Hunt, "An Acoustic Register, Tenacious Images, and Congolese Scenes of Rape and Repetition," *Cultural Anthropology* 23, no. 3 (2008): 243.
33. I have cut out some of the repetition and rearranged and truncated some passages for clarity, but have otherwise kept the testimony largely intact. Interested researchers will find the original French transcript here: "P.V. d'arrestation: Mpunzu Mikaeli," April 30, 1944, AA/AI 4737.
34. John Thornton makes a similar choice in *The Kongolese Saint Anthony: Dona Beatriz Kimpa Vita and Antonian Movement, 1684–1706* (Cambridge: Cambridge University Press, 1998). Johannes Fabian has also argued for the importance of centering archival and ethnographic texts in many of his works, but particularly in his most recent work, *Ethnography as Commentary: Writing from the Virtual Archive* (Durham, NC: Duke University Press, 2008), e-book, loc. 144. Drawing on Walter Benjamin, Nancy Hunt has also argued that historians should use techniques of "nearness" that allow historians to "listen" to the past and "bring near a human scale within the immediacy or remembering of violence." Hunt, *Nervous State*, 31. For Walter Benjamin's work on the "technique of nearness," see Walter Benjamin, *The Arcades Project*, trans. Howard Eiland and Kevin McLaughlin (Cambridge, MA: Harvard University Press, 1999), 545.
35. Bushiri's "mètre" arm emerges in a number of the interrogation records from his followers. See, for example, "Katshaka Kichuana, Audience du 13 juillet," cited in Lovens, *La révolte*, 63.
36. The bulk of those involved in the uprising were Bakumu, although there were people of other ethnic identities involved as well, including the Banianga.

37. On Nyabingi, see Steven Feierman, "Colonizers, Colonized, and the Creation of Invisible Histories," in *Beyond the Cultural Turn: New Directions in the Study of Society and Culture*, ed. Victoria E. Bonnell and Lynn Hunt (Berkeley: University of California Press, 1999), 182–216. On kubandwa, see Iris Berger, *Religion and Resistance: East African Kingdoms in the Precolonial Period* (Tervuren, Belgium: Musée royal de l'Afrique centrale, 1981); Neil Kodesh *Beyond the Royal Gaze: Clanship and Public Healing in Buganda* (Charlottesville: University of Virginia Press, 2010); and David Schoenbrun, *A Green Place, a Good Place: Agrarian Change, Gender, and Social Identity in the Great Lakes Region to the 15th Century* (Portsmouth, NH: Heinemann, 1998). On lemba, see John M. Janzen, *Lemba, 1650–1930: A Drum of Affliction in Africa and the New World* (New York: Garland, 1982). For work on healing practices more specific to the region, see Wautheir de Mahieu's work on *esomba* spirit mediumship and initiation among the Komo (i.e., Kumu, the ethnic group to which Bushiri belonged). Wuthier de Mahieu, *Qui a obstrué la cascade? Analyse sémantique du ritual de la circoncision chez les Komo du Zaïre* (Cambridge: Cambridge University Press, 1985).
38. Kodesh, *Beyond the Royal Gaze*, 20. Kodesh is writing specifically of the Great Lakes region, but he is building off of the work of scholars such as Steve Feierman, who has noted that "the number of words for 'healer' in many Bantu languages of eastern, southern, or Central African were used with equal validity for those who worked to make individual bodies whole and those who treated the body politic." Feierman, "Colonizers, Colonized," 187.
39. Janzen's work on Lemba and Feierman's work on Nyabingi support this assertion, as does Schoenbrun's work on "instrumental" and "creative" power discussed in the introduction. Janzen, *Lemba*; Feierman "Colonizers, Colonized"; Schoenbrun, *Green Place*.
40. Janzen's work on the healing cult lemba would seem to support such a reading. Janzen notes that lemba, the medicine for which the cult was named, is derived from the word *lembikisa*, "to calm." Since one of the main purposes of the association was to cure conflict within the community, particularly between the sexes, the name of the medicine, he argues, was symbolic of the larger purpose of the movement. Reading mataifa similarly, as indicative of the larger purpose of the movement, then, seems a fair interpretation. Janzen, *Lemba*, 3.
41. Recall that Bushiri was called by a similar dream.
42. On this phenomenon, see Schoenbrun, *Green Place*, 108–13. See also Feierman, "Colonizers, Colonized," 74.
43. Jane I. Guyer and Samuel M. Eno Belinga, "Wealth in People as Wealth in Knowledge: Accumulation and Composition in Equatorial Africa," *Journal of African History* 36, no. 1 (1995): 102.
44. It is important to recall that the image of the Belgians immorally hoarding power—namely, the power of the Christian God—and using it to enrich

themselves at the expense of the Congolese people during the colonial era was not unique to the Kitawalists. See, for example, Nicole Eggers, "Prophètes, politiciens et légitimité politique: Discours locaux du pouvoir et transformation religieuse dans le conflit congolais," *Politique africaine* 129 (March 2013): 73–91.

45. "Procès-verbal d'interrogatoire du prévenu Bushiri, Iterbo, 23 mars 1944," cited in Lovens, *La révolte*, 149.
46. "Procès-verbal," cited in Lovens, *La révolte*, 149.
47. Mwene-Batende, *Mouvements*, 94–98.
48. Mwene-Batende calls this process, by which Arab-Swahili occupation in the region was followed closely by European occupation, "dual colonization." Mwene-Batende, 99.
49. Lovens, *La révolte*, 28.
50. Bribosia's text was reproduced in Lovens, *La révolte*, 30.
51. Mwene-Batende, *Mouvements*, 99–112.
52. Feierman, among others, has discussed the relationship between colonial labor regimes, women's labor, food production, malnutrition, and health: Steven Feierman, "Struggles for Control: The Social Roots of Health and Healing in Modern Africa," *African Studies Review* 28, no. 2/3 (1985): 99–101.
53. "Comptes rendus d'audience," Iterbo, August 7, 1944, 159, cited in Lovens, *La révolte*, 55.
54. Dekoster, "Mesures proposées pour lutter contre le Kitawala," report sent from Dekoster to GP Bertrand, April 8, 1944, 31, cited in Lovens, *La révolte*, 30–31.
55. On this colonial perception, see Lynette Jackson, *Surfacing Up: Psychiatry and Social Order in Colonial Zimbabwe, 1908–1968* (Ithaca, NY: Cornell University Press, 2005), 72–73.
56. For an example of an oral history in which priests were implicated in such deceptions, see Eggers, "Prophètes," 73–91.
57. In a discussion of the long history of extraction in eastern Congo, a Congolese friend said to me in 2014, "You know, the Belgians were notoriously the first to do this. And they started by taking our minkisi. All of those things that made our leaders powerful . . . all those spiritual objects . . . they came in and took them. This is why they were able to rule for so long and why our leaders remain ineffective." The quote illustrates the enduring nature of such rumors. Michael Ahuka, informal discussion with author, Kalemie, DRC, July 2014.
58. I borrow the terms *theories of power* and *theories of action* from Schoenbrun, "Violence and Vulnerability."
59. Bribosia, 1944, AA/AI 4737, 2–3.
60. Chef Kahombo Mbokani, audience du 4 juillet, cited in Lovens, *La révolte*, 62.
61. Reports of witchcraft accusations and violence are commonplace in eastern Congo today, as in many parts of Africa. In March of 2013, the

NGO SOS Femmes en Danger reported that three women from a single family in Uvira, South Kivu, were publicly burned to death for witchcraft. Personal communication, Amisi Mas (field director of SOS FED), March 14, 2013.

62. "Déposition de Monsieur De Schryver," 4, AA/AI 4737.
63. Bennetta Jules-Rosette, "At the Threshold of the Millennium: Prophetic Movements and Independent Churches in Central and Southern Africa," *Archives de sciences sociales des religions* 99 (July–September 1997): 127–44. See also Cynthia Hoehler-Fatton, *Women of Spirit and Fire: History, Faith, and Gender in Roho Religion in Western Kenya* (New York: Oxford University Press, 1996), 99.
64. See Jacques E. Gérard, *Les fondements syncrétiques du Kitawala* (Brussels: Centre de recherche et d'information socio-politiques, 1969); and Philippart, "Contributions à l'étude du Kitawala," 1954, AA/AI 4737.
65. Maman Kalema, interview with author, digital recording, Uvira, DRC, April 18, 2010.
66. Berger, *Religion and Resistance;* Hoehler-Fatton, *Women of Spirit;* Jules-Rosette, "At the Threshold"; Schoenbrun, *Green Place.*
67. See Jason Stearns, "Mass Rape in Walikale: What Happened?," *Congo Siasa* (blog), August 24, 2010, http://congosiasa.blogspot.com/2010/08/mass-rape-in-walikale-what-happened.html.
68. Hunt, "Acoustic Register," 224.
69. I am of course drawing here on Michael Taussig's notion of the "colonial mirror." Michael Taussig, "Culture of Terror, Space of Death: Roger Casement's Putamoyo Report and the Explanation of Torture," *Comparative Studies in Society and History* 26, no. 3 (July 1984): 494.
70. Jean-Paul Sartre, preface (1961) to Franz Fanon, *The Wretched of the Earth* (New York: Grove Press, 2004), lii.
71. Hunt, "Acoustic Register," 243.
72. This is the crux of Hunt's article, which is about the silence surrounding sexual violence condoned by the colonial state and its repetition in the present.
73. Schoenbrun, "Violence and Vulnerability," 742.
74. Didier Gondola, *Tropical Cowboys: Westerns, Violence, and Masculinity in Kinshasa* (Bloomington: Indiana University Press, 2016), 118.
75. Joset Files, dossier no. 4583, Divers, Archives africaines, Ministère belge d'affaires étrangères, Brussels.

CHAPTER 4: UNRULINESS

1. M. Kreutz, "Objet Kitawala au 16 janvier 1956," dossier no. 4737, Affaires indigènes Series, Archives africaines, Ministère belge d'affaires étrangères, Brussels (hereafter cited as AA/AI, followed by dossier no.). It is difficult to know from the source whether these connections to the Mau Mau movement were real or were a figment of colonial anxiety, but it is certainly

possible that these Kitawalists had heard about and been inspired by the Mau Mau movement.
2. Kreutz, 4737.
3. M. Kreutz, September 5, 1956, AA/AI 4737, 3.
4. Philippart, "Synthèse des premiers résultats de l'enquête Kitawala," March 6, 1956, AA/AI 4737. Belgians—like other colonial regimes—liked to rank different ethnic groups for their perceived intelligence and capacity for work. This Walengola-Bakumu/Topoke-Lekele distinction was perpetuated throughout the administration. In a memorandum about Kitawala policy, District Commissioner Kreutz makes the same distinction, worrying that the population of Topoke and Lokele were moving closer to Kimbanguism and that this was "particularly unsettling" because they were "much more intelligent than the Bakumu or Walengola." The most notorious example of this sort of ethnic ranking by the Belgians was their policy of importing Rwandaphone immigrant workers into the mining regions of the Kivus during the 1930s because they were perceived as more diligent and capable workers than the local "Bantu" populations. On this history, see Koen Vlassenroot, "Citizenship, Identity Formation and Conflict in South Kivu: The Case of the Banyamulenge," *Review of African Political Economy* 29, no. 93/94 (2002): 499–515.
5. Philippart, "Synthèse des premiers résultats," March 6, 1956, AA/AI 4737.
6. Years later, in a colony-wide report about Kitawala, Joset wrote of this era: "Still, until the moment of the revolt, nothing particularly worrisome was reported. The logbooks at the mines report a good state of spirit among the natives. It was a spirit of optimism in which, like a bomb suddenly exploding, the news of the revolt in Utunda came." Joset Files, dossier no. 4583, Divers, Archives africaines, Ministère belge d'affaires étrangères, Brussels (hereafter cited as AA/D, followed by the dossier no.).
7. The prevalence of such fears in colonial correspondences related to "subversive religious movements" during this period is remarkable. For a good example, see the report issued by Marmitte in 1950, "Politique contre les mouvements indigènes subversifs: Mission Marmitte 1948–1950," March 30, 1950, AA/AI 4736, 11–12.
8. "Politique à poursuivre à l'égard des mouvements politico-religieux," Léopoldville, February 25, 1957, AA/AI 4736, 7–8.
9. On this turn toward development policies as a solution for "the Kitawala Problem," see Nicole Eggers, "Kitawala in the Congo: Religion, Politics and Healing in Central Africa" (PhD diss., University of Wisconsin–Madison, 2013), chapter 5. See also Dominic Pistor, "Developmental Colonialism and Kitawala Policy in 1950s Belgian Congo," in *Religion, Colonization and Decolonization in Congo, 1885–1960*, ed. Vincent Viaene, Bram Cleys, and Jan De Maeyer (Leuven: Leuven University Press, 2020), 261–84.
10. Marmitte, "Politique contre," AA/AI 4736, 5.
11. Philippart, "Rapport de la prise de contact entre Monsieur Joset . . . ," April 5, 1956 [written May 26, 1956], AA/AI 4737; D. Halleux, "Note to Minister: Objet;

rapports de mission de P. E. Joset sur les sectes secrètes," December 10, 1956, AA/AI 4737; "Report of Kitawala in Opala," 1951, dossier no. 13.939, Governeur générale Series, Archives africaines, Ministère belge d'affaires étrangères, Brussels (hereafter cited as AA/GG, followed by dossier no.).

12. Philippart, "Contribution à l'étude du Kitawala," 1954, AA/AI 4737; and "Kitawala Rapport," 1956, AA/AI 4737.

13. See Mwene-Batende, *Mouvements messianiques et protestation sociale: Le cas du Kitawala chez les Kumu du Zaïre* (Kinshasa: Faculté de théologie catholique, 1982).

14. Aparicio et al.'s characterization of unruliness as refusals and contestations that were sometimes "illegible" is relevant here. Aparicio et al., introduction to *Ethnographic Refusals, Unruly Latinidades*, ed. Alex E. Chavéz and Gina M. Pérez (Albuquerque: University of New Mexico Press, 2022), xxvii.

15. Florence Bernault and Jan-Georg Deutsch, "Introduction: Control and Excess; Histories of Violence in Africa," *Africa: Journal of the International African Institute* 85, no. 3 (2015): 387–88.

16. Marisa J. Fuentes, *Dispossessed Lives: Enslaved Women, Violence, and the Archive* (Philadelphia: University of Pennsylvania Press, 2016); Ann Laura Stoler, *Along the Archival Grain* (Princeton, NJ: Princeton University Press, 2010).

17. Fuentes, *Dispossessed Lives;* Steven Feierman, "Colonizers, Colonized, and the Creation of Invisible Histories," in *Beyond the Cultural Turn: New Directions in the Study of Society and Culture,* ed. Victoria E. Bonnell and Lynn Hunt (Berkeley: University of California Press, 1999), 182–216.

18. Lynn M. Thomas, *Politics of the Womb: Women, Reproduction, and the State in Kenya* (Berkeley: University of California Press, 2003).

19. Anjali Arondekar, "Without a Trace: Sexuality and the Colonial Archive," *Journal of the History of Sexuality* 14, no. 1/2 (2005): 12.

20. G. M. Neutens, "Report of Kitawala in Opala," 1951, AA/GG 13.939.

21. Nicole Eggers, "Authority That Is Customary: Kitawala, Customary Chiefs, and the Plurality of Power in Congolese History," *Journal of East African History* 14, no. 1 (2020): 24–42.

22. On how power was "composed" historically in Central Africa, see Jane I. Guyer and Samuel M. Eno Belinga, "Wealth in People as Wealth in Knowledge: Accumulation and Composition in Equatorial Africa," *Journal of African History* 36, no. 1 (1995): 91–120.

23. Neutens, "Report of Kitawala in Opala," 1951, AA/GG13.939.

24. This is similar to a series of conversions that reported to have happened in Lowa in 1947: "Kitawala Interrogations: Pontheirville," 1947, AA/GG 13.939.

25. Neutens, "Report." The presence of the American flag here is a fascinating detail. It is part of a broader history of "America" as symbol of potential liberation in the teachings of many Kitawalists. Note that it is also present in Bushiri's dream and in his teachings discussed in chapter 3. The meaning of the flag in this moment is not entirely clear, but it is likely connected to both the historic relationship between Watchtower and the United States

and the broader discourse about Black American liberators circulating on the continent of Africa at the time. While discussion of this aspect of Kitawala's history is outside the scope of this chapter, it does appear in other studies of Kitawala. See also John Higginson, "Liberating the Captives: Independent Watchtower as an Avatar of Colonial Revolt in Southern Africa and Katanga, 1908–1941," *Journal of Social History* 26, no. 1 (1992): 64.
26. Hirokazu Yasuoka, "Sharing Elephant Meat and the Ontology of Hunting among the Baka Hunter-Gatherers in the Congo Basin Rainforest," in *Human-Elephant Interactions: From Past to Present*, ed. George E. Konidaris et al. (Tübingen, Germany: Tübingen University Press, 2021), 469–85.
27. Neutens, "Report."
28. Steven Feierman, "Explanation and Uncertainty in the Medical World of the Ghaambo," *Bulletin of the History of Medicine* 74, no. 2 (2000): 324.
29. Neutens, "Report."
30. Neutens, "Report."
31. W. Faelens, "Report of Kitawala in Opala," September 30, 1950, AA/GG 13939.
32. David Schoenbrun, *A Green Place, a Good Place: Agrarian Change, Gender, and Social Identity in the Great Lakes Region to the 15th Century* (Portsmouth, NH: Heinemann, 1998).
33. See, for example, Jacques E. Gérard, *Les fondements syncrétiques du Kitawala* (Brussels: Centre de recherche et d'information socio-politiques, 1969), 67–71.
34. David Schoenbrun, *The Names of the Python: Belonging in East Africa, 900 to 1930* (Madison: University of Wisconsin Press, 2021), 3–13.
35. Vicky Van Bockhaven, "Anioto: Leopard Men Killings and Institutional Dynamism in Northeast Congo, c. 1890–1940," *Journal of African History* 59, no. 1 (2018): 21–44.
36. Van Bockhaven, 44.
37. Neutens, "Report."
38. Neutens, "Report."
39. See, for example, Detheir F. M., "Lettre commissaire de Orientale," October 6, 1958, AA/GG 17715.
40. Neutens, "Report."
41. Léon Debertry, *Kitawala: Roman* (Elisabethville: Éditions essor du Congo, 1953).
42. Ann Laura Stoler, *Carnal Knowledge and Imperial Power: Race and the Intimate in Colonial Rule* (Berkeley: University of California Press, 2002); Anne McClintock, *Imperial Leather: Race, Gender, and Sexuality in the Colonial Contest* (New York: Routledge, 1995). On colonial anxieties about multiracial children and intermarriage, see, for example, Carina E. Ray, *Crossing the Color Line: Race, Sex, and the Contested Politics of Colonialism in Ghana* (Athens: Ohio University Press, 2015); Amandine Lauro, "Violence, Anxieties, and the Making of Interracial Dangers," in *The Routledge Companion to Sexuality and Colonialism*, ed. Chelsea Shields and Dagmar Herzog

(Abingdon, UK: Routledge, 2021), 327–38; and Damon Ieremia Salesa, *Racial Crossings: Race, Intermarriage, and the Victorian British Empire* (Oxford: Oxford University Press, 2011).

43. "Rapport no 2 sur les agissements des relégués de la secte 'Kitawala' en Lubutu," box 7, folder 1, Maurice Martin de Ryck Congo Papers (hereafter MMRC), Michigan State University, Lansing.

44. T. J. Tallie, *Queering Colonial Natal: Indigeneity and the Violence of Belonging in Southern Africa* (Minneapolis: University of Minnesota Press, 2019), 7.

45. This is not a new observation. Black feminist scholars, in particular, have demonstrated how it has been common colonial practice to assign sexual deviance to Blackness. See, for example, Jennifer L. Morgan, *Laboring Women: Reproduction and Gender in New World Slavery* (Philadelphia: University of Pennsylvania Press, 2004); and Julian B. Carter, *The Heart of Whiteness: Normal Sexuality and Race in America, 1880–1940* (Durham, NC: Duke University Press, 2007).

46. Thomas, *Politics of the Womb*, 4.

47. Amandine Lauro, "'J'ai l'honneur de porter plainte contre ma femme': Litiges conjugaux et administration coloniale au Congo belge (1930–1960)," *Clio: Femmes, Genre, Histoire*, no. 33 (2011): 65.

48. Steven Van Wolputte, "Love, Play and Sex: Polyamory and the Hidden Pleasures of Everyday Life in Kaoko, Northwest Namibia," in *Africa Every Day: Fun, Leisure, and Expressive Culture on the Continent*, ed. Oluwakemi M. Balogun et al. (Athens: Ohio University Press, 2019), 123–32. See also Thomas, *Politics of the Womb*.

49. It is possible there are more localized personal archives in Lowa that could address these issues. As Derek Peterson's work has made clear, African political actors often kept archives. But historians' work of "cataloguing, organizing, and preserving" the archives of such actors in a region like North Kivu is greatly complicated by the reality of periodic insecurity in the region. Due to the timing of my research, I have not been able to safely travel to that region. There is also no guarantee that such "tin trunk" archives exist, awaiting intrepid historians to "disinter" them and "edit them back into the story." The reality is that the history of access to education in the more remote regions of eastern Congo is not the same as other parts of East Africa. It was delayed, and minimal when it arrived. Belgian colonial education policy was notoriously abysmal. And missions were late to arrive in this region (as outlined in chapter 3). As the works of Pedro Monaville and Amandine Lauro illustrate, none of this stopped the Congolese from writing. But it is also not clear that the habit of writing "life histories" and keeping diaries was historically as common in rural regions of Congo in this era as in other regions of Africa. To be sure, more work is needed on this subject in Congo. See Derek R. Peterson, *Ethnic Patriotism and the East African Revival: A History of Dissent, c. 1935–1972* (Cambridge: Cambridge University Press, 2012), 27–32; Pedro Monaville, *Students of the World: Global*

1968 and Decolonization in the Congo (Durham, NC: Duke University Press, 2022), 1–62; Lauro, "'J'ai l'honneur'"; and also Karin Barber, "Introduction: Hidden Innovators in Africa," in *Africa's Hidden Histories: Everyday Literacy and Making the Self,* ed. Karin Barber (Bloomington: Indiana University Press, 2006), 1–24.

50. Letter from "wasultani wa inchi ya Opienge," October 12, 1953, AA/GG 17714.
51. It is possible that such letters may exist (with the caveats about limited education access noted above); unfortunately, I was not able to consult the "native complaints and requests (women)" files that Lauro used for her work to see if there were files related to Lowa or Kitawala. Lauro, "'J'ai l'honneur,'" 65–66.
52. Peterson, *Ethnic Patriotism,* 20.
53. For an excellent summary of such research, see Chelsea Schields and Dagmar Herzog, "Introduction: Sex, Intimacy, and Power in Colonial Studies," in Schields and Herzog, *Routledge Companion to Sexuality and Colonialism,* 4.
54. On the "sacred capacity" of bodies in Central Africa, see Florence Bernault, *Colonial Transactions: Imaginaries, Bodies, and Histories in Gabon* (Durham, NC: Duke University Press, 2019), 102–7.
55. Adriaan van Klinken, *Kenyan, Christian, Queer: Religion, LGBT Activism, and Arts of Resistance in Africa* (University Park: Pennsylvania State University Press, 2019), 177.
56. R. Philippart, "Contribution à l'étude du Kitawala," 1954, AA/AI 4737, 32.
57. "Rapport no. 2 sur les agissements," MMRC.
58. "Le Kitawala in the Province of Kivu," 1956, AA/D 4583.
59. "AIMO Rapport mensuel de janvier 1957," January 31, 1957, AA/GG 17578.
60. "Menées Kitawala en territoire Lubutu," 1947, AA/D 4583.
61. It is worth noting, as I will discuss further below, that both these men were disavowing their connection to Kitawala in these interrogations.
62. Van Wolputte, "Love, Play and Sex," 128.
63. Jack Boulton, "Experimental Intimacies: Young Men's Understandings of Their Relationships with Women in Swakopmund," *Journal of Namibian Studies* 22 (2017): 25–44.
64. "Le Kitawala in the Province of Kivu," 1956, AA/D 4583; "Rapport no. 2 sur les agissements," MMRC.
65. Joset Report, 1956, AA/AI 4737.
66. "Le Kitawala in the Province of Kivu," 1956, AA/D4583.
67. "Menées Kitawala en territoire Lubutu," 1947, AA/D4583.
68. For more on colonial anxieties about unruly—or "wicked"—African women, see Dorothy Louise Hodgson and Sheryl McCurdy, eds., *"Wicked" Women and the Reconfiguration of Gender in Africa* (Portsmouth, NH: Heinemann, 2005).
69. See, for example, Sarah Watkins, "Iron Mothers and Warrior Lovers: Intimacy, Power, and the State in the Nyiginya Kingdom, 1796–1913" (PhD diss., University of California, Santa Barbara, 2014); Komlan Agbedahin, "Interrogating

the Togolese Historical Sex Strike," *International Journal on World Peace* 31, no. 1 (2014): 7–25; and Ifi Amadiume, *Male Daughters, Female Husbands: Gender and Sex in an African Society* (London: Zed Books, 1987).
70. R. Philippart, "Contribution à l'étude du Kitawala," 1954, AA/AI 4737, 37.
71. Jacques Gérard, "Le Kitawala in the Province of Kivu," 1956, AA/D4583.
72. "Le Kitawala in the Province of Kivu," 1956, AA/D4583.
73. "Le Kitawala in the Province of Kivu," 170.
74. Yolanda Covington-Ward, *Gesture and Power: Religion, Nationalism, and Everyday Performance in Congo* (Durham, NC: Duke University Press, 2016), 119–21. See also Amandine Lauro, "'Notre peuple a perdu le sens de la danse honnête': Danses africaines, catégories légales et (re)définitions européennes de l'obscénité dans le Congo colonial," *C@hiers du CRHiDI: Histoire, droit, institutions, société* 38 (2016), https://doi.org/10.25518/1370-2262.246.
75. "Rapport no. 2 sur les agissements," MMRC.
76. R. Philippart, "Contribution à l'étude du Kitawala," 1954, AA/AI 4737, 33.
77. "Le Kitawala in the Province of Kivu," 1956, AA/D 4583; "Rapport no 2 sur les agissements," MMRC. See also the set of interrogations by Émile Bastin from Isangi, "Kitawala Lowa," 1947, AA/GG 13939.
78. Watkins, "Iron Mothers," 106–17. Here Watkins is drawing on Christopher C. Taylor, *Milk, Honey, and Money: Changing Concepts in Rwandan Healing* (Washington, DC: Smithsonian Institution Press, 1992). See also David S. Newbury, "What Role Has Kingship? An Analysis of the Umuganura Ritual of Rwanda as Presented in Marcel d'Hertefelt and André Coupez La royauté sacrée de l'ancien Rwanda (1964)," *Africa-Tervuren* 27 (1981): 89–101.
79. Schoenbrun, *Names of the Python*, 102–5.
80. Daniel Biebuyck, "Organisation politique des Nyanga: La chefferie Ihana," *Kongo-overzee* 22, no. 4/5 (1956): 315–16. Interestingly, descriptions from the Kitawala archives align with Biebyuck's descriptions as well. Take, for example, a 1945 report that came from a village near Pontheirville that some Kitawalists had been arrested for performing a baptism in which the initiates "had sexual relations in the presence of the initiator" who "assisted these relations." However, the similarity between this and the "public copulation" described by Biebuyck could very well be a result of the echo chamber of colonial knowledge production, as described above. "Affaire Batiamongambo et Crts," 1945, AA/GG 17714.
81. Mary Tew, "A Form of Polyandry among the Lele of the Kasai," *Africa: Journal of the International African Institute* 21, no. 1 (1951): 1–12.
82. Didier Gondola, *Tropical Cowboys: Westerns, Violence, and Masculinity in Kinshasa* (Bloomington: Indiana University Press, 2016), 8–10.
83. On intimacy and spirituality in Africa, see Fulata Lusungu Moyo, "Religion, Spirituality and Being a Woman in Africa: Gender Construction within the African Religio-Cultural Experiences," *Agenda: Empowering Women for Gender Equity*, no. 61 (2004): 72–78.

84. That the anxieties such male authorities had about "free women" might align with those of the colonial officials should not be surprising: scholars have observed such patriarchal synergies in numerous colonial contexts. See, for example, Thomas, *Politics of the Womb*.
85. That religious spaces often provided women with such opportunities is a widely acknowledged phenomenon, not unique to Kitawala.
86. Carina Ray similarly warns against investing too much analytical weight in binaries, namely consent and coercion: Ray, *Crossing the Color Line*, 5.
87. "Affaire Batiamongambo et Crts," 1945, AA/GG 17714.
88. O. Lartiller, "Report of Kitawala Numbers in Ponthierville," 1946, AA/GG 13.939.
89. "Kitawala Lowa," 1947, AA/GG 13939.
90. Trevor R. Getz and Liz Clarke, *Abina and the Important Men: A Graphic History* (New York: Oxford University Press, 2012).
91. "Kitawala Lowa," 1947, AA/GG 13939.
92. Another girl named Basie-Tsheusi made a similar accusation against Johanne-Beyaya. "Kitawala Lowa," 1947, AA/GG 13939.
93. A girl named Igwaboko-Akoziba, for example, says that she consented to intercourse. "Kitawala Lowa," 1947, AA/GG 13939.
94. There are numerous examples of this. I discuss this phenomenon at length in my dissertation, Eggers, "Kitawala in the Congo," chapter 5.
95. Gondola, *Tropical Cowboys*, 118.
96. See, for example, "Mulonda Mission," Report, AA/GG 74.343.
97. A similar report can be found from Litoko, outside of Pontheirville (Ubundu). W. Faelens, "Report of Kitawala in Opala," September 30, 1950, AA/GG 13939.
98. John M. Janzen, *Lemba, 1650–1930: A Drum of Affliction in Africa and the New World* (New York: Garland, 1982).
99. Kairn Klieman, *"The Pygmies Were Our Compass": Bantu and Batwa in the History of West Central Africa, Early Times to c. 1900 C.E.* (Portsmouth, NH: Heinemann, 2003), 70, 151, 160.
100. "Kitawala Lowa," 1947, AA/GG 13939.
101. Gérard, *Les fondements syncrétiques*, 85–92. Gérard's 1969 study was based upon the research he had conducted during the colonial era as a "Kitawala expert." To conduct that research, he posed as a "white Kitawalist" and became initiated in the church. Interestingly, the 1969 study goes much further in critiquing colonial government than the report that he produced for the colonial government. I discuss this in greater detail in Eggers, "Kitawala in the Congo," chapter 5.
102. Philippart, "Synthèse des premiers résultats," AA/AI 4737; D. Hallieux, "Rapports de mission de M.P.E. Joset sur les sectes secretes," AA/AI 4736.
103. Placide Tempels, *Bantu Philosophy* (Paris: Presènce africaine, 1959); Gérard, *Les fondements syncrétiques*, 90.
104. Gondola, *Tropical Cowboys*, 116–46; Nancy Rose Hunt, "An Acoustic Register, Tenacious Images, and Congolese Scenes of Rape and Repetition," *Cultural Anthropology* 23, no. 3 (2008): 220–53.

105. "Kitawala Lowa," 1947, AA/GG 13939.
106. "Kitawala Lowa," 1947.
107. Report from Yalikombo, January 1957, AA/GG 17714.
108. I borrow the term *moral project* here from Derek R. Peterson, "The Intellectual Lives of Mau Mau Detainees," *Journal of African History* 49, no. 1 (2008): 75.
109. R. Philippart, "Affaire Lotika Jean," November 1958, AA/GG 921.

CHAPTER 5: RELEGATION

1. All the stories in this first section come out of two different interviews I conducted with Pastor Théophile Mulongo (and other members of the community who were present) at COLAGREL on August 9–10, 2018 (digital recording, Kasaji, Lualaba, DRC).
2. On the ubiquity of the use of the chicotte by Belgian colonial authorities—and the Force Publique as their enforcers—see the work of Congolese artist Tshibumba in Johannes Fabian, *Remembering the Present: Painting and Popular History in Zaire* (Berkeley: University of California Press, 1996). See also Marie-Bénédicte Dembour, "La chicote comme symbole du colonialisme belge?," *Canadian Journal of African Studies* 26, no. 2 (1992): 205–25.
3. Personal correspondence with Albert Van den Eynde (son of Karel Van den Eynde, the prison director at COLAGREL from 1956 to 1958), April 2021–August 2022. I am grateful to Van den Eynde for reaching out to me and sharing his family archives and memories after reading a short blog post about COLGREL that I wrote in 2020. See Eggers, "Remembering COLAGREL: Space, Memory, and Oral History," *Comparing the Copperbelt* (blog), November 19, 2019, https://copperbelt.history.ox.ac.uk/2019/11/19/remembering-colagrel-space-memory-and-oral-history-nicole-eggers/. Some of the language and content of that blog post also appears in this chapter.
4. Tamara Giles-Vernick calls such spaces "sites of recollection" and reminds us that they evoke "body memory," or memory that is felt or evoked in a space and goes beyond narrative. Tamara Giles-Vernick, "Lives, Histories, and Sites of Recollection," in *African Words, African Voices: Critical Practices in Oral History*, ed. Luise S. White, Stephan F. Miescher, and David William Cohen (Bloomington: Indiana University Press, 2001), 194–213.
5. Nancy Rose Hunt, *A Nervous State: Violence, Remedies, and Reverie in Colonial Congo* (Durham, NC: Duke University Press, 2016), 8.
6. Hunt, 5–8.
7. De Coene et al. have very recently published an article on Mpadist relégués in Opala that takes prisoner experiences very seriously. And Nancy Hunt has written about Kitawalist prisoners in Ekafera. But no such account of COLAGREL exists. Pieter De Coene, Margot Luyckfasseel, and Gillian Mathys, "Voices from Exile: The Mpadist Mission des Noirs in Oshwe's Prison Camps in the Belgian Congo (1940–1960)," *International Journal*

of African Historical Studies 55, no. 1 (2022): 89–114; Hunt, *Nervous State*, 167–206.

8. The major exception here is Nancy Hunt's *Nervous State*, which is an excellent analysis of some of the carceral techniques employed at EKAFERA, a penal colony located in Equateur that also detained many Kitawalist prisoners. De Coen et al., "Voices from Exile," is also an important exception here.

9. The idea that Kitawala freed people from both physical and spiritual slavery came up in multiple interviews with contemporary Kitawalists: Ilunga Wesele Joseph, interview with author, digital recording, Kitawala Mission, seventeen kilometers (11 mi.) outside of Kalemie, Katanga, DRC, November 11, 2010; Shindano Masubi Ayubu, Mission Kitawaliste, seventy-four kilometers (46 mi.) from Kalemie, Katanga, DRC, 2010; and Elders of Église de Dieu de nos Ancestres au Congo (EDAC), digital recording, interview with author, Uvira, DRC, September 4, 2010. While this chapter focuses on how Kitawalists attempted to mobilize forms of spiritual power to protect themselves in the context of their incarceration, such forms of resistance have been observed elsewhere in the context of imprisonment in Africa. See, for example, Ibrahima Thioub, "Sénégal: La prison à l'époque coloniale; Significations, évitement et évasions," in *Enfermement, prison et châtiments en Afrique: Du 19e siècle à nos jours*, ed. Florence Bernault (Paris: Karthala, 1999), 294.

10. That colonial states were plagued by inconsistency and fragility, subject to internal divisions and political constraints, and regularly operating in the context of multiple misunderstandings, misreadings, and misrepresentations is an argument that has been put forth by numerous scholars of colonial studies. For good examples of this kind of literature, see Frederick Cooper, *Colonialism in Question: Theory, Knowledge, History* (Berkeley: University of California Press, 2005); and Frederick Cooper and Ann Laura Stoler, eds., *Tensions of Empire: Colonial Cultures in a Bourgeois World* (Berkeley: University of California Press, 1997). For a good discussion on the "ubiquity" of resistance in colonial prisons, see Florence Bernault, "The Politics of Enclosure in Colonial and Post-polonial Africa," in *A History of Prison and Confinement in Africa*, ed. Florence Bernault (Portsmouth, NH: Heinemann, 2003), 27–29. See also David Anderson, *Histories of the Hanged: The Dirty War in Kenya and the End of Empire* (New York: W. W. Norton, 2005), 324–25; Caroline Elkins, *Imperial Reckoning: The Untold Story of Britain's Gulag in Kenya* (New York: Henry Holt, 2005), 158–59; and Dior Konaté, *Prison Architecture and Punishment in Colonial Senegal* (Lanham, MD: Lexington Books, 2018), 179. Individuals subject to containment in *cordones sanitaires*—sanitary camps set up to isolate people infected with sleeping sickness in colonial Congo—also resisted their confinement. Maryinez Lyons, "From 'Death Camps' to *Cordon Sanitaire:* The Development of Sleeping Sickness Policy in the Uele District of the Belgian Congo, 1903–1914," *Journal of African History* 26, no. 1 (1985): 81.

11. Bernault has also discussed how, in colonial Africa, some aspects of penal confinement "resonated with ancient, local forms of spatial captivity and physical seclusion," including forms of "spiritual retreats." Bernault, "Politics of Enclosure," 5. See also Marie Morelle, *Yaoundé carcérale: Géographie d'une ville et de sa prison* (Lyon: ENS Éditions, 2019).
12. "Note pour Monsieur A. Buissert, Ministre des colonies," June 15, 1957, dossier no. 4736, Affaires indigènes, Archives africaines, Ministère belge d'affaires étrangères, Brussels (hereafter cited as AA/AI, followed by the dossier no.).
13. Non-Congolese convicted of violating this decree were evicted from the colony rather than relegated.
14. The 1936 decree clarified that the 1906 decree would apply to Kitawalists. The 1943 decree stipulated that if an individual was arrested for violating the 1906 decree, they should be either released or immediately proposed for relegation rather than detained in prison. For a brief legal history of relegation, see the report from February 5, 1957, dossier no. 14 21/6 (d), Justice, Archives africaines, Ministère belge d'affaires étrangères, Brussels (hereafter cited as AA/JUST, followed by the dossier no.).
15. I've taken the term *dispersive* from a 1951 report by the assistant territorial administrator of Pontheirville (Ubundu) named M. Kreutz. In the report, Kreutz complains about the many challenges that the "*dispersion*" of the relégués has created for administrators, advocating instead for the "*concentration*" of dangerous Kitawalists. Letter from M. Kreutz to admin. of territory, July 7, 1951, dossier no. 13.939, Gouverneur générale Series, Archives africaines, Ministère belge d'affaires étrangères, Brussels (hereafter cited as AA/GG, followed by the dossier no.).
16. I have previously discussed this form of relegation in an article on Kitawala and customary authority: Nicole Eggers, "Authority That Is Customary: Kitawala, Customary Chiefs, and the Plurality of Power in Congolese History," *Journal of Eastern African Studies* 14, no. 1 (2020): 24–42. *Natal relegation* is my term and does not appear in the archive.
17. In addition to chapter 1, I discuss the history Kulu Mapenda in "Authority That Is Customary."
18. See, for example, the arrest records for Afiongo, Ilunga Levi, Kilungu Bernard, and Nduya Alphonse in "Synthèse du mouvement subversif Kitawala," 1955/56, AA/AI 1621, 1–168.
19. This official was actually describing how the policy worked in the area around Oshwe, which was mostly used for Kimbanguists and other related movements, but it worked very similarly in other areas: "Complaint about reléguée behavior," August 1937, dossier no. 1630–9184, p. 3, Service AIMO Gouvernement Générale, Archives africaines, Ministère belge d'affaires étrangères, Brussels (hereafter cited as AA/AIMOGG, followed by dossier no.). The term *résidence fixé* was used interchangeably with *résidence obligatoire* and *résidence forcée*. All three are used in one major

report on Kitawala, "Synthèse du mouvement," 1955/56, AA/AI 1621, 124, 143, and 189.
20. A number of Kitawalists also ended up relegated to the areas around Boende and Opienge. For an extensive list of names of prisoners and their relegation records, see "Synthèse du mouvement," 1955/56, AA/AI 1621, 1–168.
21. I put "free" in quotations here because other laborers were often coerced into the labor camps in a variety of ways.
22. In fact, the earliest document I have seen that suggests the idea of putting religious dissidents, in particular, in penal colonies is from 1931, but it took several years for the idea to come to fruition as policy. Untitled document, 1931, AA/AIMO 1630–9184.
23. See, for example, Prescobel, "Report on the Repression of Subversive Associations," 1938, AA/GG 17714.
24. The arrest and transfer records for these individuals, as well as 246 other individuals relegated to Malonga in this period, can be found in "Synthèse du mouvement," 1955/56, AA/AI 1621, 1–168.
25. "Note du Chef du Service des AIMO suit à sa visite de la colonie agricole de KASAJI," 1948, AA/GG 17502.
26. Hunt, *Nervous State*, 173.
27. "Rapport," February 5, 1957, in AA/JUST 15 21/6 (d).
28. Colonial officials frequently fretted, particularly by the 1950s, that the "subversive currents" of different movements would collide, not only with each other but also with communism and lead to "unification of actions." One such correspondence can be found in "Letter about Children in the CARDS," May 16, 1959, AA/GG 17687.
29. Letter from Jaegher on the subject of the new camp in Kasai, January 1956, AA/GG 17687.
30. The first "villages" for relégués in Malonga were organized in 1937 by J. Galand, who thought it was a bad idea to put leaders and "simple adepts" in the same camps. "Rapports mensuels," 1950, AA/GG 17502.
31. Many administrators doubted that any of the Kitawalists in the camp were truly reformed. In 1958, one official—F. M. Dentheir—argued that all the reformed Kitawalists were "acting in a comedy of repentance." Lettre commissaire de Orientale, October 6, 1958, AA/GG 17715.
32. See, for example, the request by the director of COLAGREL, Maurice Matton, that prisoners who were reformed should be allowed to leave the camp, lest he be called a liar who had made "false premises" to the prisoners: "Rapport mensuel mars 1951," March 1951, AA/GG 17502. See also "Notes sur les demandes et propositions de levée de relégation," n.d. [mid-1950s], AA/GG 17714.
33. F. M. Dentheir, Lettre commissaire de Orientale, October 6, 1958, AA/GG 17715.
34. For examples of letters and reports that echo similar concerns across decades of relegation, see letter from M. Kreutz to admin. of territory, July 16,

1951, AA/GG; "Politique contre les mouvements indigènes subversifs: Mission Marmitte 1948–1950," March 30, 1950, AA/AI 4736, 14; Philippart, "Contribution à l'étude du Kitawala," 1954, AA/AI 4737; and Joset, report 1956, AA/AI 4737.

35. Paul Ernst Joset, "Nouvelle politique à appliquer vis-à-vis des mouvements politico-religieux," June 15, 1957, AA/AI 4736.
36. Elkins, *Imperial Reckoning*; Anderson, *Histories of the Hanged*.
37. "Monsieur ATAP Philippart à Kasaji," 1957, AA/GG 13441.
38. "Synthèse du mouvement," 1955/56, AA/AI 1621, 124.
39. Église Kitawala, *Histoire de l'Église Kitawala: Prophète Ilunga Kadiba Émile*, Union des Missions Chretiennes du Congo (UMCC/WT). This is a history of Kitawala, specifically focused on the life of Ilunga Kadiba Émile, written by the subset of Kitawalists who consider Kadiba a prophet. It is a fascinating account that clearly draws from both oral history of the community and the "Synthèse du mouvement" (1955/56, AA/AI 1621), at least one copy of which has circulated in their community for many years. I do not know what year the history was written or the name of the author. It is also discussed in chapter 1.
40. I have no record indicating whether a specific event finally precipitated Kadiba's transfer, but his refusal to stop teaching Kitawala was almost certainly at the center of the story. According to his arrest record, he arrived at Ekafera on December 12, 1945: "Synthèse du mouvement," 1955/56, AA/AI 1621, 49.
41. "Synthèse du mouvement," 124.
42. "Synthèse du mouvement," 1–168.
43. Pastor Théophile Mulongo, interview with author, digital recording, COLAGREL, Kasaji, Lualaba, DRC, August 9, 2018.
44. COLAGREL was created under ordinance 216/AO of July 12, 1943. "Rélégues Kitawala pour colonie agricole Kasaji," 1947, AA/GG 17502.
45. On the history of the "cité-jardin," see Françoise Dubost, "Le modèle des cités-jardins: La modernité à l'épreuve du temps," *Ethnologie française* 26, no. 1 (1996): 92–99. See also Liora Bigon, "Garden Cities in Colonial Africa: A Note on Historiography," *Planning Perspectives* 28, no. 3 (2013): 477–85.
46. Most examples of the "garden city" as urban planning in colonial Africa appear to have been directed toward White residential areas in segregated cities. However, Liora Bigon has noted how colonial officials in Southern Rhodesia created a "garden city" neighborhood in Bulawayo for the "skilled" natives living in the city, which was meant, in a "spirit of paternalism and social evolutionism," to transplant African natives "from huts to houses." Bigon, "Garden Cities," 480.
47. "Note du Chef du Service des AIMO suit à sa visite de la colonie agricole de KASAJI," December 1948, AA/GG 17502a. Here again, Hunt's argument that "nervousness"—in its myriad forms—as a central mood in colonial Congo proves relevant. Hunt, *Nervous State*.

48. "Rapport pour Mars 1951," March 1951, AA/GG 17502.
49. "Création et organization colonie relégués à Kasaji," 1947, AA/GG 17502.
50. "Relégués Kitawala pour colonie agricole Kasaji," 1947, AA/GG 17502.
51. P. Montenez, "Note du Chef Du Service des AIMO suit à sa visite de la colonie agricole de KASAJI," February 7, 1948, AA/GG 17502.
52. "Situation du Director du COLAGREL," 1951, AA/GG 17502.
53. "Synthèse du mouvement," 1955/56, AA/AI 1621, 170–71.
54. "Synthèse du mouvement," 173.
55. "Manono; R. 2169 Suite du judgement du 6 janvier 1942," Maurice Martin de Ryck Collection (hereafter MMRC), Michigan State University, Lansing, cited in John Higginson, "Liberating the Captives: Independent Watchtower as an Avatar of Colonial Revolt in Southern Africa and Katanga, 1908–1941," *Journal of Social History* 26, no. 1 (1992): 71.
56. "Synthèse du mouvement," 1955/56, AA/AI 1621, 171.
57. Higginson, "Liberating the Captives," 71.
58. "Synthèse du mouvement," 1955/56, AA/AI 1621, 171.
59. "Document concernent le mouvement Kitawala," n.d., AA/AI 4737. It is unclear who authored this brief report or in which year it was produced, but it appears to have been produced at some point in the late 1940s.
60. It is possible that more of them ended up at Malonga. I was only able to confirm that thirteen were sent to Malonga based on the arrest records, but those records are by no means complete: "Synthèse du mouvement," 1955/56, AA/AI 1621, 1–168.
61. Writing about penal camps in colonial Senegal, Dior Konaté has likewise noted the ease with which prisoners in such camps were able to communicate with those outside the camps. See Konaté, *Prison Architecture*, 180–82.
62. "Rapport mensuels juin 1950," AA/GG 17502.
63. Pastor Théophile Mulongo, interview with author, digital recording, COLAGREL, Lulalaba, DRC, August 10, 2018.
64. Maurice Matton, "Rapport mensuels août 1949," August 1949, AA/GG 17502.
65. *Historia ya Kanisa: Biographie ya Baba Prophet* is a handwritten history of the church of Kitawala of Kadiba's followers that church leaders shared with me via WhatsApp in February 2019. There is no identified author. It is a version of oral history that has been written down by the historians within the church. It is a seven-page document, a copy of which I have in my personal archive. It was written in Swahili. It is also discussed in chapter 1.
66. *Historia ya Kanisa*, 4.
67. *Historia ya Kanisa*, 8.
68. Using vague language in the context of insinuating immoral or selfish behavior is a common sociolinguist practice in eastern Congo. See, for example, Nico Nassenstein, "The Linguistic Taboo of Poisoning in Kivu Swahili," in "Taboo in Language and Discourse," ed. Alexandra Y. Aikenvald and Anne Storch, special issue, *The Mouth*, no. 4 (May 2019): 117–34.

69. *Histoire*, 8. On the broader Central African phenomenon, see Peter Geschiere, *The Modernity of Witchcraft: Politics and the Occult in Postcolonial Africa* (Charlottesville: University of Virginia Press, 1997); and Wyatt MacGaffey, *Kongo Political Culture: The Conceptual Challenge of the Particular* (Bloomington: Indiana University Press, 2000), 2–12.
70. See, for example, "AIMO Rapport mensuel janvier 1957," January 31, 1957, AA/GG 17578; "Rapport sur l'incident à la COLAGREL des 14 et 15/11/1958," November 1958, AA/GG 17578-3; and "Relégués Kitawala pour colonie agricole Kasaji," 1947, AA/GG 17502.
71. "Rapport mensuel août 1949," 1949, AA/GG 17502. Elsewhere, Matton expresses that this council of regional leaders was also a ploy to sow dissent among the leadership, since he chose the "leaders" for each group that he thought would be most cooperative rather than the ones the different groups identified themselves: "Rapport mensuel déc. 1949," 1949, AA/GG 17502.
72. Caroline Elkins has written about a similar kind of dynamic in Mau Mau detention camps, where leaders from within the detainee community helped to organize the prisoners for "maximum resistance." Elkins, *Imperial Reckoning*, 158–59.
73. Ngoie is spelled "Ngoy" in the archival documents, but I have altered the spelling to match that used in the Kitawalist sources so that it is clearer that it is the same person.
74. "Rapport mensuel october 1951," 1951, AA/GG, 17502.
75. See, for example, "Sûreté Kitawala et Mulonda Mission," December 1958, AA/GG 14343.
76. The most infamous example of sabotage by Kitawalists is the Kisangani plots discussed in chapter 4. Both the Lobutu-Masisi uprising (see chapter 3) and the Manono incidents discussed above are examples of Kitawalists involved in work-stoppage and rioting.
77. "Rapport mensuel avril 1951," 1951, AA/GG 17502.
78. "Rapport de Route du Commissaire de District Assistant Galand," July 19, 1947, AA/GG 17502.
79. "Note du Chef du Service des AIMO suit à sa visite de la colonie agricole de KASAJI," 1948, AA/GG 17502.
80. "Monsieur ATAP Philippart à Kasaji," 1957, AA/GG 13441.
81. "Rapport mensuel Colagrel mars 1950," April 1950, AA/GG 17502.
82. "Fiche de punitions et fiche de renseignements, Kulu Mupenda Kandeke," September 1949, AA/GG 17502.
83. "Rapport mois de novembre 1948," 17502b.
84. "Incidents COLAGREL Kasaji," November 19, 1958, AA/GG 17578.
85. "Rapport sur l'incident à la COLAGREL des 14 et 15/11/1958," 1958, AA/GG 17578.
86. According to a letter written by Van den Eynde's wife on August 10, 1956, they had "ammunition enough to blow up the whole Belgian army" in their

bedroom. "Op 10 augustus 1956 schrijft mijn moeder vanuit Colagrel," trans. Albert Van den Eynde, Archief Karel Van den Eynde (1926–2008).

87. "Rapport sur l'incident à la COLAGREL," 1958, AA/GG 17578.
88. "Incidents COLAGREL Kasaji," November 19, 1958, AA/GG 17578.
89. "Rapport sur l'incident à la COLAGREL," 1958, AA/GG 17578.
90. "Incidents COLAGREL Kasaji," November 19, 1958, AA/GG 17578.
91. According to the Kitawalists' own history, Kadiba's previous American correspondences were letters to Judge Rutherford, who sent them Watchtower materials. *Historia ya Kanisa*, 6.
92. Pedro Monaville, *Students of the World: Global 1968 and Decolonization in the Congo* (Durham, NC: Duke University Press, 2022), 13–15, 39. On African strategies of "extraversion," see Jean-François Bayart and Stephen Ellis, "Africa in the World: A History of Extraversion," *African Affairs* 99, no. 395 (2000): 217–67.
93. Kitawala church elders, interview with author, digital recording, Kalemie, DRC, October 19, 2010.
94. "Rapport mensuel août 1951, Avis du Commissaire de District," 1951, AA/GG 17502.
95. Chikwanga is a kind of cassava bread that is fermented and steamed in banana leaves and is a popular staple throughout the region. "Fiche de punitions et fiche de renseignements, Goy Simbi David," 1949, AA/GG 17502.
96. Henroteaux, "Situation du Director du Colagrel," January 20, 1951, AA/GG 17502.
97. "Rapport mensuel mars 1951," 1951, AA/GG 17502.
98. "AIMO Rapport mensuel janvier 1957," January 31, 1957, AA/GG 17578.
99. "Rapport mensuel juin 1950," 1950, AA/GG 17502.
100. In 1955, the colonial administration had made it an official part of the agenda to "set up a team composed of 5 experienced agents having in their attributes not only the screening of leaders, but also the intensive counterpropaganda in regions deemed contaminated." M. Kreutz, 1956, AA/AI 4737, 2.
101. R. Philippart, "Rapport au sujet de la visite effectuée à la colonie agricole de Kasaji par l'administratuer territorial ASST. PPL. Philippart, Stanleyville, le 5 sept. 1956," AA/AI 4736.
102. Philippart, 5.
103. Matton was against building a school for the children, which he believed would lead to the creation of future propagandists. He thought it better to leave them in ignorance and make farmers out of them. Letter from Massart, 1947, AA/GG 17502. But, according to a letter written by his wife, Karel Van den Eynde, "general compulsory schooling until the age of 16" as "the only solution" to the "anarchist" teachings of Kitawala. Letter of September 9, 1956, trans. Albert Van den Eynde, Archief Karel Van den Eynde (1926–2008).
104. Pastor Théophile Mulongo, informal discussion with author, field notes, Kasaji, Lualaba, DRC, August 11, 2018.

105. "Rapport mensuel Colagrel mars 1950," April 1950, AA/GG, 17502.
106. She was the first woman designated as such. She was canonized during a Kitawalist conference in Likasi in 1998. Her story is told in a document titled "Biography of Mama Saint Nkulu Kwamwanya Adolphine," an official church document kept by the Kitawalist church in Lubumbashi. It is a handwritten document with no date or named author. I have a copy in my personal archive.
107. Pastor Théophile Mulongo, interview with author, digital recording, COLAGREL, Kasaji, Lualaba, DRC, August 10, 2018.
108. Letter from Bafwasende, 1948, AA/GG 17714.
109. Mission Marmitte, July 15, 1949, AA/AI 4736, 4.
110. "Rapport mensuel Colagrel mars 1950," April 1950, AA/GG 17501.
111. F. M. Detheir, Lettre commissaire de Orientale, October 6, 1958, AA/GG 17715.
112. Kitawalist mass, field notes, Kasaji, Lualaba, DRC, August 11, 2018. While most of this mass is recorded, my audio recorder was unfortunately off for the first thirty minutes or so of the service, which is when this elder testified.
113. Pastor Mulongo said of this period: "In the '60s and '70s we did not live in the houses the Belgians had built. In the '70s we started to go back in there. They were just empty. But then they said, 'These houses can't just sit empty,' so we went back in. We had built them." Interview with the author, digital recording, COLAGREL, Kasaji, Lualaba, DRC, August 11, 2018.

CHAPTER 6: POSTS

1. Mwene-Batende, "Le Kitawala dans l'évolution socio-politique récente: Cas du groupe Belukela dans la ville de Kisangani," *Cahiers des religions africaines* 10, no. 19 (1976): 94.
2. Mwene-Batende, 96.
3. Mwene-Batende's discussion of Bulukela Kitawalists' theology is fascinating. For further details, see Mwene-Batende, 96–104.
4. PP2, interview with author, digital recording, Kabalo, DRC, August 28, 2018.
5. Pastor Théophile Mulongo, interview with author, digital recording, COLAGREL, Lualaba, DRC, August 9, 2018.
6. Anonymous, *Historia ya Kanisa: Biographie ya Baba Prophete* (n.d.). This Swahili-language document was given to me by the leadership of Kitawala in Lubumbashi in 2019. They photographed it and shared it with me via a WhatsApp message. I have a copy of this document in my personal archive.
7. See, for example, Achille Mbembe, *Necropolitics* (Durham, NC: Duke University Press, 2019); Achille Mbembe, *On the Postcolony* (Berkeley: University of California Press, 2001); Richard Werbner, ed., *Memory and the Postcolony: African Anthropology and the Critique of Power* (London: Zed Books, 1998); and Kwame Anthony Appiah, *In My Father's House: Africa in the Philosophy of Culture* (London: Methuen, 1992).

8. Wamba dia Wamba and Ne Muanda Nsemi are both polarizing figures in Congo's modern history. Here I consider them not as modern political actors but as theorists whose reflections on the nature of history are worthy of consideration. Wamba dia Wamba, "Bundu dia Kongo: A Kongolese Self-Styled Fundamentalist Religious Movement," in *East African Expressions of Christianity*, ed. Thomas Spear and Isaria Kimambo (Oxford: James Currey, 1999), 222. On the history of Ne Muanda Nsemi, see Denis M. Tull, "Troubled State-Building in the DR Congo: The Challenge from the Margins," *Journal of Modern African Studies* 48, no. 4 (2010): 643–61; and Yolanda Covington-Ward, *Gesture and Power: Religion, Nationalism, and Everyday Performance in Congo* (Durham, NC: Duke University Press, 2016), 166–87. On the biography of Wamba dia Wamba, see Horace G. Campbell, "The Journey of Wamba dia Wamba and the Struggles for Emancipatory Politics in Africa," *Africa Development / Afrique et Développement* 45, no. 2 (2020): 143–66.
9. David Gordon, *Invisible Agents: Spirits in Central African History* (Athens: Ohio University Press, 2012).
10. Ramon Sarró, "Writing as Rupture: On Prophetic Invention in Central Africa," in *Ruptures: Anthropologies of Discontinuity in Times of Turmoil*, ed. Martin Holbraad, Bruce Kapferer, and Julia F. Sauma (London: UCL Press, 2019), 140.
11. Bogumil Jewsiewicki, "Figures des mémoires congolaises de Lumumba: Moïse, héros culturel, Jésus-Christ," in *Patrice Lumumba entre Dieu et diable: Un héros africaine dans ses images*, ed. Pierre Halen and János Riesz (Paris: L'Harmattan, 1997), 386.
12. Isabelle De Rezende, "Visuality and Colonialism in the Congo: From the 'Arab War' to Patrice Lumumba, 1880s to 1961" (PhD diss., University of Michigan, 2012), 394–95.
13. Filip De Boeck, "Beyond the Grave: History, Memory and Death in Postcolonial Congo/Zaire," in Werbner, *Memory and the Postcolony*, 34–39.
14. Katrien Pype, "Lumumba and Kabila: Heroes for the Present? Visual Media, Memory and Politics in DR Congo Festive Year 2010" (paper presented at the 54th Annual Meeting of the African Studies Association, November 2011); cited with author's permission.
15. Johannes Fabian, *Remembering the Present: Painting and Popular History in Zaire* (Berkeley: University of California Press, 1996).
16. Bogumil Jewsiewicki, "Corps interdits: La représentation christique de Lumumba comme rédempteur du peuple zaïrois," *Cahiers d'études africaines* 36, no. 141/142 (1996): 113–42.
17. Jewsiewicki, "Figures des mémoires," 386.
18. Jewsiewicki, 386.
19. EDAC elders, interview with author, digital recording, Baraka, DRC, June 17, 2010.
20. Wamba dia Wamba, "Bundu dia Kongo," 222.

21. Kabanga Kamalondo, interview with author, digital recording, Kalemie, DRC, October 18, 2010.
22. Letter to the governor of Orientale, December 2, 1959, doc. no. 13.939, Gouvernement générale Series, Archives africaines, Ministère belge d'affaires étrangères, Brussels (hereafter cited as AA/GG, followed by doc. no.).
23. Luise White, *Speaking with Vampires: Rumor and History in Colonial Africa* (Berkeley: University of California Press, 2000).
24. Emery Kalema, "Congolese Regimes and Lumumba's Ethics of Care" (presentation for the American Historical Association, April 22, 2021); cited with permission of author. The idea of "enmity" as politics has also been developed in Achille Mbembe, "The Society of Enmity," *Radical Philosophy* 200 (November/December 2016): 23–35, https://www.radicalphilosophy.com/article/the-society-of-enmity.
25. Kabanga Kamalondo, interview with author, digital recording, Kalemie, DRC, October 18, 2010.
26. Kamalondo, October 19, 2010; Sermy Nsenga, interview with author, digital recording, Kalemie, DRC, October 19, 2010.
27. Guy Bernard, "La contestation et les églises nationales au Congo," *Canadian Journal of African Studies* 5, no. 2 (1971): 155.
28. Bernard, 155.
29. Ordinance 71/012, December 31, 1971. For the juridical text, see Jean-Pacifique Balaamo Mokelwa, *Église et état en République du Congo: Fondements juridiques et jurisprudence (1876–2006)* (Paris: L'Harmattan, 2009), 139. Under the law, all Protestant churches were consolidated into a single organization, the Église du Christ au Zaïre. The Catholic Church, the Greek Orthodox Church, and the Kimbanguist church (EJCSK) were also officially recognized, while seven hundred independent churches were denied civil status. Bennetta Jules-Rosette, "At the Threshold of the Millennium: Prophetic Movements and Independent Churches in Central and Southern Africa," *Archives de sciences sociales des religions* 99 (July–September 1997): 153.
30. Michael Schatzberg, *The Dialectics of Oppression in Zaire* (Bloomington: Indiana University Press, 1988), 130.
31. Michael Schatzberg, *Political Legitimacy in Middle Africa: Father, Family, Food* (Bloomington: Indiana University Press, 2001), 138.
32. Emmanuel Dungia, *Mobutu et l'argent du Zaïre: Les révélations d'un diplomate, ex-agent des services secrets* (Paris: L'Harmattan, 1993), 42–49. See also Stephen Ellis and Gerrie ter Haar, *Worlds of Power: Religious Thought and Political Practice in Africa* (New York: Oxford University Press, 2004), 70–113.
33. Ellis and ter Haar, *Worlds of Power*, 92.
34. David Garbin, "Sacred Remittances: Money, Migration and the Moral Economy of Development in a Transnational African Church," *Journal of Ethnic and Migration Studies* 45, no. 11 (2019): 2048. See also Filip De Boeck, *Kinshasa: Tales of the Invisible City* (Ghent: Ludion, 2004), 207.

35. Kabanga Kamalondo, interview with author, digital recording, Kalemie, DRC, October 19, 2010.
36. Mama Marceline, conversation with author, field notes, Uvira, DRC, May 2010.
37. Ellis and ter Haar, *Worlds of Power*, 107–8.
38. Schatzberg, *Dialectics of Oppression*, 130.
39. Mwene-Batende, *Mouvements messianiques et protestation sociale: Le cas du Kitawala chez les Kumu du Zaïre* (Kinshasa: Faculté de théologie catholique, 1982).
40. I possess few verifying records for these arrests; PP2, however, did show me the release papers for his uncle—Kalenga André—from prison sentences served in 1970 (six months for refusing the census) and 1971 (sixty days, for reasons not stated).
41. PP2, interview with author, digital recording, Kabalo, DRC, August 28, 2018.
42. I put "raffia clothing" in quotes here because this is how PP2's community was uncritically described by the UNICEF writer discussed in chapter 7.
43. "Politique à poursuivre à l'égard des mouvements politico-religieux," Léopoldville, February 25, 1957, doc. no. 4736, p. 7, Affaires indigènes Series, Archives africaines, Ministère belge d'affaires étrangères, Brussels (hereafter cited as AA/AI, followed by doc. no.).
44. Ngoy Kyunga wa Nsungu, "Étude comparative de deux mouvements politico-religieux: Le Kimbanguisme et le Kitawala 1921–1960" (Mémoire présenté et défendu en vue de l'obtention du grade de licencié en pédagogie appliquée, University of Lubumbashi, 2001).
45. Maurice Matton, "Rapport mensuel d'août 1949," August 1949, AA/GG 17502.
46. Letter about Kintuadists, 1958, AA/GG 17715.
47. PP2, interview with author, digital recording, Kabalo, DRC, August 29, 2018.
48. Pieter De Coene, Margot Luyckfasseel, and Gillian Mathys, "Voices from Exile: The Mpadist Mission des Noirs in Oshwe's Prison Camps in the Belgian Congo (1940–1960)," *International Journal of African Historical Studies* 55, no. 1 (2022): 91, 112–14; Anne Mélice, "Le kimbanguisme et le pouvoir en RDC: Entre apolitisme et conception théologico-politique," *Civilisations: Revue internationale d'anthropologie et de sciences humaines* 58, no. 2 (2009): 63–65; Georges Nzongola-Ntalaja, *The Congo from Leopold to Kabila: A People's History* (London: Zed Books, 2002), 82–85, 94–96.
49. Schatzberg, *Dialectics of Oppression*, 124.
50. See, for example, Susan Asch, *L'Église du prophète Kimbangu: De ses origines à son rôle actuel au Zaïre* (Paris: Karthala, 1983).
51. Pedro Monaville, *Students of the World: Global 1968 and Decolonization in the Congo* (Durham, NC: Duke University Press, 2022), 182.
52. Monaville, 203
53. Jules-Rosette, "At the Threshold of the Millennium," 160.
54. De Coene, Lutkfassel, and Mathys make a similar argument in their recent article about Mpadists. See De Coene et al., "Voices from Exile," 91.

55. There are obvious exceptions to this. Mpadism, which did not unify with the Église de Jésus-Christ sur la Terre par le prophète Simon Kimbangu (EJCSK), is one such exception. See De Coene et al., "Voices from Exile."
56. Emizet F. Kisangani, *Civil Wars in the Democratic Republic of Congo 1960–2010* (Boulder, CO: Lynne Rienner, 2012), 12–25.
57. Gillian Mathys, *Conflict and Connection: Making the Histories in the Lake Kivu Region* (Oxford University Press, forthcoming).
58. Colette Braeckman, "Running on Empty in the Poll Booths," *Xindex: The Voice of Free Expression,* February 14, 2007.
59. De Boeck, "Beyond the Grave," 37.

CHAPTER 7: PRESENTS

1. A version of this opening vignette appeared in a blog post I wrote for the website of the History Department at the University of Tennessee, Knoxville, in 2020: Nicole Eggers, "Black Bodies, State Violence, and Covid 19: Lessons from Congo," History Department (website), University of Tennessee, Knoxville, June 9, 2020, https://history.utk.edu/black-bodies-state-violence-and-covid-19-lessons-from-congo/.
2. The initial report came from my friend and research companion, Michael Ahuka, who PP2 called initially. Later, I spoke with PP2 directly, who confirmed the report.
3. Denis M. Tull, "Troubled State-Building in the DR Congo: The Challenge from the Margins," *Journal of Modern African Studies* 48, no. 4 (2010): 643–61; Pierre Englebert and Emmanuel Kasongo Mungongo, "Misguided and Misdiagnosed: The Failure of Decentralization Reforms in the DR Congo," *African Studies Review* 59, no. 1 (2016): 5–32.
4. Achille Mbembe, *Necropolitics* (Durham, NC: Duke University Press, 2019), 9–41.
5. "DR Congo: Voter Suppression, Violence," Human Rights Watch, January 5, 2019, https://www.hrw.org/news/2019/01/05/dr-congo-voter-suppression-violence#.
6. Carl Agisha Juma et al., "COVID-19: The Current Situation in the Democratic Republic of Congo," *American Journal of Tropical Medicine and Hygiene* 103, no. 6 (2020): 2168–70, https://doi.org/10.4269/ajtmh.20-1169.
7. Theodore Powers, "Authoritarian Violence, Public Health, and the Necropolitical State: Engaging the South African Response to COVID-19," *Open Anthropological Research* 1, no. 1 (2021): 60–72.
8. Benoit Nyemba, "Profiteers Pounce as COVID-19 Threatens Congo Food Supply," Reuters, May 4, 2020, https://www.reuters.com/article/us-health-coronavirus-congo-food-price/profiteers-pounce-as-covid-19-threatens-congo-food-supply-idUSKBN22G16D.
9. Nacy Rose Hunt, "An Accoustic Register, Tenacious Images, and Congolese Scenes of Rape and Repetition," *Cultural Anthropology* 23, no. 3 (2008): 243.
10. "Tanganyika: Des inondations à Kabalo, Kongolo et Manono suite à la montée des eaux du fleuve Congo," Actualité.cd, April 2, 2020, https://

actualite.cd/2020/04/02/tanganyika-des-inondations-kabalo-kongolo-et-manono-suite-la-montee-des-eaux-du-fleuve.

11. Laura M. Bogart et al., "COVID-19 Related Medical Mistrust, Health Impacts, and Potential Vaccine Hesitancy among Black Americans Living with HIV," *Journal of Acquired Immune Deficiency Syndromes* 86, no. 2 (2021): 200; Kimberly D. Manning, "More Than Medical Mistrust," *Lancet* 396, no. 10261 (2020): 1481–82.

12. Nicole Eggers, "Authority That Is Customary: Kitawala, Customary Chiefs, and the Plurality of Power in Congolese History," *Journal of Eastern African Studies* 14, no. 1 (2020): 24–42.

13. Gérard Prunier, "The Catholic Church and the Kivu Conflict," *Journal of Religion in Africa* 31, no. 2 (2001): 155–60. I have also discussed this at length in Nicole Eggers, "Prophètes, politiciens et légitimité politique: Discours locaux du pouvoir et transformation religieuse dans le conflit congolais," *Politique africaine* 129 (March 2013): 73–91.

14. Ayo Whetho and Ufo Okeke Uzodike, "Religious Networks in Post-conflict Democratic Republic of the Congo: A Prognosis," *African Journal on Conflict Resolution* 8, no. 3 (January 2008): 63.

15. Bwimana Aembe and David Jordhus-Lier, "Within, Above, and Beyond: Churches and Religious Civil Society Activism in South Kivu," *Journal of Civil Society* 13, no. 2 (2017): 149–65; Roger B. Alfani, *Religious Peacebuilding in the Democratic Republic of Congo* (New York: Peter Lang, 2019).

16. Tull, "Troubled State-Building."

17. Mwene-Batende, "Le Kitawala dans l'évolution socio-politique récente: Cas du groupe Belukela dans la ville de Kisangani," *Cahiers des religions africaines* 10, no. 19 (1976): 81–105. The Belukela group is also discussed in chapter 6.

18. See, for example, Anne Verhoeve, "Conflict and the Urban Space: The Socioeconomic Impact of Conflict on the City of Goma," in *Conflict and Social Transformation in Eastern DR Congo*, ed. Koen Vlassenroot and Timothy Raeymaekers (Gent: Academia Press Scientific Publishers, 2004), 114; Koen Vlassenroot and Timothy Raeymaekers, "Conflict and Artisan Mining in Kamituga," in Vlassenroot and Raeymaekers, *Conflict and Social Transformation*, 150; and Filip De Boeck, "Beyond the Grave: History, Memory and Death in Postcolonial Congo/Zaire," in *Memory and the Postcolony: African Anthropology and the Critique of Power*, ed. Richard Werbner (London: Zed Books, 1998), 34–39. For example, see Colette Braeckman, "Running on Empty in the Poll Booths," *Xindex: The Voice of Free Expression*, February 14, 2007; V. Petit and J. Pittenger, "Part 2: A Trojan Horse Strategy," UNICEF, accessed June 6, 2013, http://www.polioinfo.org/index.php/communication-in-action/drc/stories-from-the-field/246-the-elephant-king-of-the-congo-making-a-powerful-ally-in-the-fight-to-end-polio-part-2 (page discontinued).

19. Ana Aparicio et al., introduction to *Ethnographic Refusals, Unruly Latinidades*, ed. by Alex E. Chavéz and Gina M. Pérez (Albuquerque: University of

New Mexico Press, 2022), xxvii.
20. "'We Will Crush You': The Restriction of Political Space in the Democratic Republic of Congo," Human Rights Watch, November 25, 2008, https://www.hrw.org/report/2008/11/25/we-will-crush-you/restriction-political-space-democratic-republic-congo. See also Tull, "Troubled State-Building."
21. Tull, "Troubled State-Building," 650.
22. "'We Will Crush You.'"
23. Before shutting off transmission from the national television station, Mukungubila's followers announced in Lingala, "Gideon Mukungubila has come to free you from the slavery of the Rwandan." "Who Is Congo's Mukungubila: 'Prophet' or Coup Mastermind?," *France 24*, December 30, 2013, https://www.france24.com/en/20131230-congo-mukungubila-profile-prophet-pastor.
24. "République Démocratique du Congo, 30 décembre 2013: Les massacres des adeptes du ministère de la restauration à partir de l'Afrique noire," Lingue des Électeurs, L.E/RDC ASBL, https://www.fidh.org/IMG/pdf/rdcligelec2014.pdf.
25. "DR Congo: Security Forces Fire on Catholic Churchgoers," Human Rights Watch, January 19, 2018, https://www.hrw.org/news/2018/01/19/dr-congo-security-forces-fire-catholic-churchgoers; "DR Congo: Repression Persists as Election Deadline Nears," Human Rights Watch, January 29, 2018, https://www.hrw.org/news/2018/06/29/dr-congo-repression-persists-election-deadline-nears.
26. Georges Nzongola-Ntalaja, *The Congo from Leopold to Kabila: A People's History* (London: Zed Books, 2002), 27.
27. Patrick M. Boyle, "Beyond Self-Protection to Prophecy: The Catholic Church and Political Change in Zaire," *Africa Today* 39, no. 3 (1992): 49–66.
28. For two excellent overviews of these different objectives, see Wamba dia Wamba, "Bundu dia Kongo: A Kongolese Self-Styled Fundamentalist Religious Movement," in *East African Expressions of Christianity*, ed. Thomas Spear and Isaria Kimambo (Oxford: James Currey, 1999), 213–28; and Yolanda Covington-Ward, *Gesture and Power: Religion, Nationalism, and Everyday Performance in Congo* (Durham, NC: Duke University Press, 2016), 187–226.
29. Tull, "Troubled State-Building," 652.
30. Alfani, *Religious Peacebuilding*, 115–22.
31. Petit and Pittenger, "Part 2: A Trojan Horse Strategy."
32. Philippart, "Rapport de la prise de contact entre Monsieur Joset," April 5, 1956, doc. no. 4737, Affaires indigènes Series, Archives africaines, Ministère belge d'affaires étrangères, Brussels.
33. Petit and Pittenger, "Part 2: A Trojan Horse Strategy."
34. See, for example, Megan Vaughan, *Curing Their Ills: Colonial Power and African Illness* (Stanford, CA: Stanford University Press, 1991), 205–6; and Henrietta Moore and Megan Vaughan, *Cutting Down Trees: Gender, Nutrition and Change in the Northern Province of Zambia, 1890–1990* (Portsmouth, NH: Heinemann, 1994), especially chapters 7–8.

35. UNICEFpolio, "The Owl's Secret: A Powerful Ally in the Fight to End Polio in DRC," March 15, 2015, YouTube video, 16:42, https://youtu.be/IOXkHzRbt7Y.
36. UNICEFpolio, "Owl's Secret."
37. Aparicio et al., introduction, xii–xxxv.
38. For the UNICEF account of the story of PP2 and the polio vaccination campaign, see the article and video on the topic published by UNICEF in 2013: V. Petit and J. Pittenger, "Part 1: Meeting the Elephant King," UNICEF, https://www.unicef.org/infobycountry/drcongo_67983.html (page discontinued); Petit and Pittenger, "Part 2: A Trojan Horse Strategy"; and UNICEFpolio, "Owl's Secret."
39. These seem to be the same Equateur Kitawalists discussed in chapter 6. See Michale G. Schatzberg, *The Dialectics of Oppression in Zaire* (Bloomington: Indiana University Press, 1988), 130.
40. Falk Grossmann et al., "Range Occupation and Population Estimates of Bonobos in the Salonga National Park: Application to Large-Scale Surveys of Bonobos in the Democratic Republic of Congo," in *The Bonobos: Behavior, Ecology, and Conservation*, ed. Takeshi Furuichi and Jo Myers Thompson (New York: Springer, 2008), 190–202. In a personal communication with the author, Lys Alcayna-Stevens likewise confirms the existence of Kitawalist villages in Djolu Territory, to the northwest of SNP.
41. Yves Nyed, "RDC: Fin de régime à Ankoro," July 16, 2016, http://mukungubila.com/rdc-fin-de-regime-a-ankoro-2/.
42. Schatzberg, *Dialectics of Oppression*, 130.
43. For another example, see Eggers, "Prophètes."
44. Eggers, "Prophètes."
45. On Bundu dia Kongo, see Wamba dia Wamba, "Bundu dia Kongo"; Covington-Ward, *Gesture and Power;* and Tull, "Troubled State-Building."
46. Eggers, "Authority That Is Customary."
47. Wamba dia Wamba, "Bundu dia Kongo," 214–15.

CONCLUSION

1. For a few examples of scholars who explore these dynamics, see Emizet F. Kisangani, *Civil Wars in the Democratic Republic of Congo 1960–2010* (Boulder, CO: Lynne Rienner, 2012); Thomas Turner, *The Congo Wars: Conflict, Myth and Reality* (London: ZED Books, 2007); Filip Reyntjens, *The Great African War: Congo and Regional Geopolitics, 1996–2006* (Cambridge: Cambridge University Press, 2009); Gérard Prunier, *Africa's World War: Congo, the Rwandan Genocide, and the Making of a Continental Catastrophe* (Oxford: Oxford University Press, 2009); Séverine Autesserre, *The Trouble with the Congo: Local Violence and the Failure of International Peacebuilding* (Cambridge: Cambridge University Press, 2010); Jason Stearns, *Dancing in the Glory of Monsters: The Collapse of the Congo and the Great War of Africa* (New York: PublicAffairs, 2011); and Gillian Mathys, *Conflict and Connection: Making Histories in the Lake Kivu Region* (Oxford University Press, forthcoming).

2. There are certainly recent works on eastern Congo that do not focus on the conflict, but they focus mainly on the region of Katanga. See, for example, the works of Donatien Dibwe Dia Mwembu, Miles Larmer, and Julia Siebert on the mining industry in Katanga and Copperbelt connections: Donatien Dibwe Dia Mwembu, *Bana shaba abandonnés par leur pére: Structures de l'autorité et histoire sociale de la famille ouvrière au Katanga 1910–1997* (Paris: L'Harmattan, 2001); Donatien Dibwe Dia Mwembu, ed., *La société de la Copperbelt katangaise: Une autopsie de sa situation socio-économique, politique et culturelle* (Paris: L'Harmattan, 2021); Julia Seibert, "More Continuity Than Change? New Forms of Unfree Labor in the Belgian Congo, 1908–1930," in *Humanitarian Intervention and Changing Labor Relations: The Long-Term Consequences of the Abolition of the Slave Trade*, ed. Marcel van der Linden (Leiden: Brill, 2011), 369–86; and Miles Larmer, "Permanent Precarity: Capital and Labour in the Central African Copperbelt," *Labor History* 58, no. 2 (2017): 170–84. See also Reuben Loffman's work on Protestantism in Norther Katanga: Loffman, *Church, State and Colonialism in Southeastern Congo, 1890–1962* (Cham, Switzerland: Palgrave Macmillan, 2019). Far less work has come out of the Kivus that does not focus on the conflict. However, in her work on cross-border migration between North Kivu and Rwanda, Gillian Mathys makes a similar observation that not enough attention has been paid to the history of connections in the region: Mathys, *Conflict and Connection*.
3. Roger Alfani, *Religious Peacebuilding in the Democratic Republic of Congo* (New York: Peter Lang, 2019), 130–36.
4. Mwene-Batende, *Mouvements messianiques et protestation sociale: Le cas du Kitawala chez les Kumu du Zaïre* (Kinshasa: Faculté de théologie catholique, 1982), 127–84.
5. David L. Schoenbrun, *The Names of the Python: Belonging in East Africa, 900 to 1930* (Madison: University of Wisconsin Press, 2021), 3–13.
6. Pedro Monaville does this particularly well in *Students of the World: Global 1968 and Decolonization in the Congo* (Durham, NC: Duke University Press, 2022). He also makes it clear that the distance—spatially and temporally—between "elite" and "nonelite" should not be overstated in the colonial era because access to education came to Congo comparatively late and many "elites" grew up in small villages. See especially chapters 1 and 2 in Monaville, *Students of the World*.
7. On some of these different conceptions of community by African elites during the colonial era (in Congo and elsewhere), see Daniel Tödt, *The Lumumba Generation: African Bourgeoisie and Colonial Distinction in the Belgian Congo*, trans. Alex Skinner (Oldenbourg, Germany: De Gruyter, 2021); Monaville, *Students of the World;* Charles Tshimanga, *Jeunesse, formation et société au Congo/Kinshasa, 1890–1960* (Paris: L'Harmattan, 2001); and Derek R. Peterson, *Ethnic Patriotism and the East African Revival: A History of Dissent, c. 1935–1972* (Cambridge: Cambridge University Press, 2012).

8. Benedict Anderson, *Imagined Communities: Reflections on the Origin and Spread of Nationalism*, 2nd ed. (London: Verso, 1991).
9. Tödt, *Lumumba Generation*.
10. See, for example, Monaville, *Students of the World*; and Anicet Mobe Fansiama, "Les intellectualités estudiantines congolaises revisitées: 1954–1965," in *Aspects de la culture à l'époque coloniale en Afrique: Presse–archives* (Paris: L'Harmattan, 2007), 115–46.
11. See, for example, Pierre-Philippe Fraiture, *V. Y. Mudimbe: Undisciplined Africanism* (Oxford: Oxford University Press, 2013); Phambu Ngoma-Binda, *Zamenga Batukezanga: Vie et oeuvre* (Kinshasa: Éditions Saint-Paul Afrique, 1990); and Horace G. Campbell, "The Journey of Wamba Dia Wamba and the Struggles for Emancipatory Politics in Africa," *Africa Development / Afrique et Développement* 45, no. 2 (2020): 143–66.
12. Monaville, *Students of the World*, 8; Gary Wilder, *Freedom Time: Negritude, Decolonization and the Future of the World* (Durham, NC: Duke University Press, 2015).
13. This is not to imply that all of Congo's emergent elites came from elite, urban backgrounds themselves. The distinction should not be overdrawn. But they were certainly more likely to come from such backgrounds.
14. Jacques Gérard, "Le caractère politique du Kitawala au Kivu," 1956, doc. no. 4737, Affaires indigènes, Archives africaines, Ministère belge d'affaires étrangères, Brussels (hereafter cited as AA/AI, followed by the dossier no.).
15. Jacques E. Gérard, *Les fondements syncrétiques du Kitawala* (Brussels: Centre de recherche et d'information socio-politiques, 1969), 106. The notion that modernity could make victims of Africans—to the point of driving them mad because of their inability to adapt—was widespread in colonial thought. Lynette Jackson discusses a similar colonial attitude in her study of colonial psychiatry in Zimbabwe. See Jackson, *Surfacing Up: Psychiatry and Social Order in Colonial Zimbabwe, 1908–1968* (Ithaca, NY: Cornell University Press, 2005), 72–73.
16. Gérard, "Le caractère politique du Kitawala au Kivu," 1956, AA/AI 4737. Mwene-Batende made a similar—though much more nuanced—argument decades later. Mwene-Batende, *Mouvements messianiques et protestation sociale: Le cas du Kitawala chez les Kumu du Zaïre* (Kinshasa: Faculté de théologie catholique, 1982).
17. Jackson, *Surfacing Up*, 72–73.
18. Sylvia Wynter, "Unsettling the Coloniality of Being/Power/Truth/Freedom: Towards the Human, after Man, Its Overrepresentation—an Argument," *CR: The New Centennial Review* 3, no. 3 (2003): 265.
19. Anonymous, "Qui est Kitawala?," *Kitawala Kamwana*, November 5, 2022. This bulletin is circulated via email periodically by members of the Kitawala community at COLAGREL. I have a copy of this issue in my personal archive.
20. Schoenbrun, *Names of the Python*, 153.

21. See, for example, Derek R. Peterson, "The Politics of Transcendence in Colonial Uganda," *Past & Present* 230, no. 1 (2016): 203.
22. See, for example, David L. Schoenbrun, *A Green Place, a Good Place: Agrarian Change, Gender, and Social Identity in the Great Lakes Region to the 15th Century* (Portsmouth, NH: Heinemann, 1998); David L. Schoenbrun, "Conjuring the Modern in Africa: Durability and Rupture in Histories of Public Healing between the Great Lakes of East Africa," *American Historical Review* 111, no. 5 (2006): 1403–39; Neil Kodesh, *Beyond the Royal Gaze: Clanship and Public Healing in Buganda* (Charlottesville: University of Virginia Press, 2010); Steven Feierman, *Peasant Intellectuals: Anthropology and History in Tanzania* (Madison: University of Wisconsin Press, 1990); and Jan Vansina, *Paths in the Rainforests: Toward a History of Political Tradition in Equatorial Africa* (Madison: University of Wisconsin Press, 1990).
23. Steven Feierman, "Struggles for Control: The Social Roots of Health and Healing in Modern Africa," *African Studies Review* 28, no. 2/3 (1985): 99–101.
24. Schoenbrun, *Names of the Python*, 3–13.
25. Nancy Rose Hunt, *A Nervous State: Violence, Remedies, and Reverie in Colonial Congo* (Durham, NC: Duke University Press, 2016), 12.

Bibliography

ARCHIVAL SOURCES

Archief Karel Van den Eynde (1926–2008). Belgium.
Archives africaines (AA), Brussels. Ministre belge d'affaires etrangères. AI Series.
Archives africaines (AA), Brussels. Ministre belge d'affaires etrangères. AIMO Series.
Archives africaines (AA), Brussels. Ministre belge d'affaires etrangères. AIMOGG Series.
Archives africaines (AA), Brussels. Ministre belge d'affaires etrangères. D Series.
Archives africaines (AA), Brussels. Ministre belge d'affaires etrangères. GG Series.
Archives africaines (AA), Brussels. Ministre belge d'affaires etrangères. JUST Series.
Maurice Martin de Ryck Congo Papers. Michigan State University, Lansing.
Zaire Colonial Documents: De Ryck Collection of Material on General Administration, Equateur, Kivu, and Ruanda-Urundi, ca. 1885–1954. University of Wisconsin- Madison.

PUBLISHED WORKS

Aembe, Bwimana, and David Jordhus-Lier. "Within, Above, and Beyond: Churches and Religious Civil Society Activism in South Kivu." *Journal of Civil Society* 13, no. 2 (2017): 149–65.
Agbedahin, Komlan. "Interrogating the Togolese Historical Sex Strike." *International Journal on World Peace* 31, no. 1 (2014): 7–25.
Alfani, Roger B. *Religious Peacebuilding in the Democratic Republic of Congo.* New York: Peter Lang, 2019.
Amadiume, Ifi. *Male Daughters, Female Husbands: Gender and Sex in an African Society.* London: Zed Books, 1987.
Anderson, Benedict. *Imagined Communities: Reflections on the Origin and Spread of Nationalism.* 2nd ed. London: Verso, 1991.

Anderson, David M. *Histories of the Hanged: The Dirty War in Kenya and the End of Empire*. New York: W. W. Norton, 2005.

———. "Mau Mau in the High Court and the 'Lost' British Empire Archives: Colonial Conspiracy or Bureaucratic Bungle?" *Journal of Imperial and Commonwealth History* 39, no. 5 (2011): 699–716.

Andersson, Efraim. *Messianic Popular Movements in the Lower Congo*. Uppsala, Sweden: Almqvist & Wiksells, 1958.

Anyenyola Welo, Jacques-Oscar. "Le mouvement Kitawala en Republique du Zaire," 1972 (3104). In *Turner Collection on Religious Movements*, 5-04-007: fiche 153.

Aparicio, Ana, Andrea Bolivar, Alex E. Chavéz, Sherina Feliciano-Santos, Santiago Guerra, Gina M. Pérez, Jonathan Rosa, Gilberto Rosas, Aimee Villarreal, and Patricia Zavella. Introduction to *Ethnographic Refusals, Unruly Latinidades*, edited by Alex E. Chavéz and Gina M. Pérez, xii–xxxv. Albuquerque: University of New Mexico Press, 2022.

Appiah, Kwame Anthony. "The Case for Capitalizing the *B* in Black." *Atlantic*, June 18, 2020. https://www.theatlantic.com/ideas/archive/2020/06/time-to-capitalize-blackand-white/613159/.

———. *In My Father's House: Africa in the Philosophy of Culture*. London: Methuen, 1992.

Arondekar, Anjali. "Without a Trace: Sexuality and the Colonial Archive." *Journal of the History of Sexuality* 14, no. 1/2 (2005): 10–27.

Asch, Susan. *L'Église du prophète Kimbangu: De ses origines à son rôle actuel au Zaïre*. Paris: Karthala, 1983.

Autesserre, Séverine. *The Trouble with the Congo: Local Violence and the Failure of International Peacebuilding*. Cambridge: Cambridge University Press, 2010.

Balaamo Mokelwa, Jean-Pacifique. *Église et état en République du Congo: Fondements juridiques et jurisprudence (1876–2006)*. Paris: L'Harmattan, 2009.

Barber, Karin, ed. *Africa's Hidden Histories: Everyday Literacy and Making the Self*. Bloomington: Indiana University Press, 2006.

Bayart, Jean-François, and Stephen Ellis. "Africa in the World: A History of Extraversion." *African Affairs* 99, no. 395 (2000): 217–67.

Beibyuck, Daniel. *Lega Culture: Art, Initiation, and Moral Philosophy among a Central African People*. Berkeley: University of California Press, 1973.

Benjamin, Walter. *The Arcades Project*. Translated by Howard Eiland and Kevin McLaughlin. Cambridge, MA: Harvard University Press, 1999.

Berger, Iris. "Rebels or Status Seekers? Women as Spirit Mediums in East Africa." In *Women in Africa: Studies in Economic and Social Change*, edited by Nancy J. Hafkin and Edna G. Bay, 157–82. Palo Alto, CA: Stanford University Press, 1976.

———. *Religion and Resistance: East African Kingdoms in the Precolonial Period*. Tervuren, Belgium: Musée royal de l'Afrique centrale, 1981.

Bernard, Guy. "La contestation et les églises nationales au Congo." *Canadian Journal of African Studies* 5, no. 2 (1971): 145–56.

Bernault, Florence. "Aesthetics of Acquisition: Notes on the Transactional Life of Persons and Things in Gabon." *Comparative Studies in Society and History* 57, no. 3 (2015): 753–79.
———. "Body, Power and Sacrifice in Equatorial Africa." *Journal of African History* 47, no. 2 (2006): 207–39.
———. *Colonial Transactions: Imaginaries, Bodies, and Histories in Gabon.* Durham, NC: Duke University Press, 2019.
———. "The Politics of Enclosure in Colonial and Post-colonial Africa." In *A History of Prison and Confinement in Africa,* edited by Florence Bernault, 1–53. Portsmouth, NH: Heinemann, 2003.
Bernault, Florence, and Jan-Georg Deutsch. "Introduction: Control and Excess; Histories of Violence in Africa." *Africa: Journal of the International African Institute* 85, no. 3 (2015): 385–94.
Biebuyck, Daniel. "La société Kumu face au Kitawala," 1957 (3117). In *Turner Collection on Religious Movements,* 5-04-007: fiche 156.
———. "Organisation politique des Nyanga: La chefferie Ihana." *Kongo-overzee* 22, no. 4/5 (1956): 301–41.
Bielo, James S. "On the Failure of 'Meaning': Bible Reading in the Anthropology of Christianity." *Culture and Religion* 9, no. 1 (2008): 1–21.
Bigon, Liora. "Garden Cities in Colonial Africa: A Note on Historiography." *Planning Perspectives* 28, no. 3 (2013): 477–85.
Biko, Steve. *I Write What I Like: A Selection of His Writings.* Edited by Aelred Stubbs. New York: Harper & Row, 1978.
Bockie, Simon. *Death and the Invisible Powers: The World of Kongo Belief.* Bloomington: Indiana University Press, 1993.
Bogart, Laura M., Bisola O. Ojikutu, Keshav Tyagi, David J. Klein, Matt G. Mutchler, Lu Dong, Sean J. Lawrence, Damone R. Thomas, and Sarah Kellman. "COVID-19 Related Medical Mistrust, Health Impacts, and Potential Vaccine Hesitancy among Black Americans Living with HIV." *Journal of Acquired Immune Deficiency Syndromes* 86, no. 2 (2021): 200–207.
Boulton, Jack. "Experimental Intimacies: Young Men's Understandings of Their Relationships with Women in Swakopmund." *Journal of Namibian Studies* 22 (2017): 25–44.
Boyer, Pascal. *Religion Explained: The Evolutionary Origins of Religious Thought.* New York: Basic Books, 2001.
Boyle, Patrick M. "Beyond Self-Protection to Prophecy: The Catholic Church and Political Change in Zaire." *Africa Today* 39, no. 3 (1992): 49–66.
Campbell, Horace G. "The Journey of Wamba dia Wamba and the Struggles for Emancipatory Politics in Africa." *Africa Development / Afrique et Développement* 45, no. 2 (2020): 143–66.
Carter, Julian B. *The Heart of Whiteness: Normal Sexuality and Race in America, 1880–1940.* Durham, NC: Duke University Press, 2007.
Colson, Elizabeth. "Places of Power and Shrines of the Land." *Paideuma* 43 (1997): 47–57.

Cooper, Frederick. *Colonialism in Question: Theory, Knowledge, History.* Berkeley: University of California Press, 2005.

Cooper, Frederick, and Ann Laura Stoler, eds. *Tensions of Empire: Colonial Cultures in a Bourgeois World.* Berkeley: University of California Press, 1997.

Covington-Ward, Yolanda. *Gesture and Power: Religion, Nationalism, and Everyday Performance in Congo.* Durham, NC: Duke University Press, 2016.

Cross, Sholto. "The Watch Tower Movement in South Central Africa, 1908–1945." PhD diss., University of Oxford, 1973.

Debertry, Léon. *Kitawala: Roman.* Elisabethville: Éditions essor du Congo, 1953.

De Boeck, Filip. "Beyond the Grave: History, Memory and Death in Postcolonial Congo/Zaire." In *Memory and the Postcolony: African Anthropology and the Critique of Power,* edited by Richard Werbner, 21–57. London: Zed Books, 1998.

——. *Kinshasa: Tales of the Invisible City.* Ghent: Ludion, 2004.

De Coene, Pieter, Margot Luyckfasseel, and Gillian Mathys. "Voices from Exile: The Mpadist Mission des Noirs in Oshwe's Prison Camps in the Belgian Congo (1940–1960)." *International Journal of African Historical Studies* 55, no. 1 (2022): 89–114.

Dembour, Marie-Bénédicte. "La chicote comme symbole du colonialisme belge?" *Canadian Journal of African Studies* 26, no. 2 (1992): 205–25.

De Rezende, Isabelle. "Visuality and Colonialism in the Congo: From the 'Arab War' to Patrice Lumumba, 1880s to 1961." PhD diss., University of Michigan, 2012.

Dibwe Dia Mwembu, Donatien. *Bana shaba abandonnés par leur pére: Structures de l'autorité et histoire sociale de la famille ouvrière au Katanga 1910–1997.* Paris: L'Harmattan, 2001.

——, ed. *La société de la Copperbelt katangaise: Une autopsie de sa situation socio-économique, politique et culturelle.* Paris: L'Harmattan, 2021.

Dubost, Françoise. "Le modèle des cités-jardins: La modernité à l'épreuve du temps." *Ethnologie française* 26, no. 1 (1996): 92–99.

Dungia, Emmanuel. *Mobutu et l'argent du Zaïre: Les révélations d'un diplomate, ex-agent des services secrets.* Paris: L'Harmattan, 1993.

Dupré, Marie-Claude. "Les femmes mukisi des Téké Tsaayi rituel de possession et culte anti-sorcier (République populaire du Congo)." *Journal de la Société des africanistes* 44, no. 1 (1974): 53–69.

Eggers, Nicole. "Authority That Is Customary: Kitawala, Customary Chiefs, and the Plurality of Power in Congolese History." *Journal of Eastern African Studies* 14, no. 1 (2020): 24–42.

——. "Black Bodies, State Violence, and Covid 19: Lessons from Congo." History Department (website), University of Tennessee, Knoxville, June 9, 2020. https://history.utk.edu/black-bodies-state-violence-and-covid-19-lessons-from-congo/.

——. "Kitawala in the Congo: Religion, Politics and Healing in Central Africa." PhD diss., University of Wisconsin–Madison, 2013.

———. "Mukombozi and the Monganga: The Violence of Healing in the 1944 Kitawalist Uprising." *Africa: Journal of the International African Institute* 85, no. 3 (2015): 417–36.

———. "Prophètes, politiciens et légitimité politique: Discours locaux du pouvoir et transformation religieuse dans le conflit congolais." *Politique africaine* 129 (March 2013): 73–91.

———. "Remembering COLAGREL: Space, Memory, and Oral History." *Comparing the Copperbelt* (blog), November 19, 2019. https://copperbelt.history.ox.ac.uk/2019/11/19/remembering-colagrel-space-memory-and-oral-history-nicole-eggers/.

Elkins, Caroline. *Imperial Reckoning: The Untold Story of Britain's Gulag in Kenya*. New York: Henry Holt, 2005.

Ellis, Stephen, and Gerrie ter Haar. *Worlds of Power: Religious Thought and Political Practice in Africa*. New York: Oxford University Press, 2004.

Engelke, Matthew. *A Problem of Presence: Beyond Scripture in an African Church*. Berkeley: University of California Press, 2007.

Englebert, Pierre, and Emmanuel Kasongo Mungongo. "Misguided and Misdiagnosed: The Failure of Decentralization Reforms in the DR Congo." *African Studies Review* 59, no. 1 (2016): 5–32.

Erlank, Natasha. *Convening Black Intimacy: Christianity, Gender, and Tradition in Early Twentieth-Century South Africa*. Athens: Ohio University Press, 2022.

Fabian, Johannes. *Ethnography as Commentary: Writing from the Virtual Archive*. Durham, NC: Duke University Press, 2008. E-book.

———. *Language and Colonial Power: The Appropriation of Swahili in the Former Belgian Congo, 1880–1938*. Berkeley: University of California Press, 1991.

———. "'Magic and Modernity': A Conversation with an Herbalist and Practitioner of Magic." *Archives of Popular Swahili*, vol. 7 (July 8, 2005). http://www.lpca.socsci.uva.nl/aps/vol7/kahengatext.html.

———. *Remembering the Present: Painting and Popular History in Zaire*. Berkeley: University of California Press, 1996.

Fanon, Frantz. *The Wretched of the Earth*. New York: Grove Press, 1965.

Feierman, Steven. "Colonizers, Colonized, and the Creation of Invisible Histories." In *Beyond the Cultural Turn: New Directions in the Study of Society and Culture*, edited by Victoria E. Bonnell and Lynn Hunt, 182–216. Berkeley: University of California Press, 1999.

———. "Explanation and Uncertainty in the Medical World of the Ghaambo." *Bulletin of the History of Medicine* 74, no. 2 (2000): 317–44.

———. *Peasant Intellectuals: Anthropology and History in Tanzania*. Madison: University of Wisconsin Press, 1990.

———. "Struggles for Control: The Social Roots of Health and Healing in Modern Africa." *African Studies Review* 28, no. 2/3 (1985): 99–101.

Fields, Karen. *Revival and Rebellion in Colonial Central Africa*. Princeton, NJ: Princeton University Press, 1985.

Fleisch, Axel, and Rhiannon Stephens. "Introduction: Theories and Methods of African Conceptual History." In *Doing Conceptual History in Africa*, edited by Axel Fleisch and Rhiannon Stephens, 1–20. New York: Berghahn Books, 2016.

Fraiture, Pierre-Philippe. *V. Y. Mudimbe: Undisciplined Africanism*. Oxford: Oxford University Press, 2013.

Fuentes, Marisa J. *Dispossessed Lives: Enslaved Women, Violence, and the Archive*. Philadelphia: University of Pennsylvania Press, 2016.

Garbin, David. "Sacred Remittances: Money, Migration and the Moral Economy of Development in a Transnational African Church." *Journal of Ethnic and Migration Studies* 45, no. 11 (2019): 2045–61.

Garrard, David J. *The History of the Congo Evangelistic Mission / Communiauté Pentecôtiste au Zaïre from 1915–1982*. Vol. 1, *The Colonial Years, 1915–1959*. Mattersey, UK: Mattersey Hall, 2008.

Gérard, Jacques E. *Les fondements syncrétiques du Kitawala*. Brussels: Centre de recherche et d'information socio-politiques, 1969.

Geschiere, Peter. *The Modernity of Witchcraft: Politics and the Occult in Postcolonial Africa*. Charlottesville: University of Virginia Press, 1997.

———. *Witchcraft, Intimacy and Trust: Africa in Comparison*. Chicago: University of Chicago Press, 2013.

Getz, Trevor R., and Liz Clarke. *Abina and the Important Men: A Graphic History*. New York: Oxford University Press, 2012.

Giles-Vernick, Tamara. "Lives, Histories, and Sites of Recollection." In *African Words, African Voices: Critical Practices in Oral History*, edited by Luise S. White, Stephan F. Miescher, and David William Cohen, 194–213. Bloomington: Indiana University Press, 2001.

Gondola, Didier. *Tropical Cowboys: Westerns, Violence, and Masculinity in Kinshasa*. Bloomington: Indiana University Press, 2016.

Gordon, David. *Invisible Agents: Spirits in Central African History*. Athens: Ohio University Press, 2012.

Greschat, Hans-Jürgen. *Kitawala: Ursprung, Ausbreitung und Religion der Watch-Tower-Bewegung in Zentralafrika*. Marburg, Germany: N. G. Elwert, 1967.

Griffin, Michael, and Jennie Weiss Block, eds. *In the Company of the Poor: Conversations with Dr. Paul Farmer and Fr. Gustavo Gutiérrez*. Maryknoll, NY: Orbis Books, 2013.

Grossmann, Falk, John A. Hurt, Ashley Vosper, and Omar Ilambu. "Range Occupation and Population Estimates of Bonobos in the Salonga National Park: Application to Large-Scale Surveys of Bonobos in the Democratic Republic of Congo." In *The Bonobos: Behavior, Ecology, and Conservation*, edited by Takeshi Furuichi and Jo Myers Thompson, 189–218. New York: Springer, 2008.

Gundacker, Claudia, Ruth Kutalek, Rosina Glaunach, Coloman Deweis, Markus Hengstschläger, and Armin Prinz. "Geophagy during Pregnancy: Is There a Health Risk for Infants?" *Environmental Research* 156 (July 2017): 145–47.

Guyer, Jane I., and Samuel M. Eno Belinga. "Wealth in People as Wealth in Knowledge: Accumulation and Composition in Equatorial Africa." *Journal of African History* 36, no. 1 (1995): 91–120.

Harding, Susan. *The Book of Jerry Falwell: Fundamentalist Language and Politics.* Princeton, NJ: Princeton University Press, 2000.

Higginson, John. "Liberating the Captives: Independent Watchtower as an Avatar of Colonial Revolt in Southern Africa and Katanga, 1908–1941." *Journal of Social History* 26, no. 1 (1992): 55–80.

Hochschild, Adam. *King Leopold's Ghost: A Story of Greed, Terror, and Heroism in Colonial Africa.* Boston: Houghton Mifflin, 1999.

Hodgson, Dorothy Louise, and Sheryl McCurdy, eds. *"Wicked" Women and the Reconfiguration of Gender in Africa.* Portsmouth, NH: Heinemann, 2005.

Hoehler-Fatton, Cynthia. *Women of Spirit and Fire: History, Faith, and Gender in Roho Religion in Western Kenya.* New York: Oxford University Press, 1996.

Hooker, J. R. "Witnesses and Watchtower in the Rhodesias and Nyasaland." *Journal of African History* 6, no. 1 (1965): 91–106.

Hunt, Nancy Rose. "An Acoustic Register, Tenacious Images, and Congolese Scenes of Rape and Repetition." *Cultural Anthropology* 23, no. 3 (2008): 220–53.

———. *A Colonial Lexicon of Birth Ritual, Medicalization, and Mobility in the Congo.* Durham, NC: Duke University Press, 1999.

———. *A Nervous State: Violence, Remedies, and Reverie in Colonial Congo.* Durham, NC: Duke University Press, 2016.

Jackson, Lynette. *Surfacing Up: Psychiatry and Social Order in Colonial Zimbabwe, 1908–1968.* Ithaca, NY: Cornell University Press, 2005.

Jaffer, Sadaf. "Women's Autobiography in Islamic Societies: Towards a Feminist Intellectual History." *Journal of Women's History* 25, no. 2 (2013): 153–60.

Janzen, John M. "Ideologies and Institutions in Precolonial Western Equatorial African Therapeutics." In *The Social Basis of Health and Healing,* edited by Steven Feierman and John M. Janzen, 195–211. Berkeley: University of California Press, 1992.

———. *Lemba, 1650–1930: A Drum of Affliction in Africa and the New World.* New York: Garland, 1982.

Jewsiewicki, Bogumil. "Corps interdits: La représentation christique de Lumumba comme rédempteur du peuple zaïrois." *Cahiers d'études africaines* 36, no. 141/142 (1996): 113–42.

———. "Figures des mémoires congolaises de Lumumba: Moïse, héros culturel, Jésus-Christ." In *Patrice Lumumba entre Dieu et diable: Un héros africaine dans ses images,* edited by Pierre Halen and János Riesz, 353–86. Paris: L'Harmattan, 1997.

———. "The Great Depression and the Making of the Colonial Economic System in the Belgian Congo." *African Economic History,* no. 4 (1977): 153–76.

Jules-Rosette, Bennetta. "At the Threshold of the Millennium: Prophetic Movements and Independent Churches in Central and Southern Africa." *Archives de sciences sociales des religions* 99 (July–September 1997): 153–67.

———, ed. *The New Religions of Africa*. Norwood, NJ: Ablex, 1979.
Juma, Carl Agisha, Nestor Kalume Mushabaa, Feruzi Abdu Salam, Attaullah Ahmadi, and Don Eliseo Lucero-Prisno III. "COVID-19: The Current Situation in the Democratic Republic of Congo." *American Journal of Tropical Medicine and Hygiene* 103, no. 6 (2020): 2168–70. https://doi.org/10.4269/ajtmh.20-1169.
Kabazo, Kikasa. *Le début du mouvement Kitawala au Katanga-Shaba, 1923–1937*. Lubumbashi: Université nationale du Zaire, Faculté des lettres, 1972.
Kalusa, Walima. "Christian Medical Discourse and Praxis on the Imperial Frontier: Explaining the Popularity of Missionary Medicine in Mwinilunga District, Zambia, 1906–1935." In *The Spiritual in the Secular: Missionaries and Knowledge about Africa*, edited by Patrick Harries and David Maxwell, 245–66. Grand Rapids, MI: Eerdmans, 2007.
Keller, Eva. *The Road to Clarity: Seventh Day Adventism in Madagascar*. New York: Palgrave Macmillan, 2005.
Kirsch, Thomas G. *Spirits and Letters: Reading, Writing and Charisma in African Christianity*. New York: Berghahn, 2008.
Kisangani, Emizet F. *Civil Wars in the Democratic Republic of Congo 1960–2010*. Boulder, CO: Lynne Rienner, 2012.
Klieman, Kairn. *"The Pygmies Were Our Compass": Bantu and Batwa in the History of West Central Africa, Early Times to c. 1900 C.E.* Portsmouth, NH: Heinemann, 2003.
Kodesh, Neil. *Beyond the Royal Gaze: Clanship and Public Healing in Buganda*. Charlottesville: University of Virginia Press, 2010.
Kollman, Paul. "Classifying African Christianities, Part Two: The Anthropology of Christianity and Generations of African Christians." *Journal of Religion in Africa* 40, no. 2 (2010): 118–48.
Konaté, Dior. *Prison Architecture and Punishment in Colonial Senegal*. Lanham, MD: Lexington Books, 2018.
Landau, Paul S. *Popular Politics in the History of South Africa, 1400–1948*. Cambridge: Cambridge University Press, 2010.
———. *The Realm of the Word: Language, Gender, and Christianity in a Southern African Kingdom*. Portsmouth, NH: Heinemann, 1995.
Langwick, Stacey A. *Bodies, Politics, and African Healing: The Matter of Maladies in Tanzania*. Bloomington: Indiana University Press, 2011.
Larmer, Miles. "Permanent Precarity: Capital and Labour in the Central African Copperbelt." *Labor History* 58, no. 2 (2017): 170–84.
Lauro, Amandine. "'J'ai l'honneur de porter plainte contre ma femme': Litiges conjugaux et administration coloniale au Congo belge (1930–1960)." *Clio: Femmes, Genre, Histoire*, no. 33 (2011): 65–84.
———. "'Notre peuple a perdu le sens de la danse honnête': Danses africaines, catégories légales et (re)définitions européennes de l'obscénité dans le Congo colonial." *C@hiers du CRHiDI: Histoire, droit, institutions, société* 38 (2016). https://doi.org/10.25518/1370-2262.246.

———. "Violence, Anxieties, and the Making of Interracial Dangers." In *The Routledge Companion to Sexuality and Colonialism*, edited by Chelsea Schields and Dagmar Herzog, 327–38. Abingdon, UK: Routledge, 2021.

Leopold, Anita Maria, and Jeppe Sinding Jensen, eds. *Syncretism in Religion: A Reader*. London: Routledge, 2004.

Likaka, Osumaka. *Naming Colonialism: History and Collective Memory in the Congo, 1870–1960*. Madison: University of Wisconsin Press, 2009.

Loffman, Reuben. *Church, State and Colonialism in Southeastern Congo, 1890–1962*. Cham, Switzerland: Palgrave Macmillan, 2019.

———. "'An Interesting Experiment': Kibangile and the Quest for Chiefly Legitimacy in Kongolo, Northern Katanga, 1923–1934." *International Journal of African Historical Studies* 50, no. 3 (2018): 461–77.

Lovens, Maurice. *La révolte de Masisi-Lubutu: Congo belge, janvier–mai 1944*. Brussels: CEDAF, 1974.

Lyons, Maryinez. "From 'Death Camps' to *Cordon Sanitaire*: The Development of Sleeping Sickness Policy in the Uele District of the Belgian Congo, 1903–1914." *Journal of African History* 26, no. 1 (1985): 69–91.

MacGaffey, Wyatt. *Kongo Political Culture: The Conceptual Challenge of the Particular*. Bloomington: Indiana University Press, 2000.

———. "Religion, Class, and Social Pluralism in Zaire." *Canadian Journal of African Studies* 24, no. 2 (1990): 249–64.

Magaziner, Daniel R. *The Law and the Prophets: Black Consciousness in South Africa, 1968–1977*. Athens: Ohio University Press, 2010.

Mahieu, Wauthier de. *Qui a obstrué la cascade? Analyse sémantique du rituel de la circoncision chez les Komo du Zaïre*. Cambridge: Cambridge University Press, 1985.

Manning, Kimberly D. "More Than Medical Mistrust." *Lancet* 396, no. 10261 (2020): 1481–82.

Martin, Phyllis M. *Catholic Women of Congo-Brazzaville: Mothers and Sisters in Troubled Times*. Bloomington: Indiana University Press, 2009.

Mathys, Gillian. *Conflict and Connection: Making Histories in the Lake Kivu Region*. Oxford University Press, forthcoming.

———. "People on the Move: Frontiers, Borders, Mobility and History in the Lake Kivu Region, 19th–20th Century." PhD diss., University of Ghent, 2014.

Mbembe, Achille. *Necropolitics*. Durham, NC: Duke University Press, 2019.

———. *On the Postcolony*. Berkeley: University of California Press, 2001.

———. "The Society of Enmity." *Radical Philosophy* 200 (November/December 2016): 23–35. https://www.radicalphilosophy.com/article/the-society-of-enmity.

McClintock, Anne. *Imperial Leather: Race, Gender, and Sexuality in the Colonial Contest*. New York: Routledge, 1995.

Mélice, Anne. "Le kimbanguisme et le pouvoir en RDC: Entre apolitisme et conception théologico-politique." *Civilisations: Revue internationale d'anthropologie et de sciences humaines* 58, no. 2 (2009): 59–80.

Meyer, Birgit. *Translating the Devil: Religion and Modernity among the Ewe in Ghana*. Trenton, NJ: Africa World Press, 1999.

Mobe Fansiama, Anicet. "Les intellectualités estudiantines congolaises revisitées: 1954–1965." In *Aspects de la culture à l'époque coloniale en Afrique: Presse–archives*, 115–46. Paris: L'Harmattan, 2007.

Monaville, Pedro. *Students of the World: Global 1968 and Decolonization in the Congo*. Durham, NC: Duke University Press, 2022.

Moore, Henrietta, and Megan Vaughan. *Cutting Down Trees: Gender, Nutrition and Change in the Northern Province of Zambia, 1890–1990*. Portsmouth, NH: Heinemann, 1994.

Morelle, Marie. *Yaoundé carcérale: Géographie d'une ville et de sa prison*. Lyon: ENS Éditions, 2019.

Morgan, Jennifer L. *Laboring Women: Reproduction and Gender in New World Slavery*. Philadelphia: University of Pennsylvania Press, 2004.

Moyo, Fulata Lusungu. "Religion, Spirituality and Being a Woman in Africa: Gender Construction within the African Religio-Cultural Experiences." *Agenda: Empowering Women for Gender Equity*, no. 61 (2004): 72–78.

Mwene-Batende. "La sorcellerie comme pratique sociale des Kumu et l'opposition au Kitawala," 1979 (3111). In *Turner Collection on Religious Movements*, 5-04-007: fiche 155.

———. "Le Kitawala dans l'évolution socio-politique récente: Cas du group Belukela dans la ville de Kisangani." *Cahiers des religions africaines* 10, no. 19 (1976): 81–105.

———. *Mouvements messianiques et protestation sociale: Le cas du Kitawala chez les Kumu du Zaïre*. Kinshasa: Faculté de théologie catholique, 1982.

Nassenstein, Nico. "The Linguistic Taboo of Poisoning in Kivu Swahili." In "Taboo in Language and Discourse," edited by Alexandra Y. Aikenvald and Anne Storch. Special issue, *The Mouth*, no. 4 (May 2019): 117–34.

Newbury, David S. "What Role Has Kingship? An Analysis of the Umuganura Ritual of Rwanda as Presented in Marcel d'Hertefelt and André Coupez La royauté sacrée de l'ancien Rwanda (1964)." *Africa-Tervuren* 27 (1981): 89–101.

Ngoma-Binda, Phambu. *Zamenga Batukezanga: Vie et oeuvre*. Kinshasa: Éditions Saint-Paul Afrique, 1990.

Nyenyezi, Aymar, An Ansoms, Koen Vlassenroot, Emery Mudinga, and Godefroid Muzalia, eds. *The Bukavu Series: Toward a Decolonization of Research*. Leuven: Presses universitaires de Louvain, 2020.

Nzongola-Ntalaja, Georges. *The Congo from Leopold to Kabila: A People's History*. London: Zed Books, 2002.

Painter, Nell Irvin. "Why 'White' Should Be Capitalized, Too." *Washington Post*, July 22, 2020. https://www.washingtonpost.com/opinions/2020/07/22/why-white-should-be-capitalized/.

Paulus, Jean-Pierre. "Le Kitawala au Congo belge (mouvement indigène à caractère politico-religieux)," 1956 (3213). In *Turner Collection on Religious Movements*, 5-04-007: fiche 173.

Peterson, Derek R. *Ethnic Patriotism and the East African Revival: A History of Dissent, c. 1935–1972.* Cambridge: Cambridge University Press, 2012.

———. "The Intellectual Lives of Mau Mau Detainees." *Journal of African History* 49, no. 1 (2008): 73–91.

———. "The Politics of Transcendence in Colonial Uganda." *Past & Present* 230, no. 1 (2016): 197–225.

Pistor, Dominic. "Developmental Colonialism and Kitawala Policy in 1950s Belgian Congo." In *Religion, Colonization and Decolonization in Congo, 1885–1960,* edited by Vincent Viaene, Bram Cleys, and Jan De Maeyer, 261–84. Leuven: Leuven University Press, 2020.

Powers, Theodore. "Authoritarian Violence, Public Health, and the Necropolitical State: Engaging the South African Response to COVID-19." *Open Anthropological Research* 1, no. 1 (2021): 60–72.

Prins, Gwyn. "But What Was the Disease? The Present State of Health and Healing in African Studies." *Past & Present* 124, no. 1 (1989): 159–79.

Prunier, Gérard. *Africa's World War: Congo, the Rwandan Genocide, and the Making of a Continental Catastrophe.* Oxford: Oxford University Press, 2009.

———. "The Catholic Church and the Kivu Conflict." *Journal of Religion in Africa* 31, no. 2 (2001): 139–62.

Ranger, Terence O. "Connexions between 'Primary Resistance' Movements and Modern Mass Nationalism in East and Central Africa." Pts. 1 and 2. *Journal of African History* 9, no. 3/4 (1968): 437–53, 631–41.

———. "Religious Movements and Politics in Sub-Saharan Africa." *African Studies Review* 29, no. 2 (1986): 1–61.

Ray, Carina E. *Crossing the Color Line: Race, Sex, and the Contested Politics of Colonialism in Ghana.* Athens: Ohio University Press, 2015.

Reyntjens, Filip. *The Great African War: Congo and Regional Geopolitics, 1996–2006.* Cambridge: Cambridge University Press, 2009.

Rotberg, Robert I. *The Rise of Nationalism in Central Africa: The Making of Malawi and Zambia, 1873–1964.* Cambridge, MA: Harvard University Press, 1965.

Rubbers, Benjamin. "Mining Towns, Enclaves and Spaces: A Genealogy of Worker Camps in the Congolese Copperbelt." *Geoforum* 98 (January 2019): 88–96.

Salesa, Damon Ieremia. *Racial Crossings: Race, Intermarriage, and the Victorian British Empire.* Oxford: Oxford University Press, 2011.

Sanneh, Lamin. *Translating the Message: The Missionary Impact on Culture.* 2nd ed. Maryknoll, NY: Orbis, 2009.

Sarró, Ramon. "Writing as Rupture: On Prophetic Invention in Central Africa." In *Ruptures: Anthropologies of Discontinuity in Times of Turmoil,* edited by Martin Holbraad, Bruce Kapferer, and Julia F. Sauma, 140–56. London: UCL Press, 2019.

Schatzberg, Michael G. *The Dialectics of Oppression in Zaire.* Bloomington: Indiana University Press, 1988.

———. *Political Legitimacy in Middle Africa: Father, Family, Food.* Bloomington: Indiana University Press, 2001.

Schields, Chelsea, and Dagmar Herzog, eds. *The Routledge Companion to Sexuality and Colonialism.* Abingdon, UK: Routledge, 2021.

Schoenbrun, David L. "Conjuring the Modern in Africa: Durability and Rupture in Histories of Public Healing between the Great Lakes of East Africa." *American Historical Review* 111, no. 5 (2006): 1403–39.

———. *A Green Place, a Good Place: Agrarian Change, Gender, and Social Identity in the Great Lakes Region to the 15th Century.* Portsmouth, NH: Heinemann, 1998.

———. *The Names of the Python: Belonging in East Africa, 900 to 1930.* Madison: University of Wisconsin Press, 2021.

———. "Violence and Vulnerability in East Africa before 1800 CE: An Agenda for Research." *History Compass* 4, no. 5 (2006): 741–60.

Scott, James C. *Domination and Arts of Resistance: Hidden Transcripts.* New Haven, CT: Yale University Press, 1990.

Seibert, Julia. "More Continuity Than Change? New Forms of Unfree Labor in the Belgian Congo, 1908–1930." In *Humanitarian Intervention and Changing Labor Relations: The Long-Term Consequences of the Abolition of the Slave Trade,* edited by Marcel van der Linden, 369–86. Leiden: Brill, 2011.

Shepperson, George, and Thomas Price. *Independent African: John Chilembwe and the Origins, Setting and Significance of the Nyasaland Native Rising of 1915.* Edinburgh: Edinburgh University Press, 1958.

Sheridan, Michael J. "The Environmental and Social History of African Sacred Groves: A Tanzanian Case Study." *African Studies Review* 52, no. 1 (2009): 73–98.

Spindler, Marc. "Le mouvement Kitawala en Afrique centrale," 1968 (1470). In *Turner Collection on Religious Movements,* 5-06-000: fiche 227.

Stearns, Jason. *Dancing in the Glory of Monsters: The Collapse of the Congo and the Great War of Africa.* New York: PublicAffairs, 2011.

———. "Mass Rape in Walikale: What Happened?" *Congo Siasa* (blog), August 24, 2010. http://congosiasa.blogspot.com/2010/08/mass-rape-in-walikale-what-happened.html.

Stoler, Ann Laura. *Along the Archival Grain.* Princeton, NJ: Princeton University Press, 2010.

———. *Carnal Knowledge and Imperial Power: Race and the Intimate in Colonial Rule.* Berkeley: University of California Press, 2002.

Tallie, T. J. *Queering Colonial Natal: Indigeneity and the Violence of Belonging in Southern Africa.* Minneapolis: University of Minnesota Press, 2019.

Taussig, Michael. "Culture of Terror, Space of Death: Roger Casement's Putamoyo Report and the Explanation of Torture." *Comparative Studies in Society and History* 26, no. 3 (July 1984): 467–97.

Taylor, Christopher C. *Milk, Honey, and Money: Changing Concepts in Rwandan Healing.* Washington, DC: Smithsonian Institution Press, 1992.

Tempels, Placide. *Bantu Philosophy.* Paris: Prešence africaine, 1959.

Tew, Mary. "A Form of Polyandry among the Lele of the Kasai." *Africa: Journal of the International African Institute* 21, no. 1 (1951): 1–12.

Thioub, Ibrahima. "Juvenile Marginality and Incarceration during the Colonial Period: The First Penitentiary Schools in Senegal, 1888–1927." In *A History of Prison and Confinement*, edited by Florence Bernault, 79–96. Portsmouth, NH: Heinemann, 2003.

———. "Sénégal: La prison à l'époque coloniale; Significations, évitement et évasions." In *Enfermement, prison et châtiments en Afrique: Du 19e siècle à nos jours*, edited by Florence Bernault, 285–303. Paris: Karthala, 1999.

Thomas, Lynn M. *Politics of the Womb: Women, Reproduction, and the State in Kenya*. Berkeley: University of California Press, 2003.

Thornton, John. *The Kongolese Saint Anthony: Dona Beatriz Kimpa Vita and Antonian Movement, 1684–1706*. Cambridge: Cambridge University Press, 1998.

Tödt, Daniel. *The Lumumba Generation: African Bourgeoisie and Colonial Distinction in the Belgian Congo*. Translated by Alex Skinner. Oldenbourg, Germany: De Gruyter, 2021.

Tonda, Joseph. *Le souverain modern: Le corps du pouvoir en Afrique centrale (Congo, Gabon)*. Paris: Karthala, 2005.

———. *L'impérialisme postcolonial: Critique de la société des éblouissements*. Paris: Karthala, 2015.

Trouillot, Michel-Rolph. *Silencing the Past: Power and the Production of History*. Boston: Beacon Press, 2015.

Tshimanga, Charles. *Jeunesse, formation et société au Congo/Kinshasa, 1890–1960*. Paris: L'Harmattan, 2001.

Tull, Denis M. "Troubled State-Building in the DR Congo: The Challenge from the Margins." *Journal of Modern African Studies* 48, no. 4 (2010): 643–61.

Turner, Thomas. *The Congo Wars: Conflict, Myth and Reality*. London: Zed Books, 2007.

Turner Collection on Religious Movements. Microform edition. Birmingham, UK: Sely Oak Colleges Library, Study Centre for New Religious Movements in Primitive Societies, 1983.

Van Avermaet, E., and Benoit Mbuya. *Dictionnaire kiluba-français*. Tervuren, Belgium: Museé royal du Congo belge, 1954.

Van Bockhaven, Vicky. "Anioto: Leopard Men Killings and Institutional Dynamism in Northeast Congo, c. 1890–1940." *Journal of African History* 59, no. 1 (2018): 21–44.

van Klinken, Adriaan. *Kenyan, Christian, Queer: Religion, LGBT Activism, and Arts of Resistance in Africa*. University Park: Pennsylvania State University Press, 2019.

Vansina, Jan. *Oral Tradition: A Study in Historical Methodology*. Translated by H. M. Wright. London: Routledge and Kegan Paul, 1965.

———. *Paths in the Rainforests: Toward a History of Political Tradition in Equatorial Africa*. Madison: University of Wisconsin Press, 1990.

———. *Oral Tradition as History*. Madison: University of Wisconsin Press, 1985.

Van Wolputte, Steven. "Love, Play and Sex: Polyamory and the Hidden Pleasures of Everyday Life in Kaoko, Northwest Namibia." In *Africa Every Day: Fun, Leisure, and Expressive Culture on the Continent*, edited by Oluwakemi M.

Balogun, Lisa Gilman, Melissa Graboyes, and Habib Iddrisu, 123–32. Athens: Ohio University Press, 2019.

Vaughan, Megan. *Curing Their Ills: Colonial Power and African Illness.* Stanford, CA: Stanford University Press, 1991.

Verhoeve, Anne. "Conflict and the Urban Space: The Socio-economic Impact of Conflict on the City of Goma." In *Conflict and Social Transformation in Eastern DR Congo,* edited by Koen Vlassenroot and Timothy Raeymaekers, 103–22. Ghent: Academia Press Scientific Publishers, 2004.

Vlassenroot, Koen. "Citizenship, Identity Formation and Conflict in South Kivu: The Case of the Banyamulenge." *Review of African Political Economy* 29, no. 93/94 (2002): 499–515.

Vlassenroot, Koen, and Timothy Raeymaekers. "Conflict and Artisan Mining in Kamituga." In *Conflict and Social Transformation in Eastern DR Congo,* edited by Koen Vlassenroot and Timothy Raeymaekers, 123–56. Ghent: Academia Press Scientific Publishers, 2004.

Wamba dia Wamba, Ernest. "Bundu dia Kongo: A Kongolese Self-Styled Fundamentalist Religious Movement." In *East African Expressions of Christianity,* edited by Thomas Spear and Isaria Kimambo, 213–28. Oxford: James Currey, 1999.

Watkins, Sarah. "Iron Mothers and Warrior Lovers: Intimacy, Power, and the State in the Nyiginya Kingdom, 1796–1913." PhD diss., University of California, Santa Barbara, 2014.

Werbner, Richard, ed. *Memory and the Postcolony: African Anthropology and the Critique of Power.* London: Zed Books, 1998.

Whetho, Ayo, and Ufo Okeke Uzodike. "Religious Networks in Post-conflict Democratic Republic of the Congo: A Prognosis." *African Journal on Conflict Resolution* 8, no. 3 (January 2008): 57–84.

White, Luise. *Speaking with Vampires: Rumor and History in Colonial Africa.* Berkeley: University of California Press, 2000.

White, Luise, Stephen F. Miescher, and David William Cohen, eds. *African Words, African Voices: Critical Practices in Oral History.* Bloomington: Indiana University Press, 2001.

Whitehead, John. *Manuel de Kingwana: Le dialecte occidental de Swahili.* Le Lualaba, Congo: La Mission de et à Wayika, 1928.

Wilder, Gary. *Freedom Time: Negritude, Decolonization and the Future of the World.* Durham, NC: Duke University Press, 2015.

Wynter, Sylvia. "Unsettling the Coloniality of Being/Power/Truth/Freedom: Towards the Human, after Man, Its Overrepresentation—an Argument." *CR: The New Centennial Review* 3, no. 3 (2003): 257–337.

Yasuoka, Hirokazu. "Sharing Elephant Meat and the Ontology of Hunting among the Baka Hunter-Gatherers in the Congo Basin Rainforest." In *Human-Elephant Interactions: From Past to Present,* edited by George E. Konidaris, Ran Barkai, Vangelis Tourloukis, and Katerina Harvati, 469–85. Tübingen, Germany: Tübingen University Press, 2021.

Index

Page numbers in *italics* refer to figures.

Alfani, Roger, 202, 211, 221n9
Alleloya, 91–92, 98–99, 103, 105, 106, 107, 109; testimony of, 94–99. *See also* Bushiri Lungunda; *dawas* (medicines): *mataifa* as; Lubutu-Masisi uprising of 1944
ancestors. *See under* healing; Kitawala; power
-anga/bwanga. *See under* power
archives: Archives africaines, 18, 226n68; colonial, 18–19, 37–38, 106, 121, 127; of Kitawalist communities, 19; and oral sources/traditions, 14, 18–21, 38, 79, 146, 227n79, 237n8; "tin trunk," 19, 38
asili (tradition), 5–6, 31–32, *61*, 61, 210, 215, 236n5
Atlantic Charter, 43–44, 163, 214

Belgian colonialism: administration of, 28; biopolitics of, 28; carceral practices during, 146–47, 152; and Catholic Church, 201; economy of, 28; as "nervous state," 15, 28, 91, 146; relegation policies of, 147–56, 166–68; violence of, 90–91, 107–8
Belgian Congo. *See* Belgian colonialism
Benzing and Paquay. *See* Lubutu-Masisi uprising of 1944: Kasese massacre
Bernault, Florence: on colonial "transactions," 13, 18, 29, 226n72; on forms of penal confinement, 256n11
Booth, Joseph, 33, 230n23. *See also* Watchtower
bulozi. *See* power: as malevolent/"eating"/*bulozi*

Bundu dia Kongo (BDK) movement, 177, 179, 199–200, 202–3, 207
Bushiri Lungunda: on America, 90, 95, 100; as Christlike figure (Yesu Mukombozi), 90, 93, 99, 103–4, 106; doctrine of *Mapendo* (Love), 90, 93, 109; dynamic theory of power, 99–100, 103–4, 106–7; as Kumu, 100, 244n37; as leader of Lubutu-Masisi revolt, 41, 90, 93, 97, 98, 109; witchcraft accusations, 91–92, 93, 104–6, 107. *See also* Lubutu-Masisi uprising of 1944

Catholic Church, 39, 184, 189, 190, 197, 198, 264n29; Lay Coordination Committee (CLC), 201. *See also* missionaries (Western): Catholic
chicotte, use of, 92, 107, 141–42
COLAGREL (penal colony), 43, 141, 144, 147, 148, 152, *154*, 159, 217; as *cité jardin* (garden city), 153; construction of, 148, 150, *153*; factions within, 159–61; Kitawalist community in, 141–46, 156–61, 165–72, 176; as powerful space, 145–47, 170–72; resistance in, 162–65, 217; women in, 166–70. *See also* Matton, Maurice (director of COLAGREL); relegation, penal practice of
conceptual history, 9, 15, 93, 214
concept-work, 9–10, 13, 212, 215–17
Congo Free State, 15, 28, 91, 107–8, 147
Congo War, First, 192, 197
Congo War, Second, 58, 197
Copperbelt region, 27–29, 37, 221n16
COVID-19 pandemic, 15; refusal of restrictions, 7, 195–96

dawas (medicines), 5, 59, 94, 98, 109, 133–35; *mataifa* as, 93–94, 98, 109, 244n40. *See also* healing, Kitawalist
Debertry, Léon. See *Kitawala: Roman* (Debertry)

Église du Dieu de nos ancêtres au Congo (EDAC): and African Watchtower, 32–33; mountains sacred to, 71–72; Patrice Lumumba as prophet of, 32–33, 178–82; and tradition (*asili*), 31–32, 61; as variant of Kitawala, 13, 30–33, 69, 71–74, 80, 138
Ekafera prison camp, 41, 147, *148*, 150, 151, 152, 176, 187, 254n7, 255n8
évolués, 212–13
extractive industries: colonial, 28; labor coercion, 28, 87, 100, 101–2, 211; mining, 28, 87, 89, 101, 192, 247n4; neocolonial, 15; resistance to, 42, 93; rubber, 15, 28, 87, 89, 94–96, 99, 100–101

Fabian, Johannes, 62, 237n8
Fanon, Frantz, 17, 108
Feierman, Steven, 6; on "peasant intellectuals," 14–15; on "ritual technology" and healing, 62–63, 116, 244nn38–39
force (Fr.). *See under* power

Garenganze Evangelical Mission (GEM), 39
Gérard, Jacques, 125, 135–37, 213–14, 253n101
Gondola, Didier, 108–9, 132
Great Depression (1930s), 28, 36, 101

healing, Kitawalist: ancestors evoked in, 60, 70–74, 82, 105, 134; and biomedicine, 58, 62–63, 70, 80–81, 83–84; *dawas* (medicines) used in, 5, 59, 94, 98, 133–35, 244n40; healers as political leaders, 97; herbs, powders (kaolin), and other materials used in, 62–74, 83, 133–35, 216; *mfumu* (healer), 59, 99, 216, 235n1; *nganga/monganga* (healer), 11, 62, 93–94, 99, 216, 235n1, 237n7, 244n38; power of, 62–63, 216–17; prayer/evocations used in, 60, 62–65, 67, 71–72, 81–82, 238n26; and refusal of colonial medicine, 133; reproductive health/fertility, 59, 69–70, 80–84, 238n27; ritual technologies of, 62–65, 73, 216;

therapeutic practices, 82–83, 116, 216; and violence, 92, 97, 217; women as healers, 75–78, 81–82, 105–6, 126–28, 216. *See also* Kitawala: healing practices in; power: and healing
Higginson, John, 4, 35–37, 220n7
Histoire de l'Église Kitawala: Prophète Ilunga Kadiba Émile (*Histoire*), 46–49, 160, 233n64, 233nn76–77, 258n39. *See also Historia ya Kanisa;* Kadiba Ilunga Émile
Historia ya Kanisa: Biographie ya Baba Prophete (*Biographie*), 46, 50, 160, 233n77, 259n65, 262n6. *See also Histoire de l'Église Kitawala;* Kadiba Ilunga Émile
Hunt, Nancy Rose: on ethnography, 225n65; on "nervous" colonial state, 16, 91, 146, 226n72, 227n79, 240n47, 243n34, 255n8, 258n47; on "tethering," 107–8

intellectual history, African, 13–14, 212–13, 217; Kitawala as part of, 6, 27, 38, 215 (*see also* Kitawala: everyday intellectuals and)
invisible transcripts, 78–79, 84, 106

Janzen, John, 80, 97–98, 134, 222n21, 224nn39–40
Jehovah's Witnesses. *See* Watchtower
Joset, Paul-Ernest, 87, 89, 91, 124–26, 147, 151, 247n6

Kabanga Kamalondo, 63–67, 71, 77, 105, 181–82, 183
Kadiba Ilunga Émile: biographies of, 38, 46–50, 233n64, 258n39 (see also *Histoire de l'Église Kitawala; Historia ya Kanisa*); conversion of, 47–48; miracles attributed to, 50, 160, 234n88; name variation, 233n76; as prophet-leader of Kitawala, 38, 50, 52–55, 57, 149, 152, 165, 206, 215; relegation/imprisonment of, 41, 50, 149, 151–52, 159–60, 163, 165, 258n40
Kamwana, Eliot Kenan, 33–34
kaolin, Kitawalist use of, 65–67, 133, 238n24. *See also* healing, Kitawalist: herbs, powders (kaolin), and other materials used in
Kasaji penal colony. *See* COLAGREL
Kasese massacre. *See under* Lubutu-Masisi uprising of 1944

kifungo (evocation), 78, 165, 181, 238n26. *See also* healing, Kitawalist: prayer/evocations used in
Kimbangu, Simon, 5, 12, 178, 187–89, 191
Kimbanguism: and Kitawala, 4, 112, 132, 147, 150, 178, 186–93, 210, 264n29; supported by Mobutu regime, 189–92
kindoki. *See under* power
Kisangani (Stanleyville), 1, 78, 144, *157*, 187; Kitawalist community at, 55–56, 112–13, 137–38, 157, 161–62, 175, 179. *See also* Stanleyville plot of 1955
Kitawala: America/Americans as allies of, 3, 12, 100, 165, 248n25; ancestors as source of power/guidance, 5, 8, 13, 21, 31–33, 50, 60, 66, 70, 71, 73–74, 105, 134, 177–78, 181–82, 184, 207; Belgian colonial views of, 17, 30, 127, 150–51, 162; as Christian and *ya asili* (traditional), 5–6, 31–32, 61, 66, 84, 136, 210, 215, 236n5; colonial attempts to suppress, 4, 28, 30, 37, 42; "communism of wives" accusation, 121, 123–26, 130, 167; in Copperbelt, 26–29, 30, 221n16; etymology and linguistic meanings of, 13, 220n7; everyday intellectuals and, 5, 7, 9, 13–16, 210, 213, 214–15; as "groupwork," 10–11, 17, 118, 212; healing practices in, 59–74, 80–82, 84, 98, 216; prayer / "prayer chambers" in, 5, 18, 29, 30, 32, 54, 67, 71, 73–74, 81–82, 162, 165, 183, 216 (*see also under* healing, Kitawalist); refusal of civic functions, 2, 185, 192, 205–8; relegation/incarceration of Kitawalists, 4, 28, 30, 40–41, 145–47, 156–61, 166, 217, 256n14, 257n30; resistance to hierarchy, 74, 128; resistance to state and customary authorities, 5, 17–18, 115–18, 194, 198–99, 206–8; rituals and ritual technologies of, 5, 62–64, 73–74, 216, 238n24; as "self-rule," 4–5, 30, 32, 74; as "sex cult," 51–52, 121–23; as "subversive" movement, 4, 42, 118, 186; as "syncretic" movement, 5, 135–36; "unruliness" of, 4–5, 7, 14, 16–18, 136, 192, 214, 217; Watchtower as source of, 6, 29, 31–35, 37, 215, 222n16 (*see also* Watchtower); women's/mamas' role in, 11, 22, 32–33, 45–46, 75–79, 105–6, 127–29, 166–70, 215–16, 262n106
Kitawala-Filadelfie, 2–3, 74, 79, 195–96, 203–6. *See also* PP2 (Pastor Paul II)

Kitawala: Roman (Debertry), 51–53, *55*, 121, 124
kujitawala (to rule oneself), 5, 30, 32, 113
Kulu Mapenda, 41–44, 45; on human rights, 43, 163–64; as prophet, 38, 41–44, 215; relegation of, 42–44; role in spreading Kitawala, 42–44

Leopold II (king), 15, 28, 101, 108, 165
Lowa, city and region of, 122, 187, 188; and Beyaya Aliso, 130–33, 136, 137; Kitawalist acts of sexual violence at, 129–30, 132–33, 136, 187
Lubutu-Masisi uprising of 1944, 4, 90–93, 217; *chicotte* use, 107; healing power, 91–93, 97–99, 104, 106–7, 109, 244n37; Kasese massacre, 87–90, 91, 108, 124; Kumu (ethnic group) involvement, 100–102, 109, 244n37; rubber collection, 94–96, 99, 100, 106, 108; socioeconomic aspects, 100–103, 107; violence directed at Congolese, 91–93; violence targeting women, 95–96, 97, 104–8, 109; witchcraft discourse, 90, 91, 92–93, 97, 102, 107, 109. *See also* Bushiri Lungunda
Lumumba, Patrice, 144; assassination of, 32, 175, 178–80, 182; Kitawalist devotion to, 178–84, 193; "politics of life," 182–83, 193; as prophet/Christ figure in collective memory, 32–33, 175–76, 178–82, 210 (*see also under* Église du Dieu de nos ancêtres au Congo)

Malonga prison camp, 43, 45, 141–42, *148*, 155, 156, 161, 257n30; Kitawalists interned in, 149, 152, 158–59, 163, 169–70
Maman Kalema, 58–60, 62, 75–76, 80–81, 82, 105–6
mashetani (evil/demonic spirits), 59–60, 80–81, 235n1
Mathys, Gillian, 66, 270n2
Matton, Maurice (director of COLAGREL), *144*, 154–56, 159, 161–63, 167, 172, 257n32, 260n71, 261n103. *See also* COLAGREL
Mau Mau (Kenya), 110, 151, 246n1
medicine. *See* healing, Kitawalist
mfumu (healer). *See under* healing, Kitawalist
migrant workers, 4, 28; of Copperbelt, 28–29; and transmission of Kitawala, 4–5, 28, 31, 33–37, 40, 43; violence targeting, 28, 102

Index ~ 289

missionaries (Western), 6, 28, 34, 101, 123; Catholic, 28, 39, 103, 123; Kitawalists' suspicions of, 17, 31, 39, 48–49; and opinions of Kitawala, 16, 103, 123, 135; Protestant, 28, 39, 49, 101; schools run by, 28, 101

Mobutu, Joseph-Désiré, 7, 16, 178, 182, 184–86, 190, 192, 201, 207, 211; and Kimbanguist Church, 189–91; Kitawalist antagonism with regime of, 176, 178, 183–86, 191–93, 195, 207; "occult power" of, 184, 186; "politics of enmity" and, 182–85, 192–93; populism of, 192–93; and program of *authenticité*, 190, 192; religious policies of, 184, 189, 264n29

Mukungubila, 200–203, 206–7, 268n23

Mulongo, Pastor Théophile, 57; alternative reading of *Kitawala: Roman*, 51–54, *55*; on healing practices, 67; on relegation and COLAGREL, 141–46, 152–54, 159, 161, 168–69

Mutombo Stephano: and Kituadists/ Kibanguism, 187–89; as prophet/ preacher of Kitawala, 25–27, 38–41, 44, 46–48, 215, 232n50; relegation of, 40–41, 45, 138, 151–52

Muyololo Kabila, 38, 41, 45–46, 128, 149, 151, 152, 159–60, 215

Mwene-Batende, 4, 100, 175, 177, 211, 245n48

nganga/monganga (healer). *See under* healing, Kitawalist

Ngoie Maria, 38, 45–46, 105, 128

NGOs, 205

nguvu. See under power

nkisi/minkisi (empowered objects), 5, 12, 59, 67, 83, 216, 245n57

occult, 12

oral history, 19–20, 78, 216; interviews and fieldwork, 20–22, 77, 225n65

Philippart, R. (Belgian colonial administrator), 31, 33, 55–57, 111–12, 123, 125–26, 138–39, 168

pouvoir. See under power

power: ambivalent meanings of, 7–12, 93; of ancestors, 5, 8, 71–74, 177–78, 181–82, 184, 193, 207, 234n89; *-anga/ bwanga*, 8, 11, 80, 239n27; body/spirit, 113–14, 120–21, 122–23, 129, 139, 215; conferred by religious persecution, 43–44; to do miracles/*ajabu*, 50, 82, 160, 181; economy of, 12–13, 44, 83, 97, 103, 135; empowered objects (*minkisi*), 5, 12, 59, 67, 83, 216, 245n57; etymology and linguistic meanings, 8–13, 239n27; Europeans' hoarding of, 49, 102; *force* (Fr.), 8, 239n27; of God, 8, 12, 34, 46, 56, 73–74, 102–4, 177, 181–82, 184, 193, 207; and healing, 11, 62–63, 70, 83–84, 93, 193, 216–17; instrumental vs. creative, 10–11, 106; invisible forms of, 12, 29, 78–79, 97, 180, 184; *kindoki,* 11; legitimate vs. illegitimate, 11–12, 93, 102–3, 186, 207; as malevolent/"eating"/*bulozi*, 8, 11, 12, 64, 93, 186, 210; *mamlaka*, 56–57; *nguvu*, 8, 10, 60, 63, 64, 70, 72, 76, 188–89, 240n44; places/spaces of, 29–30, 66, 71–72, 74, 145; *pouvoir/puissance*, 8, 10, 63, 181, 239n27; of religious leaders, 3, 12, 44, 99, 106, 207; spiritual, 8, 12, 46, 146–47, 162, 177–78, 184, 197–98, 206, 208, 255n9; therapeutic, 7, 60, 216; *uwezo,* 8, 10; as witchcraft, 8, 11, 80, 97, 239n27; of women, 60, 75–79, 82–83, 97, 105–6, 215

PP2 (Pastor Paul II), 2–5, 8, 27, 31, 38, 176, 195–96, 205, 215; and "bible in their head," 2, 7, 31; and COVID-19 restrictions, 195–96; on "DEMONcratic Republic of Congo," 12, 189, 195, 203–6; on Kimbanguism and Kitawala, 187–89; as leader of Kitawala-Filadelfie, 2–3, 74, 185, 195, 203–5, 208; on Mobutu era, 185–86; UNICEF's portrayal of, 195, 203–4; on women, 79

refusal, ethnographic concept of, 16–17, 91, 205–8, 209–10, 214

relegation, penal practice of, 30, 40–41, 44, 112, 146–50, *148*, 186, 217, 256n14; and acts of resistance among *relégués*, 110–11, 161–66, 217; CARDs (Agricultural Camps for Dangerous Relégués) and, 110, 149; concentrative, 41, 149–50; dispersive, 148–49, 256n15; natal, 40, 148, 256n16; penitentiary schools and, 168, 261n103; as powerful experience, 139–40, 145–47, 152, 160; of women and wives, 78, 166–70. *See also* COLAGREL; Ekafera

290 ~ Index

prison camp; Kitawala: relegation/incarceration of Kitawalists; Malonga prison camp
ritual technologies. *See under* healing, Kitawala
Russell, Charles Taze, 33, 52

Schoenbrun, David, 10–11, 92, 99, 117, 127, 236n1
Stanleyville plot of 1955, 110–12, 120, 139, 144, 182, 260n76. *See also* Kisangani (Stanleyville)
syncretism, 5, 135–36

transmission: divine, 29, 51, 57, 215; forms of, 27–31, 57; of ideas, 15, 28; oral, 29, 54, 57; reception, 29, 57; textual, 50–54, 57

umpafu tree (*Canarium schweinfurthii*, or African elemi), 62, 64–65, 67, 69, 71, 237n12
UNICEF, 195, 203–5, 208
uwezo. *See under* power

vaccines: Kitawalist refusal of, 2, 195, 203–5; polio, 195, 203–5
Van den Eynde, Karel (director of COLA-GREL), 164–65, 260n86

Wamba dia Wamba, 177, 181, 209, 263n8
Watchtower (Watch Tower Bible and Tract Society): African variant of, 30–31, 215; American roots of, 3, 31–37, 43; in Copperbelt, 27, 28, 29, 30, 37, 222n16; and critique of colonial authority, 31, 35; and equality of believers, 6, 34; as global movement, 31, 214; as "millenarian," 6; radio broadcasts, 31, 33; as source of Kitawala, 6, 30–32, 37, 215, 222n16; transmission of, 6, 27, 30–34, 37; universalism, 215. *See also* migrant workers: transmission of Kitawala
wazimu/*bazimu* (spirits), 60, 83. See also *mashetani* (evil/demonic spirits)
witchcraft, 8, 35–36, 74, 90, 91, 102–6, 129, 160, 200, 208; women accused of, 42, 90, 97, 104–6. *See also under* Lubutu-Masisi uprising of 1944; power
women in Kitawala: as ceremonial leaders, 11, 75, 79, 127–29; and "communism of wives" accusation, 121, 123–26, 130, 167; creative power of, 11, 106, 127–29, 216–17; as healers, 62, 75–78, 81, 105–6, 126, 128, 216; role in prayer / "prayer chambers," 11, 58–59, 67, 76–79, 81–82, 105–6, 167; "secret" knowledge/power of, 60, 75–79, 106, 215–16; and sexuality and fertility/reproductive power, 123–25, 128–29 (*see also* power: body/spirit); sexual violence committed against, 92, 107–8, 129–33, 139 (*see also* Lowa, city and region of). *See also* Maman Kalema; Ngoie Maria; power: of women; witchcraft: women accused of

Index ~ 291

Printed and bound by CPI Group (UK) Ltd, Croydon, CR0 4YY
10/01/2025

14623881-0001